Julius Wilhelm Albert von Eckardt, Edward Fairfax Taylor

Russia Before and After the War

Julius Wilhelm Albert von Eckardt, Edward Fairfax Taylor

Russia Before and After the War

ISBN/EAN: 9783337298715

Printed in Europe, USA, Canada, Australia, Japan

Cover: Foto ©ninafisch / pixelio.de

More available books at **www.hansebooks.com**

RUSSIA

BEFORE AND AFTER THE WAR

BY THE AUTHOR OF

'SOCIETY IN ST. PETERSBURG' &c.

TRANSLATED FROM THE GERMAN

(WITH LATER ADDITIONS BY THE AUTHOR)

BY

EDWARD FAIRFAX TAYLOR

SECOND EDITION

LONDON
LONGMANS, GREEN, AND CO.
1880

TRANSLATOR'S PREFACE.

TWENTY YEARS AGO, Prince Dolgorouki, the author of 'La Vérité sur la Russie,' prefaced his indictment against the administration of his country with the remark, 'A book on Russia must be by a Russian; my country resembling no other.' Largely as our knowledge of Russia has increased during this eventful interval, the observation still holds good. It is of some importance, therefore, that English readers should know that the author of the work, now translated, with some additions, from the lately published German original, not only writes with the authority of one familiar with the conditions of social and political life in Russia, but deals with the subject as a Russian. Opinions proceeding from such a source have a representative value of their own, irrespective in one sense of the views of foreign critics, but none the less indispensable for a calm and impartial estimate of the circumstances which have directed the attention of Europe to a State as unique in its composition as it is exceptional in its historical development. Keenly as this attention has been excited since Russia re-emerged from her diplomatic obscurity which followed the Crimean war, to play a part, for good or for evil, in European politics, which will form an epoch in her history, and momentous as are the possible issues involved in this change, still, the problems of foreign policy and the questions connected with international relations deal rather with effects than causes. What, as Englishmen, we are called on to decide, is the practical result of a certain line of action, or perhaps the probable consequences of a certain diplomatic act. What, as foreigners, it is difficult but most desirable to understand is, the motive power which determines the collective action of a State where, in the absence of representative institutions and the virtual silence of the Press, a barometer of public opinion, in our meaning of the term, does not exist. It may be doubted whether a foreigner, however able and acute, who speaks from observation rather than experience, is qualified for the office of instructor in this respect; his competency is still more doubtful if his previous experience has been gained in the free atmosphere of a constitutional country. Accustomed to see the ripple on the surface denote the faintest movement of the popular mind, he runs the risk of ignoring, or at least imperfectly studying, the undercurrents of political life in other countries where such tests are not immediately apparent. To analyse the ingredients and examine the various phases of discontent; to distinguish between a temporary ebullition and a permanent sentiment, between legitimate aspirations for reform and the wild dreams of revolution; and to trace the secret causes of events—is a study which must be approached with feelings other than those of mere impatience with the intrigues of a court camarilla or the corruption of a bureaucratic class.

And yet with no other country is such a study more important than with the Russia of the present time. Her days of isolation from Western influences are past. The official dread of publicity—and especially of European publicity—is a silent testimony to their power. Even the Slavophils, on the other hand, and those who, while championing the cause of progress against the reactionary stubbornness of bureaucratic absolutism, profess to purify the national life from the taint of foreign elements, fight in reality with weapons borrowed from the armoury of European ideas. Nor again, as regards the relations between the government and the governed, can the former afford to divorce itself from that public opinion at home which it learned to recognise upwards of twenty years ago, and since then, by a mutual interchange of action, has largely contributed to develope. Add to this the probable consequences of the recent war. Apart from the dangers of a foreign policy dictated by a spirit of military aggression—dangers which European action, if united, will always be able to allay—it is impossible to suppose (Russian precedents of this century forbid the supposition) that a foreign war, of the character and magnitude of that from which Russia has recently emerged in a military sense victorious, can fail to affect the internal condition of the Empire. In so far as popular forces dictated its commencement, those forces must survive its termination—the more so as, in this case, the manner in which the war has been conducted and concluded has entailed a heritage of discontent and disappointment at home. Hopes and aspirations have been excited which can never be permanently suppressed by a state of siege, or a recurrence to the stale devices of despotic coercion. Whatever form the remedy may take, it is necessary in the first place to know the origin and symptoms of the disease. The better Europe comes to know Russia, the better chance there will be of Russia knowing herself. If the enlightened patriotism of Russia is forced to address the nation through the medium of the foreign press, the fact of contributing something to this self-knowledge, the condition and essence of all real progress, contributes also to the prospect of the peaceful regeneration of a people who, in spite of all the faults and follies of their rulers, deserve a nobler future than that of barbarism,—deserve to be happy and free.

E. F. T.

WEYBRIDGE: *December* 1879.

CONTENTS.

INTRODUCTORY.

FROM GENERATION TO GENERATION . . 1

CHAPTER I.

Early life of Constantine—His relations with his father—Assassination of Paul—Posthumous reputation of Constantine—Character of Alexander I.—Prince Galytzin and Photi—Weak conduct of the Emperor—His minister removed 6

CHAPTER II.

Incapacity of former governors—Military officials—Shirkovitch's appointment as Governor of Simbirsk—A New-year's masquerade at the Winter Palace—Araktchéyef and his nominee—Life at St. Petersburg under Nicholas 21

CHAPTER III.

Radical members of the nobility—the old and the new eras—Griboyedoff's sketches of high life at Moscow—Memoirs of Herzen and Passek—Early life of Passek—Family of the Jakovleffs—'Count Feodor the chemist'—Parental home of Alexander Herzen—His early life and education—Demoralising influences—Later defects of character—His friends Granovski and Belinski—Old Russian aristocrats 34

CHAPTER IV.

False ideas of Russian peasant-life—Ismailoff, the 'Nestor' of Griboyedoff—His story told from official sources—Brutal ill-treatment of his serfs and servants—Connivance of the local authorities—His ultimate punishment—Vices of his generation 56

CHAPTER V.

PRINCE P. A. WJÄSEMSKI.

His birth and ancestors—Altered position of the nobility after the death of Catherine II.—The Nicole Institute at St. Petersburg—Wjäsemski's early studies—High-life at the capital—Introduction to official duties—A volunteer in 1812—Mania for Liberalism after the French War—His removal to Warsaw—The Emperor's scheme of 'Polish reconciliation'—Wjäsemski in the Ministry of Finance—His first literary efforts—The 'Arsamass' Club—Friendships with Pushkin and Wielehorski—His irresoluteness of character—His literary dilettantism—His self-estimate . . . 63

⁕CHAPTER VI.

MICHAEL BAKUNIN AND RADICALISM.

Bakunin's birth and education—Reactionary *régime* after the conspiracy of December 1825—Popularity of revolutionary ideas—Bakunin's military life—His 'circle' at Moscow—Stankevitch—Early Hegelian studies—Bakunin at Berlin—at Dresden—Ruge and the 'Jahrbücher' of 1842—Bakunin's contributions as 'Jules Elizard'—His negative Philosophy of Revolution—At Paris in 1843—Relations with Proudhon—Forced to leave for Switzerland—temporary return to Paris—Removal to Germany—Slav Congress at Prague, 1848—With Bohemian revolutionists at Leipsic—August Röckel—Bakunin at the Dresden outbreak—A State prisoner—Escape from Siberia—With the London exiles—Advocacy of Panslavism—Father Pafnuty's mission—Bakunin's influence over Herzen—Nihilist tendencies of the *Kolokol*—Polish Revolt of 1863—The Working-men's Association and the Peace League of the International—Fanatical theories of destruction—The 'Alliance Internationale'—Connection with Netchayeff—The champion of the French proletariate—With Cluseret at Lyons—Exiled to Switzerland—His death 88

⁕CHAPTER VII.

PRINCE V. A. TCHERKASSKI, THE REORGANISER OF POLAND AND BULGARIA.

Tcherkasski's early life—Connection with the Slavophil movement—Society at Moscow—Emancipation of the serfs—Miliutin and his opponents—Tcherkasski's mission to Poland—His quarrel with Berg—Rebuff at St. Petersburg—Panslavonic Congress at Moscow

—His anti-Polish speech—His Mayoralty at Moscow—On the Slav committee—Appointed Civil Administrator of Bulgaria—His preparations—Military character of the administration—Harsh treatment of the Bulgarians—Agrarian and communal organisation—Despotic nature of its 'system'—The higher and lower clergy—Russian evacuation and its consequences—Discouragement of the Russian army—Tcherkasski 'interviewed'—His death—Subsequent exposure of his administration—Bulgarian prospects—Russian policy and the National party 137

CHAPTER VIII.

THE RUSSIAN UNIVERSITIES.

I.

Imperial Ukase of 1849—Universities of Dorpat and Helsingfors—of Moscow—of St. Petersburg—The Medico-Chirurgical Academy—Universities of Charkoff, Kasan, and Kieff—Statute of 1835—Government restrictions—Tyranny of provincial curators and inspectors—Unenviable position of professors—Paucity of competent teachers explained—Invidious treatment of students.

II.

Personal reminiscences of the author at St. Petersburg University—Fellow-candidates for matriculation—The 'Marchirovka'—Political apathy of the students—Social characteristics of student life—The Curator—Academical restrictions—Legal studies.

III.

Reforms under Kowalevski's ministry—Liberal movement at the Universities—Reactionary policy of Count Putiätin—His successor Golownin—The Statute of 1863—Instability of academical rights—Vacillating policy of the government—Consequent distrust of the students—Their fondness for conspiracies explained. . . . 187

CHAPTER IX.

FEMALE EDUCATION IN RUSSIA.

Private boarding-schools described by Gogol—Superficial requirements at State Institutes—Russian and foreign governesses—Western influences under Catherine II.—Private schools in Wigel's time—Tatjana Passek and her school—Want of religious instruction—Defective education of the middle-classes—Elementary schools—Establishment of female gymnasia—Insufficiency of local efforts—Apathy of the government—Self-emancipating movement—Female medical students—Revolutionary tendencies 227

CHAPTER X.

JURI SAMARIN AND THE BALTIC PROVINCES.

The Moscow Slavophils under Nicholas—Samarin appointed to Chanykoff's Commission in Livonia—Suppression of municipal rights—Russification of the Baltic provinces under Golownin—Conciliation policy of his successor Suworoff—Samarin's anti-German tendencies—His interview with Nicholas—Refuses service in the State—His literary labours—His pamphlet on the 'Russian Frontiers'—His advocacy of national democracy—His influence with the government—Causes of his success—Vices of bureaucratic legislation in Russia—Death and character of Samarin 248

CHAPTER XI.

THE RUSSIAN POPULAR VIEW OF THE EASTERN QUESTION.

Antiquity of Russia's connection with Constantinople—Early Slavonic invasions of Byzantium—Influences of Græco-Byzantine Christianity—Mongol invasions of Russia—Establishment of Turkish supremacy in the East—Marriage of Ivan III. with Sophia—Turkish fears of Russia in the sixteenth century—Growing hostility of the Czars—The Will of Peter the Great—His far-sighted policy of aggrandisement—Treaty of Kutchuk-Kainardji—Premature ambition of Potemkin—Catherine II.'s scheme of a Græco-Slavonic empire—Failure of her designs against Constantinople—Her project thwarted by Austria—Incorporation of Crim-Tartary into Russia—Peace of Jassy—Removal of barriers between Turkey and Russia—Progress of anti-Turkish popular sentiment in Russia. . 267

CHAPTER XII.

THE RUSSIAN POPULAR VIEW OF THE EASTERN QUESTION (continued).

Greek influence on the early Russian Church—Hostility between the White and Black clergy—Eastern orthodoxy and the Russian National Church—Byzantine tendencies of the higher clergy—Spiritual affinity with the East—Idea of ethnological unity—Greek jealousy of Slav predominance—The Greek-Bulgarian Church conflict—Decision of the Russian Synod—Recent origin of Slavo-nationality—The movement of 1876. 283

CHAPTER XIII.

THE WAR AND THE DYNASTY.

Influence of foreign wars on domestic policy—Absolutist system of Nicholas—The Crimean War and its lessons—National humiliation and popular discontent—Reaction after the Polish revolt of 1863—Centralisation and 'National Development'—Russian parties and the Turkish War—Authors and origin of the war—The Moscow Nationalists and the Servian insurrection—Triumph of Panslavistic doctrines—The so-called Russian popular movement—Ivan Aksakoff and the Czar's speech at the Kremlin—Aspirations of the Moscow National party—Expectations founded on the war—Constitutionalism and revolution 203

CHAPTER XIV.

THE WAR AND THE DYNASTY (*continued*).

The war not desired by the Government—The Manifestos of 1854 and 1877 compared—Imitation of Prussian military precedents—Want of competent Russian Generals—Bombastic utterances of Panslavism—Commencement of hostilities—Bad news from Armenia—First repulse at Plevna—Popular discontent and despondency in the army—Pessimist spirit at St. Petersburg—Aksakoff's memorial to the Czarevitch—Blunders of military administration—Increase of paper currency—Second repulse at Plevna—Demoralisation of the public mind—The Grand-duke Michael—Trial of the 183 Nihilists—Revolutionary spirit at Odessa—Poland and Lithuania remain tranquil—The Moscow National party and the war. 310

CHAPTER XV.

THE WAR AND THE DYNASTY (*continued*).

Fall of Plevna—The Czar's return to St. Petersburg—His despondency amidst the general joy—Differences of opinion in high quarters—Passage of the Balkans—General desire to continue the war—Treaty of San Stefano—Its effects on Russian society—Russian disappointments—The British Fleet in the Bosphorus—European demand for the revision of the treaty—Schouvaloff alone insists on peace—Attempts to coerce the government—Menacing language of the National party—The Treaty of Berlin—Popular indignation—Damage done to the government and dynasty by the war. . . 337

CHAPTER XVI.

INCIDENTS AND LESSONS OF THE WAR.

Popular appetite for news of the war—Complaints of mismanagement—Inferiority of Russian weapons and equipment—Want of trenching tools at Plevna—General absence of maps—Defects of the Field-post and of telegraphic arrangements—Want of telescopes—Breakdown of the Intendance and Commissariat—Jobbery of army contractors—Military peculation—Scandalous condition of the hospitals—Incapacity of the Army Medical Department—Want of transport for the wounded—Admirable arrangements of the Red Cross Society—Excellent behaviour of Russian officers and troops—Absence of military offences early in the war—The nation and the government—Popular estimate of Russian strength. . . 354

CHAPTER XVII.

THE NEW SITUATION AND THE NEW MINISTERS.

Acquittal of Vera Sassulitch—Recent frequency of political murders—Cases of incendiarism—Ministerial changes—The new Minister of Finance—Fallacious estimates of the Budget—Urgent need of retrenchment—The Eastern Loan of 1877—The Ministry of the Interior—Arbitrary restrictions on the Press—The Plague in Astrachan—Alleged cases at St. Petersburg—M. Botkin and the German doctors—The Minister M. Makoff—Solovieff's attempted assassination of the Czar—Martial law in Russia—Solovieff's trial—Wide extent of Nihilist conspiracies—Apathy of the public—M. Nabokoff, the new Minister of Justice—Count Tolstoy, the new Minister of Public Instruction—Tyrannical treatment of the Universities—Turgenieff and Young Russia—Count Schouvaloff and Constitutionalism—Makeshift policy of the government—Foreign relations—Russia demands a constitution—Dangers of revolution in case it is refused. 381

CONCLUSION (Additional) 431

RUSSIA

BEFORE AND AFTER THE WAR.

INTRODUCTORY.

FROM GENERATION TO GENERATION.

THE FAILURE of most foreign observers, even the most competent and the most acute, to arrive at a correct understanding of Russians and Russian life; the fact that, again and again, men who have learned to know the country, its inhabitants, and its language, are puzzled by the peculiar phenomena of Russian life, and forced to confess that they have come to the end of their knowledge—all this is due to one pervading cause, as patent as it is commonly overlooked, to the ignorance, in a word, shared by most foreigners alike, of the conditions which only a few generations ago were paramount in the great Monarchy of the East, and have determined the growth and progress of the present generation. The ordinary rule of daily life, that a man makes some inquiries about the family, the origin, and the antecedents of those with whom he cultivates acquaintance, is almost habitually neglected where international relations, and especially those with Eastern nations, are concerned.

That underneath the polished and elegant exterior of officers of the guard, aristocrats, officials, and others of that sort, whom foreigners have been taught to recognise as the representatives of the Russian nation, lurks not unfrequently the nature of an Asiatic despot ; that the quick-witted men of business and merchants of Moscow and St. Petersburg, familiar with the technical details of the commerce of Western Europe, betray at times the character of religious fanatics of the deepest dye ; that the gentle, amiable, and patient *muzhik* (peasant) surpasses, under certain circumstances, the savagery and barbarism of Turks and Circassians ; and that over and over things are done on the Neva, the Volga, or the Moskva, which in other parts of Europe would seem impossible—all this never ceases to be the subject of amazement to Germans, French, and English. And yet a single obvious reflection more than half suffices to solve the apparent enigma. The Russians of the second half of this century are either the sons and grandsons of serf-proprietors, or the descendants of former serfs, or men who themselves have tasted the bitterness of serfdom. Astonishment at what now is possible or impossible will be lessened according as we become familiar with the state of things which constitutes the traditions of the Russia of to-day. From whatever side we approach the social history of the nation, whether we fix our eyes upon the antecedents of the Imperial house and the high nobility, or those of the bureaucratic, the burgher, or the peasant class, it is equally plain that even the cradle of the present generation has been surrounded by an atmosphere which can be described by no other name than that of barbarism. The mild and enlightened Autocrat, who abolished serfdom and the knout, is the grandson of that Emperor

Paul, who seemed to belong not to the Christian era, but to the age of the Cæsars. His uncle was that Grandduke Constantine, whose roughness amazed the Congress at Erfurt, and who himself confessed his inability to rule a modern State. The fathers of the statesmen, who have given laws to modern Russia, led her armies, and conducted her diplomacy, have been actors in the palace conspiracies of 1762 and 1801—men who despised anyone below a colonel, and who harried their subordinates just as they were harried by the emperor. The clergy, whose duty it is to humanise the emancipated peasants and teach them to read and write, have been ordained for the most part by dignitaries of the Church, who regarded as their chief mission the persecution of heretics, and whose folly was only surpassed by their cruelty—men, in fact, who even till quite recently were accustomed, at least once a year (on December 24, o.s.) to curse with bell, book, and candle all the heretical nations of the West. With a few insignificant exceptions, there is not a single Russian merchant whose father was not a serf, and obliged to pay for the privilege of settling in a town a poll-tax to his lord, who fixed the amount at his pleasure. The older generals have been eye-witnesses of Araktchéyef's system of military colonies, of which the Russian soldier speaks with horror even now, and which sought to introduce into the first quarter of the nineteenth century institutions of the days of the Bactrians and Medes. In the military academies of St. Petersburg there still survives the recollection of those days when the cadets were trained by the discipline of stick and rod, and purposely kept from all knowledge of those 'unhappy people of antiquity, whose predilection for the republican form of state is at least excusable from their ignorance of the blessings of monarchical institutions.'[1] What the Russian peasant lived through before 1861, there is no need for us to say. Among the Russian historians of the first rank there is not one who has not contributed at least something to the tale of sufferings which those unhappy people underwent.

A nearer acquaintance with those conditions of political and social life in Russia, which have not yet passed into history, has for a long time been all but impossible. To supply this defect, there was nothing but a number of misunderstood anecdotes, taken from Herbert's 'Russian Favourites,' the writings of Custine and Haxthausen, and other less authentic sources, and repeated again and again in a hundred variations. So incredible sounded the stories of the rose of the Empress Catherine, which was tended for twenty years, of the Emperor Paul's ordering a whole regiment to Siberia, of the tallow-candle of Alexander I. that cost 20,000 roubles, and of the Emperor Nicholas's sorrowful exclamation, 'My son and I are the only people in the country who do not steal!' that sober-minded men never troubled themselves about Russian matters, and put down as doubtful whatever came from the right bank of the Vistula and was not officially authenticated. These times are now long past. Within the last twenty years there has arisen a Russian literature of Memoirs, which at no very distant date will nearly rival that of Germany, and perhaps even that of France, and the extent of which may be gathered from the fact that two

---

[1] Compare the regulation of General Rostovzoff in 1849. Of all the Commandants of the School of Cadets, General von Klinger has left behind him the worst reputation. His harshness is a by-word to this day, as is also the fact that he knew only three words of Russian, 'Off with him to prison (*Na turmu jevo*).'

monthly periodicals have devoted their columns exclusively to the publication of state papers, old letters, diaries, family reminiscences, &c., and make it their chief object to reveal the dark side of former days. The study of these journals, which derive their materials from the most various sources and circles, is the more instructive, as not only do they treat of the now fabulous times of the Muscovite Grand-dukes, but dwell with especial care on the latter part of the last century and the first half of the present one.

The object of these pages is to contribute some information from contemporary notices, about the characteristics of the generation immediately preceding the present one—to tell, in short, of the fathers of the people who constitute the Russia of to-day. Whoever has appreciated the justice of the remark, 'Quid leges sine moribus?' will understand that a knowledge of the manners and customs which these sons have learned to imitate from their fathers, suffices to answer the question why the whole mass of the Russian legislation of the last four-and-twenty years has not availed to alter a single essential feature of the moral constitution of the Russian people and of Russian society, and why the men and the conditions which govern that Eastern quarter of Europe still resemble far more closely their much-abused predecessors, than those Western models whom they strive with such passionate haste to imitate.

CHAPTER I.

Early life of Constantine—His relations with his father—Assassination of Paul—Posthumous reputation of Constantine—Character of Alexander I. —Prince Galytzin and Photi—Weak conduct of the Emperor—His minister removed.

THE sanguinary traditions of the eighteenth century in Russia are interwoven as closely with the family history of the Imperial house as with that of many of the subjects of the present emperor. Nicholas and his brother knew the murderers of their father as well as any of the conspirators or favourites of their grandmother Catherine II. When this remarkable woman closed her career in November 1796, Alexander I. was only nineteen, and his brother Constantine only seventeen years of age. Educated under the eye of their grandmother, and intentionally estranged from the court of their father, who was living in retirement at Gatschina, the two youths came first into closer contact with their father when the latter, then in his forty-second year, ascended the throne—a man embittered and morbidly irritated by incessant neglect. His eldest son, Paul treated from the first with a mistrust that bordered on hostility, and even his favourite Constantine never lost the feeling of mortal terror of his father throughout the five years of his reign.

Even if we knew nothing more of Constantine's early history than what has recently been gathered by Karnovitch from the notes of Count Komarovsky and Colonel Sablukoff, we should know enough to understand why

Constantine Paulovitch was bound to become what he was—a compound of despotism and servility. The first sign of paternal confidence which was given to this boy of seventeen opened his eyes to the moral degeneration of his family. It was he, not his elder brother, the heir to the throne, who witnessed the sealing of the mysterious document, countersigned by Suboff, Markoff, and the Vice-Chancellor Besborodko, which the last-named had received from the Empress Catherine a few weeks before she died, and had delivered, immediately after her death, to the new sovereign. This paper contained an Imperial manifesto, intended for publication on November 24, 1796 (the empress had died on the 7th), by virtue of which Paul was to be excluded from the succession in favour of his son Alexander. But the knowledge of this secret was not the only reason why the Grand-duke 'trembled and changed colour' directly the word 'court-martial' was pronounced. The smallest oversight of military duty, the most trifling deviation from the instructions, given to him as Inspector-General of the Cadet Schools, Commander of the *Chevalier-garde* regiment,[1] temporary Governor of Peterhof, &c., roused the emperor to fits of rage, the consequences of which might be as critical to his children as to any other of his subjects. The military propensities of the father corresponded exactly with those of his son: in sternness and the pedantry of spatterdash discipline the former was even surpassed by the latter, while for political affairs and intrigue the Grand-duke had neither taste nor aptitude. Nevertheless, Constantine could scarcely ever please the emperor, who in turn could never shake off the dread

[1] The *Chevalier-garde* was the bodyguard of the empress, the *Garde à cheval* the emperor's regiment. [TR.]

of intrigues on the part of his son. Sasonoff, the adjutant of one of the regiments commanded by the Prince, was attached to him as a secret spy, with instructions never to let him go out of his sight. The young officer thought it prudent, however, to take account of the anger of his superior no less than the disfavour of the emperor, and accordingly never troubled himself to report the private life of the Grand-duke, pretending that there was nothing to report, and that the personal adjutants of his Imperial Highness must necessarily be better informed than himself, a simple regimental adjutant. To watch Sasonoff, therefore, and the other officers attached to the Grand-duke, valets were occasionally employed, whom the unhappy monarch at times interrogated in person.

By his *entourage*, especially the officers and soldiers placed under his command, the savage, passionate, and reckless young man was feared as much as his father, for he sought to compensate himself for the ill treatment he suffered and the constant state of fear in which he lived, by surrounding his own person with double terrors. Hand-in-hand with this harshness towards his subalterns, went a dependence on the favourites of the emperor, very little honourable to himself. Although it was a public secret, that Paul's chief confidant, Ivan Kutaissoff, who had risen from a boot-cleaner to be chief master of the horse and Lieutenant-General, systematically incited the emperor against the members of his own family, Constantine regularly invoked his powerful intervention, whenever it served to avert his father's wrath. Kutaissoff was called in to intercede, when the Grand-duke, through a misunderstanding, had omitted to make the usual evening report, which formed part of his duty as Military Governor of Peterhof. Kutaissoff was called in again, to get the Prince and his wife removed from the icy palace of Zarskoye-Selo, which had not been warmed for years, and whither he and his regiment had been sent for a slight mistake in manœuvring. In all probability it was Kutaissoff also who had smoothed down the great quarrel of 1799. Constantine, on his return from Italy, where he had fought by the side of Suvaroff against the French, and been rewarded with the title of 'Cæsarevitch,' usually confined to the heir to the throne, had been looked upon not only by the public, but even by his father, as a hero and a competent judge of military matters. In this capacity he had proposed certain alterations in the uniforms of the army, and attempted to explain them by a model. The emperor at first listened in silence, but suddenly he exclaimed, with a voice trembling with rage, 'Why, that is just the cut of Potemkin's uniforms! You are siding with my enemies; away from my sight, you traitor!' The mere mention of his mother's paramour, and the enemy of his youth, sufficed to rob the unhappy monarch of his senses, and to plunge the unsuspecting Grandduke into a depth of disgrace, the consequences of which it cost much difficulty and long negotiations to avert.

This malevolent distrust of Paul I. towards his son lasted, as is known, till the death of this sovereign; and the apprehension entertained by the Court circles of some sudden and violent outbreak of this animosity had a decided bearing on the catastrophe of March 11 (23), 1801. The emperor's remark to the Princess Anna Gagarin, 'Sous peu je me verrai forcé de faire tomber des têtes qui jadis m'étaient chères,' was interpreted as indicating his intention to put aside the two Grand-dukes, and to proclaim as his successor Prince Eugene of Württemberg, then only thirteen years of age, and it gave the signal for the execution of the plans which Pahlen, Bennigsen, and Suboff had already secretly matured. On the day before the tragic event, so we learn from a memorandum of Sablukoff, both Grand-dukes had been confined to their rooms by the emperor, and their servants had received orders to report at once any visitor to the prisoners. When Sablukoff, on the evening of March 11 (23), appeared in the Michailoff Palace, in order to give to Constantine his daily report as Regimental-Adjutant of the *Chevalier-garde*, a valet who knew him, cautioned him against entering the apartments of the Cæsarevitch, saying that he was bound to report it immediately to the emperor. Sablukoff, however, was firm, and was at length admitted. He found the Grand-duke pale, and trembling in every limb. Shortly afterwards, Alexander entered the room, painfully labouring to conceal the traces of strong inward excitement. At last, by another door, the emperor himself appeared, with solemn step as if on parade, in gala uniform, and carrying in his upraised hand the staff of command. At his entrance, Alexander flew into the next room, but Constantine remained standing, like one rooted to the spot. Paul listened to the Adjutant's report, and then withdrew. Constantine remained behind for a moment, and then dismissed Sablukoff, after admonishing him to observe the strictest caution; he and his brother were under arrest, and would have to take an oath before the Procurator-General Oboljaninoff. In the night Sablukoff was called up by a command from Constantine, ordering out his regiment, fully equipped. An hour later, all was over, and Alexander I. was emperor; but Constantine, at the news of his father's death, made a vow never, and under no circumstances, to accept the Russian crown.

On none of Paul's sons did the impressions of these years of youth and early manhood operate with such lasting and powerful effect as on the 'Cæsarevitch.' Alexander, to whom Constantine was closely attached by those days of common trial, let his brother have his way as far as possible; but he could never conquer a certain awe of his wild and capricious nature, and found himself repeatedly compelled to interfere against his acts of brutality and fury. Nicholas throughout his life treated his elder brother, who had renounced the succession in his favour and was looked upon, accordingly, as a great man by the masses, with respect and deference, but, nevertheless, he always kept him at a distance. Both he and Alexander possibly felt that the licentious habits and Asiatic nature of their brother, whom their grandmother had destined to be Emperor of Byzantium, were no longer congenial to an age so widely severed from the era of palace revolutions, Boyar conspiracies, and assassinations of emperors, and which, with all the rigour of absolutism still remaining, strove earnestly to imitate the forms of European government. Although well-nigh a mythical person in the traditions of the Imperial house, and especially of its younger generation, Constantine's memory, nevertheless, has outlived his death (June 27, 1831), and has served to illustrate the type of a rough and straight-forward son of the Czar. His bravery at Austerlitz, his proud bearing at his interview with Napoleon at Erfurt, his mysterious renunciation of the throne (January 26, 1822), his romantic relations with the Countess Grudrinska (Princess Lowicz), who captivated and finally became the second wife of this unruly prince, his strange conduct towards the Polish army, which he treated so badly and yet passionately loved, and the countless camp-stories related of him, had made of Constantine a sort of Russian Condé, the Paladin of an epic cycle, who for years had been the hero of the nursery and servants' hall of the Imperial palace.

The real Arthur of this round-table, however, was not Constantine himself, but his elder brother, the Emperor Alexander I., the 'Blessed,' the *Ange blanc*, who had vanquished the Corsican Imperator, and in official phraseology had 'driven the Gauls from the soil of Holy Russia, together with two-and-twenty nations, their allies.' Strange, indeed, that in the traditionary estimate of his character those mild and amiable qualities with which the emperor captivated the whole of Europe, figure far less prominently than certain peculiarities of temperament and mode of life, which, though they find a warrant in history, harmonise ill with the customary ideal. Alexander's immoderate proneness to licentiousness, the sudden fits of rage to which at times he gave way, and the system of unexampled despotism established under the patronage of Count Araktchéyef, the one man in whom he trusted to the end of his life, have occupied succeeding generations far more than the services he rendered in humanising the political life of Russia. Measured, indeed, by the standard of what was done in the way of libertinism during the first twenty years of this century, and paid for out of the secret service money entrusted to General Solomka, the whispered profligacy of the Russian grandees of to-day wears a tolerably innocent aspect. Outbreaks of a Sultan's caprice, such as the censor of the 'Constitutionnel' and the Imperial aide-de-camp, Colonel Bartholomäi,[1] experienced, were quite as impossible under the

---

[1] This censor was sent to Siberia, by a summary order of the emperor given at his table in the first paroxysm of rage, for having overlooked on

Emperor Nicholas as the barbarities of Araktchéyef's military colony, and the gross vulgarities which the disciple of the 'philosopher' Laharpe, the friend of Baader and Frau von Krüdener, submitted to from the coarse and savage fanatic Photi in 1824.

The main features of the priestly intrigue by which Prince Galytzin, the youthful friend and long-trusted confidant of Alexander, was overthrown and removed from the Ministry of Public Worship and Education, are well known. The details, however, of this story, so illustrative of the character and culture of the monarch, then in his forty-eighth year, have been first brought to light by Miropolski's 'Monograph on Photi,' the Archimandrite (Abbot) of the Jurjev Monastery, which appeared last year, and by the publication of Photi's own Diaries.[1] Recommended to Araktchéyef by a distinguished and wealthy patroness, the old, bigoted Countess Anna Orloff-Tchesmenskaja, Photi set his whole heart on the dismissal of Galytzin, who had become odious to the clerical party of reaction as the founder of the Russian Bible Society, and on the removal, with him, of his so-called Protestantising friends, including Alexander Turgenieff, Popoff, and Labin, and several high dignitaries of the Greek Church. The main offence charged against the Minister was the encouragement he had given to the translation into Russian of several manuals

---

the outer sheet of the *Constitutionnel* a printed advertisement of a pamphlet on the murder of the Emperor Paul. Bartholomäi, whom Alexander had loaded with testimonies of his friendship, and during his first visit to Paris had made his constant attendant, fell into disgrace and was never again favoured with a word from the emperor, simply because, in the course of a walk over Montmartre, he had compared the prospect of Paris from that eminence with the panorama of Moscow from the Sparrow Hills, and by so doing had reminded the monarch of the presence of Napoleon in the old capital of the empire.

[1] *Russki Archiv*, 1873.

of devotion and tracts of Gossner, Jung-Stilling, Fessler, Eckartshausen, and other 'heretics' who inclined to Mysticism. In a series of letters, full of frantic invective, which were secretly presented to the emperor in April 1824, the monk, expressly summoned for this purpose from Novgorod to St. Petersburg, denounced Galytzin as guilty of secret complicity with revolutionary and anti-ecclesiastical intrigues, aiming at the overthrow of throne and altar; accused him of being a forerunner of Antichrist, of seeking to introduce a new religion, and so forth. By an appeal to apparitions from heaven, which were represented as having commissioned him to combat Satan and his followers, and in a speech fit for Bedlam, as full of ignorance as of eccentricity, Photi urged the emperor to place his whole confidence in the 'true and loyal' Araktchéyef, and take at once the necessary measures for the extirpation of ungodliness. In answer to his fervent prayers for enlightenment in the battle against revolution he had been vouchsafed the following as a direct revelation of the Divine will :—

1. The Ministry of Ecclesiastical Affairs, and two other Ministries as well, must be purged of their present occupants.

2. The Bible Society must be dissolved at once, as there are enough Bibles already, and no more are wanted.

3. The Synod, or Upper Church Consistory, must be restored to its former footing, and the clergy entrusted with the conduct of education, so that nothing may be taught against the government and the faith.

4. The privy-councillor Koscheleff must be removed, Gossner and Fessler expelled, and the Methodists driven over the frontier.[1]

[1] Letter III., presented April 27, 1824.

After the number of these letters—in which Galytzin was described as the 'spiritual Napoleon,' and the emperor thereby reminded that just twelve years had elapsed since his war with the temporal Napoleon—had reached to five, Alexander showed himself so deeply agitated by their contents that Galytzin was warned by his friends to come to an explanation with the Archimandrite, whom he had himself recommended and treated with distinction. A conférence ensued; but the crafty monk lied throughout so skilfully that the unsuspicious minister was satisfied. The conspirators then proceeded to deal their *grand coup*. Photi fixed upon the Metropolitan Seraphim, a weak and insignificant man, to seek an audience of the emperor and 'prepare' him accordingly. The audience having proved successful (it lasted so far into the night that Photi began to fear the Metropolitan had fallen into disgrace, or even been 'sent away'), Photi received command to go to the emperor, 'in the deepest secrecy, by a hidden stair leading straight to the Imperial cabinet, so that nothing might transpire in public.' The emperor evidently thought it desirable to leave Galytzin in the illusion that matters remained exactly as they were before. In an audience which lasted three hours Photi unfolded in detail his 'God-given' programme sketched above. 'The emperor,' so Photi himself reported, 'was deeply agitated; he saw that the Lord Himself had sent him deliverance from a grievous danger. Again and again he exclaimed, "O Lord! how gracious and merciful art Thou towards me! Almost direct from heaven hast Thou sent to me a messenger to announce to me righteousness and truth."' After having besought the monk, who was going on with the most terrifying prophecies, to 'put his plan all down in writing,' the emperor sank, 'like one broken down,' upon his knees, and begged for the prayers and blessings of his visitor, to whom he solemnly promised the removal of all the evil already done.

Beaming with delight, Photi hastened back to the palace of the Countess Orloff, where he had taken up his abode. The next day a conference took place between the Metropolitan, Photi, and Count Araktchéyef, who appeared on behalf of the emperor. So completely had the pliant monarch fallen under the influence of the rude fanatic, that he formally begged for mercy to Galytzin, the friend of his youth, and proposed making matters up. The Metropolitan wavered, but Photi insisted on his demand that the minister should be dismissed, and that his 'programme' should be ratified to its full extent. On being pressed, the Metropolitan was forced to declare that for the chance of saving the minister, he would resign his spiritual dignity. With this reply, which corresponded with his own wishes, Araktchéyef returned to the emperor. The latter delayed, however, a few days longer: Gossner, indeed, was expelled by a decree of the ministerial committee, but Galytzin still was not dismissed. The monk, now assured of success, determined to take in person the initiative for the removal of his hated enemy. Meeting the prince in the palace of the Countess Orloff, he loaded him with the most furious invectives, called him a son of Satan, who should be silent when the Lord spoke to him through the mouth of his anointed, and ended by pronouncing an anathema upon the man who, in reality, was still his superior. Galytzin had nothing left but to withdraw, and demand satisfaction from the emperor. This was the very thing that Photi wanted, and it explained why, when Galytzin had left the house, he received the terrified Countess with the exclamation of triumph, 'The Lord is with us!' He knew well enough that Alexander could never venture to break his promise, given to the 'messenger from heaven;' and by noising abroad the scandalous incident as much as possible, he forced Galytzin to repair without delay to the emperor. Alexander was at first surprised; but the persuasions of Araktchéyef, of Gladkoff the Chief of the Police, and of General Uvaroff the Commander of the Guard, and an accomplice of the conspirators of 1801, prevailed with him to consent to the downfall of the 'hopelessly compromised' minister. Two more letters from Photi, presented privately to the emperor by Uvaroff, assured the triumph of the plot; and on Ascension-day, May 15, 1824, an Imperial decree was issued, allowing Galytzin to hold office as Postmaster-general, but removing him from his posts as Minister of Public Worship and Instruction, and Procurator-general of the Synod, and abolishing at the same time the Ministry of Public Worship. Photi's programme had been carried out to the utmost.

But the vindictive fanatic was still not satisfied. Although properly he ought to have returned to his monastery, he remained at St. Petersburg, to deluge the emperor with a whole flood of fresh letters, to persist in his denunciations of persons he disliked, including even Philaret, the worthy Metropolitan of Moscow, to mark out, as dangerous to Russia, the multitude of 'heretical foreigners' at Court and in offices of dignity, and, lastly, to calculate, for the emperor's benefit, that the year 1836 ($18=6+6+6$ and $36=6\times6-6$ the cypher of the Apocalyptic year) would be the year of doom mentioned in Revelation. He seemed, however, at last to have outworn the emperor's patience. On August 6,

1824, he received a command to appear 'privately' in the Imperial cabinet. Of this second audience his own notes record as follows :—The monarch received the Archimandrite with coolness and severity, and reproached him for his conduct towards Galytzin. On Photi's attempting to open his mouth in his defence, the emperor harshly bade him hold his peace, and went on to upbraid him for his unchristian behaviour. 'Does Photi,' he ended, 'understand what the Czar has said to him?' The Archimandrite listened in silence till the emperor seemed to have given vent enough to his displeasure. Then he began in a long harangue to portray the purity of his zeal and the extent of the dangers which had threatened Church and State. 'Saint Nicholas' (so his well-weighed reply concluded) 'did not hesitate to smite Arius publicly in the face for a lie, and allow himself to be unfrocked for it by the Fathers.' 'You see, then,' broke in the emperor, 'how it fared with the saint for his excess of zeal.' Photi had only waited for this objection. 'The Fathers condemned him,' he retorted with emphasis, 'but the Lord has blessed him;' and therewith he drew from his pocket a carefully-prepared dissertation on the fall of St. Nicholas, and gave it to the astonished emperor to read. Alexander perused the paper, and returned it with a look expressive of confusion. But Photi now saw his opportunity, and took from the pockets and sleeves of his dress, and lastly from his boots, every possible paper and document, by which to prove the 'diabolical' schemes of his enemies, and the vastness of his own services to throne and altar, in having 'unmasked them;' and in extracting these papers, managed to manipulate so cleverly that the emperor caught sight of the penitential hair-cloth, with iron rings, which he wore next his naked skin.

The crafty monk had now won his game. 'The Czar was seized with remorse, and reddened as with a holy fire of shame.' At length he sank upon his knees, begged the modern prophet Nathan for his blessing and intercession, and left him to retire with the consciousness of having once more achieved a signal triumph.

The character of this sovereign, with whom the coarse and low-minded Archimandrite of Novgorod was able to play such an extraordinary game, is introduced by the Russian historian Pypin [1] with the remark that, ' even the personality of an absolute ruler is but a product of the relations surrounding it—essentially such as circumstances make it. In the person of Alexander I. were reflected the most opposite and contradictory tendencies of the time. Together with aspirations after enlightenment and liberty, there were embodied in him leanings, thoroughly reactionary, tending to oppression and arbitrary power; indeed, from the weakness of his character, he followed at times simultaneously both one and the other bent.' Viewed in connection with the incident above related, these self-contradictions will only explain his conduct on the supposition, that the basis of the collective Russian life of that time was essentially barbaric, and wholly unaffected by those influences of European culture which merely touched the surface. And yet the typical representative of this period—the sovereign wavering in such marvellous fashion between extremes, but in his inmost nature still remaining a barbarian—has for years been treated by official historians as a higher being, looked up to

---

[1] *The Movement in Russian Society under Alexander I.*: St. Petersburg, 1871. Pypin for this work was elected a member of the Academy of Sciences, but the minister, Count Tolstoy, induced him to decline the honour.

with admiration as a superlatively liberal-minded potentate, called '*notre Ange*' by his slighted and neglected consort, and 'the blessed' by the spokesmen of a great nation! In the worship of his memory the present emperor and his brothers have been brought up from their infancy, and have been accustomed all their lives to venerate the eldest brother of their father as one of the greatest men of all times. To reach up to Alexander I. has for years been the aim and object of Alexander II. Meanwhile, however, Court tradition has sufficiently instructed the present representatives of the Imperial house to let them know what has been compatible with the holiness, the ideal aspirations, and the liberalism of their idol.

CHAPTER II.

Incapacity of former governors—Military officials—Shirkovitch's appointment as Governor of Simbirsk—A New-Year's masquerade at the Winter Palace—Araktchéyef and his nominee—Life at St. Petersburg under Nicholas.

FEW things have provoked such general and bitter ridicule, both in Russia and abroad, as the incapacity of the higher officials of the government, the mode of their selection and employment, and the peculiar rule by which their performances are judged. Of some kinds of high functionaries it might be said without exaggeration, that they have become comic characters in the literature of their country. What Russian does not know that the 'exalted official' in Griboyedoff's comedy, M. Famussoff, is a Moscow Senator? Who has not seen the shrugging of shoulders that regularly takes place, whenever it is said of anyone that he has been promoted, or as the saying goes, has 'tumbled' into the Senate?

Even the governors in former days fared no better than the *patres conscripti*. The governor in Gogol's 'Dead Souls' is chiefly remarkable for his skill in embroidery and other feminine employments. Alexander Herzen declares that among the innumerable chiefs of governments whom he had met, he only knew one, who had qualified himself even decently for his post, and this was the Greek Kuruta, who had entered the Russian service. The governors in Saltykoff-Schotschedrin's

'Provincial Sketches' are regularly the dupes of their subordinates, and even the modern, humane, and intelligent governor whom Turgenieff commends as a tolerable administrator of the province committed to his charge, and as the owner, by the way, of an incomparably soft and well-tended pair of moustachios, is a semi-comical figure.

To this proconsular dignity there was formerly but one means of approach. This was to have commanded a regiment—if possible, a regiment of the Guard—and by services of some sort or another to have attracted the notice of the emperor. Twelve years have passed since the well-known writer Juri Samarin declared that no military man had a chance of acquiring the legal and political training demanded for the administration of an extensive district. The remark was made at a time when the influence of this writer and his friends was at its highest, and it appears to have made a great impression, like the mass of misstatements in whose company it was first published. Of the sixty-four provincial governors, now holding office in European and Asiatic Russia, more than twenty are still military men by profession; and out of the remainder there are a large number who only in riper years exchanged the military for the civil service. And as with the post of governor, so with ministerial and other high offices of State. The late Minister of the Interior, General Timascheff, was formerly a cavalry officer; Makoff, his colleague and afterwards his successor, doffed his Uhlan uniform only a few years ago; Greig, the Minister of Finance, was formerly in the Chevaliergarde; Possiet, the Minister of Public Works, was an old sailor. And besides these military ministers, and the sons and brothers of the emperor, who likewise belong to the military class, no less than nineteen generals belong to the Plenum of the Council of State.

That certain primitive defects of Russian administration, that in particular the habit of arbitrary rule, the violation of the forms of justice, and the restriction of the rights guaranteed to the estates and provinces, are part and parcel of the customary system of utilising military men for the higher posts of the civil service; and that the barrenness of the representative system in government circles, called into life in 1862, is to be ascribed to three-fourths of these military governors, and to their inability to tolerate contradiction—on these points no difference of opinion any longer exists among those who are acquainted with the real state of things. When, if ever, it shall be resolved to separate the various branches of the administration, to insist upon a certain measure of education from all higher officials, and to discard the notion that a general can be converted at once into a financier, a professor or teacher into an Administrator of Domains, a Treasury official changed with impunity into the Curator of a University, the Director of the Court theatre or the President of a court of justice—then, but not till then, will some improvement be possible.

That the present government has not yet resolved upon this seemingly impending reform, is due to various reasons, among others, to the fact that the number of State servants, who possess a competent education, is still comparatively small; for instance, the appointment of none but trained jurists to judicial offices, as required by law, has not been fully practicable to this day. But the chief thing to be considered in this respect is that the generation now ruling has been brought up under customs and traditions, the power of which cannot be broken at once, and which represent the right of persons, favourably known by the emperor, to any employment that the latter chooses to bestow, as an indispensable attribute of absolutism. How naïvely this doctrine was practised under the former government, is known, for instance, from the history of the Finance and Post departments. The customary mode of appointing governors, which has passed, without any essential modifications,[1] into the *succum et sanguinem* of the new era, has been described only a few years ago with such incomparable liveliness by Shirkovitch, himself a former governor, that a short summary of his narrative will make any further details superfluous.

M. Shirkovitch served with distinction in the artillery, and rose to be major-general; but in the year 1839 was compelled, by a disagreement with a superior, to tender his resignation. The father of a numerous family, and wholly destitute of private means, he resolved, in order to avoid starvation, to go and try his fortunes at St. Petersburg, and 'look out for a place.' With a small sum, laboriously scraped together, in his pocket, and without any friends at Court to look to, the general, in a faint-hearted and seemingly desperate humour, reached that city where, as the saying goes, 'hearts are always dry and the streets are always wet.' His one hope lay in a cursory acquaintance, dating many years back, with the Minister of Marine, Prince Alexander Sergejevitch Mentchikoff, who, after having begun his career as *attaché* of the Imperial Embassy at Vienna, among other things had served in the artillery.

---

[1] Under the present government, it is true, several competent governors have been appointed from among the provincial nobility. But many of them appear to have given umbrage by their independent line of conduct.

With beating heart the applicant entered the house of this grandee, so feared for his haughty manners and his biting tongue, who recollected, however, the acquaintance of early years, and seemed willing to help him in his difficulties. On being asked by the prince what kind of service he had thought of, the honest old soldier answered that he wished for a post under the Minister of War; about the Civil Service he knew nothing. 'That will never do,' replied Mentchikoff, 'I am on bad terms again with Tchernytcheff.[1] But I could recommend you to Bludoff, who is a good friend of mine, and could give you perhaps a governor's appointment.' Armed with a short note given him by Mentchikoff, Shirkovitch announces himself next day to the Minister of the Interior, a complete stranger to him. Count Bludoff is in a good humour; he receives favourably the *protégé* of the Minister of Marine, enters into conversation with him, introduces him to the Director of the Chancellery, the actual[2] State Councillor Lex, and asks him to come again another day. At his second visit Shirkovitch learns that his new acquaintance is not indisposed to think of him for the next vacant post of governor; meanwhile Bludoff advises him to get himself made an actual State Councillor in the Ministry

---

[1] Prince Alexander Tchernytcheff, the Minister of War, laboured under the weakness of considering himself the real conqueror of Napoleon, and took every opportunity that offered of recounting his great exploits in war, and thereby became the constant butt of Mentchikoff's mischievous wit. 'Comment s'appelle donc la ville qu' Alexandre avait pris?' asked Tchernytcheff's wife once at a large party, while holding up her husband as the Alexander *par excellence*. 'Vous pensez sans doute à Babylonne,' was Mentchikoff's reply.

[2] The word 'actual' applied to a Councillor of State or a Privy-Councillor, indicates the higher grade of these respective dignities. But the official rank or Tchin does not designate necessarily actual office. The Privy Council in Russia has been extinct for more than a century. [TR.]

of the Interior. No sooner said than done. The very next day Shirkovitch is dressed already in the civil uniform of one of the officials of the fourth class attached to the Ministry of the Interior ' for special duties,' and takes the oath of office before the assembled Senate—a ceremony entailing, sad to say, the payment of forty roubles, which have to go as ' tips ' to the various porters and couriers of the Minister and of the Chancellery of the Senate. Now begin the duties of office. The honest fellow who, by his own confession, had never had the remotest experience of civil administration, prepares a memorandum on administrative reforms in the German colonies of the Volga, which gains the entire approval of Bludoff and of the high and mighty M. Lex. Next, he is made member of a Commission, appointed under the presidency of Baron Villiers, physician in ordinary to the emperor, to inquire into the remodelling of the Academy of Medicine and Surgery at St. Petersburg. Here also Shirkovitch conducts himself to the satisfaction of his high superiors :—Villiers himself, the presient, of course never appeared at the sittings. A few more days pass by, and the lucky Shirkovitch learns that he has been nominated Governor of Simbirsk, and that his nomination has already been confirmed by the emperor. Bludoff, after a few words of congratulation, sends him to the Director of the department of the Executive Police, Privy-Councillor Sämjäkin, who will inform him as to details. From Sämjäkin he learns that, first of all, two things are necessary—the due obtaining of a gala-uniform, in which the new governor of the fortunate province may be presented to His Majesty, and after that, the prompt execution of an Imperial decree, by which the Domain peasants of the province were to be made peasants of the Appanage Administration.[1] Shirkovitch, as he confesses, is wholly in the dark as to what are Domain peasants and what Appanage peasants; but, with the instinct of a born statesman, he gathers that to obtain the gala-uniform in time is the most important thing at present, and on this he centres all his efforts. *Fortes fortuna adjuvat*; and within four-and-twenty hours the necessary ceremonial costume is procured :—so momentous, indeed, was the matter, that Bludoff had given orders to be awakened, if necessary, in the night, as soon as his *protégé* had succeeded in duly fitting himself out for the occasion. Arrived in the Imperial ante-chamber, Shirkovitch overhears the monarch, who was then in his cabinet, inquiring who the new governor of Simbirsk really is, and in what branch of the army he has served : as to any further testing of his capability, not a word is said. Another ex-general, who has also been made a governor, enters by chance the ante-chamber, and both gentlemen have to wait for ten minutes. Shirkovitch during this interval is seized with grave apprehension ; his new colleague has a different kind of boots on from his own. One of them, it is evident, has committed a breach of etiquette, which may lead to serious consequences. At last the signal is given for admission. The emperor, in the undress uniform of the Ismailoff regiment of the Guard, stands at his writing-table ; he lets Shirkovitch explain his military antecedents, addresses a few words to him about the importance of transferring the Domain peasants to the Appanage department, and courteously dismisses the man, now promoted to rule a million of his subjects.[2] 'I promise,' adds Shirkovitch to himself,

[1] Perhaps it may be useful to remind the reader that the Appanage estates are those reserved for the maintenance of the Imperial family. [TR.]
[2] The Government of Simbirsk is nearly twice and a half as large as the Kingdom of Würtemberg.

'punctually to perform the will of my gracious sovereign, and to dedicate to him all my energies.'

Filled with this praiseworthy resolve, Shirkovitch arranges to make further official visits, and seek for instruction from his new superiors. The number of these superiors is Legion. First, he has to present himself to Bludoff's civil adjutant, Count Stroganoff; then to the Director of the Chancellery, M. Lex; then to Sämjäkin, the director of the department; after that, to Perovski, the President of the Appanage department; to Perovski's superior, the Minister Prince Wolkonski; to Daschkoff, the Minister of Justice, and of course to the 'great Count Benckendorf,' the Chief of the Administration of all Administrations, namely, that of the Political Police. In these interviews no mention is made of any real business ; the utmost that is done is that Sämjäkin condescends to point out by name those persons with whom the new governor will have most to do, and warns him against certain 'bad men,' such as Besstusheff, the administrator of the Appanage estates of Simbirsk—a 'downright rogue.' Pity only, that this same Besstusheff had been pictured before to Shirkovitch by Count Perovski, the President of the Appanage department, and afterwards Minister of the Interior, as the 'pillar of the service,' and a worthy man, whose confidence he should obtain at any price. Daschkoff, the Minister of Justice, knows of nothing better to do than to tell the new governor of Simbirsk about his estates in that province and to beg him to be kind to the local administrator who (of course without any fault of his own) has got the reputation of being a very 'peasant-flayer.' Shirkovitch answers that he will do all in his power, but of course in this matter he must 'keep the law well in view.' Daschkoff thereupon points out that in the case of a recommendation conveyed by a Minister of Justice, this is taken for granted, and he compliments his new acquaintance upon the manliness he has shown as a 'genuine' governor, and calls the choice made by his friend Bludoff a first-rate one in every respect. Leaving behind him twenty-five roubles for the valet who congratulates him on his appointment, and five roubles for his excellency's porter, Shirkovitch proceeds on his round. Benckendorf, in a few sententious phrases, touches on the importance of preserving a good understanding (unhappily so often disturbed) between the organs of the ordinary and the superior police.[1] The 'benefactor' Mentchikoff displays the severe and imperious air which a minister is bound to study when he has to do with a private acquaintance who has become an official subordinate. There remains now the visit to Field-Marshal Prince Wolkonski. Before the door of this magnate, who, as Minister of the Imperial Court, is also supreme head of the Appanage Administration, Shirkovitch first receives a check; His Highness declines to receive anyone, having lost a grand-daughter. Shirkovitch explains that he has to receive from the minister his instructions respecting the Domain peasants in Simbirsk, who are to be placed under the Appanage department, and he is finally admitted. The Prince is unexpectedly gracious; and vouchsafes Shirkovitch a longer interview, when he touches on every subject but that of business, to say nothing of Appanage peasants. At the end of his round the new Governor of Simbirsk knows just as

[1] The powers of the officers of the Gendarmerie, who have charge of the 'political police,' not being adequately defined, and their chief duties consisting in the private supervision of all officers, administrative and judicial, it is a rule that the governor of a province and his subordinates are at daggers drawn with the local gendarmerie, and that both branches of the administration do all in their power to injure each other.

much about the matter, the carrying out of which had been represented to him by his sovereign as his cardinal duty, as he did at the beginning—in other words, nothing at all.

Fully to appreciate this instructive narrative, which bears every trace of being true to life, we require perhaps to know the somewhat prolix language of Shirkovitch himself. Nowhere in his account do we find a shadow of surprise at this manner of conducting business. As a man of experience, he had long since learned that things could not be carried on differently; and he accepts it all just as naïvely as the other actors in the farce. They all knew well enough that for the proper selection of high officials there was but one method, and that the Emperor Nicholas only did what had been done before him by Alexander I., by Paul, by Catherine the Great, and by the Russian of Russians, Elizabeth. The practices above described are in fact immemorial, bequeathed from one generation to another, and all public functionaries, including the highest, have never known any other. Elsewhere also, no doubt, it happens that influences and pressure of a social kind invade the territory of politics; but in Russia only does the rule prevail, that social qualifications and none other determine the fitness of candidates for employment by the State; and that the personal infallibility of the sovereign is a maxim of universal application, and regarded as the necessary outflow of absolutism. So, indeed, tradition demands; and with tradition it is always difficult to break—most difficult of all, where it fits in with inclination. How deep-rooted and ineradicable among our emperors is the habit of personal government—that is to say, of deciding according to accidental impressions —can hardly be exemplified more clearly than by the following well-authenticated extract from the life of Alexander I.[1] :—

Up to the year 1835 the whole of the Winter Palace was regularly on New Year's Eve thrown open to everyone without ticket, for a masquerade, which consisted of the Court, dressed in domino, going in procession through all the rooms. In the Theatre of the Hermitage the Court had supper. The public filled the palace in thousands; peasants in sheepskins crowded in. It had been the custom since the time of Alexander I. to ask the names of the first person who entered and of the last who left the building, and to report them the next day to the emperor. The chief of a section in the Ministry of War under the all-powerful Araktchéyef had never yet been to a masquerade or a theatre; his whole life long he was in bed at ten o'clock and up with the sun. A sister of his wife comes up from the country, and the old man determines to go to the January masquerade. To his misfortune, he goes. At eleven o'clock he is so sleepy that he does not know what to with himself. Now in some of the passage-rooms of the large parterre of the palace there are a series of small, unlit cabinets, with arm-chairs. He slips into one of these, and tells his wife to follow the crowd, make the tour of the rooms, and fetch him away when all is over. This, alas! is impossible; the curtains have been lowered, the cabinets are many, the procession endless. The ladies in despair drive home, but the old man is awakened in the morning by the *frotteurs*. He had been the last, but also the first, in the hope of getting away all the quicker. A year goes by: Araktchéyef recommends some of his subordinates for rewards, including the chief of his section, who is his right-hand man. The emperor confirms his recommendation, but strikes out the name of this particular nominee. Araktchéyef summons courage to speak, but the emperor interrupts him with the remark, 'You ministers, what do you know about it? This official visits every masquerade : he is the last as well as the first; he is not a man to work.' All representations were in vain; the man was forced to resign, and yet he had never left his house but to go to the Chancellery : there he had been the last and the first.

---

[1] Compare the German *St. Petersburg Zeitung*, No. 23, of Jan. 23 (Feb. 4), 1878:—' Schicksale eines Livländers in St. Petersburg von 1833 bis auf die Gegenwart, I.' The author of these very readable sketches, which have been translated into Russian, formerly held high office in the State.

To the danger of being accidentally deceived, and diverted from large and important interests by mere social trivialities of daily life, the Emperor Nicholas was even more exposed than his brother. Putting aside their common fondness for military parade and that constant soldiering which no princes of the house of Holstein-Gottorp seem able to dispense with, these two sovereigns resembled each other as little in their habits as in their dispositions. Whilst Alexander I. lived, generally speaking, so retired that, with the exception of a few older confidants, he saw scarcely a soul, Nicholas, especially when a young man, was extremely sociable and accustomed, from the number of his acquaintances, to take an active interest in the daily trifles of St. Petersburg life. Of the inanity of this life and the petty interests that stirred it, no one can have an idea who has not had a personal insight into it, and learned to know the men and the doings that agitated the capital between 1840 and 1860. To a St. Petersburger of to-day it sounds like a myth that there have been times when blowing soap-bubbles was a pastime of fashionable *salons* and the pretended discoverer of the art was the hero of the day; when the naturalisation as a French subject of an insignificant singer, the tenor Ivanoff, in 1844,[1] was resented by the Autocrat of all the Russias, and by a large number of his faithful subjects, as an affront to the national honour; and when the question (ultimately referred to the emperor) 'whether the officers of the Guard, appointed to the Army-corps of the Caucasus, should wear caps or hats during their stay in the capi-

---

[1] The painter Aivasovski, who was staying in Paris at this time, thought it necessary for his safety to contradict, in a letter addressed direct to the minister, Prince Wolkonski, the rumour of his intended settlement in France.

tal,' was able to split high society for several weeks into two hostile camps.[1] The generation which grew up under those influences sits to-day at the helm of State; can anyone then wonder that important differences of principle are still treated as mere personal questions, and decided with reference to social convenience and custom?

[1] Gleboff and Massloff, two of the Hussar officers of the Guard appointed to the Caucasus, wore, during a leave of absence spent at St. Petersburg in 1841, the fur caps prescribed for the Army of the Caucasus, instead of the customary shako, and by so doing gave occasion to an animated controversy between the Commander of the Guard and the Governor-General, Count Woronzoff.

CHAPTER III.

Radical members of the nobility—The old and the new eras—Griboyedoff's sketches of high life at Moscow—Memoirs of Herzen and Passek—Early life of Passek—Family of the Jakovleffs—'Count Feodor, the chemist'—Parental home of Alexander Herzen—His early life and education—Demoralising influences—Later defects of character—His friends Granovski and Belinski—Old Russian aristocrats.

THE spokesmen of modern Radicalism in Russia are sprung in great measure from the high nobility of their country. Bakunin's cousins and brothers figure still with some distinction as Adjutants-General and Marshals of Noblesse. Prince Michael Krapotkin, so often mentioned during the trial of the Socialists in the spring of last year, is a brother of the Governor of Charkoff, who was murdered for his vigorous prosecution of the Nihilists. Prince Alexander Urossoff, famous as the defender of Netchayeff and other Nihilists—the same man who, after having been banished from Moscow only five years ago as a political *suspect*, was appointed in 1876 Assistant in the Department of State for Poland, and transferred to St. Petersburg in that capacity only last year—boasts of being cousin of the Chancellor of the Empire. A son of the late Adjutant-General, Count Jacob Rostovzoff, was imprisoned in 1862 for being a correspondent of Alexander Herzen's 'Kolokol' ('The Bell'). Herzen himself was the illegitimate son of an aristocrat of rank, and nephew of a lieutenant-general and a senator who had been ambassador at the court of King Jerome. Herzen's companion, Ogareff, belonged likewise to an ancient and noble family, and was the son of a senator. His rival, Prince Peter Dolgoruki—the author of one of the most venomous books that has ever been written against the Russian government—boasts a direct lineage from the house of Rurik the Varangian, and has a reigning prince among his ancestors. Ivan Golowin has sprung from a house whose name was mentioned five hundred years ago in the register (*Barchatnaja Kniga*) of the high nobility.[1] All these men have risen to high places under the traditions of the old *régime*, and were brought up by parents who were the most exclusive aristocrats and the staunchest conservatives of their time. Very many of their contemporaries even now make no secret of their predilection for serfdom and its sister institutions, and do their best to counteract and frustrate the results achieved by the reforms after 1860. The bulk, however, of this generation vacillates helplessly between the old and the new era, and unites with occasional aspirations of an advanced liberal or even a radical character, habits and inclinations that are usually found only among downright 'Junkers' and men of unbridled passions and unlimited power.

Certain common peculiarities, however, occur among all the representatives of this generation without distinction of party. The same incapacity for consistent, methodical work, the same hankering after self-will and boundless indulgence, the same aversion to all that even looks like subordination to external authority, which constitute a reproach to Russian statesmen and aristocrats, who have risen under the *ancien régime*, are as plainly discernible in the radical leaders of young

---

[1] It is notorious, we suppose, that all those who took part in the conspiracy of 1825 belonged to the high nobility.

Russia. Both parties have their origin in the same school; both are the fruits of the same tree, differing far more materially in the shell than in the kernel.

Of the kind of society, under whose auspices the present generation of Russian nobles has been trained, we have several, and in their way, classical illustrations; above all, those which Griboyedoff has given in his immortal comedy, 'Sorrow comes from Sense' (*Gôre ot umà*). It is not only that the chief characters in this piece, such as the senator Famussoff, who hates all business, the secretary Moltschalin, unable to express an independent opinion from his 'humble rank,' the book-hating blusterer Colonel Skalosub, the profligate actor Repetiloff, the notorious swindler, but universal favourite, Anton Antonitch Sagorezki, represent types of a widespread species; but even the seemingly most trifling allusion to contemporary persons and events, which abound in this incomparable play, give an insight into the history of the manners of that time which is instructive in the extreme. Thus the 'Nestor of high-born rogues,' who 'would sell his two oldest and trustiest servants for a pair of greyhounds,' is the famous Bluebeard of his time, General Ismailoff. The 'genius of the first rank —the duellist, bully and gambler who scoffed at decency and law,' is the so-called 'American' Tolstoy, whom, in spite of his criminal propensities bordering on the insane, and even of his escape from Siberia, Alexander I. always received back into favour. The Prince Feodor, however, of whom his relatives report with horror, that—

> The Prince eschews all titles, rank, and stars—
> To dream of plants and dote upon his 'jars.'
> He's turned a full-blown 'chemist'—and so shy,
> He's but to see a lady, and he'll fly—

is Herzen's cousin Jakovleff. And though we cannot perhaps literally apply to the *frondeurs* and brawling Nationalists what Repetiloff says of the circle of friends and politic-mongers, who assemble for 'secret purposes' every Thursday evening at the English club at Moscow, still of those, too, it may be said :—

> So learnedly we argue and so loud,
> None hears his voice amid the wrangling crowd—
> Of Byron's poetry and Constant's prose,
> The sacred rights of man and nations' woes,
> Juries, and Parliaments—small things and great—
> And metaphysics and affairs of State:
> A glorious noise, my brother, how it spreads
> Warmth through our hearts and fancy through our heads!

Griboyedoff's sketches of high life at Moscow are largely filled up, as is well known, and in some places exaggerated, from Alexander Herzen's Autobiography. The portraits which the founder of the young Russian school has drawn of his father and his father's brothers and sisters, of the 'Revel Merchant,' Karl Ivanovitch Sonnenberg, and others, possess a value, not only as being superior specimens of what the modern memoir literature of Russia has to show, but as illustrating the study of Russian life and manners in a way that cannot be too highly appreciated.

That these indictments against the *ancien régime* and its boundless demoralisation are not exaggerated—that Herzen drew from nature, and has in some cases rather softened down than overdrawn, is strikingly confirmed by the Memoirs of his contemporary and relative, Tatjana Passek. The literature of memoirs affords, perhaps, no other example of two autobiographies such as these, each written with a different object and from opposite points of view, so perfectly supplementing each other and leading to exactly the same conclusions.

It is strictly accurate to say that since Passek's revelations have appeared, no doubt or obscurity can exist any longer as to the true nature of the events and persons depicted by Herzen. In themselves the two books, of course, are widely different. The power of Herzen's representation lies in the author's eminent talent for unfolding traits of character, in his discrimination between the essence and its accidents, and in the justice with which he brings out the better features of even the most corrupt and depraved natures. It was just because he aimed at representing 'pure fiction' that the author of 'Byloje i dumi' was able to produce an historical picture of the times, which will remain quite as intelligible to posterity as it was to his contemporaries, and is exempt for ever from the danger of growing stale. Tatjana Passek, on the other hand, keeps to the individual and concrete; she calls things by their real names. She strives throughout to adhere to historical narrative, and compensates by faithfulness of detail for what is wanting in her of descriptive talent and depth of literary power. She has left behind her, not indeed a work of art, but an excellent photograph of those events which Herzen elaborated into a picture, as rich in colour as unrivalled in fidelity to life. The chief merit of Madame Passek's narrative consists in the proofs, amounting almost to demonstration, which it affords that Herzen and his friends do not differ essentially from their surroundings; that they are the creatures of, and in many respects responsible for much of what they have afterwards learned to condemn. The authoress herself has followed no fixed bent; she has simply wished to narrate. The circle of young revolutionists, who gathered round Herzen, and whose later action left a permanent impress on the Russian Liberalism of the present day, is introduced to us in its every-day dress; and what its members did, and what they left undone, are described by an eye-witness. The moral of her narrative, though not expressly told, is plain. Enough is seen in this collection of examples, culled apparently at hap-hazard, to show that the men of the revolutionary period, represented in her pages, are types and creatures of a species to whom the very names of duty and morality are unknown, and whose vices have infected all their descendants alike, even those of most opposite views and opinions.

We have mentioned that Tatjana Passek (Kutschin was her maiden name) was a relative of Alexander Herzen. The history of this relationship is so remarkable in connection with what remains to describe, that we must dwell upon it for a moment. At the end of the last century there lived in Moscow a Boyar, Alexei Jakovleff,[1] of boundless wealth, and belonging to the higher nobility, who, in addition to a number of married daughters, including a Princess Chovanski and a Madame Golochvastoff, left behind him four sons. All of these became fathers of a numerous progeny; but their descendants and their name have died with them, since none of them ever made a prudent or judicious marriage. The eldest son Peter, when a lieutenant-general and a man of mature age, ran away with a young Swiss girl, a former governess in the house of General Suchtelen, lived with her for many years, and made her the mother of a number of daughters, of whom the eldest married a M. Kutschin, and ultimately became the mother of our authoress. *In extremis* the

---

[1] The Jakovleffs boasted a common ancestry with the house of Romanoff; and, like the latter, derived their origin from Weidewut, King of ancient Prussia, and his son, Andreas Kobyla. It is said that Weidewut emigrated into Russia in 1341, and was there baptized.

age-stricken general married a widow of bad repute, Madame Ulski, with whom he had been for many years on intimate terms. The second brother, Alexander, had taken his discharge from the service when a young officer, and on the strength of his share of patrimony, led the life of a reckless 'peasant-grinder' of the old school, surrounded with a whole harem of favourites. No sooner had his elder brother died, than he commenced a lawsuit against the widow, took possession of the family estates, broke open one night the writing-desk of the deceased, and secretly burned the will, by which the latter had formally emancipated all his servants. A tyrant of the true Asiatic kind, he ransacks the estate to fill his harem, allows the property itself to go to ruin, ill-treats the peasants, and finally falls out with his co-heirs; to annoy whom he marries, when almost on his death-bed, one of his former mistresses, leaving the son who was born of this union the sole heir of his enormous property.

This son is the 'Chemist' Count Feodor of Griboyedoff's comedy—a strange creature, who devotes himself exclusively to the study of natural science, takes up his quarters in a single room of his wealthy father's mansion, lets the splendid household of his ancestors sink miserably to decay, and withdraws himself altogether from the world. His illegitimate half-brothers and sisters, who are counted by dozens, he releases from servitude: he portions them off liberally, and behaves to them with kindness, but purposely avoids giving any of them a decent education; they must remain, as they are, half-civilised, so as not to encumber him at any time with claims.[1]

---

[1] Tatjana Passek thus describes a visit to the house of the 'Chemist,' who, by the way, became Herzen's brother-in-law, and exercised much influence

Ivan and Leo, the two youngest sons of Jakovleff's family, were brought up in the European manner. Ivan, after resigning his captaincy in the Guard, had lived for ten years in Germany, France, and Italy, and on his return to Moscow, in 1811, had brought with him the daughter of a Stuttgard citizen, Henriette Haag, who began by officiating as his coffee-server, then bore him two sons, and ended by remaining the companion of his whole after-life. This Henriette (the name being unpronounceable by the Russian domestics, and the common idea being that all German men are called Ivan, she was called all her life Louise Ivanovna) was the mother of Alexander Herzen. The name 'Herzen' had been added by M. Jakovleff to both his sons, whom otherwise he treated very differently, to express his '*heart*-felt attachment to their mother.' With this lady he lived under one roof, and treated her with a certain amount of consideration; but he never had the courage to give her his own name and rank.

over him:—'In the ante-room we were received by a numerous array of domestics, whose sole employment was smoking and playing cards. One of these idlers conducted us through a series of vast apartments, never lighted and never warmed, and just in the same state they were left in by their late owner when he set out for St. Petersburg. On the floor all around were standing huge chests, crammed promiscuously with costly vessels and utensils of crystal, marble, and porcelain. On marble tables and bronze *étagères* lay objects of every sort and kind. On the walls hung costly gilded frames, emptied of their pictures, which leaned in dozens against the panelling. Half-broken chandeliers hung from the ceiling. Everything was covered finger-deep with dust, and reflected in melancholy grandeur by the pier-glasses that reached from ceiling to parquet. Stumbling over every conceivable obstacle, we came at length to a room which was inhabited. Alexander opened a door hung with tapestry, which led to the 'Chemist's' cabinet and laboratory. He was sitting motionless, amid a chaos of books, retorts, and chemical utensils, upon a divan covered with a tiger-skin, which was exchanged every evening for pillows and coverlet. The same piece of furniture, which he used at daytime when eating and working, served him for sleeping on at night.'

Jakovleff's youngest brother Leo, commonly known only as 'the Senator,' was also a member of this household about 1820. At the end of his year's instruction in the Guard, the necessary qualification for every aristocratical profession, he entered upon his diplomatic career, and after serving as ambassador in turns at Stuttgard, Cassel (at the court of King Jerome Napoleon), and Stockholm, was enrolled among the *patres conscripti* of Moscow, where he was then almost a stranger. That a distinguished gentleman, such as he was, with a French education, and now a full-blown *diplomat*, should know nothing whatever of the laws he had to administer, and next to nothing of the language in which those laws were written, was a matter of no surprise; and it nowise hindered him from leading a life as active as it was enjoyable. He had been so early accustomed to lead a purely titular existence, that this seemed to him to be the only proper form of statesmanship. He had entered regularly upon his duties as ambassador shortly before the rupture of diplomatic relations between Russia and the Courts concerned. He had then been removed, as actual Chamberlain of the Imperial Court, to Moscow—a place where the Court appeared once in every three years at the outside, and then always for a short time only. Beloved on all sides, during the many years he lived with his brother and his brother's children, for his good-nature, his amiability, and his indestructible youthfulness, the old gentleman filled the offices of Senator, of honorary member of the department of supreme guardianship, of president of the Alexander Institute, and chief director of the Mary Hospital, besides the dignities of Chamberlain and Privy-Councillor. His coat, covered with stars, looked like a map of the firmament. So far, however, from being oppressed with this load of business, the worthy old man, always healthy, always merry, and always busy, led the simplest and most innocent life in the world. In the morning, after signing his papers, he would attend the various sittings and committee-meetings—for he was an active member of societies, medical, agricultural, archæological, and philanthropic—at midday he was off to some official or semi-official dinner, then to the French play; at teatime he would make his appearance in the rooms of Louise Ivanovna, to tell the news and bandy arguments with his usually morose elder brother, whom he treated with more politeness than he received; after that he generally went to some ball or rout. On Sundays there was a family 'spread' at the Princess Chovanski's, the eldest and ultimately the centenarian sister of these brothers; an uneducated aristocrat, fossilised in bigotry and old Russianism.

To describe this household in detail would be superfluous after Herzen's incomparable sketches, which have been translated into German and most of the other leading languages of Europe.[1] Some notices, however, borrowed from the narrative of Madame Passek, will probably be of interest, even to those who are acquainted with her writings:—

> Not less than sixteen men-servants and maid-servants were employed to look after two old gentlemen, a lady of an anomalous position in society, and two children. Alexander Herzen, when a baby, was tended by three nurses: his father, who hardly ever drove out, kept a dozen horses, two coachmen, and two outriders, whose sole occupation consisted in fetching every evening the 'Moscow Gazette,' and in fighting and drinking. The winter was spent in one of M. Jakov-

---

[1] Compare *Memoiren eines Russen*: Hamburg, 1854, and *Jungrussisch und Altlivländisch*: Leipzig, 1870. Second edition, 1871.

leff's palatial mansions in Moscow, two of which were never used at all. The summer was passed in the country, where half a dozen big estates vied for the honour of a visit from their lord. Joy, indeed, this visit could bring to nobody. Ivan Jakovleff was a man in whom the libertinism of the Voltairian school, mixed with old-Russian indolence, love of ease, aristocratical arrogance, and a tendency to hypochondria, nurtured by imaginary illness, made a compound as disagreeable as eccentric. Prematurely old, hindered by his peculiar relations with the woman who shared his home from entertaining in his own house the company to which he was accustomed, he became, in time, a torment to himself and all around him. Men he openly and without exception despised; the one thing which he claimed from them were the forms of good breeding. The *convenances* of life were to him a kind of moral religion. Every affable approach he resented as familiarity, every spark of feeling as sentimentalism; and yet at the bottom he was a weak man. That he was not happy can easily be imagined; that his presence scared away all pleasure from others he was well aware. A constant *malade imaginaire*, he had always three doctors to attend him, and besides this, he never ceased to plague himself with household cares. He was always being robbed and cheated by his stewards, and so he kept double watch over everything he had about him. He would lock up the ends of candles and the half-empty decanters; but let himself be robbed of a whole forest on one of his estates, and of a whole crop of oats on another. Every evening his valet had to report to him exactly whether all the lights were out and the doors locked; but never did this scrupulous master examine whether his orders had been carried out. He allowed his empty houses to stand unlet to avoid any danger from fire, or risk of injury, and yet he insured them, while dooming them to certain ruin through the neglect of all repairs.

More extraordinary still were the internal arrangements of M. Jakovleff's household. The intercourse of this pretentious and formal old aristocrat with the outer world was limited to the numerous and, for the most part, wholly uneducated illegitimate offspring of his elder brothers, to some poor fellows whom he had taken under his protection, and to the school-fellows and tutors of his sons. With his female relations Louise

Ivanovna associated on a footing of equality; but from society she was excluded, notwithstanding her good manners, her numerous attendants, and her splendid residence. His social relations were on a par with all the rest; they were such as chance or the whim of the moment dictated. At times the whole house swarmed with men of eminence whom Ivan and 'the Senator' had known in early days. When the Court was at Moscow young Herzen and his brother would play their childish pranks in the company of the highest dignitaries of the empire. Count Miloradovitch, the Governor-General of St. Petersburg, General von Essen, the Governor of Moscow, Lieutenant-General Staal, Prince Jussopoff, the Director of the Kremlin Administration, Count Komarovski, the Adjutant of the Grand-duke Constantine, Prince Obolenski, and many others, were among their nearest acquaintances and friends; and when the Grand-duke Constantine, after having become a big man by his renunciation of the throne, came to Moscow, Ivan was obliged to squeeze his sick and pampered body into a court dress and spend an evening with the Imperial companion of his youth. Then came again weeks and months of isolation, during which the children never saw a single soul, except their governors and tutors[1] and M. Sonnenberg, the 'Merchant of Revel.'

This M. Sonnenberg was one of the most singular creatures in the world. An adventurer in the first instance, who had found his way from Esthonia to Moscow, he had filled in turn the parts of merchant,

---

[1] Alexander Herzen's education was divided at first between an ex-Abbé of Jacobin tendencies, the son of a Russian priest, and Herr Mess, an old German, from Sarepta. Several other tutors were afterwards added to this list.

tutor, agent, and steward of grandees. He had been saved from drowning, in the presence and by the order of Jakovleff, by a Cossack, who was rewarded, at Ivan's suggestion, by being made a non-commissioned officer. Jakovleff himself, a consummate idler in his way, accustomed to let chance govern all he did, and flattered by the consciousness that he had done two men—the rescuer and the rescued—a good service, so far interested himself in this ignorant and needy fortune-hunter, who had 'suffered every trouble that can befall a man without wit or money, with an ugly face, a servile spirit, and, especially, a German origin,' as to obtain for him, first the post of tutor in the house of the senator Ogareff, and afterwards to attach him to his own household. Here he employed him to play with the children, and to attend to 'particular commissions,' which were hardly ever executed. Ivan, in short, quartered him in one of his empty houses, loaded him with errands, received him at his table, and let him tell him the news. That the poor wretch had a hard life of it, under the constant teasings and fits of ill-humour of his noble patron, may readily be imagined; nor, on the other hand, is it strange that he became at length indispensable to Jakovleff, passed on, after his death, as an heirloom to his children, and remained till he died a client of the family which had rescued him from the water.

Much the same happened with a number of other persons whom chance brought into contact with the old hypochondriac, whose goodwill was as precarious and fickle as his displeasure. Some who had come only for a visit remained for years under his roof; others would come and go as accident or his caprice determined. Tatjana Passek, when at a boarding-school at Moscow, regularly spent her holidays in the house of her great-uncle, and a moralising letter which she wrote to Alexander so won the old man's heart that he took her away from school and had her educated in his own home. The daughter of a civilian's widow, who had nursed Alexander Herzen in an illness during his exile to Vyätka, was educated by old Jakovleff at his own expense at Moscow, and taken for months into his house. And yet, with all these traits of natural kindness, he would systematically disregard his duties towards his nearest relatives, grudging even trifling sums, which would have been invaluable to them, and ignominiously ignoring those who lacked the all-important *esprit de conduite*. His talented eldest son he spoiled, with a degree of weakness bordering on crime. The younger son, Jegor, notwithstanding his exemplary character, was so slighted and neglected that his brother was obliged to take his part and to frighten their father with the threat that, if it lasted, he and his mother would leave the paternal roof for ever.[1]

In order to secure the rights of nobility, indispensable for a suitable position in society to his sons, as children of a citizen of foreign extraction, Ivan not only had them carefully educated—they learned Latin, strange to say—but already, in their infancy, had them enrolled as civil officials of the Kremlin Administration. The chief of this department, Prince Jussupoff, was an old friend, and, as such, took care that the boys were regularly promoted, so that by the time they reached their majority they were already in the 'eighth class,' and entitled, accordingly, to the rights of hereditary nobles. Nothing, of course, was done for their moral education, and the peculiar circumstances of their position added

[1] Strangely enough, Alexander Herzen, in his otherwise so copious Memoirs, has not made the slightest mention of this brother.

to the mischief engendered by this defect. The servants' gossip taught the boys in early years the secret of their birth, and the family relations of their uncles on the father's side. The social contrasts between children born in and out of wedlock were revealed to them by the occasional indiscretions of their father, and the anomalous position of their mother, who, in spite of her excellent conduct and the tact and amiability of her deportment, was never able to win a footing of equality. The example daily set them was, as may well be imagined, of the very worst and most dangerous kind. As the father and his brothers behaved, so did all with whom they held most intercourse. Every matter of daily life gave evidence of dissoluteness, indifference to the moral law, submission to the whims and humours of the high aristocracy, and of other people worse than these. *Les convenances, les apparences*—these were the sole passport to an honourable position, and no man could shine in society without them. As for any respect for religious influences, such a thing was out of the question. The father was a devotee of Voltaire, and regarded the forms of worship as a requirement of circumstances which a man of the world must manage to comply with as cheaply as he could. The mother was a pious Lutheran, in the sense that she read Zschokke's 'Hours of Meditation,' and every Sunday took her children, who belonged to the Greek orthodox religion, to the Lutheran church of St. Peter and St. Paul, to listen to a wearisome rationalistic sermon. By the side of the French tutors, who had been trained in the school of the eighteenth-century philosophy, and who were entrusted with the chief instruction of his sons, the harmless Greek priest, in his function as a teacher of religion, naturally played a very wretched and pitiable part. Of course, no ecclesiastic ever crossed the threshold, except during the lesson-hours; this was as well understood in M. Jakovleff's house as in that of all other grandees of the orthodox Russian Empire. 'Reasons of health' forbade Ivan ever to go to church, and he carefully eschewed all contact with priests, even to dispensing with the customary house-consecration of Twelfth-night. The usual five-rouble note was presented by a servant to the pious fathers, waiting with cross and vestments in the antechamber, with the remark that the proffered blessings of the Church were taken as given and received.

The young naturally chimed in with the old. In his thirteenth year Alexander Herzen, who, when a child, as our authoress informs us, had had a warm and deep-seated religious feeling, and used to read the Gospel history with enthusiasm, was already such a desperate freethinker that the priest who admitted him *ad sacra* made a cross before him, and pronounced him a lost soul. His moral was just as defective as his religious education. These children of Jakovleff, watched over by servants and tutors of every sort, anxiously screened from every draught of air, and daily spoiled and kept in leading-strings, were in reality, at the decisive period of their life, left quite as much to themselves as were most of their noble contemporaries, educated on similar principles and under the same sharp contrasts. They had seen, heard, read, and learned all that was possible; but as for notions of duty, of authority, and of subordination to a moral law, independent of self-will and caprice, they were spared the very knowledge of such matters.

That Alexander Herzen was endowed not only with

brilliant intellectual gifts, but also with striking features of character and disposition, is confirmed by all testimonies about him, and especially by that of the female companion of his youth. When quite a boy he showed the warmest and tenderest sympathy with the sorrows of others, a passionate aversion to all that was mean and vulgar, and an abhorrence, allied to hatred, of the injustice done to the peasant-serfs and servants of his father. So spiritual was his bent of mind, that, in spite of the dependence of all about him on brilliant externals and worldly success, he rejected even in his childhood the prospect of the military and diplomatic career which was held forth to him, and set his heart on the idea of becoming, either as historian or poet, the benefactor and teacher of his countrymen. Before he was half-grown up he had gained a thorough knowledge, in its most various aspects, of the frivolous French literature of the eighteenth century; but his first acquaintance with Schiller and Goethe sufficed to imbue him with enthusiasm for true artistic taste, and a thoroughly ideal view of life. Contrary to the express wish of his father, he determined to pursue his studies at a University, and to enter the Faculty of Natural Science, although it offered to him no sort of career, and although his younger brother was already decorated with an order while he himself was still attending lectures. At an age when his companions knew no other pleasures than dissipation and the follies of fashion, he married, to the vexation of the whole family, a poor, but modest-minded cousin, who, as half-sister of 'the Chemist,' had been brought up and ill-treated in the house of the bigoted Princess Chovanski. Not the noble companions of his father, but young *savants*, enthusiastic for freedom and the dignity of human nature, were his favourite associates when he returned from the exile which he had brought upon himself by his devotion to the liberal ideas of the time.

But over all these promising beginnings and qualities fell the shadows even then of those vices which were the hereditary bane of the fashionable life and education of Russian grandees — the utter want of energy, of concentrative power, and of moral earnestness, and, above all, the *ljenj*—the genuine Slavonic addiction to idleness, combined with constant hankering after pleasure, which have afflicted the most illustrious minds of Russia. Spoiled and petted as a boy by all around him, Herzen already, as a young man, was tortured with such immoderate vanity that he could never bear a whisper of criticism or contradiction, while a single word of dissuasion or reproof was enough to destroy for half the day his otherwise amiable temper. This same vanity undermined in time his relations with his wife, a remarkable woman in her way, and whom he tenderly loved. It alienated also many of his best and most sincere friends, and betrayed him into follies and mistakes for which, from his own standpoint, there was no excuse. With Belinski he fell out for years over a difference of opinion about a poem. He could never forgive his wife for keeping aloof, after the death of a child, from society and those intellectual circles in which to him it was a necessity to shine. So completely had vanity, bad example, and early acquired habits enslaved his better nature, that he, the mortal enemy of all aristocratical pretension and social prejudices, would not scruple, when in grand and brilliant company, to ignore his best friends, if they happened to be in modest circumstances, and simple and unobtrusive accordingly. So far was this arch-democrat and Socialist from renouncing his position as a dandy of the first water, that he never hesitated to run after the merest simpleton he came across, if only they were fashionable, and would recite, to the despair of his wife, his poems and essays to ladies who had not the faintest notion of what they meant. During his exile at Vladimir the relations between husband and wife had been exemplary, and there seemed no end to their happiness; but the haughty demagogue was as powerless to resist the fascinations of high life at Moscow as if he had been a simple lieutenant. The first *contrariété* at home was enough to plunge him into dissipation, which made him even more unhappy than his wife, and which he put down, after the manner of weak characters, not to himself, but to circumstances. After the death of his father, who left him nearly half a million roubles, Herzen, so far from steadying himself with the reflection that he was now a wealthy man, only irritated his most intimate friends by his want of tact, and by one of these, the historian Granovski, he had formally to be called to account. As for regular occupation and earnest study, neither Herzen nor his friends ever dreamed of such things. They read and argued together *ad infinitum*; they carried the study of Hegel's philosophy to a mania, and wasted weeks and months in discussing the most insignificant pamphlets of the young Hegelian school; but quiet, really productive work was only an occasional result. Three-fourths of their time was claimed for sociable converse, highly intellectual and ambitious enough, it is true, but still so vague and desultory as to lose at length all particular interest. So engrossed were these young men in 'understanding' and 'doing justice to' each other, and in mutual admiration, that they ended by losing all sober estimate of their own and other persons' performances. If ever any of them gathered up his energies for an independent piece of work, the effort passed for heroic. When Granovski appeared in public with his lectures on mediæval history he created a sensation, which could not have been greater if the talented young lecturer had discovered the philosopher's stone. For whole months together literally nothing was talked of but these lectures; they were perpetually being brought out, examined, and admired. Public displays, indeed, of this kind were permitted to few; for the censorship and the secret police made nearly all activity impossible, unless devoted to the service of the ruling system. Up to a certain point these external difficulties were convenient to this circle which had gathered round Herzen, and frittered away its best energies in theological discussions and fantastic dreams of the future. What Madame Passek says about these worthies brings home the suspicion that their own personal inclinations had most to do with their way of treating life, and that the greatest abuse was made of the plea that circumstances were fatal to the exercise of independent energy. Herzen and his friend Ogareff (a poetically gifted, good-natured *dilettante*, but without any character, who under the rule of his vain wife had become an elegant fop, and consequently allowed Herzen first to make a demagogue of him, and finally to run away with his wife,) were both of them, as young men of rank, idlers *par excellence* by profession. Neither was open to much reproach, indeed, for living without any definite vocation, and having time enough and to spare for social vanities as well as for the study of Hegel's and Schelling's philosophy. Granovski, the historian, and Belinski, the famous critic, did in fact the same, although they were not of high rank and, moreover, had an occupation. Granovski, at the time in question, had just begun to read, but was not yet a professor; his position therefore was such as would have incited anyone not a Russian to exert his utmost energies; and yet we are told of him, that his talents were even surpassed by his laziness and his fondness for cards. For weeks together, when he visited Herzen in the country, he would idly lounge about, waste his time with disputations, idle dreams, and tobacco, and then sit down at the card-table, not to rise from it for whole days and nights. The longer he lived the more madly did this passion develope itself, until at last it threatened to make this gifted and well-intentioned man altogether incapable of any mental work.

The same was the case at this time with Belinski, whom the short-sighted authorities of the Moscow University had dismissed 'for idleness.' He also was too lazy to fill up halfway the gaps in his early education, and his nearest friends, including Alexander Herzen and Ivan Turgenieff, were forced to allow that he was wanting all his life in the veriest rudiments of knowledge.

And all this took place in the green leaf of the *élite* of the Russia of that day, among a generation which plumed itself on its superiority, which made a clean breach with the past an axiom, and which exercised a lasting and still active influence upon the development of the generation that followed it. Is any further explanation required of the incurable worthlessness of the average representatives of aristocratical old Russia and their descendants? Need we explain why even the first champions of reform never rose throughout their lives above hopeless paradoxes and criminal puerilities?

Beyond a mere negation of what existed the 'sons' were never able to attain, just because, for real productive work and concentrated energy, their powers were as inadequate as those of their 'fathers;' because, like these, they acted not on principle, but from the whim and impulse of the moment, and were accustomed to make themselves and others subservient to their own self-will. Insubordination, indolence (*ljenj*), and a passive apathy fatal to any power of initiation, have been the ruin of all those who lived under the influence of the *ancien régime* in Russia, just as of their opponents, the Radicals and Nihilists. That a high-minded, shrewd thinker like Herzen could have come to such a pitch as to preach cosmopolitan revolution, even after the experiences of 1863 and 1864, to his fellow-countrymen, just emancipated from the bonds of serfdom; that he, the humane idealist of European education, should have succumbed to the influence of a wild, but energetic fanatic like Bakunin, serves as a guide to explain the conditions under which he and his contemporaries had come to the front —a guide which, rightly employed, elucidates all the anomalies and self-contradictions which make up the Russia of the present day.

CHAPTER IV.

False ideas of Russian peasant-life—Ismailoff, the 'Nestor' of Griboyedoff—His story told from official sources—Brutal ill-treatment of his serfs and servants—Connivance of the local authorities—His ultimate punishment—Vices of his generation.

OF Russian peasant-life, such as the old unbroken rule of serfdom had made it, Russian literature unfortunately gives us no account from those who actually took part in it. The 'village tales' of Russia are a product of modern art, founded on German and French models, and attributing to the rude victims of the tyranny therein depicted the refined feelings of indignation excited in the breasts of educated persons. Whoever has read Turgenieff's 'Diary of a Sportsman,' Herzen's 'Byloje i dumi,' and S. T. Aksakoff's 'Chronicle of a Family,' and has taken note of any of the official reports on 'peasant-tyrants,' who were brought to justice, need scarcely trouble himself with the imitators of German village annalists. A Russian Jung-Stilling has yet to be discovered.

We have no intention, however, of contributing to the natural history of the Russian peasant. Our object is limited to reproducing the substance of an official report, published a few years ago, on what had passed for a quarter of a century, from 1802 to 1827, on the estates and in the household of Major-General Ismailoff, who, as we have mentioned above, escaped the fate of being forgotten with the many other provincial tyrants of his time, by the allusion to him in Griboyedoff's comedy :—

> Who 's he, to whom I curtseyed when a child ?
> Of high-born rogues the Nestor he is styled ;
> His oldest servants, who had served him well,
> Just for a pair of greyhounds he would sell.

After it had leaked out some time ago, that this 'Nestor' was Ismailoff, a later critic contrived to procure the papers relating to him, and with their help brought to light the following facts, remarkable, indeed, and much talked of at the time in question, but by no means isolated or exceptional in their nature.

In 1802 Alexander I. ordered the Governor of Tula to report on the condition of Major-General Ismailoff's estates, concerning which very sinister rumours had reached his Majesty's ears. Whether this order was ever carried out, and the report in question drawn up, remained for a long time a mystery. Certain it is, however, that more than twenty years passed by, before even the first step was taken towards giving effect to the design which had underlain the Imperial command. That during this long interval, the disorder existing on Ismailoff's estates had become a matter of public notoriety and been noised about at Moscow, and that it was viewed with indulgence by the authorities whose duty it was to protect the peasants, is evident from the fact, that Griboyedoff's piece, in which 'Nestor' was thus branded for all ages, was not written till about 1820, and the criminal inquiry into his conduct not instituted till 1827. The marvel is that, with circumstances as they were, and in the face of the connivance of the local authorities of Tula, this inquiry was ever instituted at all ; and the fact is reassuring as a proof that sometimes, even in Russia, 'necessity,' as the proverb runs, 'will break iron.' The poor terrified peasants had gone straight to the emperor and prevailed upon him to interfere in person. Their necessity, indeed, had reached a point beyond endurance; and common wrongs had made allies of two classes of men, the household servants and the peasants, who otherwise had very little in common. The former of these, who numbered no less than two hundred and seventy persons of both sexes, were employed partly in domestic service, partly in the garden and workshop attached to the estates. The number of housemaids alone was twelve, the number of men who looked after the horses and dogs was still larger. The huge, rambling mansion in which the General lived wore a gloomy and uncomfortable aspect, notwithstanding its size and the splendid furniture of some of its rooms. Its innumerable windows were darkened with gratings, through which were seen the faces of pale and pining men and women; a heavy, anxious atmosphere seemed to hang about the place. On looking closer, it was seen that one wing of the building was used as a prison. Here the unhappy victims of the General's anger were locked up, not only for hours and days, but for weeks and months together. So completely were the internal arrangements adapted to the purpose, that there were cells of various grades and classes, some even with chains and fetters, the number of prisoners reaching at times as high as forty. The house of correction consisted of a huge workshop, kept open day and night, where, besides the regular *employés*, a number of domestic servants as well as peasants, sent thither for punishment, were continually at labour. Whilst other tyrants, even those of worst repute, had usually restricted imprisonment and bodily punishment to the servants of the household, and had been content, as regarded their peasants, with draining the fruit of their labour and plundering their cattle and other goods, Ismailoff, on the contrary, made it a rule to extend the blessings of his paternal discipline to both classes of his subjects, and to make no invidious distinction between them. The number of the serfs who languished in his dungeons and places of correction was at times as large as that of his domestics; rods and sticks were brandished daily over the heads of all alike. Each class alike furnished its victims to this monster, and helped to make up the thirty inmates of his harem, who subsequently appeared before the commission of inquiry, tamed to his will by ill-treatment, incarceration, and hard labour in the workshop. The gross brutalities of this wretch are not fit to be described, but are recorded in the evidence taken by this commission. Daily, for the smallest oversight, men and women were whipped till the blood came; daily this tyrant would break up families, and give away or sell their members. The famous barter, to which Griboyedoff alludes, actually occurred in 1823, when four persons, who for thirty years had been servants of Ismailoff, were exchanged for two couples of greyhounds. According to the evidence of the local clergy, the ex-General strictly forbad his domestics ever to go to church; he himself had not profaned it with his presence for twenty years. Neither servants nor peasants were allowed to marry, and if they did so against his will, he considered it his privilege, as lord of the manor, to dissolve the marriage. Once, when a peasant refused to surrender his daughter to him, he gave orders to have the man's roof burnt over his head.

Such were the infamies of this household, which, notwithstanding the emperor's command above referred to, were winked at by all the governors, vice-governors, procurators fiscal, and officers of the rural police (*Ispravniks*), who from 1802 to 1827 were supposed to administer and look after the government of Tula; when, at length, the peasants, driven to desperation, got a petition and memorial of grievances drawn up and sent direct to the emperor at St. Petersburg. The Post-Office, of course, had no more welcome task than to be the medium of making known these audacious proceedings, so compromising to all the local authorities at Tula, and of compelling the offending grandee, who was backed up by all the big people of the province, to confess the error of his ways. Ismailoff, however, was equal to the occasion. He charged the persons suspected of having sent the petition, with having concocted a revolutionary plot (*bunt*) against their lawful lord and master, and with the help of a number of bribed and interested witnesses, got the local court of justice to institute criminal proceedings against the petitioners and have several of the suspected persons locked up; the rest, of course, were privately bastinadoed and put in irons. The chief actor in this infamous affair was a Tulan official, who, under the pretence of being an 'emissary of the Czar,' cross-examined the complainants. A number of innocent men were on the point of being sentenced to the knout and to exile in Siberia, when fortunately, in 1828, Captain Shamschin, an officer of the Gendarmerie, sent direct from St. Petersburg, arrived at Tula, and simply by his appearance struck such panic into the guilty parties, that matters seemed about to take another turn, and to cost the governor and his gang their places. A host of Ismailoff's official accomplices and confederates were cashiered off-hand; the local tribunal was reprimanded, and administrators were appointed for the estates, which had been the scene of such unheard-of infamies.

Thus roughly startled from their enjoyment, the whole band of rogues and cowards joined together to deprive justice of her victim. Testimonials, so numerous and so favourable, of the good character and conduct of his Excellency the Major-General were showered upon the Captain of Gendarmerie by the Tulan authorities, the district Marshal of Noblesse, the neighbouring land-owners and others interested in his cause, that this officer got puzzled, described the statement of grievances as open to suspicion, and finally consented that, pending the proceedings instituted against Ismailoff, two persons should be appointed *curatores bonorum*, who, in fact, let the old tyrant have his own way and did as he told them. It was not until two years had elapsed, and matters had got into confusion worse confounded, that a peremptory order from the emperor in 1830 commanded that the administration of the estates should be placed in other hands, and Ismailoff deprived for ever of the disposition of his property, on account of his abuse of his powers, and interned for the rest of his life in a district-town of the government of Tula. Nicholas, however, strict as he was, and in similar cases often wholesomely despotic, never thought of administering any formal punishment to this profligate tyrant. Perhaps, even in this matter his advisers had allowed their counsel to be governed by the maxim professed a few years later by Prince Orloff, the Chief of the Gendarmerie, in a report addressed to Prince Schtscherbatoff on the doings of another 'consummate rogue,' the Tolstoy already mentioned. 'It is always,' he said, 'a matter for grave consideration, when an individual of inferior rank gains the day over a member of the higher classes.'[1]

The generation to which General Ismailoff belonged, and its relations with that which succeeded it, are alluded to by Griboyedoff as follows:—

> The good old times!—Nay, rather the reverse;
> Our proverb holds 'the older is the worse.'
> Show me but one who's honest, and I'll say
> 'There goes a *man* of that degenerate day,
> When title-traffic and the pride of birth
> Concealed the want of honour and of worth.'
> Yet still in endless homilies we're told—
> 'Be like your sires, and imitate the old.'

Such was the sentence passed by the foremost Russian satirist and moralist of his time on the fathers of the present generation of his countrymen, and on the paths that generation were instructed to tread.

---

[1] Tolstoy had inveigled into his house a citizen of Moscow, with whom he had quarrelled, and had had him bound, and had wrenched out one of his teeth. The citizen complained, but Tolstoy so contrived that the complainant was not only dismissed, but put in prison for slander. The historian, N. F. Pauloff, a member of the prison administration at Moscow, took up the matter and procured a fresh inquiry. Prince Schtscherbatoff, the Chief Director of the Prisons in that city, brought the matter to the knowledge of the Chief of the Gendarmerie, and received from him the above answer, together with orders to remove M. Pauloff from his appointment. This took place shortly before 1840.

CHAPTER V.

PRINCE P. A. WJÄSEMSKI.

His birth and ancestors—Altered position of the nobility after the death of Catherine II.—The Nicole Institute at St. Petersburg—Wjäsemski's early studies—High-life at the capital—Introduction to official duties—A volunteer in 1812—Mania for Liberalism after the French War—His removal to Warsaw—The emperor's scheme of 'Polish reconciliation'—Wjäsemski in the Ministry of Finance—His first literary efforts—The 'Arsamass' Club—Friendships with Pushkin and Wielehorski—His irresoluteness of character—His literary dilettantism—His self-estimate.

ON November 22, 1878, the newspapers announced that the former Assistant Minister of Instruction, the actual Privy-Councillor Prince Peter Andrejevitch Wjäsemski, grand cupbearer, Member of the Council of State, and a Knight of almost all the high orders in Russia, had died at Baden-Baden in his eighty-sixth year. Of the many who read this announcement, a few only would have known that with this man, so celebrated in his time, but now nearly forgotten, there was carried to the grave the last representative of an entire movement, the last witness of the so-called classical age of Russian literature;—a poet eminent in his way and typical in the largest sense of the word. So strikingly does the progress of his life reflect the peculiarities and contradictions not merely of one, but of three periods in the development of modern Russia, that a survey of the official, as well as the private career of this latest champion of Russian Romanticism, cannot fail to be of interest in connection with the moral and ethical history of his country.

Prince Wjäsemski was born at Moscow on July 12 (24), 1792, in the days of the Empress Catherine. He sprang from a very ancient and highly respected family of Boyárs, who traced back their origin to Rurik the Varangian, and ruled over Smolensk and subsequently over Wjäsma during the time when Russia was divided into several independent principalities. One of his ancestors had been the boon companion of Ivan the Terrible, and Head Steward of the 'Order of the Brethren,' instituted by that monarch, and notorious for its excesses. Another had figured as general of the second pseudo-Demetrius. A third had been implicated in the designs of the Czarevitch Alexei Petrovitch, the son of Peter the Great, and suffered death by the hands of the executioner. A fourth, Prince Alexander Wjäsemski, who died the same year our hero was born, was Procurator-General of the Empress Catherine II., and gained the reputation of being one of the most corruptible and reprobate of statesmen. The father of the late Prince filled no office in the State, but lived as a grand seigneur at Moscow towards the end of the last century. Peter Andrejevitch's childhood was passed in the times of the Emperor Paul, and amidst the panic that unhappy monarch had spread through the high nobility of his empire.

This class, which had been the dominant one from the death of Peter the Great down to the accession of Catherine II., was now being degraded to a level which precluded all comparison with their former position. The old nobles, full of self-importance and solemn dignity, had been accustomed, as recently as the time of Catherine, to be treated as exceptional beings—a compound of *hauteur* and ferocity, they were insensible to the feelings of others. With the customary loud voice and nasal utterance of their class, they addressed with contempt every Russian below the rank of colonel, and looked on foreigners as mere human creatures, but nothing else. These aristocrats were now suddenly reduced to the level of common mortals, and treated likewise as mere shuttlecocks by the emperor. To their terror they found that the latter carried out his saying to the letter: 'On n'est grand seigneur en Russie, que quand on me parle, et pendant qu'on me parle;' that he trod so unsparingly under foot whatever came in his way, and overturned so completely all existing customs, that those only could enjoy to some extent their life and liberty who lived outside the glare of the Court's sun, and were too insignificant to be noticed. Men who yesterday had climbed to the top of the ladder were flung back to-day into the void, and rejoiced if only they escaped a journey to Siberia. In silence they packed up their trunks, and harnessed the peasants' horses to their smart but cumbrous coaches, to disappear as unnoticed as they could into the solitude of their country estates, which they had inherited from their ancestors, but which they had previously only known by name. Here they passed away their days in laborious or inactive idleness, and built small mansions, which the next generation again allowed to stand empty and go to ruin.

Prince Peter Andrejevitch was, happily for himself, only nine years old when the catastrophe of March 11 (23), 1801, put an end to the reign of terror which all of his rank had had to endure. By the time he came to St. Petersburg, the days had just gone by, when to put on a modern coat had been dangerous to one's life,

F

and when one of the chief duties of the first Imperial officer of State was to see that no waltz was ever danced. Still a vague idea may possibly have remained with him, that, under certain circumstances, the position of a Russian grandee might be a very bad thing, and that discretion was after all the better part of valour.

In his parents' home the boy had been left, as was customary in Russia,[1] to French, German, and English tutors, who alternately spoiled and ill-treated him, without any notice being taken by his father. Of the first of these tutors (who, of course, were always changing), the Frenchman Lepierre, the Prince says that he used to beat him, when only five years old, with the strap on which he sharpened his razors. At St. Petersburg his education was continued in an institution which is one of the few surviving creations of the Emperor Paul. This unhappy monarch's dread of revolution had been worked on with consummate adroitness by Father Gabriel Gruber, the head of that branch of the Jesuits, which had established itself in Russia, to obtain the emperor's permission to found a private educational institute, conducted by one of the members of the order. Its director, the Abbé Nicole, knew the people he had to deal with quite well enough to accommodate himself to their requirements. His terms were 1,500 roubles a year; all instruction was conveyed

---

[1] We hire a host of tutors, all who'll come,
The more the better, for the smallest sum.
Then comes the learning—'tis a simple thing,
What Heaven has destined or our luck may bring.
Be pedagogue, professor, if you will;
Teaching's a thing of choosing, not of skill.

. . . .

The rod will teach what Russian lads should know,
'No hope, unless you're German, top to toe.'
    Griboyedoff's *Sorrow comes from Sense*, act i. sc. 7.

in French: only sons of the highest Polish and Russian nobility were admitted, and the chief stress was laid on the propagation of good—that is, anti-revolutionary—principles. All this did not fail to have due effect, and to make the Nicole Institute the favourite resort for young nobles. Gradually then, and unobtrusively, this 'private' institute was transformed into an official seminary of the order. Gruber himself drew up the rules; and before long it received within its walls a number of Russian celebrities, including the Princes Galytzin and Odojevski, the Counts Tolstoy, Schuvaloff, Stroganoff, Novossiltzoff, Rostopschin, Mussin-Pushkin, and finally, also our Prince Peter Andrejevitch.

If the pupils of this institute retained a vestige of their Russian nature, it was surely not the fault of its managers and teachers. With the happy *insouciance* of an age, to which the principle of nationality was not even known by name, their parents in their innocence regarded it as a special favour of Providence that their sons should enjoy the opportunity of obtaining a 'foreign education,' of receiving all instruction in the French language (at the cost, it is true, of being surrounded by none but Frenchmen), of learning the classical languages, if only as a pastime, from priests who actually spoke Latin, and of gaining the shortest and easiest road to being 'Europeanised.' Of course it could only further this grand object, that their 'orthodox' children should receive the bulk of their religious teaching from a highly-cultivated, and therefore 'unprejudiced,' disciple of Loyola, and that their instruction in the doctrines of the State Church should be limited to one hour in the week. Besides, did not everyone know that the Russian priest whom Father Gruber had hired for this purpose was a coarse old fellow, addicted to drink, whose example could be of no use to the pupils, in respect either of morality or patriotic sentiment?

Wjäsemski remained for several years at this institute, which he always remembered with gratitude, and to which he really owed the better part of his culture—that is, some ideas of the nature of classical antiquity, and a tolerable intimacy with the French language and literature. He had also a certain knowledge of his native tongue, in which most of the other pupils were deficient, and which he owed to the fact that his father was somewhat of a *dilettante* in Russian literature, and that he had frequently seen at home, and sometimes heard speak in Russian, several prominent authors of a former period, such as Karamsin, Shukovski, and Dimitrijeff, afterwards Minister of Justice. This had left its effect upon the boy. By his own account the Odes of Dershawin had produced a kind of intoxication upon him, and he declaimed them with even greater enthusiasm than the pieces of his then favourite poets, Voltaire and Racine. Among the Russian authors of his day, Prince Shatiloff—an imitator, grown ridiculous by his exaggerations, of Karamsin—ranked high in his youthful estimation; he admired him as a great literary star for his 'Travels in Little Russia' (1804), and his 'Journey to Cronstadt' (1805). His chief interest, however, was centred in French literature, and he remained loyal to it, even after he himself had acquired a reputation as a Russian author. 'What attracts us in the French,' he used to say, 'is not the Latin but the Gallic element in their nature. Because this element is most congenial to the Russian, we understand the French better than do any other Europeans. For this reason their theatre has become ours. Like them, we are also light-hearted and sociable: *Mon jour est mon siècle* is the motto of us both.' His classical studies were limited to a tolerably superficial acquaintance with Horace and Ovid. 'I am not great at Latin,' he said; 'the classical languages do not strike root among us Russians, for we have neither an historical nor national soil for them to thrive in.'

The Catholic propaganda, carried on by the teachers at this institute with such zeal and success, passed by Wjäsemski without leaving any trace on his happy and joyous disposition. His friendship to the Jesuits was confined to his insisting, in opposition to most of his associates with whom he sympathised, on the cultivating influence of the college, and condemning throughout his life as 'illegal' its abolition, which took place a few years after he left it, and was carried out in a most harsh and summary manner. In his opinion the Russian hatred of the Jesuits was only an imitation of the French. 'From time immemorial,' he says, 'we have been accustomed to put up our umbrellas by the Neva when it rains at Paris.'

After exchanging the College of the Jesuits for the academy conducted by Engelbach, and not long after released altogether from the discipline of school-life, this attractive young man, equally favoured by nature and circumstances, plunged headlong into the whirl of high life at St. Petersburg, which was then at the height of its gaiety and splendour. The nobles had not yet spent their large fortunes. The Boyárs had been reinstated in most of their former bureaucratic and social privileges. The storms of the Revolution and the French war seemed to have been laid by the Peace of Tilsit, and the pleasures and luxuries of life at the capital could be enjoyed to the full, and without any disquieting afterthoughts by those who were admitted to its ban-

quets. 'Festivities crowded thickly on each other.
One noble family vied with the other in magnificence
and display. So numerous were the houses where daily
"receptions" were given, so boundless the hospitality
of their wealthy private occupants, that a man of good
family needed nothing more than a night's lodging, a
good coat, and a carriage, to be on a par with the
rest, and take his equal share of the pleasures of life.'
Whoever belonged to the ruling caste enjoyed almost
absolute liberty of action. The liberal tendencies of
the Government favoured the progress of that form
of national literature which had come into fashion
since Karamsin, and promoted a certain interest in all
efforts for the public good, of which the Freemasons'
lodges, now in fashion, had become the centres. Intercourse increased with foreign countries, and a host
of literary and political adventurers and *beaux-esprits*
of every sort and kind crowded every year to the banks
of the Neva. It was an accepted maxim, that young
men of high birth should regard enjoyment as the
chief object of life; or at least, if they engaged in any
serious occupation, were it military or bureaucratic, or
the study of some 'free art,' that they should do so
merely for variety's sake and as *dilettanti*. Was it not
written in the book of Fate that, by the time they were
seventeen, they would be Gentlemen of the Chamber,
or Lieutenants of the Guard; when twenty-five, either
Chamberlains or Adjutants; and after their marriage,
'Ambassadors, provincial Governors, Procurators, Commanders of regiments, or high dignitaries at Court, free
from the irksome and humiliating service in the chan-
celleries and colleges, so wearying from its monotony?'
Speranski, a priest's son, raised to the dignity of Secretary of State, took in hand the remodelling of the

Government Colleges, and laid the foundation of the bureaucratic organisation as it now exists. But before him, it literally happened that young men of rank did not know whether they had an appointment in the Civil Service or not, or where their appointment was, and had never even seen the door of their bureau from the inside. Wigel, the well-known Councillor of State, tells us in his 'Memoirs,' that during the first part of the reign of Alexander I., he had been under the impression for two years that he was a member of the Statistical Committee of the Ministry of the Interior, and that afterwards he learned that in reality he had been dismissed all the time. He says also, that when in active service in the Foreign Ministry, his official duties were confined to sitting once a fortnight or three weeks in the anteroom of Prince Kurakin, and introducing to him whatever couriers might happen to arrive. And Wigel, as the son of the Governor of Pensa, who had toiled to rise, did not even belong to the class of the most highly favoured ones, in the midst of whom Wjäsemski had been born. Nominally, indeed, our young prince was attached to the Chancellerie of Obresskoff, the Director of the Surveying Department, who sent him occasionally, on account of his 'intimate acquaintance with the actual condition of his country,' on a 'special mission' into his district. By these means Obresskoff took an opportunity of securing rapid promotion for his noble *protégé*; but, as a matter of fact, Wjäsemski, like the rest of his class, looked upon enjoyment as the main object of his life.

The events of 1812, however, interrupted for some time this happy *dolce far niente*. The young prince, in common with most other young men of his standing, took up arms at the news of Napoleon's invasion. He served for several years as a volunteer in the Moscow

Landwehr regiment in Russia, Germany, and France, and was present, among other battles, at Borodino. At the close of the campaign, however, he left the service, and returned to St. Petersburg.

Here, in the capital of the empire, a new epoch began with the return of the Russian armies, who had lived for several years in foreign countries, and learned to know, from personal experience, the civilisation of the West. The officers who had fought at Borodino, Kulm, and Leipzig, and 'seen Paris at Moscow and Moscow at Paris,' brought home with them feelings of chivalrous self-respect and patriotic sympathy, very different from the torpor and submissive apathy of former generations. The necessity of reform in the head and members of the State, and of a radical change in its organisation, so as to correspond with the institutions of the West, was loudly and publicly discussed. The abolition of serfage was talked of as a measure as urgent as inevitable; and the government was seriously advised to delay no longer the introduction of the intended constitution. The higher the social scale, the more zealous were the worship of liberal ideas and the agitation for establishing Freemasons' lodges and associations for the public welfare, after the model of the *Tugendbund* in Germany. Whoever wished to be of any importance, was bound to be able to talk with others about Tracy and Benjamin Constant, and to contribute some information about the difference between the constitutions of France, England, and the kingdom of Poland, now suddenly raised to the rank of a constitutional State. Even the older generation, though not immediately affected by the current ideas of this time, showed themselves more humane and independent than any of the high dignitaries of the empire before them. 'Brave, good-natured, but thoroughly dissolute,' says Herzen, ' as loyal to the religion of buttoned-up uniforms as to that of honour, the men who owed their rise to the wars with the French monopolised not only all military, but nine-tenths of civil appointments. Without the smallest knowledge of business matters, they signed papers they had never read. They loved the soldiers, though they flogged them daily; for flogging, they were firmly convinced, was the only way to teach them. They spent their money lavishly, and when none was left, they took to pilfering from the public funds; for were not dogs, books, and State money ' common property ' from time immemorial? In justice to these men, it must be said that they were neither informers nor spies, and were ever ready to go through fire and water for their subalterns. Often uncouth in manner, and always noisy and demonstrative in speech, accustomed to judge in matters that they never understood, and condescending only to give an answer when the humour took them, the generals of this stamp, nevertheless, had the immense advantage over others that they were imbued with true feelings of honour, and would sacrifice their lives, if necessary, for right and truth.' Count Miloradovitch, who fell a victim to the December insurrection in 1825, was perhaps the most thorough type of this genus now extinct. ' Brave, brilliant, extravagant, and reckless, always steeped in debts, though the Emperor Alexander paid them ten times over; an inveterate gossip, and yet one of the most amiable men in the world, the count was the idol of the soldiers, and a tolerably successful governor-general of the capital—a post which he filled for several years, without ever having known a single law.'

It was under the auspices of men like these that

Prince Wjäsemski had risen into notice and grown to manhood; and now, on his return to St. Petersburg, he was ready to continue his service in the Surveying Department. This kind of work, it is true, could scarcely be considered a preparation for a diplomatic career. Still, for a functionary of high birth, and well thought of for the courage he had shown at Borodino, it was not a difficult thing to find promotion to some high political post. In 1815 he was attached to Count N. N. Novossiltzoff, the Imperial Plenipotentiary and Commissary of the Government of Poland, and an intimate friend of Alexander I.; and, as an official in his chancellerie, he removed for several years to Warsaw.

Affairs in Poland at this time were in a state of marvellous confusion. Contrary to the counsel of all his Russian and German advisers, the emperor had effected its restoration as a constitutional kingdom, and entrusted the administration to those who had risen into notice either towards the close of the French Republic or during the Napoleonic period, and who made no secret of their exclusively Polish sympathies. The office of viceroy was filled by the veteran general Zajonczek, a republican of Kosciusko's school, who had served in the Napoleonic campaign in Russia, and lost a leg on the Beresina. The portfolios of the minister were given to the Counts Wielehorski, Potocki, Matuszewicz, Sobolevski, and other members of the high Polish nobility; and it was in the company of these men that Novossiltzoff was to exercise his functions as the representative of Russian interests and the mediator between Russia and Poland. The difficulty of such a task was obvious, and it was increased by the fact that while the emperor's sympathies were on the side of the Poles, he demanded from Novossiltzoff a secret *surveillance* over his Polish ministers and all around them. Add to this, that most of the officials 'attached' to the Imperial commissary were Poles, and, as such, either the tools of the ministers and councillors of State, like Prince Adam Czartoriski, curator of the university at Vilna, and the youthful friend and influential adviser of the emperor, or else intriguers on their own account; and it must be confessed that Novossiltzoff and his Russian *attachés* were placed in a very difficult position if they wished to do their duty.

These difficulties Count Novossiltzoff seems to have taken entirely on his own shoulders. Having spent several years at Warsaw, he was sufficiently familiar with the posture of affairs to see how impossible it was to carry out the emperor's project of reconciliation. At the same time, frequent experience had taught him that his Imperial majesty did not like being undeceived, and was sincerely desirous of removing all causes of quarrel between Russians and Poles. Hence the count was forced to temporise and pursue a waiting policy. Hated by the Polish leaders, looked upon with suspicion, and therefore isolated in society, he no doubt thought it useful that his subordinates should intermix socially with the Poles.

Wjäsemski's official duties at Warsaw consisted chiefly in translating French documents into Russian, the reports of the Polish ministers being written in French, and requiring to be so translated, to be of any use in the bureaus at St. Petersburg. He did the same with the speeches of Alexander I. in the Parliament at Warsaw, which were delivered in French. Meanwhile he made himself a thorough master of the Polish language, which proved as important to him in his official as it was in his literary labours. To literature already he was zealously devoted. His biographers mention that the first-fruit of these studies was a translation of Mickewicz's 'Taurian Sonnets,' executed with 'philological exactness.' Whether it was he who discovered the mistake that Adam Czartoriski had made in his Polish translation of the Organic Statute, originally written in French, we are not told;[1] but it led to the downfall of that statesman, and has become a matter of history. Wjäsemski appears, however, to have kept aloof from all *haute politique*, and never to have taken any part in suppressing the intrigues of the Polish patriots against the Russian Government. 'Reconciliation between Russians and Poles' had been the official order of the day, and a Russian grandee, educated in cosmopolitan principles, would find no difficulty in giving practical effect to such 'reconciliation' in the gayest and most sociable capital of Eastern Europe. He divided his time between the enjoyment of high life and stirring intercourse with Polish authors and poets, who celebrated in prose or verse the restoration of their country, and were wise enough to impress upon the Russians who lived at Warsaw that they gratefully joined with Frau von Krüdener in her veneration of the '*Ange blanc*,' as the greatest and most liberal sovereign that the world had seen.

After a residence of several years at Warsaw, Wjäsemski returned to St. Petersburg, and as in duty bound, devoted himself to promoting ' a *rapprochement* between the two great Slav races.' He was received most graciously by the emperor, and honoured with a long audience, during which political matters, as well

---

[1] The details of this remarkable incident, so illustrative of the state of things at that time, are given by Th. von Bernhardi, in his excellent work, *Geschichte Russlands und der Europäischen Politik*, vol. iii. p. 622 sqq.

as others, were discussed. Alexander I., still an ardent Liberal, refused to surrender his faith in the final triumph of his experiment of a Polish constitution, and among others made the following remark ;—' Quelques-uns pensent, que les désordres dont nous sommes parfois témoins, sont inhérents aux idées libérales, tandis qu'ils ne sont que des abus de ces idées et principes.' After living for a while in private, Wjäsemski entered the Ministry of Finance, presided over since 1823 by Count Cancrin. In a country where ' everybody understands everything without ever having learned anything,' and where the rule is. that, in the interests of the public service, soldiers are made judges and administrative officials, and worn-out hacks of a *chancellerie* appointed generals,[1] no one could be surprised that a young official in the Surveying Department, since exchanged for a diplomatic career, should be transformed without further ceremony into a financier. Had not, indeed, Cancrin's own predecessor, Count Gurjeff, been made a minister of finance for no other reason but his incapacity, and retained in this post for thirteen years? And why ?—Just because Speranski at that time, in 1810, was all-powerful, and wished to acquire a hold over the department.

Once securely planted in this office, Wjäsemski was duly promoted, in the course of a few years, to the Vice-directorship of the Board of Foreign Trade, then to the banking department, and finally made a member of the Committee of Ministers. ' Heaven protects the innocent,' this amiable prince would add, after speaking of his profound aversion to

[1] Cancrin, who had never carried a gun, was metamorphosed, when sixty years old, from a privy councillor into a lieutenant-general, in order to save the Emperor Nicholas the daily sight of his civil uniform.

figures and calculations, and relating the wonderful fact that during his long years of public service, the accounts he handed in should sometimes have been found correct.

His chief interest, however, had never been in his public duties, but had centred in studying the literature of Russia, then struggling into fresh existence, and in developing, with the aid of his refined taste for language, his poetical talent. At a time when the ignorance of their mother-tongue passed as *bon ton* among Russian gentlemen and ladies of distinction, and when even business matters in high quarters were conducted in French, to be able to write Russian with elegance was a rare accomplishment, and valuable even in a bureaucratic sense. Wjäsemski had won his spurs as a financier by his cleverness in weeding his predecessor's official reports from the Germanisms and grammatical errors with which they teemed.[1] The same talent enabled him to write verses, unexceptionable in their way, and to shine as the writer of 'occasional pieces,' chiefly humorous and satirical. Already, when a volunteer in 1812, he had made acquaintance with the poet Shukovski (a friend of his parents, and who, like himself, hastened from Moscow to enlist), also with Karamsin, Alexander Turgenieff, Pushkin, whose first literary efforts had made him popular, and with other men of the so-called Romantic school. 'Romantic' these poets and authors were called, because they were the first to introduce to their countrymen

[1] Although Cancrin was quite young when he left Hesse and came to Russia, this most famous Minister of Finance of his time had never learned to express himself even tolerably well in the language of his adopted country. In spite of his atrocious pronunciation and incorrigible habit of bad grammar, the old gentleman considered himself a thorough master of Russian, and took Wjäsemski's corrections most ungraciously.

the creations of the modern literature of Germany and France, and to break with the old pseudo-classical traditions, represented by Schischkoff, the opponent of Karamsin in his endeavours to bring about a simple style of writing; Prince Schachovski, and others. Kryloff, the celebrated writer of fables, and Shukovski, were particularly friendly to this young literary star; and even Karamsin, though at first mistrustful, began after 1816 to acknowledge his talent as a poet.

At the time when Wjäsemski first became intimate with Pushkin and Shukovski, a great battle was raging between these men and the representatives of the old school, the result of which was that the new school banded themselves together into a regular club, the 'Arsamass,' or society of humoristic poets. Its composition, indeed, was motley enough; but the main object of its members was the same, to establish the worship of the modern ideas of the day, and to combat every kind of stiffnecked and antiquated routine. Shukovski acted as secretary, and was called 'Swetlana' in the club, from one of his ballads. He had shortly before this been summoned to the court, as Russian master to the Grand-duchess, afterwards Empress Alexandra. Pushkin was nicknamed 'Whim;' he had just been recalled from exile, and was known as an ardent Liberal. Batuschkoff, the famous lyric poet of his time, was named 'Achilles;' Nicholas Turgenieff, the well-known Liberal statesman, was called 'Warwick,' from his energy and boldness of mind; his brother Alexander (the historian' was called 'the Harp.' Besides these and other writers, who have become more or less celebrated, there were two men, who subsequently gained notoriety and influence as the reactionary advisers of the Emperor Nicholas One of these was Bludoff, afterwards minister, but then a young official of ultra-Liberal views, who proposed once to inscribe over the door of certain ministers, '*Lasciate ogni coscienza, voi chi entrate.*' The other was Sergei Semenovitch Uvaroff, afterwards Minister of Instruction and President of the Academy of Sciences. Among other members of this club were Wigel, who abhorred all Germans, and Count Capodistrias. Wjäsemski was received into it also, and for his witty sarcasms received the nickname of 'Asmodeus.'

Real political 'tendencies,' however, were as foreign to the Arsamass club as to its 'Asmodeus.' Its members were liberal, because the times were liberal, and because they fancied they stood on the pinnacle of a civilisation and culture, the diffusion of which throughout the empire formed the recognised mission of the government. To yield to the humour of the sovereign in small matters; to combine the practice of a rigid aristocrat with the most liberal theories in existence; and, conformably with the changing fashion of the day, to be now an ardent oppositionist and to-morrow fanatically loyal—all this was far too inveterate a custom in the society in which Wjäsemski moved for either him or his friends to depart from it. All that this Arsamass fraternity really had at heart was to preserve a correct taste in literature; as for the rest, these aristocratic and liberal authors were content, like well-meaning and humane patriots, to rave about the freedom and greatness of their Fatherland, and to follow the impulses which Western Europe had imparted to the State-life of Russia. When the wind changed to another quarter, and the successor of Alexander I., terrified by the December insurrection of 1825, proclaimed a strict isolation from Europe and the repression of all liberal ideas throughout his empire, nothing of course was left to men accustomed to better traditions but silent submission to the will of the great Autocrat who had pledged himself to think and act for sixty millions of Russians. Wjäsemski, like his friends Shukovski and Pushkin, had to bid farewell to the liberal dreams of his youth. He was forced to accommodate himself, as best he could, to the harsh and benumbing rule which for the next thirty years aimed at upsetting and counteracting all that had been held valuable during the last quarter of a century. The 'Arsamass' was dissolved, and its members forgotten amid the stir of social and bureaucratic life which surrounded them on every side.

Wjäsemski lived chiefly in the 'circle' of Pushkin and the Wielehorskis,—a *coterie*, closely connected with elegant society, of aristocratic writers, poets, and art-amateurs, who divided their days between fashionable pleasures after the French kind, and the cultivation of Russian literature and classical music, and who differed only from the courtiers and men of the world about them in their superior refinement and culture. The Counts Wielchorski themselves were well known as genuine friends and connoisseurs of music. There were also General Lyvoff, a distinguished violinist and composer, the author of the 'Tarantass,' the 'Bear,' the 'Apothecary's Wife,' and other pieces; Count Solohub; Tjutscheff, the diplomatist and poet; Alexander Turgenieff; Prince Obolenski; the two Wenjevitinoffs, and a number of other talented men, who sought compensation from the emptiness of the social life around them in æsthetic and refined pleasures and in literature and art, and found that compensation so complete that they were scarcely to be distinguished from the thoroughgoing adherents of the existing *régime*. Closely allied

to the Court and the Imperial family by the ties of
habit and tradition, accustomed, like men of the world,
to swim with the stream and to let things go as they
were, these men, in spite of their French culture and
mode of thought, in spite of the unsparing severity with
which they criticised all abuses and noted down the
symptoms of national bankruptcy, were far too easy-
going and indolent, far too engrossed with themselves
and their personal affairs, to attempt even to give practical and earnest expression to their views, however
widely these differed from those of the official world
about them. If, indeed, they ever did use their influence, it was always for some good object, as, for
instance, to mitigate the senseless rigour of the censorship, or to give a helping hand to rising talent. It was
mainly due to the members of this circle, especially
Shukovski and Wjäsemski, that Gogol's and Griboyedoff's
pieces were allowed to be performed, that Gogol's 'Dead
Souls' was permitted to be printed, and that Lermontoff
and other proscribed poets were not condemned to
absolute silence. Wjäsemski had been one of the
earliest and most ardent admirers of Gogol's remarkable talent, and was altogether as warm-hearted
and enthusiastic in acknowledging the performances of
others as he was modest, nay sceptical, with regard to
himself.[1] He could never quite shake off the liberal-

---

[1] Wjäsemski relates with much humour how once in his life he was even
a 'classical' poet. 'I was staying,' he says, ' at my small estate, Krassnoje,
in the Government of Kostroma. One Sunday, after Mass, the priest addressed to me in the church a discourse of welcome. After enumerating all
my virtues as a citizen and landlord, he added, pointing me out to his congregation, "Brethren in the Faith! you are not all aware what kind of
master the Lord has given us. He is a Russian Horace, Catullus, and
Martial." At each of these names the whole congregation turned to me with
low obeisances, and almost made the sign of the cross. Imagine my feelings
and the face I made at being thus publicly exposed and tortured.'

minded and enlightened man he had been in the better era of Alexander I. In the days of the most shameful and pitiless oppression, he had liberal moments; and even when actual privy councillor and a colleague of the ministers, he would write verses which terrified the press censor, and were struck out, regardlessly of the author's high rank, by Krassovski, the watchdog of Uvaroff's Ministry of Instruction, and a man of bad repute. On the whole, however, he was compelled, like most of his contemporaries, to follow the line laid down by the Emperor Nicholas. Wjäsemski never succeeded in becoming, like Bludoff, his brother-member of the Arsamass, a favourite and confidant of the soldier-emperor; the reason lay not in his want of will, but in his indestructibly sound and noble nature, and above all, in the instinctive abhorrence of Nicholas fróm all close contact with men of liberal minds. Trained in obedience to the spirit of the day, and infected with that irresolution of character which is the weak point in all Slavs, Wjäsemski was not ashamed, even in those times of hopeless bureaucratic imbecility, to continue his career as a public functionary and the servant of a system, the corruption of which he had never doubted for an instant. Never before, in all probability, had the senseless hatred of all culture, shown by the military *régime,* and the glaring absurdities in the Ministry of Instruction, been lashed with such bitter and scathing sarcasm, as is found in his ' Satires,' most of which appeared under the present government. Not even Pushkin or Lermontoff had ever treated with such unmitigated contempt the literary sycophants of Nicholas. No other Russian writer had ever denounced so fiercely the arrogance and brutality of those Nationalist fanatics, who thought to convert the mortal enemy of the 'heathens of the West' into a champion of Slav autochthony. And yet this same Wjäsemski condescended to go on serving indefatigably, and simply because custom so dictated, a Ministry of Finance, whose every step was retrograde, and of the business of which he knew nothing at all. Nay, worse than this—this friend of Pushkin voluntarily tuned his lyre to celebrate the Emperor Nicholas on his return from the Hungarian campaign of 1850; and to glorify him, in his poem 'Holy Russia' (*Swätaya Russi*), as the Saviour of civilisation, the 'Monarchical and Religious Spirit,' which had preserved Russia from revolution! It was only when this shibboleth of 'Holy Russia' and 'Russian Genius' became stereotyped in official phraseology, and was proclaimed by the National party at Moscow as the rallying-cry of a crusade against all that denoted European culture, that he ate his former words, and made the 'Russian National Genius' the subject of a satirical poem, which to this day delights the heart of every Radical of 'Holy Russia':—

> Genius of our ancient nobles;
> Shoeless slaves, with humbled brow,
> Boyárs greet thee, slaves in spirit,
> Russian Genius—it is thou!

> Genius of the knout and cudgel,
> All the nation hails thee now;
> Shield and shelter of the Germans,
> Russian Genius—it is thou!

Remarkable, indeed, it is, that the very people who read these verses (circulated of course privately) received them with as much enthusiasm as they had shown to the loyal hymn of 1850, and the commentaries Shukovski had added to it; and that nobody expressed any surprise at a high dignitary in office throwing ridicule, so soon after, on the ruling system. A high dignitary, however, in the strict sense of the term, Wjäsemski did not become until after the death of Nicholas; when, in June, 1855, he was removed to the Ministry of Instruction under A. S. Noroff, a man as good-natured as he was ignorant and puzzle-headed.[1] In the days of Nicholas, not even the most accurate observers of the Court barometer could ever say with certainty what the emperor thought of Wjäsemski, and how the latter stood with the Autocrat of all the Russias. Wjäsemski used to tell of the despair of one of his best friends, a man of high position, who, when in expectation of an Imperial visit, never felt quite sure whether he ought to allow the portrait of Wjäsemski to remain on the wall of his room.

In literature, Wjäsemski had to content himself with a secondary rank. Notwithstanding his natural talent and his extraordinary technical skill, he could never disembarrass himself from dilettantism, and he was conscious of this defect. Among his poetical pieces, his epistles and occasional poems are the best. His prose writings, mostly *critiques* and monographs on Russian poets, contain, amidst a wealth of admirably acute and pointed observations, such distorted and singular views, as can only originate in a man, who, as he himself confesses, 'had been too lazy and careless to make literature his profession, or to treat it otherwise than as a guest.' Elsewhere, in his 'Autobiography,' he says, 'I have never written for, nor scarcely ever thought of the

---

[1] Wjäsemski was after December 2, 1839, a member of the Russian Academy, a separate and national branch of the St. Petersburg Academy of Science. He scarcely ever attended the *séances* of this learned body, and at the most was only seen there on solemn occasions. His post as Ministerial colleague he resigned in March, 1858.

public. There are readers and real readers, as there are writers and those who *write*; the former are in the majority, but I have always been on the side of the minority. No doubt figures are figures, and a thousand roubles are worth more than ten; still my opinion remains, that it is better to gain the approval of ten persons of sense than that of a thousand blockheads.' In this indifference to public opinion, Wjäsemski showed at once the genuine aristocrat of the old school, as much as his own crotchetty nature, which was often blamed, and which, in spite of his personal trustworthiness, rendered his judgment, in political and literary questions, wholly unreliable. Even after the great changes of 1850-60 he was unable to rise superior to the contradictions that marked the times. The Radicals and Nationalists of the new era remained to this contemporary of Alexander I. and Count Miloradovitch just as much strangers in mind and spirit as the partisans of the Nicholas *régime* had been in their day. He stood outside of parties; he could never make up his mind to adopt any settled programme; and from time to time he amazed and embarrassed friends and foe alike by his remarks, which however uncompromising, were always witty and to the point. One of the last sayings of this remarkable man [1] reminds us of the latest experiences of Russian life. 'Whatever we do,' he says, 'is the result of intoxication in some idea or other. We never get free from this kind of periodical dipsomania, and when we have slept ourselves sober, we hardly ever remember our own attacks. This is the case with our juries, for example, whenever they give

---

[1] In 1868 Wjäsemski's sixtieth anniversary as an author was celebrated with marks of general interest, and on this occasion a complete edition of his works was prepared, to which he wrote an autobiographical introduction.

a verdict in criminal cases.' Still more severely did he judge himself and his own work. 'In fact,' he says, 'I have always followed the stream. When young, I let myself be ruled by the liberal ideas of the time; when a man, by considerations of State-service; and finally, by the cares and vexations of old age.' To some qualities, however, he remained true, notwithstanding the fickleness of his temperament. He was to the last a noble-minded and humane man, thoroughly able and kind-hearted, and always ready to be generous and to assist. These virtues explain why the name of Peter Andrejevitch has remained popular, after all appreciation, even in Russia, of the generation that witnessed the wars of Freedom began to fade away.

CHAPTER VI.

MICHAEL BAKUNIN AND RADICALISM.

Bakunin's birth and education—Reactionary *régime* after the conspiracy of December 1825—Popularity of revolutionary ideas—Bakunin's military life—his 'circle' at Moscow—Stankevitch—Early Hegelian studies—Bakunin at Berlin—at Dresden—Ruge and the 'Jahrbücher' of 1842—Bakunin's contributions as 'Jules Elizard'—His Negative Philosophy of Revolution—At Paris in 1843—Relations with Proudhon—Forced to leave for Switzerland—Temporary return to Paris—Removal to Germany—Slav Congress at Prague, 1848—With Bohemian revolutionists at Leipsic—August Röckel—Bakunin at the Dresden outbreak—A State prisoner—Escape from Siberia—With the London exiles—Advocacy of Panslavism—Father Pafnuty's mission—Bakunin's influence over Herzen—Nihilist tendencies of the *Kolokol*—Polish revolt of 1863—The Working-men's Association and the Peace League of the International—Fanatical theories of destruction—The 'Alliance Internationale'—Connection with Netchayeff—The champion of the French proletariate—With Cluseret at Lyons—Exiled to Switzerland—His death.

MICHAEL BAKUNIN, like most of those men who have gained a reputation as champions of Russian Radicalism, belonged by birth and education to the ruling class. He was born in 1814, about the same time as Alexander Herzen, Belinski, and Ivan Turgenieff. His father was a wealthy landed proprietor, descended from an ancient Boyár family, and who had settled in the Torshok district of the government of Tver. Though his namesakes and predecessors never played any prominent part in Russian history, they figured from time immemorial among the aristocracy of their country, who not only fill all military and civil posts of importance, but enjoy a traditional claim to the highest offices of state.

At the present day a near relative of the agitator is the Adjutant-General of the emperor, and another is Marshal of the nobility in one of the governments in the interior. For a Russian gentleman born in 1814 the military profession was his natural destiny. Service in the Guards was an essential requisite for an aristocratical career, and of the bare possibility of an existence outside the service of the State Bakunin's father had as little idea as any of his contemporaries. After the usual imperfect education received from French tutors, he entered, when about twenty years of age, the School of Artillery at St. Petersburg, an institute for young cadets, modelled on a military pattern, and differing only so far from other schools of this kind that pupils of exceptional talent might possibly acquire, with some effort, a knowledge of the rudiments of mathematics. In all other respects it exhibited the same anomalies which governed the entire Russian life of those days, and which the events of 1825 brought so strongly into relief as to take everyone by surprise. The young generation of nobles, and of the military class, had grown up under those liberal traditions to which Alexander I. was wedded during the first half of his reign, and which, in consequence, as we have seen, of the wars of liberation and the protracted residence of the army in France, had become the common property of the higher classes.

The insurrection of these young nobles, which broke out immediately after the death of Alexander, was the fruit of this training and these traditions, and a practical protest against the continuance of absolutism. It was put down with bloody severity, and brought about a reaction such as Russian society had never experienced before. The Government, which, except during the short reigns of Elizabeth and Paul, had ever since the days of Peter the Great been the promoter of ideas of progress, and the champion of European civilisation, now came forward as the avowed and determined enemy of this civilisation, and in the name of National principles, exerted every effort to repress it. Russian literature, just then in the blossoming-time of fresh vitality, was cramped by the fetters of the strictest censorship; all intercourse with Western Europe was checked, and foreign artists and men of learning were well nigh excluded from the country. Admiral Schischkoff, successor of Galytzin in the Ministry of Public Instruction, undertook to uproot the whole crop of humane and liberal culture which had sprung up during the reign of Alexander I., and to substitute a system of mere drill. The military training schools suffered most of all by this change. Within a short space of time they degenerated into places of intellectual and moral barrenness, where every offence was pardoned, but that of studying the best and noblest productions of the times.

The consequences of this reaction may easily be imagined. Whilst the great mass of the rising generation were dwarfed by their utter want of culture and morality, and by their incapacity to appreciate anything but the idols of fashion and the passing vanities of the hour, the more able and thoughtful among them gradually learned to identify the welfare of their country with the negation of all existing things. Those foolish young enthusiasts who had done incalculable mischief by their ill-advised attempt at revolt on December 14, 1825, and had to expiate their errors on the scaffold, or in the desolate wastes of Siberia, became saints and martyrs in the eyes of the young pupils in the military schools, whose homage to them was the more zealous and devoted as it was paid clandestinely. While outwardly all was deadened by strict obedience and stagnant uniformity, copies of Ryléjeff's and his friend Besstusheff's poems circulated by hundreds, and were transmitted as sacred records from one generation to the next. It was considered a privilege to be in any way connected with the 'victims of the December catastrophe,' and a kind of merit to be able to point to former colleagues among the number of the conspirators. Next to the first Cadet corps, the institute where young Bakunin received his training was particularly favoured in this respect. The artillery, as the 'scientific branch' of the service, had from time immemorial enjoyed the reputation of a certain liberalism, and its officers, more than any other, were known by that sure symbol of 'advanced opinions'—whiskers cut after the English pattern. Again, the poet and rebel Conrad Ryléjeff had belonged to the artillery of the guard,[1] as had also the two Borissoffs, Gorbatschevsky, Betschanoff, Pestoff, Kiréjeff, Colonels Borstel and Jentalzoff, and a number of other 'Decembrists.'

Whether Michael Bakunin, during his years of cadetship, distinguished himself by any peculiar revolutionary zeal, or whether he was content with the average measure of liberal acquirements, we know not.

[1] Ryléjeff had been trained in the first Cadet corps, which, in consequence of this fact, and the importance attached to it by the pupils, was looked upon as *suspect*, and apparently not without reason. In this respect, some passages in the *Memoirs of a Russian Dekabrist* are very significant. The author, Baron Rosen, who atoned for his complicity by ten years' hard labour in Siberia, held in 1825 the rank of a lieutenant in the Finnish Chasseurs of the Guard. He says: 'My brother, a cadet in the first corps, wrote to me that his fellow-pupils were proud of finding several names of former members of their institute among the number of the condemned, and that they pitied me for not having shared the honourable fate of their former comrade Ryléjeff'—Ryléjeff had been hanged.

That the contrary currents which agitated the Russian life of that time, and made the danger of falling into extremes almost a matter of necessity for the rising generation, had had their influence upon him as well as upon others, cannot indeed be doubted, and a peculiar concurrence of events prevented the germ, thus planted in him in his youth, from being choked by the influences he received in manhood. For the more competent and assiduous cadets it was a matter of course that, after being quit of their 'pass-examination,' they should be transferred to the Guards, and thereby be placed in a position, as witnesses and partakers of the splendours of life at the Court and the capital, and the intoxication of endless festivals and entertainments, to forget as rapidly and completely as possible their youthful dreams. But although Bakunin had passed a brilliant examination, and although the good circumstances of his family gave him ample means to afford the expenses necessary for an officer of the Guards, he was placed, not there, but in the Line—in other words, he was doomed apparently to waste his days in a miserable peasant-village in White Russia, far away from the centre of Russian civilisation. Alexander Herzen, who had been a friend of Bakunin since his youth, tells us that this change was the result of a quarrel between Bakunin and his father, who chose that way of punishing him; according to another, and not improbable version, the Director of the School of Artillery had grown jealous of his former pupil. However that may be, he left the capital, when a young man of twenty-one, to spend the next year of his life in a peasant's hut, which had been assigned to him for his quarters. To be told off to the society of rough or even frivolous comrades, and that not for a short period of transition, but possibly for the rest of his life, was to Bakunin an idea destructive of all his cherished projects. Naturally of a meditative turn of mind, and brought up from childhood in a society which looked upon indolence as the natural calling of men of good birth (for the so-called busy people of that day were, taken at bottom, only *très-occupés à ne rien faire*), the young officer of artillery sank into a state of lethargy, which was all the more remarkable in one who, at first sight, seemed endowed with an impetuous, nay, choleric temperament, and an unusual amount of energy. He gradually abjured all social intercourse with his comrades, isolated himself entirely, and (here also we follow a statement of Herzen's) dreamed away whole days in his dressing-gown and on his bed. This, of course, could never last. There were loud complaints about his neglect of duty, and nothing was left to the Commander of the division, who in other respects was well disposed towards him, but to give the young misanthrope the choice between a stricter performance of his duty and sending in his papers. Bakunin chose the latter alternative. At the early age of twenty-two, he brought his career in the service to a close, and retired to Moscow to live there as a private gentleman, upon the earnings of his serfs.

Here, indeed, he found plenty of companions. The number of young men who were living at Moscow in those days, under circumstances akin to his, and in whose circles the ex-Lieutenant of Artillery had to seek his society, was legion. Whoever had been unlucky in the Civil Service, at the Court, or in the army; whoever fancied himself slighted or overlooked, whoever despaired of rising to the standard of apathy required for a Russian country gentleman of the old style, or had grown tired of German baths, or life at Paris, regularly retired in the days of the Emperor Nicholas to Moscow. As opposed to St. Petersburg—uniform, Europeanised, bustling, and always ruled by the whims and humours of the Court—this old metropolis of the empire—'the "white-stone" mother Moscow of many cupolas'—managed to acquire a sort of social independence and old-fashioned propriety. Here social position was determined by other considerations than those of rank and position; here nationality had still a certain value; here there were people who, in spite of their unpopularity at Court, still played a part in society, and were not afraid of expressing an independent opinion; here, at least within certain limits, a man could read, talk, and do as he pleased without waiting for permission from the police. All those who in their choice of residence were not straitened by external considerations, and who set any value on their independence, repaired, as a matter of course, not to St. Petersburg, but to Moscow, and sought in this city their 'circle.'

Monotonous and insipid enough was the character of most of these 'circles.' 'Do you know what a clique, a social "circle," is called in Moscow?' Turgenieff makes his Hamlet of Schtchigroff's 'circle' ask. 'Such a circle is the ruin of all independent development—a musty, barren kind of social intercourse, to which one gives the form and importance of a rational entity. It substitutes mere gossip for conversation, and utterly unfits a man for all work. It infects its members with a mania for scribbling, and robs every soul of all freshness and innocence. Dulness and boredom are offered in the place of friendship and brotherhood, frivolity and pretension instead of frankness and sympathy. In a clique of this kind no man has a clean or untouched place left in his heart, for each one claims the right to probe with unwashed fingers the most silent recesses of his neighbour's soul.'

The 'circle,' however, into which Bakunin was received did not belong to the sort here described. It included the most conspicuous young talents of the Moscow of that day, and was filled with interest in a subject which had occupied the attention of all Europe, and even in Russia was destined to produce important effects. This was German, and in particular Hegel's philosophy.

German philosophy had been taught since 1826 at the Moscow University. The first prophet of this teaching, till then wholly unknown, was a Professor Pawloff, who introduced his lectures on physics with quotations from Schelling's and Oken's system of natural philosophy, and had enjoined it as a duty on his pupils to consult the works of these writers for their answers to such questions as—What is nature? What means the investigation of nature? and then to pass on to the study of single branches of the science. Hegel was first introduced to the Russian youth, some eight or ten years later, by a pupil of Pawloff, named Stankevitch, a well-to-do private gentleman, who held neither a professorship nor any public office, but preached the system of the Berlin philosophy to a select circle of his friends.

To this circle belonged a number of men who have made an epoch in the history of Russian literature and civilisation. Belinski, the Radical critic, who subsequently became a Russian literary magnate, Granovski the historian, and Alexander Herzen represented the extreme left of this *coterie*. Chomjäkoff and K. Aksakoff, the founders of the Slavophil party, believed to have found in Hegelian literature a confirmation of their

Conservative-romantic conception of state and society. Stankevitch knew how to quicken the enthusiasm of his young friends in the new teaching. 'Whole nights,' says Herzen, ' were spent in animated disputations over single paragraphs of Hegel's " Logic," the " Encyclopædia," and the two volumes of his " Æsthetics." Friends, who in other respects had been inseparable, fell out for weeks together over their various conceptions of the nature of Absolute Intelligence and the Relation of the *per se* to its contrary (*An und für sich sein*). The most insignificant *brochures* that appeared at Berlin on German philosophy, if they only mentioned Hegel, were bought with eagerness—no matter what the cost or trouble—and devoured for days and nights with inexhaustible zeal, until they had been literally read to pieces and useless.'

Little indeed did Hegel know what extravagant conclusions his Moscow disciples drew from the doctrines of their master. According to the theories extolled by Herzen and his friends, including Bakunin, there was no real difference between the substance and spirit of the Berlin philosophy on the one hand and French Socialism on the other: this philosophy was simply the 'Algebra of Revolution.' ' After I had resolved,' says Herzen, ' to drink *ex ipsâ fonte*, and had gained a knowledge of Hegel's terminology, I perceived plainly that his views were far closer allied to our own Socialistic theories than to those of his nearer disciples. His philosophy makes men free, in a way that no other teaching does; it leaves no stone in Christendom unturned; it liberates the world from obsolete traditions; but it is—and very likely intentionally—badly formulated.'

Whilst the ' true meaning ' of the new system popularised by Stankevitch was regarded for years with suspicion by the 'wider' circles of Moscow philosophers, whilst Stankevitch himself came to no definitive conclusion, and men like Samarin, Aksakoff, and others took over to the camp of Slavo-Byzantine orthodoxy the weapons they had forged in this school, Bakunin himself, and later on Belinski also, declared for the theory of Herzen. Bakunin passed for the ablest philosopher and the profoundest *savant* of the whole circle. He who till then had passed his life as a visionary idler, allowed his talents to rust, and wasted his days in moody reveries and reading, as aimless as promiscuous, now took to learning German, plunged into the writings of Kant and Fichte, succeeded in understanding Hegel's 'Logic' to perfection, and made its propagation the formal profession of his life. Belinski's conversion had been regarded as peculiarly his work; Herzen he impressed by his incomparable 'revolutionary tact.' The boldness of his conclusions and the strength of his dialectic passed as irresistible: in the opinion of his friends he had reached at his first effort the pinnacle of contemporary culture and development. He left Moscow after Stankevitch's circle had begun to be dissolved in 1839, and his two most intimate friends had gone to settle at St. Petersburg. He went to Berlin, as Katkoff and Granovski had done before him, to continue the studies commenced at Moscow, and conclude them with the help of German teachers.

Hegel himself, when Bakunin arrived at Berlin, had been dead nine years; but his system was then at the climax of its fame in Germany, in Prussia, and especially at Berlin. 'Most of the chairs of philosophy were given away to his disciples: to obtain a post as teacher, it was indispensable to know at least the technical terms of his school. A host of enthusiastic and talented young men applied his ideas with success to various departments of science and learning. Jurisprudence and politics were arranged, to the amazement of the old-fashioned jurists, according to the categories of *An sich*, and *Für sich*, and *An und für sich*. Painters, poets, and actors consulted the "Æsthetics," and people even thought of establishing an Hegelian theatrical school at Berlin. The history of culture seemed to have reached a point, beyond which no further progress was possible.' Just as ten years earlier, young men from all countries, Poles, Russians, New Greeks, Scandinavians, &c., crowded the lecture-rooms where the wheezy and coughing lecturer had with difficulty and constant repetition got out his magic words of wisdom, and which had since become historical. 'Each and all of them,' as Rosenkranz remarks in his 'Life of Hegel,' 'felt themselves to be fellow-actors with him in a grand, world-historical transformation. They were all elevated by this sublime pathos, and a new life trembled through their young hearts and heads.'

Amidst the hearers who surrounded Michelet, Hotho, and others of that school, our tall Russian student, so emotional, so prompt for disputation, and so remarkable for his dialectical acuteness, had become, as some of his contemporaries may remember, a conspicuous and familiar figure. But after the first intoxicating impressions of this new world had faded, Bakunin remained chiefly in the circles of his fellow-countrymen. Turgenieff for a long time shared his home; Katkoff and Granovski were his constant guests at table. Where all had a touch of Radicalism and fully believed in the advent of a new era, the pronounced character of Bakunin's views could scarcely attract especial notice.

If at times he frightened his friends with his wild and extravagant deductions from commonly accepted doctrines, and his demands for their immediate realisation, still eccentricities of that sort were too common in those days to allow any particular importance to be attached to them. With the examples of others daily placed before him, it could hardly pass for strange that a young, ill-educated man, the creature of wholly heterogeneous and half-barbarous conditions, and now suddenly launched into the metropolis of intelligence, should lose the power to discriminate between dreams and realities, and with nothing but the 'Algebra of Revolution' to assist him, should indulge in calculations of the boldest and most questionable kind.

How long Bakunin's stay at Berlin lasted we cannot say for certain. At the beginning of 1842 we find him at Dresden, whither he had removed, in order to gain a nearer acquaintance with Arnold Ruge, the interpreter of Hegel with whom he most sympathised, and a man who was held in high esteem by the entire school of young Russian philosophy. The annual periodicals (*Jahrbücher*), published at Halle, had been part of the gospel of Stankevitch's circle: Herzen and Belinski were downright intoxicated with them. They were delighted with the boldness with which the editor denounced war against all national prejudices, championed the cause of France and its Socialistic literature, and roundly declared that salvation was only to be looked for from the West and its darling metropolis. All this language not only suited the personal leanings of these men who, with impulses first received from Fourier and Proudhon, turned afterwards to Hegel and his school, but furnished also effective weapons in the battle against the 'friends of former days,' the national fanatics of the Slavophischool, whose growing influence was regarded with apprehension.

With Ruge Bakunin soon became on such friendly terms, that the former invited him to co-operate with him in his *Jahrbücher*. The young Russian philosopher, now twenty-eight years old, had long since mastered the German language as thoroughly as the Hegelian terminology. Accordingly, he did not hesitate to comply, and published in Nos. 247 to 251 of the *Jahrbücher* of 1842, under the pseudonym of 'Jules Elizard,' a treatise on the 'Reaction in Germany.' This treatise is remarkable, and in order to estimate its value correctly, it is necessary to look more closely at the nature of the *Jahrbücher* of 1842, now only known by name.

Periodicals of this kind would be impossible in these practical and matter-of-fact days. Three hundred and ten numbers annually, each number containing eight closely printed pages, devoted exclusively to the criticism of whatever appeared in the fields of literature, science, art, and especially philosophy, and written in a style intelligible only to those who possess at least some acquaintance with Hegelian terminology—where could be found in modern Germany an editor, a publisher, or readers for a *magnum opus* of this kind? Notwithstanding the variety of subjects discussed, the one-sided tendencies of the editor are revealed with a crudity and harshness, unparalleled even in our own days, when the one-sidedness of party spirit penetrates all society to the core. It is almost comical now to observe the self-assurance with which the editor insists that his ideas of what constitutes a State must be put at once into practice. The smallest incident of the day is magnified into a symptom of the coming great revolution. Three-fourths of his space are taken up with philosophy and theology; the names of Hegel, Strauss, and Feuerbach recur on almost every page, nearly as often as the comparisons between the German literary and the French political revolution. An idolatrous admiration of the French, and an open affectation of Radical opinions, are expressed in dictatorial language, and with a conscious air of infallibility. In the very first article the editor announces that ' the entire past of the Christian world had been rolled together and made a stepping stone to the Heaven of modern times'; that the ' exclusion of mankind from his earthly paradise had reached its term,' and that ' the universal effort to shake off the past was the sign that a new era had already been born.' His contributors followed suit. The golden age assuredly was at hand, and the old idols of the world must sink into the dust before the splendour of the coming light. 'A new German Drama,' writes Adolph Stahr, is approaching—' the Drama of the most civilised nation on earth, and destined to reign supreme in the literature of the world.'[1] To stamp out effectually the trash of former days, the Lyric Muse had only to follow in the steps of Herwegh and Prutz, whose writings breathed the 'freshness of a new spring-time.' Nothing found favour with these *Jahrbücher* writers of 1842, but what had reference to the ' ideas of the time,' or served to strengthen their proposition of the superiority of the French. Accordingly, Gutzkoff is reproached for ' want of principle and feeling,' because his 'Letters from Paris' betrayed, benaeth a mass of egotistic verbiage, a German mind, and because he had been too cowardly to launch out boldly,

[1] This prophecy was inspired by a representation of Gutzkoff's *Patkul*. Somewhat similar opinions had been expressed when the *Antigone* of Sophocles was first represented at Berlin.

and with enthusiasm, upon the ' living ocean of a grand national life.' Accordingly, Börne is eulogised as a man unique in German history, the John the Baptist of a new era, without whose influence, supplemented by the larger spirit of Hegelianism, the system which Hegel introduced, might never have obtained free scope and play. Equally grotesque and dictatorial were the verdicts passed on unpopular, and therefore ' insignificant' writers of the time. Charles Dickens is nothing but a coarse Sterne, whose productions (speaking of ' Nicholas Nickleby') are unworthy of the name of art, and belong to the amusing but superficial class of reading, serviceable only for daily use. Schopenhauer is anonymously relegated to the dead, as a dilettantist and insignificant scribbler. Pfitzer is plainly told that his allusions to Prussia's future in Germany will not ' earn the thanks of those who dislike to see Philosophy take a retrograde step.' As for Greece, it had already been settled as an axiom, that she was approaching a great future, and that even now her national character and natural capabilities offered no obstacles to the establishment of a better state of things.

Such was the tone of the periodical which in 1842 claimed to march at the head of German progress, and under the patronage of which Bakunin (Jules Elizard) made his *début* as a public writer. His friend Ruge had not omitted to herald this event with an editorial flourish of trumpets, and to preface the pretended ' Fragment by a Frenchman ' with an introduction of his own. Our readers must really allow us to quote from it, for it illustrates the general tendency of these *Jahrbücher*. ' We communicate,' he says, ' in these pages, not merely a remarkable production, but an important fact. German philosophy has ere now produced in other countries *dilettanti* and servile disciples, like Cousin and others; but men who have been the philosophical superiors of German philosophers and politicians have hitherto not been found outside our frontiers. Thus then, for the first time a foreign country tears the laurels from our brows; and we may hope that this new phenomenon of a Frenchman understanding German philosophy will stir up many a sluggard from his indolence. M. Jules Elizard is perhaps right in promising us a " great practical future," but surely he has mistaken us, if his example does not induce us to put aside our arrogance, voluntarily resign our fancied prerogative, and, *horribile dictu!* become true Frenchmen.'

The 'important fact,' thus pompously announced, and from which such profound consequences were foreshadowed, was simply the elaboration of a series of propositions, more or less unintelligible, and embedded in a mass of sophistical jargon. Dismissing as unworthy of notice all 'enemies of the principle of Revolution,' except the reactionary party throughout Europe, who in Politics have gained the name of Conservatives, in Jurisprudence that of the Historical School, and in Speculative Science that of Positive philosophers, Bakunin proceeds to glorify the Democratic principle as the true lever of the world, and to claim for the Democratic party, whose imperfect appreciation of their true principle he laments, the exclusive right to existence. Blind indeed are the Reactionists not to see that the Positive exists only as the contrary of the Negative, and that the destruction of the one would be the completion of the other. 'But we can forgive them their blindness,' he says; 'for our " principle " allows us to be generous. We—the champions of the Revolutionary principle—are something more than the mere Negative party, the uncompromising enemies of the Positive; that which sustains and elevates us as a party is the all-embracing principle of absolute Freedom.' With similar arrogance he rejects all notion of mediation or compromise between the Revolutionists and their enemies the Reactionists. Mediation implies the recognition that of two opposite and conflicting tendencies both are equally one-sided, and therefore equally untrue. The supposed equality does not exist. So far from being a mere equipoise of the Positive, the Negative alone determines the balance, and comprehends the totality of the contrast. The Negative, therefore, alone is absolutely true,

It is scarcely worth while to observe that Hegel's own theory of the identity of contraries supplied an answer, such as it was, to this last-mentioned paradox of his admirer. Nor shall we drag our readers through the columns of nonsense in which Bakunin proceeds to explain the gradual transformation of the Negative into an ' independent principle,' and the corresponding transition of Nature into a World of free Intelligence. ' Have you not read,' he says to the advocates of mediation, ' the mysterious and dreadful words *Liberté, Egalité, et Fraternité*, in front of the Temple of Liberty erected by the French Revolution; and do you not know and feel that these words mean the total annihilation of the existing world of politics and society?' Then, after treating of the Socialistic-religious associations in France and England, which ' are wholly foreign and opposed to the present world of politics, and derive their life from sources altogether new and unknown to us,' Bakunin concludes as follows :—' The air is sultry; it is charged with storms. Let us therefore cry aloud to our blind brethren, "Do penance, do penance; the Kingdom of the Lord is at hand!" To the Positivists we say, "Open your spiritual eyes: let the dead bury their dead; and be convinced at last that the Spirit of Intelligence (*Geist*), the ever-young, the ever new-born—is not to be looked for among the ruins of the past." Let us also put our trust in this everlasting Spirit, which destroys and annihilates only because it is the fathomless and ever-creating fountain of all life. The joy of destruction is also the joy of creation.'

That this rigmarole of senseless phrases and hollow abstractions could have appeared in 1842 in the most advanced German periodical of the time, and been lauded by its editor as the *ne plus ultra* of modern philosophical and political wisdom, is a fact too significant of the character of the time and the mental development of Bakunin, to be passed by unnoticed. The half-educated ex-Lieutenant of Artillery, left to himself for years, had gone to Germany with the intention of submitting to revision a teaching received in a crude state from his friend Stankevitch, of repairing and compensating in the Western world of culture the defects of his youthful education, and of learning the aims and methods of those who had been named to him as the leading exponents of the civilisation of that time. And what had these heralds and representatives of culture, to whom the entire youthful generation of those days looked up with astonishment and awe—what had they to offer him? The same rubbish of mystic formulas, the same 'Algebra of Revolution,' with which he and his friends had wasted their time at Moscow; the same blind faith in the universal efficacy of subtle abstractions which had deluded Herzen and Belinski into imagining that the true conception of the State had only to be proclaimed to be carried at once into practical effect. Not as a disciple, but as a friend and equal, had Bakunin entered the circle of those vain *doctrinaires*, who accounted themselves the forerunners of a new and better dispensation, and looked down upon the world of reality with as much arrogance as himself. It was the glory of this tyro of philosophy to have mastered the conceptions of religion, of nationality, and of history. His maiden effort was lauded as a masterpiece. The wild energy of his passion for destruction was admired as manly decision of character. His belief in the absolute truth of the Negative principle—the depositary, as he called it, of all intelligence—was strengthened into an article of faith. Was it to be wondered at, that with the firm resolve to give immediate and complete effect to his infallible theories, with ' the light in front, and the darkness behind him,' Bakunin went his own way, and soon pretended to give laws to and dictate the development of the world of culture, which he had just begun to be acquainted with, and of whose real nature he had scarcely even a superficial idea?

In Germany Bakunin now fancied he had learned all there was to learn. In January 1843 he quitted Dresden for Paris, to gain acquaintance with that city of wonders, which his German friends had taught him to worship as the Mecca of Revolution. When Bakunin arrived at the French capital, the Duke of Orleans had been dead six months, and the Ministry of Guizot and Soult, which three years before had taken the conduct of affairs, was still at the height of its power. The influential circles of Parisian society, however, had already begun to look beyond the July monarchy and its attempts at Constitutionalism, and to seek in the literary productions of the Socialistic school some consolation and compensation for the *ennui* from which their country, as Lamartine expressed it, was suffering. Eugène Sue, a celebrity since the publication of his 'Deux Cadavres,' began his 'Mystères de Paris' in the *feuilleton* of the 'Journal des Débats,' and managed to enlist such passionate interest in the so-called hero and heroine of his story as to make educated people forget for a while all customary ideas of morality. Alfred de Musset had already preached in his 'Paresse' the omnipotence of money. George Sand, under the influence of her friend Michel, had made the 'Countess of Rudolstadt' the vehicle for proclaiming plans for a radical regeneration of the universe. Michelet, in the fervour of his crusade against the Jesuits, developed a degree of Radicalism which created all the more sensation, as no one had suspected, in this solitary student of the closet, the man who, as Heine remarks, ran the greatest danger of becoming a 'villain as bad as Robespierre and Marat.'

The three chief works of modern Socialism, Cabet's 'Icarie,' Proudhon's book on 'Property,' and Louis Blanc's 'Organisation of Labour,' though published only three years before, were still in everyone's hands, and had begun to bear fruit among the educated. A dim feeling that the old society resisted the new claims more from the necessity of self-defence than from a consciousness of right, had begun to take possession of the people of rank and station even, who were the readers of the 'Mystères' and the Socialistic romances of Sand.

That Bakunin should surrender himself a willing victim to the impressions which swayed the greater part of Parisian society was to be expected from his antecedents. Once resolved to take part, not as a mere spectator, but as an actual combatant, in the great contest of the time, he allied himself with the various leaders of the Socialist party and with the numerous Polish conspiracy-mongers, who, by the indulgence of Louis Philippe's government, lived as emigrants in the French metropolis—with all, in short, who were noted for 'decided views' and revolutionary recklessness. His favourite was Proudhon, with whom he found a bond of union in their common admiration of Hegel's philosophy. A lasting intimacy between them was impossible, for Proudhon in 1843 removed to Lyons as agent for a transport company, and Bakunin was induced by his Polish friends to go to Switzerland, then the head-quarters of all Communists and revolutionary intrigues, in order there to establish that wide-spread connection which enabled him, wherever the standard of Revolution was hoisted, to be on the spot and take a prominent part. His removal was to some extent determined by the fact, that the Russian residents at Paris were strictly watched by secret agents; and Bakunin, moreover, had excited so strongly the suspicions of the government, that an extension of his *permis* was refused. For years he was forced to pass his life without the necessary *légitimation*, and completely at the mercy of the police—a fate easier to bear in Switzerland than in the France of Louis Philippe.

Shortly before the outbreak of the February revolution—namely, in November 1847—Bakunin, after whiling away five years in the Swiss valleys, paid another flying visit to Paris. His native rights being definitely forfeited by his ostracism from Russia, he could now come forward publicly, and surprise the world in the novel character of a Russian political refugee. For the first time his name was hailed in wider circles with applause; and soon after he had the satisfaction to see printed, and then translated into various languages, the speech he delivered, in the presence of numerous representatives of French Radicalism, at the annual Polish banquet held November 29, 1847, to celebrate the seventeenth anniversary of the last rising at Warsaw. The substance of this oration, which formed the prototype of countless other speeches of Russian and Polish revolutionists, may be readily guessed. Acknowledging the grievous injustice done to the Polish nation by Russia, he promised that the Revolution of the future would not only make amends for this, but would remove all the differences still remaining between the two leading families of Slavs, and unite the lands east of the Oder into a proper and beneficent federative Republic. Original indeed this idea was not, for the Dekabrists of 1825 had had visions of a similar scheme, and had gained for it the approval of the Patriotic Union at Warsaw. Still its public proclamation by a Russian made an extraordinary impression, and one that soon extended to France and Paris. Nicolai Kisseleff, who after the recall of Count Pahlen in 1841, conducted the Russian embassy as chargé d'affaires, received instructions from Count Orloff to demand the expulsion of the venturesome orator from France—a demand with which Guizot did not hesitate to comply. Watched at every turn by Russian agents (the government at St. Petersburg is said to have offered a reward of 10,000 roubles for his capture), Bakunin fled to Belgium, until the February revolution removed the former obstacles to his residence in France, and he was able to return again to Paris, whither in the meantime refugees from all countries of Europe had flocked together, to celebrate the spring-time of the Universal Revolution, so long awaited and now close at hand.

His joy was of short duration. Before the new

Republic was four weeks old, it was plain that the Provisional Government, in spite of all their cosmopolitan phrases, abjured the notion of figuring as the leaders of Revolution in Europe, and that the difference between Blue and Red Republicans was far wider and deeper than that which separated the Blue from the Liberal Monarchists. The real reason why the Government of February 24 were so liberal as to give passports and travelling-money to the Poles who left France in order to revolutionise their own country, was not any active sympathy with Polish affairs, but the wish to get rid of these inconvenient foreigners, for a long while the allies of Blanqui and Barbès. Bakunin, who, for want of a Russian revolutionary party, had looked to the Poles for the overthrow of the Czardom and the establishment of the Slav Republic of the future, found his prospects crushed by the failure of the insurrection of May. All hope was now over of the triumph of French Radicalism, and of furthering by its means the cause of Revolution in Europe. He left France, and went to Germany and Austria, where the universal confusion furnished at once a prospect of fishing in troubled waters, and an opportunity for realising his darling objects. Without departing from his philosophical cosmopolitanism and his enthusiasm for the 'Sainte alliance des peuples,' the pupil of Hegel had remained sufficiently Russian at the bottom of his heart to regard the idea of a universal Slav Republic, organised on federal principles, as the most vital and important concern of mankind, and to subordinate to this object all other considerations, even those of an alliance between freedom and the civilisation of Western Europe. He was convinced that the Slav Congress, convened at Prague on June 1, 1848, would render far greater services to the cause of universal revolution than either German or French democracy, mixed up as it was with civic elements. And this conviction was strengthened by his belief, which forty years before had been accepted also as a dogma by the party of opposition in Russia, that the want of freedom at home was chiefly the work of German hands, and that the final emancipation of the Slav race would be impossible, until Germany's influence over Eastern Europe was broken, or at least restricted to the narrowest possible bounds.

Accordingly, early in June 1848, Bakunin came to Prague, where he joined the Polish section, presided over by Libelt, of the Slav Congress, and at once exercised a permanent influence over its deliberations. With the Croats and Czechs, who formed the Conservative element of the assembly, he fraternised on the strength of their common aversion to all that was German. His object was to join hands with Poles and Servians over the ruins of the Austrian Empire, and to undertake a revolutionary crusade against the universe. He and a monk of the Old Faith, who had been sent from the Bukovina to represent the grievances of his co-religionists against the Governments of Vienna and St. Petersburg, were the only representatives of Russia at this Congress. Bakunin, therefore, as representing the most numerous of all Slav races, played a conspicuous part, and largely contributed to the triumph of the revolutionary party. But this triumph was only momentary, and proved fatal to the whole enterprise. Bakunin was compelled to fly, and the furious enemy of the German element in Austria actually sought refuge in Germany.

Here he was welcomed with open arms by the Radicals, and remained concealed for some time, first at Berlin, then at Dessau, Cöthen, and various towns in

Saxony. Everywhere pursued and turned away by the police, he was a wanderer for nearly a twelvemonth; until, at the end of April, 1849, he succeeded in finding employment, under a false name, at the University of Leipsic. Here a circle of Bohemian students accepted unreservedly, not only his revolutionary, but also his Panslavistic doctrines. With the leaders of the Saxon and German democracy he remained on terms of unbroken intimacy; nor was the least offence taken, either at his doings at Prague the year before, or at the eccentricity of his schemes of Panslavism. Strange to say, August Röckel,[1] in a work written as recently as 1865, eulogises his old comrade as the exponent of the 'noblest humanity, untainted by national exclusiveness,' although Röckel himself had borne eloquent witness to Bakunin's political incapacity, and in his book above referred to has the following passage on that subject:—

> By means of his friends, the Bohemian students, Bakunin thought to rouse Bohemia from the state of torpor and discouragement which followed the unfortunate and somewhat aimless conflict of June in the previous year. What at first, however, he only wished and strove for, his impatience falsely pictured to him as accomplished, and he awaited with confidence a speedy and general rising in Bohemia. Judging by the aspect of affairs in Germany, it seemed now a matter of the utmost importance to guard carefully against every single indiscretion, and Bakunin easily induced me to go to Prague, in order to confer with the leaders in that city, counselling them to defer a rising until affairs in Germany, which were rapidly hastening to a crisis, should permit a hope that the movement would at once become general.
>
> At Prague, however, I found matters very different from what they had been represented to me. Czechs and Germans were more bitterly estranged than ever. The loss of Vienna in the previous

---

[1] *Sachsen's Erhebung und das Zuchthaus zu Woltheim.* Frankfort-on-Main: E. Adelmann.

October, so far from being felt as a common calamity, had been regarded by the Czechs with a certain satisfaction as a just retaliation on the Germans for deserting them in the June insurrection. Even the great struggle in Hungary had not met with that sympathy from the Bohemians which kindled such fervour among us Germans, it being looked upon simply as an attempt of the Magyars to maintain their supremacy over the Slav population of Hungary. The want of unity of sentiment—a want so much lamented in Germany—was even more hopelessly expressed in Austria, where differences of nationality and the traditional system of government combined to perpetuate it. The various peoples regarded each other with mutual jealousy and distrust, and instead of uniting their forces against the common enemy, each thought, by oppressing the other, to win the victory for itself, until all alike became re-united in the common fate of bondage. Instead of that powerful and widely ramifying union, of which Bakunin fancied himself the head, and by means of which he thought to set the mightiest agencies in motion, I found scarcely a dozen of young people, whose excited imagination could not even deceive them about their impotence. I spoke with a few of them, who had been pointed out to me as being possibly in favour of an appeal to force. I met also with a ready acquiescence in self-sacrifice; but everything that I saw around me only served to confirm my first impressions of the situation of affairs. As experienced patriots assured me, months would be still required to make it generally perceived that nothing but an active cooperation of German and Austrian democracy could stem so far the prevailing reaction as to give a prospect of exchanging words for deeds. The Austrian Government demonstrated indeed, soon after, by its rigorous persecution of all my associates, during my short visit to Bohemia, how insecure it felt its own position, and how it dreaded even the remotest attempt at a popular rising. I had scarcely been three days at Prague when I was called away again by the wholly unexpected news of the movement at Dresden.

Bakunin also, like Röckel, hastened at the news of this movement to the capital of Saxony. We find him on May 5, 1849, taking part at a conference, held at the town-hall, between Heubner, Tschirner, and Todt, the three heads of the Provisional Government, and Heinze, the Commandant of the National Guard. Far above his associates in decision, in rashness, and in physical and moral obstinacy of purpose, the Russian revolutionist exercised over this German attempt at insurrection, kindled in the name of the constitution which he abhorred, an enduring influence. From the 6th to the 9th of May he was the very life and soul of the defence of Dresden against the Saxon and Prussian troops. From him, not from Röckel, came the orders to pile up combustible materials in the town-hall, and to prepare the brands which 'for strategic reasons' were thrown into the 'Zwinger' and the Opera-house. It was he who uttered the infamous words, 'Never mind the houses; let them be blown into the air!' It was he who, regardless of the forlorn nature of the insurrection, and the weariness and despair of Heubner and Todt, addressed a speech on the afternoon of the 8th to the Communal representative of Leipsic, who attended the meeting of the Provisional Government, on the 'European importance' of this desperate enterprise; and on the morning of the 9th, when all was lost, gave the order for a general retreat to Freiberg. Seized at Chemnitz on the 10th, and delivered up to the pursuing troops, Bakunin knew how to preserve to the last a proud and courageous demeanour. Twenty-seven years afterwards one of the Prussian officers, who had guarded the prisoner on the way through Altenburg, still remembered the calmness and intrepidity with which the tall man in fetters replied to a lieutenant, who interpellated him, that in politics the issue alone can decide what is a great action and what a crime.[1]

The 10th of May, 1849, determined the next ten years of Bakunin's life. From the following August,

[1] Von Varchmin, *Die Sociale Frage*. 1876.

till May, 1850, he was kept prisoner in the fortress of Königstein, and being sentenced to death by the Saxon tribunal, was delivered up to the Austrian Government, in pursuance of a resolution passed by the old Diet of the Bund in 1836. Once more condemned to death (May, 1851), his sentence was commuted to imprisonment for life; but, at the request of the Emperor Nicholas, he was handed over to the political police of his native country, and taken, in the autumn of 1851, through Warsaw and Vilna, to St. Petersburg, to be locked up in the casemates of the Peter-Paul fortress. The silent respectfulness of the Poles, who, in spite of strict orders to the contrary, had collected in large numbers in the streets of Vilna, baring their heads as the orator of November 27, 1847, drove past them in a sledge, surrounded by gendarmes, was probably the last ray of light that Bakunin took with him into the dungeons which for the next six years shut him out from the world. At the outbreak of the Crimean War he was removed to the casemates of the dreaded Schlüsselburg, which actually lie beneath the level of the Neva; but when the new emperor, Alexander II., at his coronation in August, 1856, issued his Ukase of Amnesty (extending to the condemned conspirators of 1825), Bakunin, at the intercession of his relatives, was released from prison, and banished to the eastern part of Siberia. There he lived for several years as a penal colonist, until, in 1859, the then Governor-General, Count Muravjeff-Amurski — or, according to others the Civil Governor, Korssakoff — gave him permission to settle in the lately annexed territory of the Amur. Here he was allowed to move about almost as he pleased; and being granted a pass, which of course referred only to the province, and favoured by all around him on account of his relationship with Muravjeff, he found it no difficult matter to extend his excursions as far as Novo-Nikolaievsk, where he secretly got on board an American vessel, and escaped to Japan. From thence he went to North America; and finally came to London in 1861, where Herzen, Ogareff, and the other Russian refugees welcomed with open arms the veteran of the revolutionary party of Russia, who, although forty-seven years of age, was physically and mentally full of freshness and energy. His wife and children, whom he had left at the mouth of the Amur, now rejoined him; and once on English soil, he found himself secure against all the dangers and persecutions which his earlier memories had conjured up to his imagination.

We cannot here enter into the details either of his years of exile in Siberia or of the romantic journey which restored him to the European world. According to his own statements and those of his friends, not once, not even in Siberia, did Bakunin recant the opinions which caused his exile; he owed his freedom solely to himself, to his boldness and his enormous physical strength. His enemies, on the contrary, tell of things which place his conduct in a very questionable light. In bureaucratic circles in Siberia, which pass for very liberal and unprejudiced, it is still asserted that his escape was due to a shameful abuse of confidence practised by him towards the Governor and his subordinates. Charges even worse than this have been made against him by Russian exiles, and have since been repeated and believed even in France. According to these, he sneaked into the favour of the government by intriguing against Petraschevski, the chief instigator of the conspiracy at St. Petersburg in 1848; it is represented as 'past all doubt' that he had a hand in bringing about the banishment of this man to the desolate regions of the White Sea, who was living at that time in a town of Central Siberia, and that he defended this act of the Government in an article he wrote for the 'Kolokol.' He is accused also of having sold to unworthy persons his influence with the Governor-General of Irkutsk, of having carried on a traffic in patronage, and of having prevented the establishment of a Siberian University.

That most of these charges are founded simply on calumny, and a spirit of malicious scandal fostered by the *ennui* of idle emigrants, may be taken for certain; but still there are several of his actions, more or less equivocal, which Bakunin has never been able to explain. No doubt he became demoralised by his many years of imprisonment and his life of adventure. At any rate, it is a fact that his recklessness, his extravagant demeanour, and his cynical way of expressing himself, shocked the London friends of Herzen and his *coterie*. It is equally plain that the effect produced by his life in Siberia was far from beneficial to his character, and that his influence upon the 'Kolokol,' the editorship of which he undertook, was unfavourable in the extreme. The original object of this paper, as founded by Herzen, had been to expose the defects of Russian life and Russian government, and, as such, its utility had been acknowledged even by its political opponents. That, from a Radical, it now became a Revolutionary journal, which put itself in the wrong with regard to the St. Petersburg Government, preached subversion instead of reform, and subversion indeed at any price, even at the expense of a general chaos, was mainly the fault of its new editor, Bakunin. Number upon number of the 'Kolokol,' after

1861, exhibited tendencies now scarcely distinguishable from Nihilism, such as Herzen had not only never professed, but had repeatedly spoken of with horror. The same 'pleasure of destruction' which twenty years before the youthful Jules Elizard had eulogised as the logical consequence of the 'Negative principle,' and the necessary condition of a true creative spirit, became at length the ruling motive of all his actions, thoughts, and wishes. Not once, even when some distinct and defined revolutionary object was in view, could he moderate, if only for the moment, his fanatical hatred against existing things. Religion, art, literature, and science, as well as State organisation—he would spare nothing that had the appearance of a positive existence. So indiscriminate was his rage for destruction that even the champions of systematic subversion, the men of the International, looked upon it as a mania and a crime. The history of the last fifteen years of Bakunin's public career is the history of a revolutionary fanaticism, which reached eventually the lowest depths of Radical infatuation.

Once fairly settled in London, he announced his intention of devoting the remainder of his life exclusively to the task of revolutionising Slavdom. His language showed the same want of principle, which had changed the cosmopolitan into a Panslavist, and the Panslavist into a champion of German revolution. 'It is a bad thing,' he wrote in a manifesto dated February 15, 1862, 'to exercise one's energies in a foreign country. My experience has sufficiently taught me that neither in Germany nor France have I ever struck root. My fullest and most ardent sympathies will be directed, as before, to the liberation of mankind in general; but what remains to me now of life and activity I intend to restrict exclusively to the service of Russians, Poles, and Slavs. Of all Slav nationalities, that of Great Russia alone has understood how to preserve her nationality. Let us, therefore, banish the Tartars to the East, and the Germans to Germany. Let us be a free and purely Russian nation.'

This theoretical devotion to Russian nationality and the interests of Slavdom was carried into practice in a very singular manner. The very year this vow was made he alienated for ever his own and his friends' cause from that of the Russian nation by opposing the wishes of the latter with far more determination and harshness than even a Romanoff would have done. A monk of the Old Faith had come in 1861 to London, charged by his co-religionists with a mission that might have been of marked importance to the grand work of Russian revolution on which Herzen and Bakunin were engaged. The object of Father Pafnuty, as representing his fellow-sectaries oppressed both by Church and State, was to establish a connection with the party of emigrants, to enlist their interests on behalf of his sect, and to prepare on English ground a home for their Superior, who had been expelled from his domicile in Austria. Herzen welcomed this opportunity of an alliance with the lower strata of the Russian nation, who numbered millions, and he entered zealously into their cause. His friend Vassily Kelssieff was intimately acquainted with the singular and delicate nature of Russian sectarianism, and with his assistance a supplementary sheet in the interest of this body was added to the 'Kolokol,' and various schismatic works were printed. Both of these men, in dealing with their spiritual negotiator, evinced a degree of caution and suppleness which, with their contempt of Church and religion, must have been extremely difficult. To spare Pafnuty's superstitious prejudices, they abstained, in his presence, from smoking, from eating forbidden dishes in Lent, and from using expressions that might hurt his feelings. All was going on smoothly until Bakunin began to interfere. But the fanatic of Negations found it impossible to humour, even for a moment, the religious views of his fellow-countryman, or to restrain his hatred of all that savoured of religion. His cynical manners and language made at once the most painful impression on the suspicious monk. After having had to listen to his humming the hymns of his liturgy as if they were light opera songs, and to hear him bantering Kelssieff upon his theological wisdom, Pafnuty broke off all intercourse with the emigrants, and returned to Moscow. He explained, in terms, to his committee, that there could be no question of any communion of the 'just' with the 'worldly children' of wicked London, and that all intercourse with them must be shunned as fraught with ruin to the soul.

Thus broke down for ever all hopes of an alliance— and of the only possible alliance—between the mass of the Russian people and the revolutionary agitators of their country. The hopes of these *émigrés* were narrowed to a certain number of students, cadets, and revolutionary *frondeurs* at St. Petersburg and a few University towns. The reforms begun by Alexander II. in 1862 gradually cut the ground from under the editors of the 'Kolokol,' by convincing the educated and intelligent portion of the Liberal Opposition that what was really wanted to effect a wholesome change in Russian life was not systematic conspiracies and underground intrigues, but an active interest in the newly created institutions of the State. The increased popularity of the periodical press of St. Petersburg and Moscow, now treated with a certain amount of liberality, contributed more than anything to lessen the circulation of the 'Kolokol.' Nevertheless, a large field would still have remained open to Herzen and his party, if only they had known how to practise moderation, to grapple with existing facts, and to supply the defects left by the prohibitive severity of the censorship, and by the government's nervous terror of all that savoured of Constitutionalism. That this was not done, that on the contrary every number of the 'Kolokol' became more and more violent and fanatical, attacking in an offensive manner the emperor himself, and finally defending the mad incendiaries at St. Petersburg in May 1862—all this was chiefly Bakunin's work. To cope for any length of time with his impetuosity, his determination, and the undeniable energy of his nature, was impossible for a man of the easy-going and conciliatory temperament of Herzen, especially as the latter had never had a positive programme of his own, and had exhausted in Negative criticism all he had to offer. Whether he liked it or not, he was forced to say Amen, while Bakunin preached the necessity of a radical rupture with all existing order, and plainly stated that the fruits of many years of culture—whether artistic, literary, or scientific—would have to be placed on the proscription list of the future. Never, in his wildest days of Radicalism, had views such as these found favour with the gentle Herzen, the warm admirer of Goethe and Schiller, of Pushkin and Byron, and the grateful disciple of modern Natural Science. Gradually, as Bakunin's ascendency increased, the 'Kolokol' adopted the tone of pure Nihilism. Already in the summer of 1862, it became evident that Herzen must either change his course or renounce all hope of promoting the cause of Russian progress.

So long as the *régime* of Nicholas lasted, the mass of educated people had thought little of the Socialistic *velléités* in which the paper occasionally indulged. But now, with the prospect of practical politics before them, the time was come to reckon with such eccentricities, and to trace the limits of allegiance to the leader they admired.

Six months later (January, 1863) came the Polish rising, and with it the crisis that decided the future of the party of emigrants. Many, though not most of the Russian Liberals, could not at first withhold their sympathies from the cause of Poland; but on one point they were nearly all united. There could be no question, they agreed, of surrendering White Russia and Lithuania to their former rulers, the Catholic priests and Polish aristocrats: these provinces, whose inhabitants for the most part were neither Poles nor Catholics, must remain an integral portion of the Russian State. This condition became the test of Russian patriotism, and determined the current of popular opinion. After the revolt had spread to the province of Vilna, and the cruelties of the Polish gendarmes had made the peasants turn against their Polish masters and join the cause of the government, the whole of Russia followed their example. The dangers of Western intervention and Katkoff's unrivalled skill in kindling religious and national passions, led to a triumph of the Russian State-system so complete as to take even the government by surprise.

The London exiles were the first victims of this new turn of events. No sooner was it known that Herzen and Bakunin had espoused the cause of Mieroslavski and the Polish claim to the North-west provinces, than their staunchest adherents deserted and denounced them. Bakunin, the devoted Panslavist, had gone over to his old Polish friends. He had actually exhorted the Russian officers who were fighting in Lithuania to turn faithless to the Czar, and join the Polish guerilla rebels, who were instigated by the monks. He had pointed to the brilliant prospect of an invasion of Holy Russia by the Western Powers; and when such an invasion was seriously mooted, had gone to Stockholm to lead a band of refugees to the assistance of the Polish combatants and import cosmopolitan revolution into Russia. This was quite enough to sign his political death-warrant, and to deprive him of all the popularity he had enjoyed for many years, as a 'victim of despotism,' with the majority of liberal Russians. This part was now played out.

Beyond this point it is needless to pursue the history of the 'Kolokol,' which in 1865 was transferred to Geneva, and soon after came to an end. Of its editors, Herzen died in 1870; Ogareff had never taken an independent part; and Kelssieff made his peace with the Russian Government. Bakunin, after having been the ruin of the London exiles by his insane Radicalism, changed colours again when that party was broken up, and rejoined the flag of Cosmopolitan Revolution, trying first to form a connection with the International Peace League, and supplementing these efforts by carrying on his Russo-Slavish propagandism. In the autumn of 1867 we find him settled at Geneva, as a member of the permanent Committee of the Peace League, and occupied in establishing an alliance between the old middle-class democratic party of revolution and the young Socialist Working-Men's Association of the International. In spite of all his zeal for Socialism, Bakunin, as a genuine man of 1848, belonged by sympathy rather to the former than the latter faction, whose clear and definite aims little suited his extravagant theories and his passion for secret societies. His object in bringing the two associations together was twofold. He hoped to inspire the International with his holy ardour of Negation, and he hoped to offer to the Peace League, which in itself was unimportant, a wider field of activity.

The Second Congress of the International was now sitting at Lausanne, from September 2 to 8, 1867 (Marx, as is well known, was not present); and to further his object, Bakunin laid before them the plan of an offensive and defensive alliance, by which the 'working-men were to promise to support the middle-class in the reconquest of political liberty, while the latter pledged themselves to co-operate in the economic liberation of the proletariate.' He was so far successful as to persuade the Working-Men's Association to send delegates to the Peace Congress at Geneva, who received their brethren from Lausanne with open arms. Bakunin now seemed to be in his element. In July 1868 he joined the Central Section of the International at Geneva, and sent out a solemn circular, full of grand 'European' phrases, which was to prepare the consummation of his scheme, and recommend it to the next Congress of the International. 'The Peace League,' he said, 'can only accomplish its task by opposing the alliance of working-men to the alliance of oppressors; by representing, in short, the cause of the labouring millions. Our League must be the political mouthpiece of the great economic interests and principles which the vast international union of working-men in Europe and America have triumphantly proclaimed and spread abroad.'

But the managers of the International, taught wisdom by their experience in France, prudently declined to compromise their firm organisation by an alliance with the devotees of the Peace League. Bakunin made several speeches at Brussels, but his offers were declined; and a resolution was passed which, while leaving it open to send delegates to the Congress of the League at Berne, expressly stipulated that the delegates should vote in their personal capacity, and not as members of the International. This decision was resented by the League as a vote of want of confidence; and as the project of an alliance had emanated from Bakunin, they poured upon him the vials of their wrath. 'Either you doubted the result of our invitation,' wrote their president Gustave Vogt, 'in which case you have compromised us; or you were aware of the surprise your friends of the International had prepared for us, in which case you have most unworthily deceived us.' Bakunin replied by an elaborate statement, throwing the blame upon Marx and other 'German intriguers,' and promised to give a full explanation at the next Congress of the League. This Congress met at Berne; but of the 110 members who were present, only 30 supported Bakunin and his motion; and no other course was now left him, but to leave the League, and form a new brotherhood, the *Alliance Internationale de la Démocratie Socialiste*, of which, of course, he constituted himself the head.

Before describing, however, this new society, called the party of the Bakunists or Nihilists, we must briefly recur to Bakunin's proposals at Berne. In the course of an elaborate speech he demanded *the abolition of the State, as such*; the extirpation of all religion, and of all hereditary rights; the absolute equalisation of all individuals; the substitution of Collectivism for Communism. Some passages in this oration serve to illustrate these demands.

Your fine civilisation, gentlemen of Western Europe, of which you are so fond of boasting to us barbarians of the East, was founded from time immemorial on the forced labour of the enormous majority, condemned to lead the lives of brutes and slaves, in order that a small minority might be enabled to live as human creatures. This monstrous inequality is part and parcel of your system, that of Western Europe. It will never mend itself, for it is a necessary consequence of your civilisation, which rests upon the absolute separation between head-work and hand-labour. But this abomination cannot last; for in future the working classes are resolved to make their own politics. They insist that instead of two classes, there shall be in future only one, which shall offer to all men alike, without grade or distinction, the same starting-point, the same maintenance, the same opportunities of education and culture, the same means of industry; not, indeed, by virtue of laws, but by the nature of the organisation of this class, which shall oblige everyone to work with his head as with his hands.
. . . . . Communism I abhor, because it is the negation of liberty, and without liberty I cannot imagine anything truly human. I abhor it, because it concentrates all the strength of society in the State, and squanders that strength in its service; because it places all property in the hands of the State, whereas my principle is the abolition of the State itself. I want the organisation of society and the distribution of property to proceed upwards from below, by the free voice of society itself; not downwards from above, by the dictate of authority. I want the abolition of personal hereditary property, which is merely an institution of the State, and a consequence of State principles. In this sense I am a Collectivist, not a Communist.
. . . . . Give to all your children, from their birth, the same maintenance and education; then give to all men, so educated, the same social *status*, and the same means of providing for their wants by their own labour; and you will see that many of the inequalities, now considered natural, will disappear, because they are merely the effects of an unequal distribution of the conditions of development. Improve nature by society, and you will make all things, for all men, as equal as they can be—the conditions of development as well as those of labour—and you will exterminate many crimes, many follies, and many evils.

After insisting on the necessity of extirpating all religion, he concludes:

> To destroy religious superstition by means of education, societies, newspapers, and other methods of propagandism, is a sheer impossibility. Religion is by no means a mere aberration of the brain; but a protest of human nature and the human heart against the misery and the narrowness of the real world around us. Meeting here with nothing but stupidity, injustice, and wretchedness, man creates for himself a better world with the aid of his imagination. . . . . . Not until happiness and brotherhood are restored to earth, will religion have lost its *raison d'être*. An intellectual crusade will never destroy it; a social revolution is required for that purpose.

The last part of this harangue, monstrous as it was, and delivered in a tone of self-conscious infallibility, met with lively sympathy from many of his audience, though the majority of the Congress, as we know, voted against the adoption of Bakunin's 'system.' Thirty persons only joined the new 'Alliance Internationale;' amongst these were Bakunin's own wife, a Russian lady named Alexeieff, the German democrat Philip Becker,[1] an English lady, Mrs. Gay, a French police-agent named Albert Richard, and a Russian, M. Shukovski, who was the secretary of this society. This tiny band of irresponsibles now seceded with great solemnity from the League, declaring at the same time their intention of continuing their connection with the International, though the latter had distinctly disavowed them. They quitted Berne for Geneva, whence they issued a grandiloquent programme, proposing to abolish all States and governments and reduce them to mere administrative machines. Next followed a grand scheme of organisa-

---

[1] This was M. Becker of Geneva, one of the Vice-Presidents of the Working-Men's Congress at Lausanne. He must not be confused with Bernhard Becker, the friend of Lassalle, and his successor in conducting the *Allgemeinen Deutschen Arbeiterverein*.

tion, with sections, bureaux, committees of supervision, &c., encompassing half the world. Within his public 'Alliance Internationale' Bakunin created a secret 'Alliance,' which he called the 'Secret College of International Brethren.' To the profane world this represented the *bureau central*, or executive organ of the outer body; but in reality its functions were those of surveillance, not only over the 'Alliance' itself, but over the International, according to a pre-arranged plan. The 'Brethren' were to 'acknowledge no fatherland but Universal Revolution;' they were to regard every movement as reactionary, unless directed to the triumph of their principles. The majority transferred their powers to the 'Citizen Bakunin,' who, as their central point, was to conduct the 'National Committees' of the various countries, and so organise them as to subordinate them always to the control of the 'Bureau Central'—in other words, of the Citizen Bakunin. The object of this vast, but visionary association was to be the universal abolition of Church and State, with all their institutions, religious, political, economic, judicial, financial, police, and university—and, of course, marriage, 'as a political, religious, legal, and social ordinance.' This object once accomplished, 'anarchy, *i.e.* the absence of a State, would be proclaimed; a free society would be organised; and, above all, the erection of a new revolutionary State would be prevented.'

This wild idea of annihilating the whole civilised world and establishing a dictatorship of Citizen Bakunin upon its ruins might well appear fabulous, were it not for documentary proofs, published now several years, and never contradicted, that it was actually and seriously entertained. But even this does not exhaust the measure of the monstrous and incredible. Hun-

dreds of fools were really found who made Bakunin's
'system' their rule of action, and thereby brought ruin
and misery upon a vast number of their fellow-dupes.
In Spain and Italy, particularly, the adherents of this
'Alliance' became so numerous among the members of
the International Working-Men's Association that the
International repeatedly felt the danger of being
swamped by Bakunin's secret society. The minority,
who at the Basle Congress in September, 1869, voted
against the Bakunin-Richard motion for the complete
abolition of all hereditary rights, were not very numerous; and Bakunin, even after his expulsion from
the Swiss section of the Association (June 1870), still
continued to agitate in its name against the decrees of
the General Council in London, until he and his followers [1] were formally repudiated and proscribed by
the Congress of the International at the Hague in 1872.
This sentence led to the secession of four Spanish, five
Belgian, two Dutch, one American, and two Swiss delegates from the Jura district, and many of the most
zealous and devoted sections at once dissolved. Bakunin succeeded in getting together a counter-Congress,
which declared the decrees of the International null
and void, and resolved ' that any organisation for the
union of existing revolutionary authorities was a sham
and a snare, and would involve the proletariate in the
same dangers that they incurred from the present
governments.' Thus open war was declared against
the International. The Universal Revolution, which was
not to leave one stone upon another throughout the
world, now turned its weapons against the only revolu-

---

[1] Of these the foremost had been Guillaume, Schwitzgebel, Richard, and
G. Blanc.

tionary organisation that could possibly endanger existing rule and order.

The climax of folly was now reached—the point at which, in the language of Jules Elizard, 'Negation negatives its own self.' There is no need to pursue further the revolutionary ravings of Bakunin, but simply to notice briefly his personal fortunes after his latest attempt to outdo the Radicalism of the International, and his expulsion from that body as a social and political madman.

Although his most numerous following was in Italy and Spain, Bakunin, during the latter years of his life, turned his chief attention once more to Russia and France. In resuming his connection with Russia he employed as his instrument a man who has since then been handed over to public execration by one of the most remarkable criminal trials of modern times. This man was the assassin Netchayeff. Having arrived at Geneva in March, 1869, under pretence of being invested with full powers by the 'organised' academical students of St. Petersburg, he was forced, soon after his acquaintance with Bakunin, to confess that he had no such commission at all, and that the pretended student-organisation did not exist. In spite of this, the grandfather of Russian Nihilism, now a man of fifty-five, took this young impostor, corrupt to the very marrow, so completely to his heart that he entrusted him with the special conduct of the Russian branch of his 'Alliance,' and sent him to Russia as its representative to enlist recruits for the cause of universal revolution. Boundless ignorance, and an idolatry of all connected with 'foreign countries and emigration,' were the time-honoured characteristics of the sanguine young Nihilists of Moscow and St. Petersburg, and hence, Netchayeff had only to produce his credentials from Bakunin, stamped 'Alliance Révolutionnaire Européenne, Comité-Général, le 12 Mai, 1869; No. 2771,' to create a downright sensation in the revolutionary circles of school-boys, students, and lieutenants of the Russian capital, and to become the idol and master of a number of young men who yielded him implicit obedience. Constantly boasting of his 'secret Superiors,' and of the conspiracy whose network already overspread the whole of Russia, Netchayeff was able to spread his snare so skilfully as to catch these foolish young enthusiasts by the dozen, and seriously to compromise others, by manifestos or instructions sent to their addresses. At St. Petersburg he declared that the head-quarters of his invisible Lodge were at Moscow; his friends at Moscow were constantly told of his 'circle' at St. Petersburg. Those who began to suspect their seducer, and sought to disengage themselves from him through fear of the police, he threatened with the vengeance of the Committee, and by impressing upon them his 'unlimited authority,' extorted large sums by way of ransom, which of course found their way into his own pockets. In many cases, young men whose Radical opinions were known were purposely compromised, and thus driven into the arms of his propaganda. The end of all these doings is well known. A student of the Agricultural Academy at Moscow, named Ivanoff, found out, at length, that this much-talked-of Committee was a pure invention, and that Netchayeff was a mere swindler and pickpocket. Netchayeff in revenge surprised him unawares, and killed him. The murderer fled into Switzerland; but was delivered up by the Federal Government as a common criminal, and the systematic imposture he had carried on was brought to light by the judge at his trial.

- Bakunin probably did not learn at once the details of Netchayeff's nefarious proceedings, but this much is certain, and remains a fact, that he attempted to the last to justify this infamous wretch, and that he lent his name to cover the imposture. The trial brought to light a mass of pamphlets and proclamations which Bakunin had circulated in Russia by means of his tools and agents. Their contents surpass all that has ever been written by the vilest Revolutionists. We have before us some extracts from two of these pamphlets—'A Word to the Young Men of Russia,' and 'Publications of the Society of Popular Justice.' The reader will judge for himself from these specimens :—

> Under the Czar Alexei [says the writer] it was the robber chieftain Stenka Rasin who took the right way to liberate the Russian people. And who is the Stenka Rasin, for whom the people are waiting at the present day, and whose services they sorely need? It is the state-destroying spirit of Young Russia, proceeding from the very depths of Nationalism. Stenka's place will be supplied by the legions of 'unclassed' young men, who are part of the national life, and collectively represent the ancient hero. . . . . . National 'robberdom' is one of the most venerable facts of Russian national life : he who does not understand or sympathise with it has neither understanding nor sympathy for our national life. . . . . . The Russian robber is the true and only Revolutionist—no dealer in empty phrases and theories, no mere subverter of politics and class. The robbers who are scattered over the forests, steppes, and villages of Russia form a compact and single world—that of true Russian Revolution. He who desires this revolution must repair to this world. Let us therefore take this road; let us throw ourselves among the people; let us join the insurrectionary tumult of peasants and robbers. . . . . Leave the academies, universities, and schools; dismiss all thought of literature and science, which in their present form are simply official trammels intended to cramp and unman you. This is the opinion, this the counsel of the best men of the West.

Karakasoff, the would-be assassin of Alexander II. (April 4, 1866), is praised for having inaugurated this 'holy work;' but he is cautioned not to make any further attempt on the Czar's life, because the emperor must be spared for the judgment of the National Tribunal. To sum up, the last and greatest object to be attained is universal destruction and the restoration of chaos. 'If even a single old form is spared, this form would become the embryo from which all the old social forms would be begotten again.'

While Russia was being deluged with these and other[1] crazy but mischievous productions, which brought ruin on a whole generation of credulous young simpletons, the arch-agitator himself resided now in Switzerland, now in France. The German victories and the fall of the Napoleonic empire suggested to the old enemy of Germany the liberation of France, as the next and most important object of the Revolution. In the middle of September, 1870, we find him busied in summoning the proletariate of every country to the defence of France. For the moment his darling theories of the objectionableness of all State-systems *per se*, and of the imbecility of political republics, were set aside, and in a pamphlet, entitled 'L'Empire Knouto-germanique et la Révolution Sociale,' he proclaimed the cause of the fourth French Republic as synonymous with the 'cause of humanity.' 'A France subjugated to a rule chartered with Prussian bayonets would be the greatest misfortune, in regard to liberty and progress, that could happen to Europe and the world. Destitute of all

---

[1] Among these especially are the *Catechism of Revolution* and the *Missive to Russian Officers*, both of which preach the duty of political murder and the necessity of blind obedience on the part of the Revolutionist to his superior.

liberal ideas for the last three hundred years, the Germans live quietly and contentedly like rats in a cheese; animated by one wish alone, that this cheese might grow as large as possible. With the discipline that was hammered into them by custom, and with their voluntary self-enslavement, it was easy for them to gain the victory over a France disorganised and demoralised.' These premisses are followed by an elaborate explanation of the thesis, that 'France can only be saved from German invasion by a grand social Revolution!' For this purpose he proposes to remove all civil officers, to sentence all Bonapartists to the galleys, to send about agents into all the villages, and establish local bands, inspired with and organised upon revolutionary principles. The object of these free corps would be to gain the respect of the rural population; and this would be effected best by abolishing all communal administration, by imprisoning all landed proprietors and the clergy, by establishing revolutionary committees composed of 'converted peasants,' who were to enjoy all the property of the State and the middle-classes. Thus, and thus only, it would be possible to inspire the peasantry with a genuine enthusiasm for the cause of Revolution, while the ground would be prepared for the ultimate abolition of all private property. The State being abolished, all property would lose the benefit of its sanction and guarantee, and would thus sink down into a mere fact which had ceased to be a right. Bakunin recognises, indeed, the danger that a revolution of this sort might kindle a civil war at a time when everything depends on uniting all the forces of the nation to combat the foreign enemy. 'All this,' he says, 'may perhaps not be brought about in a very peaceful manner: possibly even something may arise which is called civil war. But better far to have civil war than to deliver over France to the Prussians. . . . . A new life, a new world will arise; and history has taught us that nations have never been more powerful abroad than when excitement and confusion prevail at home.'

Fresh from the announcement of these theories of salvation, Bakunin no sooner heard of the communal outbreak at Lyons, than he hastened thither to put his theories into practice, and head the movement in the name of his 'Alliance.' He arrived there on September 20, the day that the mob had captured the Hôtel de Ville, and taking at once a footing, together with his friends Richard and Gaspard Blanc, in the council constituted under the auspices of Cluseret, he strove to incite the members to pass high-sounding resolutions for the abolition of State and property, and to declare the 'Holy Revolt' *en permanence.* Four-and-twenty hours later the National Guard had retaken the Hôtel de Ville, scattered the assembly to the winds, and put Bakunin in the train for Geneva. The great moment of 'action' had come a third time; and, as at Prague in 1848, and at Dresden in 1849, for the third and last time it had been lost!

The rest of Bakunin's life was nothing but disgrace and disaster. He had sown the whirlwind and he now reaped the storm: contempt and ruin stared him in the face. The French Radicals turned with scorn from the author of the 'Empire Knouto-Germanique.' The Russian Radicals, to some extent responsible men, would have nothing to do with the ally of Netchayeff. The suppression of the revolt at Carthagena decided the fate of the Spanish section of the new 'Alliance.' Mazzini, in the name of the Italian Radicals, pronounced the anathema on his 'Alliance' as well as on the International. From the German Radicals he had already estranged himself, by his agitation against the General Council of the International and his enmity to Marx. The sentence of the Congress at the Hague in 1872, already mentioned, was fatal to his further political career; and Marx took care, in a number of pamphlets published under his direction, to make the conspirator against the Working-Men's Association incapable for ever of figuring as a missionary of Panslavism in Western Europe. Surrounded by a small, but ever-dwindling band of Polish, Swiss, and Russian friends, who could not be taught better, the grey-headed conspirator continued for some years his revolutionary doings at Geneva, Zürich, and Berne, until he suddenly died at the last-named city, in the summer of 1878.

CHAPTER VII.

PRINCE V. A. TCHERKASSKI, THE REORGANISER OF POLAND AND BULGARIA.

Tcherkasski's early life—Connection with the Slavophil movement—Society at Moscow—Emancipation of the Serfs—Miliutin and his opponents—Tcherkasski's mission to Poland—His quarrel with Berg—Rebuff at St. Petersburg—Panslavonic Congress at Moscow—His anti-Polish speech—His Mayoralty at Moscow—On the Slav committee—Appointed Civil Administrator of Bulgaria—His preparations—Military character of the administration—Harsh treatment of the Bulgarians—Agrarian and communal organisation—Despotic nature of his 'system'—The higher and lower clergy—Russian evacuation and its consequences—Discouragement of the Russian army—Tcherkasski 'interviewed'—His death—Subsequent exposure of his administration—Bulgarian prospects—Russian policy and the National party.

On the very day, March 3, 1878, when the Peace of San Stefano was signed, there died in that town Prince Vladimir Alexandrovitch Tcherkasski, known as the leader of the Russian National party, no less than as Civil Commissioner of the Imperial Commander-in-Chief, head of the Civil Administration of Bulgaria, and former reorganiser of the kingdom of Poland. In each of these capacities his conduct has been so remarkable, and the results he achieved so important, that he may well be numbered among the foremost Russian politicians of modern times. A survey, therefore, of his public career, embracing the last twenty years, cannot fail to offer many points of insight into the course and characteristics of Russian progress.

Prince Tcherkasski was born in 1821, in the circle

of Weden, and government of Tula, of a family who count among the wealthier and better known of the nobility. Originally they came from the Caucasus, but were not recognised as Russian princes until 1798. The names of their ancestors appear already in the days of the first three Romanoffs, Michel, Alexei, and Feodor, as office-bearers at Court and Boyárs. Contrary to the custom of his time and rank, Prince Vladimir Alexandrovitch was educated neither at St. Petersburg nor for the military profession; but, after having finished his school studies, was sent to the University at Moscow, which in those days (1830–40) was looked upon as 'liberal' and 'dangerous.'

This step determined the whole subsequent course of his life, since the years of his study at the University were those when the Slavophil fraction was just starting into life. Founded a short time before, under the auspices of Chomjákoff, a former officer in the Guards, and carried on by the brothers Constantine and Ivan Aksakoff, Juri Samarin, the two Kirejevskis, and others, this fraction became the precursor and pioneer of the Russian National party of the present day. Its salient tendencies are sufficiently known. Its great aim, as we have already stated, was to free Russian civilisation and society from the influences of Western Europe, and found an independent national culture on the basis of popular conceptions and Byzantine orthodoxy, forsaken since the time of Peter the Great. At the same time the Slavophils, from the first, were friends of the peasants, and in a certain though not the customary sense, Democrats, inasmuch as they looked to the lower classes, as untainted with Western culture, for the restoration of Russia nationality, and rested their hopes of victory on an undivided communal property.

The young pupils of this school, in its time so much lauded and so much derided, belonged all of them socially to the aristocracy. Their head-quarters were at the house of the elder Aksakoff, the father, a wealthy nobleman of ancient family; the places of their propagandism were the fashionable *salons* of Moscow, where some of them figured in the sleeveless velvet coats and red silk shirts of national cut and antique fashion, but made by a fashionable French tailor. M. Chomjäkoff, the originator, as we have said, of this movement, had passed his early days in the emperor's *Garde à cheval*. Mons. D. Waluieff, another member, was a cousin of the late minister of that name. Juri Samarin was a wealthy landed proprietor; Koscheleff, a millionaire. These young enthusiasts did all in their power to be 'National.' They occasionally mixed with the masses; they took part in the Easter disputations between the Old Believers and the Orthodox; they forswore the use of the French language, and abjured Parisian hats and fashionable clothes. And yet, with all this, they remained what they had been at first —men who, in spite of the earnestness of their convictions and their devotion to the cause of nationality 'pure and undefiled,' could never change their skin; who had started with aping the culture of Western Europe, and therefore never were, and never could be popular. The keystone of their doctrine—at least originally—was devotion to the Orthodox Church, which they believed was destined by Providence to regenerate Western Europe, already lost in the 'heathenish arrogance of civilisation,' and to conquer and rule the world by means of an undivided communal property. These worthies had borrowed their philosophy from Schelling, but the real founder of their system of political economy was the German traveller, Baron von Haxthausen, who was then on a visit at Moscow.[1]

So far as we can judge from all that has been written about this Slavophil movement between 1830 and 1850, Prince Tcherkasski was a mere *pater minorum gentium* in the circle of his youthful friends. In theological and patristic learning he was far surpassed by Peter Kirejevski, in mystic profundity by Chomjäkoff. As a writer he was far inferior to Waluieff, Samarin, and the younger Aksakoff; as an agitator he lacked the poetical enthusiasm and the impetuous *verve* of Constantine Aksakoff. In the eyes of his contemporaries he was looked upon as a man of intelligence, but of cool temperament, and inclined to scepticism, who differed chiefly from other mortals in his immeasurable self-consciousness and self-confidence; as one, in short, of that species, to be found throughout Russia, who imagine their *aplomb* can accomplish all they wish, who are omniscient without the trouble of learning, and who regard a proper *esprit de conduite* as the sum total of all wisdom and the substance of human life. Quite as incapable of religious enthusiasm as of any devotion to a political ideal, a Realist and Egotist in the full sense of the expressions, the young Prince seemed so little fit to champion the fervid theories of his friends, that he might well have appeared to them to be taking up Slavophilism as a pastime of the hour, with the intention of becoming a grand gentleman ere long, if not ultimately the enemy of his youthful aspirations. In society this muscular, fair-haired aristocrat, with his golden spectacles and lofty manners, had

---

[1] Compare what Haxthausen says of his friends, *Russian Empire*, vol. ii. p. 182, *sqq.* [TR.]

always been welcomed for the piquancy of his wit, the pithiness of his sayings, and his familiarity with nearly every modern language. But among his friends he was never popular; he was too self-conscious and pretentious to call forth sympathy in others, and not warm-hearted enough himself to respond to it, if evoked. He was incapable of all *abandon*; he was a stranger to that devotion which constitutes the chief ingredient of Russian amiability, and the cardinal condition of real and permanent success in society, and the want of which is nowhere pardoned with such ill grace as among his countrymen.

After Tcherkasski had finished his studies at the University, he lived alternately at Moscow and on his estates. Having passed the most important years of his youth in good and really cultivated society, he was superior to most around him in culture, as he excelled them in bodily vigour; and by abstaining from all service in the State, and continuing the part of a *frondeur* among those who shared his opinions, he acquired the reputation of a man of character. Such was the state of Russia under Nicholas that a *rôle* of this kind was rather grateful, and on the whole not dangerous for those who were above the common cares of life, and understood how to temper with moderation the profession of their political creed. Just then it was a sign of *bon ton* at Moscow to sulk with the government, to sneer at the incapacity and corruption of the bureaucracy, to know everything better than those in power, to deduce from Adam Smith the impracticability of Cancrin's financial system, and from Bentham the bungles of criminal administration, and to cite against the German advisers of the emperor the saying of Lemonossoff that Russia was rich in Platos and Newtons. The *salons* of Moscow aristocrats had long been the asylum of broken-down or disappointed officials of St. Petersburg; and even before the Crimean War, thinking people had satisfied themselves that Nicholas's system of isolation and tutelage, brought to a pitch since the Hungarian campaign of 1849, was bound to collapse with the death of its author. Since the confusion of 1853-54, all those who looked for future profit, made up their minds to eschew State service under the existing government, and to keep their powder dry.

Tcherkasski knew this as well as other people, and shaped his course accordingly. Not until after Alexander II. had succeeded to the throne, and the movement for Serf Emancipation had begun, did he consent to accept public office, and then only as the nominee of his fellow-nobles, not as a functionary of the government. To assist the preliminary discussion of the measures which were necessary to regulate emancipation, Provincial Committees, chosen by the nobles, were appointed in 1858, whose duties were to express their opinions on the cardinal questions at issue, and in particular on the agrarian organisation of the future—in other words, the relations of the emancipated peasants with the soil they cultivated. A bitter feud broke out at once between the Liberal minorities, who wished to see the manumission of the serfs accompanied by a redemption or freehold purchase of their homesteads and allotments, and the adherents, on the other hand, of the *status quo*, who would listen to nothing beyond the grant of personal liberty, and abhorred the scheme of agrarian reorganisation as the precursor of a dangerous revolution. A third party, scantily represented on the Committees, but actively supported by public opinion, went so far as to demand the gratuitous cession of the lands to their peasant cultivators, and the proclamation of the indivisibility of Communal property as the groundwork of the new agrarian system. Tcherkasski, the leader of the Liberals of the Government of Tver, made no secret of his predilection for Communal property, and avowed so openly his sympathies for a scheme of redemption in favour of the peasants that he was looked upon as a Radical, and as much detested by his enemies as he was idolised by his friends. While a large number of the nobles clung to the reactionary opposition, the minority, on the other hand, enjoyed the especial favour of the government; and it was plain that an active co-operation in the scheme of emancipation was the surest way to Imperial patronage and promotion.

How far these latter motives prevailed with Tcherkasski may be a matter of question; the main fact is, that the Prince did his best to attract public notice as a leader in this war of principles, and that in this he was perfectly successful. He was one of the deputies of the nobility, who in 1859 were summoned to St. Petersburg to take part in revising the proposed Edict of Emancipation. He was a member also of the Committee of Organisation, and together with the Privy Councillor Nicholas Miliutin and his young Moscow friends Samarin and Koscheleff, formed the extreme left of that body. Miliutin, the recognised head of the democratic-bureaucratic party, enjoyed just then the particular confidence of the Grand-duchess Helena (the widow of the Grand-duke Michael Paulovitch, and the sister-in-law of the late, and aunt of the reigning emperor), who regularly assembled the Coryphæi of the new-fashioned Russian Liberalism in the *salons* of the Palais Michel, sought to play a part in politics by favouring emancipation, and, in spite of her German origin, was inclined to coquet with Nationality. Miliutin's friends were *habitués* of the Grand-duchess's apartments; they discussed there every evening the most far-reaching schemes, argued questions concerning the future constitution of the empire, and soon were looked upon by public opinion as men destined to wield the fortunes of modern Russia. Among these, Tcherkasski produced such an impression by the assurance of his demeanour, his sarcastic and decisive language, and his Radical views, that he became the especial favourite of the Grand-duchess, and passed for a man who knew everything, could do everything, and shrank from no hazard. Aristocratic self-consciousness, social flexibility, and a doctrinaire's conceit of infallibility had combined to make his character peculiarly congenial to that remarkable time, so stirred by the strangest contradictions. Enough had still survived of former prejudices and habits to make birth, means, and a distinguished *savoir faire* the fundamental requisites, as before, of every statesman who studied the 'grand style.' It suited the requirements of the day, that the Prince looked down with contempt on the existing order of things, that he demanded the opposite of whatever had hitherto been valued, and proclaimed aloud the gospel of the providential mission of 'the people,' surrounded as it was with all the charms of novelty, and scarcely known by name to the exclusive society in which he moved. Slavophilism had become fashionable for the moment and in favour with the *salons*. Whoever wished to make a mark, had to profess the doctrine of 'National principles;' and the privilege of being a patriot and Nationalist *de la veille* was not to be compared with any other. Thus the youthful friend of

Aksakoff and Kirejevski vaulted lightly into the position of a Liberal and national hero of the *salons*, and passed for one of the men of the future, though in reality he had done no more than a hundred others in the commissions of the various districts and governments, and in the Committee appointed to carry out the programme of Miliutin, whose policy he not only adopted, but artfully declared his readiness to push, if necessary, to extremes. As for any administrative experience, Tcherkasski, like most of his companions, had never had the opportunity of acquiring it, or turning it to account. But in the eyes of the then spokesmen of popular opinion, even this defect was regarded as a merit. Salvation could only come from political neophytes, for these alone were not yet corroded by the rust and routine of old officialism, and had not yet lost the 'inborn energy of determination.'

Useful as the government found these liberal Emancipationists, they took care not to let their ardour soar too far. Inside the Committee of Organisation Nicholas Miliutin only partially prevailed with his theories. For a while he withdrew himself from public life, and travelled abroad, leaving his adherents in the cold. There was no question yet of Tcherkasski or his friends entering the service of the State; indeed, it looked as if the enemies of the new school would keep the upper hand, and the growing influence of Radicalism upon the masses of the population drive the government to a closer alliance with the Conservatives. Tcherkasski, in receiving an Order, was honoured with a mark of distinction far beyond his class, being then only a titular Councillor. He returned, however, from St. Petersburg to his province without any higher office in the State being offered to him; though his patrons and patronesses at the Palais Michel took such good care to keep alive his memory, that at the next political change of importance, he was placed in one of the most important posts there was to give away.

This change took place in the spring of 1863, two years after the Emancipation Ukase had been published, and was due to the deep impression produced on the Russian Government and society by the outbreak of the Polish-Lithuanian revolt. The government resolved to abandon the scheme of reconciliation, elaborated under the auspices of the Polish Marquis Wielopolski, and entrusted for execution to the Grand-duke Constantine, as Viceroy of Poland, and to adopt the extensive plan which Miliutin had proposed for the reorganisation of the former kingdom. The stone which the builders of 1859 and 1860 had rejected was made the corner-stone of the new edifice to be reared on the Vistula. A remodelling of agrarian regulations and of Polish administration was taken in hand, which aimed at removing the nobles and clergy, as political incorrigibles, from their historical position and the enjoyment of their property, and making the Russian domination over the 'province of the Vistula' rest upon the sympathies of the Polish peasant class, now suddenly converted into proprietors. The system of emancipation and reorganisation, so favourable to the peasants and so injurious to the nobles, which had been rejected for Russia, was applied to Poland in its harshest form, and Miliutin, its author, was entrusted with its execution. He went to work with the zeal of a genuine fanatic. His first step was to put the most important offices into the hands of political volunteers, his friends and associates of 1859; to declare the Russification of Poland a holy mission; to exclude all Poles from any share in the administration of their country; and to get despatched to Warsaw whole troops of youthful devotees of the new Gospel of Slavism. The titular Councillor Prince Tcherkasski became suddenly an actual Councillor of State, Director of the Government Commission at Warsaw for internal and ecclesiastical affairs, and a member of the Polish Council of State, now transformed into a Committee of Organisation. Koscheleff, another Slavophil and administrative *novus homo*, was entrusted with the management of the national finances; and so with other appointments. Miliutin, who afterwards received the office and title of Secretary of State for Poland, introduced the men in his confidence to their new offices, but returned, when this was done, to St. Petersburg, in order to promote his policy with effect, and to be able to meet the attacks which soon were made from all sides against this monstrous enterprise of converting a compact Polish country into a Russian province, and in Tcherkasski's own words, of ' uprooting Latindom to replace it by a thoroughly Slav civilisation.'

This ' spirited saying ' was not the only one in which this statesman in his teens had professed the very principles that Muravieff, the Governor-General of Vilna, and former Minister of Domains, had first endeavoured to carry into practice. Before he put his foot for the first time on Polish soil, Tcherkasski declared that he was taking with him ' a scheme of administration complete in all details,' in which there would be nothing to alter. On his arrival at Warsaw he replied to an old official, who had noticed the difficulties of obtaining a competent knowledge of the complicated institutions of Poland, with the remark that everything necessary to know had been already discussed by himself and Miliutin on the journey from St. Petersburg. Evil tongues reminded Tcherkasski, who had climbed to fame by his power of spirited repartee and *grands aperçus*, of his saying at a banquet in Vilna, reported by the opposition organ, the *Vesstj*, that 'a Greek-orthodox atheist is always better than a Catholic believer.'

His subsequent proceedings corresponded with this beginning. Institutions, which it had cost tens of years to establish, were removed or remodelled in as many days. Whole libraries of new laws and ordinances were published to the world. Agrarian regulations were issued which ruined the nobles without enriching the peasants. Bishops were deposed and schools closed. Catholic and Uniate Churches were transformed into Greek-orthodox ones. Attempts were even made, with the happy innocence of doctrinaires too wise to learn, to abolish by decree the Latin alphabet and substitute for it the Cyrillic—attempts, of course, withdrawn as soon as the necessary mischief had been done.[1] Backed up by public opinion, lauded daily in the 'Moscow Gazette' as the missionary of the 'good cause,' and furnished by Miliutin with almost unlimited power, the Prince for a while could give free rein to his disposition for absolute autocracy and his passion for self-aggrandisement. In a few months he succeeded in tearing to shreds not only the laborious results of Wielopolski's organisation, but nearly all the institutions dating back to the time of Napoleon and the year 1830; in upsetting all former relations of property, and in throwing the Polish peasant class into a confusion of ideas, which

---

[1] To a Polish proprietor, a general of German extraction, who in vain begged permission to repair a decayed Catholic church, and warned him against an accident happening from neglect, Tcherkasski replied that the tumbling down of a building devoted to the Latin worship could not be considered an accident, but only a piece of good luck.

found vent in the destruction of forests, and the neglect of road-making and agriculture, and the consequences of which, notwithstanding the benefits lavished by the government on their new *protégés*, have never been repaired to this day. On paper, indeed, the new organisation of Poland—a thoroughly Russian one, of course—was complete. But in reality no such thing existed, and Count Berg, the Adlatus and afterwards the successor of the Grand-ducal Viceroy, found himself compelled to take measures to prevent the increasing disorganisation of the country, and publicly to oppose Miliutin's administration as well at St. Petersburg as at Moscow.

Between Berg and his opponents, the myrmidons of the Ministerial Secretary of State, who as such fancied themselves independent of his authority, a deadly quarrel now broke out, which was fought on the Vistula by Tcherkasski and on the Neva by Miliutin, with fortunes that wavered for several years. Berg was a man of the old school, who had come to the front under Alexander I. and Nicholas. He was, moreover, an aristocrat, a German, and a soldier; and as such he entertained a rooted aversion to all National vagaries and experiments of Liberal administration. Inferior far to Tcherkasski in education and refinement, he combined with an administrative experience of many years' standing, acquired under circumstances of peculiar difficulty, so sound a political instinct, that his first reports sufficed to destroy the emperor's confidence in the schemes of Miliutin and Tcherkasski. Still, so powerful had grown the influence of the National party between 1863 and 1866, that an immediate change of system appeared unadvisable; and accordingly an attempt was made in many circles to effect a compromise for a while between the two extremes, and to smooth down the sharp points of both. Did not the antagonism between Berg and Miliutin reflect the differences, apparently incurable, that prevailed also in the Imperial Cabinet, between Waluieff, the Minister of the Interior, on the one hand, and the Ministers of Domains, of Education, and of War on the other? Tcherkasski therefore was counselled to observe moderation, and to come to an understanding with Count Berg, who was assured that the evils denounced by him were due not to the system itself, but to the manner of its execution and the novelty of the whole thing. The matter first took a decisive turn, when Miliutin had an apoplectic seizure in December 1866, while Count Berg was present at St. Petersburg to lodge fresh complaints against the doings of the Committee of Organisation and its two leaders, Tcherkasski and Koscheleff. At the news of Miliutin's illness Tcherkasski at once telegraphed to Count Berg for leave to go to the capital. He was anxious to go straight to the emperor himself, and flattered himself with the hope of succeeding his friend Miliutin. As Berg took no notice of the request, the Prince turned to the Grand-duchess Helena, who procured for him the permission he desired. But when Tcherkasski reached the capital, it was already too late. Count Berg had laid his plans so successfully, that his rival failed to meet with, in the cabinet of the Czar, and at the hands of Count Schuvaloff, then his chief adviser, the favourable reception he had found in the patriotic *salons*. The post of Secretary of State for Poland had been taken up temporarily by Schuvaloff himself, to be handed over to the Senator (now Minister of Justice and Secretary of State) Nabokoff, one of the earlier advisers of the Grand-duke Constantine at Warsaw, and a man, who having served under Wielopolski, was an utter stranger to the new 'system.' Tcherkasski, foiled in this design, essayed an extreme step: trusting to the indispensableness of his services, of which his friends and admirers had convinced him, he begged leave to resign. To his astonishment his resignation was accepted, and accepted so readily that he thought it better not to return at once to Warsaw, but, with Koscheleff, his friend and fellow-sufferer, to shake off the dust from his feet against the ungrateful capital, and seek a more congenial home at Moscow. But as a missionary of the Slavs, his occupation was gone for ever. The emperor's confidence had been transferred to men of peace and moderation, whom Tcherkasski only knew as his mortal enemies.

Had this so-called 'catastrophe' not occurred in the days that witnessed the establishment of the North German Confederation, it might perhaps have created some part of the sensation in Europe, on which Tcherkasski in his vanity had counted. All that actually resulted was a Russian sensation and the homage heaped by Katkoff and Ivan Aksakoff, the literary lions of the National party at Moscow, upon their fellow Nationalist on his arrival in the capital of Old Russia. Tcherkasski could now figure as a patriotic martyr of reactionary intrigues and a political agitator of the first rank; and, as such, he performed his part, with the success to be expected from his energetic character, first in the circles of his immediate friends, and afterwards before the public at large.

Circumstances offered an opportunity, seldom found in Russia, and earlier in his case than could have been expected, for his appearance on the public stage. A few months only after his rebuff at St. Petersburg, an

Ethnological Exhibition was arranged at Moscow, at the instance of the 'Society of Friends of Science,' in that city. All branches of the Slav family, non-Russian as well as Russian, were invited; for, under the patronage of the leaders of the National party, the idea soon broadened into that of a Panslavonic Congress, intended to represent to Western Europe, then occupied with the restoration of Germanism, the unity and high culture of the youngest and most numerous branch of the European family. The Exhibition itself was restricted to very modest dimensions; it consisted of some dozen model-houses, intended to exemplify the peculiar architecture of Great and Little Russia, of Ruthenians and Poles, and a collection of costumes, domestic utensils, weapons and harness, which had been hastily gathered together and grouped by skilful hands. The central feature of the affair was to be the meeting and conference of the national leaders from all Slavonian countries; the idea being to imitate the national rifle and gymnastic meetings which had come into vogue a few years ago in Germany, and on the pattern of these to inaugurate something like a National Slavonic Union.

On May 5, 1867, the Exhibition was opened with great solemnity in the great Riding-School near the Moscow University. A few weeks later the guests, invited from South and West, began to assemble, and the usually silent streets of 'Mother Moscow' wakened into life. At Czenstochau, on the Polish frontier, congratulations had been showered on the deputation which represented the Austro-Slavonic branch. Next came brilliant festivities at Warsaw and St. Petersburg, a grand reception by the Grand-duke Constantine, the reading of numberless addresses, odes of welcome, and masses celebrated in the Cathedrals,

The Czechs were represented by Palatzky and Rieger, the younger Schaffarik, Hamernik, and others; the Banat by Dr. Polisch. Miletitsch appeared for Servia, Peter Damilo von Zara for Dalmatia. The Croats had sent Subotisch; the Bulgarians a student named Bogoroff; and to give a spice of humour to the proceedings, the Saxon, but 'genuine Slavonic' Lusatia was there too. Its representatives, Schmaler, Pech, and Deutschmann, had assumed the euphonious names of Smolyár, Pek, and Dutschmán, and outdid all the rest in their National devotion and their enthusiasm for the cause of the 'leading Slavonic State.' All the more painfully apparent were the facts that the darlings of the Moscow propagandists, the Ruthenians of Galicia, had been prevented, by the mistrust of the Austrian Government, from sending a deputation of their own; and that the Roman-Catholic element, richly represented to all appearances in other quarters, deprived the Congress, to a large extent, of its Eastern Catholic character.

The preparations for this remarkable gathering are too elaborate to be described. Enough to say, that their main object was to impress upon the foreign guests, in spite of all the homage lavished upon them, the necessity of an entire subordination of non-Russian Slavs to the Russian conception of State, and to point out Greek orthodoxy as the indispensable condition of true Slav development. In this sense the Metropolitan of St. Petersburg, on the occasion of the gala mass in St. Isaac's Cathedral, had preached on the Shepherd and his flock. This was the meaning of Barsheff's grand speech, the Rector of the Moscow University. With this view the writer Tjutsheff had lauded the unity and solidarity of Slavism in contrast with the loose fabric of the West. Another speaker, the historian Schtschebalski, had soared so high as to demand a common language, and, together with the Bulgarian Bogoroff, proclaimed the supremacy of the Russian idiom as the sole legitimate vehicle for literature. Not a word of protest was raised against these extravagances. Those of federal views among the guests refrained from expressing their dissent, preferring to wait for an opportunity of testing by a concrete example the doctrines they had heard, and of bringing forward a matter, the discussion and settlement of which was the principal object of the Czechs.

This matter was the Polish question; the opportunity chosen for its discussion, a grand banquet given in the Sokolniki park, which was to form the crowning feature of the whole 'Slavonic week.' The hostess was 'Mother Moscow' herself; the emblem under which she assembled her guests was the banner, planted in the park, of the two Slavonian apostles, St. Cyril and St. Methodius. The old Panslavist Pogodin opened the debate. ' Our fraternal assembly,' he began, ' is, alas! not complete: Poland is not represented amongst us. She alone, of all countries of the Slavs, still holds aloof; and whilst all the sons of our common family embrace each other as brothers, Poland remains in alliance with the immemorial enemies of the Slavs. But far be it from us to exclude for ever these our brethren from our company. Much rather would we profess the hope and the wish that they will purge themselves some day of their blindness, and acknowledge their wrong. When first the Poles agree to let bygones be bygones, to put aside their hostility, and trust to the magnanimity of our beloved sovereign, then, but then only, will the joy of the Slavs be full.' The ball was now fairly set rolling, and the apostrophe of Ivan Aksakoff about the voluntary exclusion of Poland from the Slav family, favourably as his remarks were received, was no real answer to this challenge of debate. All the world knew that Rieger meant to reply, and that he had pledged himself, at a conference held at Paris with the Polish leaders of the emigration, to represent the deserted branch of the Slavonic family. Taking his stand under the banner of the two Slav apostles, the famous party-leader of the Czechs reminded his audience that it was the law of love which Cyril and Methodius had preached to the peoples of the East. That law was binding to this day, and must be observed also towards the country of the Piasts. Whilst all Western Europe had sympathised with Poland in the rising of 1863, he (Rieger) and his friend Palatzky had never doubted for a moment that the insurrection was a national wrong, and an unjustifiable refusal of Russia's legitimate demands. The wrong done by Poland was an old one, reaching back for centuries. It lasted even to that hour, for it was the Poles alone who hindered the general union of the Slav populations and their common espousal of the Eastern question. But since an end must now be put to the quarrel, in the interest of all parties, and since the main fact to be recognised was that Poland lay vanquished at the feet of Russia, prudence as well as mercy demanded that the conqueror should initiate the offer of reconciliation, and hold out the hand of peace to the conquered. The brother must raise up again his fallen brother. Russia must say 'I am the conqueror: I could take your life; but inasmuch as I am righteous, and you are my brother, I grant you your life.' The moment to be chosen and the means to be adopted for healing the wounds that had been inflicted, it was not necessary for him to specify. He made bold in this respect to trust to the heart and the head of Alexander II., who was not only a great sovereign, but also a noble and large-minded Slav. A generous way of dealing such as this would undoubtedly convince Poland of the wrong she had committed: of that he was as confident as that the Russians would know how to forgive. 'I know well,' he concluded, 'that your hearts are now full of bitterness; that your wounds are still rankling. But if once the Poles will acknowledge the rights of Russia, I confidently hope that you, as good Slavs, as members of a mighty nation, conscious of its power, and as true and loyal sons and disciples of our holy apostles, will know how to find the word of love and forgiveness.'

Although this harangue had been skilfully framed to captivate Russian self-love and exclude whatever could savour of offence to old prejudices, yet the impression it made upon the audience was painful in the extreme. As to the futility of any real understanding, the Russians then present were thoroughly agreed. But they were equally unanimous about the necessity and the difficulty of a reply. An interval of silence ensued, broken only here and there by angry murmurs, when Tcherkasski, confident and self-complacent as ever, rose to his feet, to take his place under the Apostolic Standard and defend the policy of Polish annihilation, which he had been the foremost to advocate. The National side of the question, upon which everything hinged, was dealt with in a couple of sentences. The question, he asserted, was purely administrative and political. Administratively, Russians and Poles were on a common footing of equality. The same laws, the same system of taxation, the same regulations prevailed alike in the Province of the Vistula and in the rest of

Russia. The duty on brandy, levied on the Vistula, was lower indeed than that on the Neva and at Moscow. Russia had done all that could be demanded; she had amply fulfilled her duty to Poland, and now, in the face of Europe and her Slavonic brethren, she could boast a conscience thoroughly pure and clean. Touching the political question, it must be remembered in the first place that it was Russia alone who had created Poland. In 1815 there was no such thing as a Poland, for her existence as a State had been destroyed by Europe. Russia then had granted her political liberty, but that liberty was definitely forfeited by the insurrections of 1830 and 1863; and by those events 'the old account between Poles and Russians had been closed for ever.' To alter now the relations once existing between the two branches of the Slavonic family was as impossible as to turn back the course of a river. 'Reconciliation will only be possible when the Provinces of the Vistula renounce all idea of separate existence. When Poland, not in a spirit of defiance, but as the repentant prodigal of Scripture, humbly returns to the paternal roof, then, but not before, we will open our pardoning arms to receive her. Then, indeed, no fatted calf of ours will be good enough to be slain in honour of the grateful feast. Poland's future depends upon the Poles themselves; Russia owes her nothing.' And as if enough had not been done by thus insisting on the necessity of a united Slav State, to the exclusion of all liberty in particular branches, Tcherkasski concluded his address by calling for cheers for the mortal enemies of Polish freedom and Austrian federalism—for the Ruthenians of Galicia, the champions of Russian nationality.

With this speech, which flatly forbade the 'beloved

guests' to discuss the most important of all 'Slav questions,' and curtly defined Panslavism as the domination of the elder over the younger brother, Tcherkasski climbed to the pinnacle of popularity. For weeks the 'Moscow Gazette' filled its columns with paraphrased portions of his address, concluding always with a panegyric of the 'genuinely national' statesman, whose eloquence had taught his Slavonic brethren, once and for all, the importance of the 'real Russian State' to the interests of Slavdom.

This 'statesman' meanwhile had taken up his residence for the winter at Moscow; where he kept himself before the public eye as a member of the Slav Committee, and qualified himself finally, as a householder, to become a candidate at the municipal elections. These elections, since the introduction of the new civic institutions, were to some extent useful, as well as fashionable, with the higher classes at Moscow and St. Petersburg. They offered a suitable scope for the much-needed exercise of public activity, and for the realisation of party purposes, whether political or those of class, which in their earlier form no longer ventured otherwise to find expression, since the government had once more asserted its dictatorship. Municipal offices, which ten years before had been filled exclusively by merchants and second-rate men of business, and had been regarded by State dignitaries with unconcealed contempt, were now coveted by aristocrats of high birth and political agitators, who comforted themselves and their neighbours with the reflection that Mirabeau also had not scrupled in his time to descend to the ranks of the *bourgeoisie*. The first Mayor of Moscow, chosen under the new municipal organisation, had been a Prince Schtcherbatoff, and Ivan Aksakoff and Juri

Samarin had been prominent members of the Town Council. At the new election in 1868 Prince Tcherkasski consented to be nominated for the mayoralty, and was elected by an overwhelming majority. The bearded merchants of the Bazaar (*Gostinoi-Dvor*) boasted with delight that the chief magistrate of their Commune was an ex-Minister of Poland—a man who was not only an office-bearer (*Sannovnik*), but a magnate (*Welmoscha*), who was superior in rank to His Excellency the Marshal of Noblesse of the Government, who treated the Governor-General as his equal, and who, at an Imperial *levée*, had claimed and triumphantly asserted, as the second dignitary of the Province and the representative of the first provincial city of the Empire, precedence over the Governor himself. Could not the older of these electors remember the day when their Mayor (*Govodskoi Golová*) had not been thought worthy by the Imperial officers of the Guard to sit next them at table, at a banquet given to them in honour of the emperor's coronation-day!

But beyond enjoying these pretentious externals of municipal representation, the good citizens of 'Mother Moscow' were not intended to go. The new Mayor treated his colleagues and subordinates so harshly and imperiously that angry quarrels and dissensions soon arose, which were well-nigh fatal to the working of the Communal machinery. His predilection for corporal punishment, which not even the peasants' friend of 1859 and the democratic reorganiser of Poland was able to conceal, was an obstacle, in particular, to harmony. Even his friends and partisans were forced to shrug their shoulders when they heard that no word was so constantly on his lips as the old national, but long since unfashionable, rod (*Rosgi*). All parties at length were heartily glad when the Prince resigned the dignity he had so eagerly canvassed for, and thereby enabled his friends to say that the narrow sphere of municipal duties was unsuited to a statesman accustomed to deal with larger questions. The fact that a reprimand administered to him for taking part in an anti-government demonstration of the Moscow nobility had been accepted by Tcherkasski, as a pretext for resigning an office, which had nothing whatever to do with his position as a noble, excluded, to be sure, the possibility of talking of a second 'martyrdom;' but it availed, nevertheless, to put a good face on his retirement, desirable as it was on other grounds. Moreover, employment in elective municipal offices had by this time passed out of fashion again in good society, and had fallen back upon the burghers. The mayoralty of Moscow had passed from the illustrious houses of Schtcherbatoff and Tcherkasski to a simple M. Schumacher (who was imprisoned afterwards as an accomplice of the swindler Strousberg); and this episode in the life of the 'National statesman' was either forgotten, or remembered with a sigh of regret for the 'immaturity' of political life and the difficulties to be encountered in modern Russia by men of real independence. Tcherkasski's popularity had not suffered by this affair; it had simply not been increased.

For some years after this Tcherkasski contented himself with administering his tolerably extensive estates, and delivering speeches, after his own fashion, among his fellow-nobles at Moscow and at the meetings of the Slav Committee. This Committee had been founded in 1857 by the Privy-councillor Bachmetieff, the Curator of the educational district and University of Moscow, and originally had only been intended to support the Southern

Slavs, namely, the Servians, Slovenians, and Bulgarians, in their efforts after civilisation. It was under Bachmetieff's successor as president, Professor Pogodin, who had looked to the Crimean War for the establishment of Russian supremacy over the East and West, that this committee began to play a part in politics. Under the influence of Ivan Aksakoff and after the outbreak of the revolt in the Herzegovina, it became the centre of the agitation, which extended throughout Russia, for supporting Servia in the war with Turkey. The Slav Committees reached the zenith of their activity in the summer of 1877, while the Czar and Prince Gortchakoff were in Germany; and already then their *fiat* had gone forth, that Tcherkasski must be placed at the head of the administration, to be entrusted with the reorganisation of the Slav countries. The necessity of appointing this administration, in the event of a declaration of war, was derived from the fact that a similar one had followed the German occupation of Alsace and Lorraine, and that the imitation of the German precedent of 1870-1 had become a fixed idea among the ruling circles at St. Petersburg. This *fiat* was repeated by Aksakoff, Katkoff, and their friends at every opportunity that offered. It was taken up by the reckless and time-serving hirelings of the press, and ultimately found its way to the Court. In November 1876, after the chief command of the army had been divided between the Grand-dukes Nicholas and Michael, Tcherkasski was informed that His Imperial Highness the Generalissimo of the Army of the Danube, by the advice of Miliutin, the Minister of War (the younger brother of the former Secretary of State for Poland), had proposed his nomination as Civil Commissioner and Chief of the Civil Administration, and that a complete scheme of organisation

M

was expected from him. His friends took good care that this scheme, whatever it might be, should be so pre-announced and puffed, that the Government was well-nigh pledged to give effect to it, at any price, when it appeared.

The preliminary arrangements with Tcherkasski in the winter of 1876-7 were so speedily concluded, that his appointment was already settled before the declaration of war (April 24, 1877). The Prince had proved himself, as before, a true master in the art of turning circumstances to his advantage, and of imparting to others his confidence in his own infallibility. With the air of one who had been taught by experience the fickleness of opinion at head-quarters, he had declared that he could only accept the post offered to him under certain conditions. A man called upon to conduct affairs of an extraordinary kind must have extraordinary trust reposed in him. The 'system,' for which he had declared himself, required a strict subordination of the executive instruments to its author, and for the latter, absolute liberty of action. He was ready to undertake the whole responsibility for its success; but, in return, he demanded that he alone should be responsible. He had no idea of letting himself be thwarted a second time by self-constituted critics in the execution of his matured plans. He must insist that the administration committed to his charge should be looked after by officials of his own selection, and that he should have absolute power as to their appointment and dismissal.

These conditions were accepted. As nobody had formed a clear idea of the proper nature and extent of the new administration, and as the whole thing had come upon the government, so to speak, unawares, they were glad enough to see the conduct of these difficult transactions entrusted to firm hands; they were, moreover, so engrossed in carrying out their new and wholly untried system of mobilisation, that they had no time to spare for other questions. The public augured success from the appointment, as a proof that its wishes had been consulted, and asked no questions about details of execution. There was no end to the rejoicing when in April 1877 Ivan Aksakoff informed the Slav Committee — now changed into a Slav Benevolent Society—that the emperor, at the proposal of the Civil Commissioner of the Commander-in-Chief of the Army of the Danube, had consented that the society should enter into direct relations with the Grand-duke and send a deputation to his head-quarters. A little later the Central Committee of the Red Cross Society nominated Tcherkasski as their general-plenipotentiary. Loaded with congratulations and marks of confidence of every kind, Vladimir Alexandrovitch entered upon his new grand 'mission.'

Once in possession of full powers, and with a view to confine the 'civil administration of the territories to be occupied' to men of his own choice, Tcherkasski took a step, which even the most devoted friends and admirers of the 'man of the situation' received with surprise. With the exception of a couple of officials to manage the technicalities of finance, and a few university professors, who were valuable from their knowledge of Slavonic, and particularly of Bulgarian, law, the new administrator surrounded himself exclusively with young officers selected from the various regiments of the Guard. That these gentlemen knew next to nothing about administration, and as regards the countries in which their active duties lay, knew nothing but what they had picked up from geographical primers, was in

Tcherkasski's eyes their chief recommendation. He himself wished to be the sole director of affairs, and to have at his disposal instruments implicitly obedient and accustomed to strict discipline—men, in short, who understood by the word 'service' nothing but the performance of orders. As the Imperial Guard, by the nature of their constitution, took no part in active warfare, but were intended to remain at St. Petersburg, most of the officers, now designated to civil employment, willingly responded to the summons. Those who considered the matter at all soon allowed themselves to be allured by Tcherkasski's vaunted reputation for high administrative capacity and his decided Liberal views; and the prospect of large salaries removed whatever scruples might remain. The majority accepted, because the newly-opened service had come into fashion. Some allayed their misgivings by imagining that the instructions promised to them would sufficiently enlighten them about their duties. Others fancied that residence in a foreign country would be more useful and instructive than remaining in their garrison with a division of the army shut out from active service. The well-known writer, Eugene Utin, whose sketches, 'Bulgaria during the War,'[1] form at present one of the chief sources of information respecting the history of Tcherkasski's administration, had frequent opportunities, during their tenure of office, of making acquaintance with these sons of Mars, so suddenly transformed into administrators; and he assures us that their amiability, good nature, and sense of honour were only exceeded by their ignorance of business and incompetence for civil affairs. They were all filled with the best wishes towards their chief and unbounded confidence in his capacity. They had all

[1] These appeared first in the *Véstnik Evrópy*.

travelled in post haste to the Roumanian frontier, but were bitterly disappointed on their arrival. The two things on which they had reckoned in particular, namely, a settled organisation and a plan for the administration of the territories intended to be occupied, were so entirely wanting, that the new officials were forced to dawdle about for weeks in Roumanian villages and kill the time, before even they were put in a position to gain a nearer acquaintance with their future duties. 'At St. Petersburg,' so Utin heard a young captain complain, 'we were told we must make haste to get to the Bulgarian frontier, and that the matter was urgent in the extreme; but here on the spot we are told that we have come far too soon, for there is nothing yet for us to do.' The so-called 'organisation' which they found on their arrival, consisted simply of creating a multitude of grandiloquent titles and fixing an exorbitant standard of salaries. Even before the Imperial army had crossed the Danube (June 29, 1877), Tcherkasski's head-quarters were crowded with governors, vice-governors, and superintendents of districts for every part of Bulgaria, and with commandants and majors *de la place* for all the strongholds that lay between the Danube and the Bosphorus. All these rulers *in partibus*, ever since they had crossed the Roumanian frontier, drew enormous salaries and a liberal allowance of daily pay, which Bulgaria had to provide. Each governor drew 7,000 roubles, and had, besides that, a separate fund of from six to ten thousand roubles to dispose of, for which he was not required to account. The vice-governors had each 3,500 roubles, together with a similar fund in proportion. The superintendents of districts and heads of police had 2,500 roubles and another 1,500 roubles for travelling expenses. All these salaries were paid in hard gold; every official, moreover, had received in advance his military pay for the year, and (as had been the custom in Turkestan) a double allowance for travelling expenses. When doubts were expressed about the wisdom of saddling with such serious burdens the Bulgarians 'whom they were about to liberate,' the answer was forthcoming at once, that the Turkish pasha government, at any rate, had been still more expensive, and that the blessings of political liberty could not be purchased too dearly. It was doubly vexatious that the commandants and officers of the Danube fortresses were appointed and received their titles, even before those places were in Russian hands. The holders of these posts knew, indeed, that they were objects of ridicule to the officers of the active army; and they bore their high-sounding titles with some aversion and discomfort.

Of the instructions promised to the officials of the civil administration, not one, at the outbreak of the war, was ready. Tcherkasski, as the hero of the 'system' and a connoisseur in such matters, thought it necessary to collect at once 'materials for the study of Bulgaria,' and to have them worked up by a specially appointed commission for the use and behoof of his subordinates. What Utin says of this *opus* seems incredible; but it has since been confirmed in detail by the specimens of it which have penetrated into Russia. On April 30, 1877, the commission, after having received from Tcherkasski a detailed programme of its intended labours, was ordered from Kischineff to Bucharest. On May 3 the commission assembled; eighteen days after, the first volume of the 'materials,' consisting of nine sheets, was already printed. Considering that the setting-up and printing must have required some time, since it was issued from a small Bulgarian printing office, served by only two compositors, it follows that this commission must have finished their labours in two or three days. Accordingly, the contents of the work were limited to the translation of fragmentary extracts from a couple of foreign *brochures*, which chance had thrown into the hands of the commissioners. Two circumstances seemed to account for this apparently objectless over-haste. One was the total ignorance of everyone about Bulgaria; the other was the illusory notion that in two or three months the Russians would have pushed on to Constantinople, and made themselves masters of all the Bulgarian territory. Whether the five following volumes of this production, compiled under the patronage of Tcherkasski, were as hastily put together we are not in a position to say; that they differed not, however, from the first instalment, was the unanimous opinion of even advanced Russian critics of the day. Of the fourth volume, devoted to the 'relations of landed property in Bulgaria,' Maxim Kowalevski, the Moscow historian, testifies that it had been compiled in perfect ignorance of the whole subject and of the simplest and most familiar facts. Fortunately however, adds the writer, the whole work was issued in so small a form, and was accessible with such difficulty, that it could do no harm, and at the most could only be regarded as a proof that its authors themselves were ashamed of their production.

Equipped with these materials, the young lieutenants and captains of cavalry, suddenly called upon to reorganise Southern Slavdom, went to work after the greater part of the territory, fixed upon as the scene of their exploits, had been occupied at the end of July by the Russian forces. The promised instructions were postponed from week to week; and when at length they appeared, most of them proved to be useless, and so contradictory that nobody knew what he was about. The simplest thing, under these circumstances, would have been to maintain the existing institutions, to let the Bulgarians govern themselves, and to be content with controlling this self-government, which, in its fundamental aspect, already prevailed. But to this Tcherkasski would not listen. Just as if it had been intended to make the very name of Russians hated by those 'brethren' whom they came to free, the supreme civil administrator played the part from the first of an absolute master, who had come to model all he found after his own pattern. Even before the Russian troops had crossed the Danube, a deputation of Bulgarian notables, consisting chiefly of representatives of the so-called Young Bulgarian party, arrived at Plojeschti, who solemnly welcomed the emperor and his generals in the name of the nation, and sought to unfold in detail their wishes and aspirations. His Majesty and the old Prince Gortchakoff received them with unusual amiability, and honoured them with a long audience. Just as unamiable, not to say hostile, was the reception these gentlemen met with from Tcherkasski. 'In the most offensive terms,' so an eye-witness relates, 'they were told they must not fancy they were there to represent the Bulgarian people. Bulgaria had no national assembly, and would not obtain any. In tones of downright menace he warned them to get rid at once of any political chimæras of that sort. When one of the Bulgarians attempted to make a statement in reply, he was peremptorily stopped with the remark, "We have no need of your wisdom. You have to listen and obey, not to argue."'

What followed was of a piece with this instructive beginning. Notwithstanding the pompous announcement at head-quarters of the institution of a new agrarian system and the abolition of existing taxes, throughout most of the occupied territory an arbitrary state of rule prevailed, under which the Turks who remained behind and their Greek adherents found themselves much better off than the 'liberated brethren,' whom the new civil administration addressed not in the Bulgarian but the Russian language, and in the Russian manner of the old school, namely, with whip in hand. Among Tcherkasski's first measures, published already in the Imperial proclamation, had been the promise that the tax paid by the Rayahs for exemption from military service and the tithes levied on all natural products should be abolished 'for ever.' The news of this boon was still in every one's mouth, when the civil administration announced that the latter impost would continue to be levied for the present, wherever the Russian troops were, for the proper provisioning of the army. As the whole country bristled with soldiers, the promised blessing profited nobody. But the bad feeling aroused by this counter-ordinance was universal, and was heightened to discontent and embitterment, when after a month it was announced that the tithes would be levied not in natural produce, as before, but in hard cash, that is to say, in a form at once the most inconvenient and oppressive to the landed tax-payers. The iniquity of this proceeding was crowned by the fact that its origin was not disguised; and that all the world was taught what Tcherkasski's much vaunted energy and independence really meant. The levying of tithes in hard cash had been the work of the three great army contractors Horwitz, Greger, and Kohan, who found it inconvenient, as a matter of business, to collect the natural products, and had used all their influence to bring about the change.

The same was the case with the remodelling of the agrarian system and of the local communal administration. Guided by his Polish experiences, Tcherkasski had drawn up a plan, the object of which was to expropriate altogether the aristocracy of the so-called *Tchorbadji*, who had grown up under Græco-Turkish influence, and who, as possessors and farmers of the Crown lands and *Vakuf* Estates, were the lords of the rural communes, while, as magistrates and tax-farmers, they fleeced the people right and left. The will and energy required to carry out this object of wholesale expropriation were not wanting, of course, in the man who had recklessly trampled on the clergy and nobility of Poland; but what Tcherkasski did want was circumspection and perseverance. Most of the district superintendents had no instructions at all; and so they took politics into their own hands and organised autonomy after their own fashion, without the least regard to the ultimate objects of their chief, of whom sometimes nothing was to be heard for weeks and months together. To many of these young aristocrats, trained in the traditions and by the discipline of the Guard, such things as democratic institutions and the independence of the communes committed to their charge, were simply an abomination; and the comparatively educated, clever, and pliant *Tchorbadji* suited their tastes far better than the rough peasants and village priests, whom it was their duty to protect. Total strangers to their new position, and tormented with the fear that beneath the aspirations of the so-called Young Bulgarian party there might lurk the same revolutionary and

Nihilist tendencies which they had had to combat in their native country, the soldier-civilians of Tcherkasski's administration looked to the enforcement of strict discipline and unconditional obedience as the sum and substance of their mission. The imperious demeanour of their chief, who brooked no contradiction, and was bent on carrying through his radical 'system' with all the means and appliances of absolutism, had deluded them into thinking that his objects would be better served by a vigorous use of the Cossack's whip (*Nagaika*), than by fulfilling the hopes of the Bulgarian nation. 'I feel as if I were stuck in an enchanted wood,' said a district superintendent to M. Utin; 'I am burdened by a mass of duties, without knowing how to perform them. My only comfort is, that it is the same with others; and that nobody really knows what he has to do, and what he may do.' 'The best emancipation for the Bulgarians,' said another, 'is the *Nagaika*. I am quite aware that our brethren, as we call them, cannot endure me; but I am equally indifferent to their affection or their hatred. These people are good for nothing, and must be kept under strict discipline. They fear me now, at all events, for they know that I let no misconduct escape me. Whoever does wrong, has twenty-five lashes counted out to him; and then there is an end of it.' 'What do I care?' said a third. 'I insist that they shall live quietly and peaceably with each other. The much-abused Turks do as I bid them, and leave the Bulgarians at peace. I insist that the latter shall do likewise. Whoever stirs a finger against his neighbour, gets a taste of the *Nagaika*.'

With such a disposition among the numerous servants of the administration, it is not surprising that they proceeded very irregularly in dealing with the communal and agrarian organisation, and repeatedly acted in direct opposition to the intentions of the government. In many parts the old rule of the *Tchorbadji* was simply retained as it was, and dignified with the name of the new organisation. In others, everything was senselessly and indiscriminately overturned, and a mob reign of terror was instituted, which, after the catastrophe at Plevna and the evacuation of much of the newly occupied territory, was naturally followed by a fearful and bloody retribution by the Turks.

But all these experiences did not shake Tcherkasski in his purpose. He stuck to his opinion, that the liberation and reorganisation of Bulgaria must be accomplished without any Bulgarian co-operation, by Russian instruments and according to a Russian plan. Not even the semblance of an active share in the administration was allowed the natives. Not one of the educated Bulgarians, who tendered their services to the Russian Government, received a post of any importance. The authorities had settled once for all that 'this people' were fit for nothing; that the idea of granting them autonomy or a constitution was absurd; and that a strong Russian dictatorship was wanted to develope among their Bulgarian 'brethren' the capacity for 'genuine Slavonic freedom.'

It is easy to guess what effect such opinions had upon the 'brethren,' expressed as they were at every opportunity, and without the least regard to their feelings. The more educated among them paid the Northern 'liberators' back in their own coin for their contempt of everything Bulgarian, and gave them now and then to understand that they at any rate had eyes to see, and could criticise with cutting sarcasm the system impersonated in Tcherkasski, and the weakness of Russian administration. They lost no opportunity of openly declaring that, urgently as they had desired to be freed from the Turkish yoke, they had no wish to be united to the Russian Empire—a possibility already contemplated by several of Tcherkasski's officials. 'The reason,' M. Utin heard a Bulgarian say, 'why you cannot discover among us any useful men, is not that they do not exist, but that you do not want to look for them, because you are victims of the prejudice that a man of any independence must necessarily be a semi-Revolutionist. Those of Young Bulgarian sympathies are in your eyes mere revolutionary firebrands. If once you could shake off this superstitious terror of the Red Spectre, you would very soon perceive that there are plenty of men among us, who are not only willing, but well qualified to serve their country—plenty of them, I say, though perhaps they may not always be found with the same degree of so-called European culture. If you would only enable us to protect our interests according to our own judgment, our actions would soon prove to you that it was quite unnecessary to look outside our country for governors, heads of districts, and other rulers of that kind.'

But words of wisdom like these were lost on Tcherkasski and his satellites. In the eyes of the supreme Civil Governor the necessity of a bureaucratic administration, filled exclusively by Russians, was as clearly established as the infallibility of all the other fundamental principles of the system which he had brought from his native country ready made.

One of these fundamental principles was the belief that the lower clergy of Bulgaria (having remained national) were a credit to the country and one of the mainstays of social order. Tsherkasski had learned from the Græco-Bulgarian ecclesiastical dispute, that the lower clergy had been arrayed against the bishops and abbots (who were either Græcianised or imported direct from the Fanar at Constantinople), and had been mainly instrumental in obtaining the appointment of Church dignitaries from among their own race and the performance of public worship in their native language. This was quite enough to determine Tcherkasski's Church policy at once. He resolved to demand from the higher clergy an entire separation from the Œcumenical Patriarchate, and to cede to the secular clergy an extensive influence upon local administration.[1]

[1] In the Archdiocese of Bulgaria, as elsewhere throughout the Greek-Orthodox Church, a sharply defined contrast exists from ancient times between the Monastic or Black clergy, who hold the higher offices and episcopal sees, and the Secular or White clergy, who fill the lower offices. The 'popes' or secular clergy must all be married; they conduct worship in the town and country churches, and administer the cure of souls; while the monastic clergy, who alone enjoy wealth and social influence, monopolise the government of the Church and the management of her revenues. For many years all higher offices in Bulgaria were held exclusively by Greeks of Fanariot origin, whose object was to spread the language, manners, and authority of their own people, and to drain their diocesans in favour of the Œcumenical Patriarchate. They practised the most scandalous simony, and laboured systematically to efface all remembrance of the former self-government of the Bulgarians and their independence as a State. With this view they attempted also to influence the lower clergy, whose members had little prospect of promotion or of any favour being shown them unless they adopted Greek culture and the Greek language, and put off their own Bulgarian nature. A reaction against this Grecianising system became perceptible early in 1860, and was supported by Russia, while the Turks took the part of the Greeks and the Patriarchate. Thanks to the influence of the Ambassador Ignatieff, the Bulgarians obtained, after a struggle of many years, the independence of their Church province, and the right to elect their own clergy and to perform service in the Bulgarian language; for which, on the other hand, they were solemnly excommunicated and treated as schismatics by the Patriarch and the Synod of Constantinople and the Church of the Hellenic kingdom. It was only a year or two before the late war that some signs appeared of a *rapprochement* between these two communities, the Exarch Joseph being considered the chief mover. The lower clergy had taken a lively interest, so far as their dependence on the pashas allowed, in the struggle against the Greek oppressors. Thus,

The Moscow Slavophil Catechism of 1830 had established it already as an *à priori* principle, that the bearers of orthodoxy, in so far as they remained National, should be the leaders of the Slavonic nations. By this rule Tcherkasski proceeded, and kept to it firmly, regardless of the result. The Exarch Joseph, who had remained at Constantinople since the beginning of the war, received an order from the Prince to repair at once to Tirnova under pain of deposition. This order the Exarch disobeyed, and was forced to disobey, for any attempt on his part to leave Stamboul would have cost him his head. Thereupon he was threatened with the election of another Arch-diocesan of Bulgaria, and a schism in the Church seemed imminent. That it was averted is due solely to the fact, that the turn of military events after the first battle of Plevna caused the whole affair to be forgotten. Undeterred, however, by this experience with the higher clergy, Tcherkasski persisted in his design of exalting their secular brethren who were Nationalists, notwithstanding the unfavourable impressions which the want of education and the rapacity of this class, who were universally unpopular and frequently the creatures of Turkish influence, had produced, and were bound to produce, upon every attentive observer. A deputation of Bulgarian notables presented an address to Tcherkasski, requesting him to exclude the clergy altogether from interfering in administration. This memorial, drawn up of course in tones of deep humility, was answered by a fulmination which effectually frightened them from any further enterprise of the kind. The petitioners were

at the time of the Russian occupation, there were two Church parties in Bulgaria, an Hellenic and a National one. The former was prevented from giving any support to the Russians by the influence of the Patriarchate.

told, in the harshest and most offensive language, that they must beware in future of that sort of reasoning, and that it was natural the clergy should have an influential part assigned to them, since it was they who had preserved to the people their nationality and language. This reply concluded with a few commonplaces about religion being the foundation of the State and of society, and respect for the clergy a political duty. Can it be wondered at that the Bulgarians at last suspected Tcherkasski's administration of the intention to establish a firm and permanent footing in the country; and that soon the fear became universal, that his object was to deprive the nation for ever of all independence and of the slightest influence or control over its own destinies?

Such was the state of things when, in August 1877, there came the sudden crisis brought about by the Turkish victories of Plevna and Ezki-Saghra. A large part of the Bulgarian territory, recently occupied by the Russian troops, who had been the sole support of Tcherkasski's rule, had to be evacuated by them in all speed and under cover of night. The governors and heads of districts, having been for some weeks the masters of the country, followed the divisions of troops, which were now being hurriedly concentrated, and thus obliged to expose large districts to the vengeance of the Turks. The favours shown in some places to the *Tchorbadji* and to the Turks who had remained behind, were now punished as mercilessly as the acts of violence committed in other districts against the representatives of Turkish rule. Whole communities, which, under an energetic leader, might well have been able to oppose the Turkish hordes now breaking in upon their homes, were induced by the district officials to submit unconditionally, as soon as the last Russian soldiers were gone, just because nowhere had an attempt been made to give them an organisation capable of life and independent action from within. Wherever Turks and friends of Turks had been pushed aside or ill-treated, these now came forward to accuse their fellow-countrymen who had been used as Russian tools, and who were hanged without mercy by hundreds. A panic seized upon the whole country. No one knew where to remain or whither to go. Everywhere Russian troops were called for, but nowhere was it known for certain whether there were any left in the country or not. Even the garrisons left behind for the protection of the towns remained cut off for some days from all communication with the divisional bodies of the army.

Matters were still worse, as might be expected, in the Bulgarian districts south of the Balkans. Here the Russian evacuation was complete; and here all that the civil administration had done was to appoint a few hundred communal officials, who of course were so many victims for the Turkish police. The road leading from the Shipka Pass to Tirnova was covered with thousands of fugitives, who had saved nothing but bare life, and who dragged their fainting and famished limbs to those districts where the Russian administration still remained. It could not have been difficult to find shelter for these miserable creatures, with so many villages, once inhabited by Turks and Tartars, standing empty. It only wanted someone to take the matter in hand, to direct this crowd of wretched fugitives, and to see that at any rate they should have the necessary food. It is, perhaps, the heaviest charge to be laid against Tcherkasski's administration, that in this respect it ignored altogether its plainest duty, and never even made an attempt to save these miserable creatures from starvation. 'We have no money—none has been assigned to us for this purpose. We are here to govern, not to practise benevolence and play the philanthropist;' such were the answers given, with the calm and superior air of 'statesmen,' to those who appealed to the civil administration in the name of humanity and the most elementary dictates of political prudence. The same officials, who had drawn millions of roubles from Bulgaria, who had continued to collect all the rates and taxes as fixed under Turkish rule, and who had then in their hands a special fund for unforeseen expenses, according to the rules laid down in the 'Project for the administration of Bulgarian finance'—these very men asserted that they were unable to raise the comparatively trifling sums required to keep these unfortunate people from starving, who had had to pay with the loss of all their property for their rash confidence in the invincibility of the Russian soldiers. With a shrug of the shoulders they declared that assistance could not be given for 'political reasons.' The knowledge that Russian authorities were providing for Bulgarian fugitives would multiply their number tenfold, and would lead to endless difficulties. It was the business of the Slav Committees to practise benevolence. The sufferers should apply to these, and if their appeal were ineffectual, the civil administration could not be held responsible.

Such was the language spoken and acted upon, whilst the whole world was horrified by the fearful news from Kazanlik, whose unhappy inhabitants were literally given over to butchery by the premature withdrawal of the Russian garrison and their obedience to the civil administration of Tcherkasski. The indignation at this proceeding was as universal as it was passionate, especially in military circles, and contributed more than anything to make the pessimism, diffused through the army since the beginning of August, exceed all bounds. 'Where this is possible,' was the general remark, 'everything is possible.' Neither officers nor soldiers concealed their aversion to the civil and military administration of Tcherkasski. His subordinates had daily to endure the bitterest scorn and sarcasm, and, as is natural in such cases, to suffer blame for things of which they were wholly innocent. Despondency and embitterment were universal; and doubts were expressed, openly and in no flattering terms, whether even the most moderate termination was possible for a campaign begun so confidently. The same men who in June and July had reckoned with supreme assurance on a pleasant autumn residence on the Bosphorus, now sank to gloomy prophecies about having to retreat across the Danube and abandon the whole of Bulgaria to the soldiers of Osman and Suleiman Pasha. For months there was no longer any question of the reorganisation of the country or of the scheme of civil administration proposed with such confidence. All they wished and hoped for was to regain the military positions they had lost during that disastrous August. Nobody cared any longer for Tcherkasski or his 'system': his part seemed to be played out for ever. The abler members of his staff of officials, whom he had gathered round him in April, resigned their appointments on hearing that the Guards had received orders to march, intending to join their regiments. These young officers openly avowed that they would never have left them for an hour, could they have foreseen that the much-talked-of civil administration would be nothing but a very bad farce.

The author of this farce, however, seemed determined to play the part, once undertaken, as long as possible. Incapable of making a name among his countrymen by deeds, he sought to refresh their memory of him by the medium of the press. For this purpose he 'interviewed,' at the end of September, the war correspondent of a St. Petersburg daily paper.[1] In a speech which was obviously carefully prepared, he remarked on the weakness of educated Russians for telling phrases and anecdotes—'our chief disease,' as he called it—and next on the strange, but thoroughly Slavonic phenomenon, that the war had not produced a single man of eminence, but that the really decisive part had been assigned to the Czar and his people. The whole of the Russian press received this announcement with amused indifference. One short passage only deserves notice, in which the acknowledged spokesman of the Russian War-party, self-satisfied as ever, assures his listener that he had never really wished for the war, and had expressed his opinion from the first that Russia was not sufficiently prepared. Only a few days before this, General Ignatieff had been telling another 'Interviewer' exactly the same story; and had caused a witty journalist of St. Petersburg to ask—How a war, desired neither by the government, nor by diplomacy, nor by the National party, had ever come about? But Tcherkasski was not discouraged by his failure to achieve distinction. He resumed his peculiar confident demeanour, and continued to play his part as a reformer of Southern Slavdom, whenever circumstances would permit. Immediately after the fall of Plevna, he procured a commission from the Commander-in-Chief to re-establish

---

[1] This curious speech of Tcherkasski, given to the correspondent of the *Novoe Vrêmya*, will be found *in extenso* in the *Times* of Sept. 26, 1877. [TR.]

the administrative apparatus which had collapsed in the disastrous days of August and September. He began again exactly where he had left off. For a second time, and heedless of past experience, he started by appointing a purely Russian Staff, by introducing Russian bureaucratic rules and ordinances, and by treating the people, for whose liberation they had crossed not only the Danube but the Balkans, as a flock of sheep without a will of their own. The only difference was, that this time they set in earnest about the promised formation of a Bulgarian Militia, and took care to have them trained by Russian officers and sergeants.

Twelve weeks after the catastrophe of Plevna, Prince Tcherkasski, who had followed the head-quarters of the Grand-ducal Commander-in-Chief, suddenly died. A fortnight before he fell ill, the February number of the *Vêstnik Evrópy* had appeared, and Russia had learned for the first time, and with a certain amount of details, the real nature of the Civil Administration of Bulgaria, and of the 'system' of the first Apostle of the Slavophils, who had climbed to dignity and office. Rumours, it is true, had already reached St. Petersburg and Moscow as to the true character of the propaganda, which the friend of Nicholas Miliutin was carrying on amongst the Southern Slav 'brethren,' but these rumours were now confirmed by M. Utin, and by the criticisms published a few weeks later of Kowalwesky and Stassulevitch. The impression produced by these revelations upon the many admirers of the Prince, who had hailed him as the pioneer of a new era of freedom and national development, can be gathered best from the following words of Stassulevitch :—' The example before us teaches us,' he says, ' that if our present Slavophils were suddenly to attain to power and influence in Russia, they would not be a whit more liberal than the men now in power, whom, as types of the "St. Petersburg period," they have criticised so severely. They would use exactly the same means—such as the employment of military persons for civil administration, the appointment of a large and costly staff, the suppression of all independence among those who are subject to their rule; they would resort, in a word, to Absolutism pure and simple. The same people who were always prating about the departure from our "natural basis," as a peculiarity of the St. Petersburg period, have shown, at the first opportunity offered them for a display of practical politics, that they too are incapable of shaking off for a moment the bureaucratic traditions of those days.'

One statement, however, in this passage is incorrect; namely, where the writer speaks of the Bulgarian Civil Administration as the 'first' opportunity given to the National party and their leaders for the exercise of political activity. He forgets that the farce enacted during the previous summer between the Danube and the Balkans, was substantially a reproduction of that performed on the Vistula between 1865 and 1867. In both cases 'emancipation' was the ostensible object; in both cases the attempt was made to carry out emancipation by force, and in obedience to a 'system' prearranged without any regard to existing relations or the wishes of those immediately concerned. Employing military men for civil administration, terrorising the people who were to be made happy, trying to replace one agrarian system (which was not understood) for another, the effects of which could not be watched—all this had been done before, and its results already experienced, when Tcherkasski had taken in hand the domestic administration of Poland, and pledged himself to 'exorcise the Latin spirit by means of that of Slavo-Byzantinism.' The essential difference between 1865 and 1877 was this: that the experiment of vindicating liberty and equality by means of despotism, and of preparing the self-government of a country by gagging its natural spokesmen, revealed its utter want of common sense far more strikingly in Bulgaria, a country to be liberated and on a friendly footing with Russia, than in the anti-Russian kingdom of Poland, kept prostrate by forcible means; and that this time the Russian nation had no interest in letting themselves be deceived about the true state of affairs, or yielding implicit belief to those who acted in their name. The most prejudiced and short-sighted of the Moscow patriots could not but acknowledge that this violent and despotic policy, carried on in Bulgaria in the name of the Slavish National cause, was entirely counter to all Russian as well as Slavish interests; besides creating the danger of bringing the Russian name into ill repute in the South Slavonic countries of the East, just as it had done in the countries of the former Poland and Lithuania. For the failure, moreover, notwithstanding all the efforts of a century, to bridge over the gulf between the Slavs of Great Russia, Lithuania, and Livonia, the differences of history and creed could be alleged as an excuse. But no such excuses could be alleged in the case of Bulgaria. And in Servia matters were already even worse. Here the crusade against Turkey in 1876 had been undertaken by Russians and Servians in common, and had ended in a common defeat, and painful quarrels between the leaders of the allies. What would be the result, if the proverbially patient and pliant Bulgarians were likewise to renounce their friendship to Russia and declare her rule incompatible with the freedom and dignity of man? What prospect was left for the establishment of a great empire of the future, extending from the Volga to the Moldau, if every Russian attempt to restore a genuine National organisation was to end in failure and disunion between the liberators and the liberated? if that incapacity for establishing civil order, which the Novgorodians of 862 complained of to the Varagian chief,[1] should be the epitaph on the grave of Slavo-Russian development?

If conclusions, as regards the future, may be drawn from the past, we cannot predict for Bulgaria that 'free Constitution' which Stassulevitch and his friends consider necessary for the interests of Russia. In the first place, the recent war has brought the Russian and Bulgarian nations into contact in a manner which secures for any democratic-constitutional experiments on the slopes of the Balkans the certainty of an important reaction upon the internal condition of Russia. In the second place, the passion for self-aggrandisement is implanted far more deeply in the great nation of the East than her liberal spokesmen care either to know or confess. Tcherkasski was no accidental, but the typical impersonation of that tendency which, with all its faults and exaggerations, seems likely to assert its influence over Russian society for some time to come. The urgent desire of the nation to take an active share in political

---

[1] According to the narrative of Nestor of Kieff, the oldest of Russian chroniclers, who died in 1114, the Novgorodians, Tchudi and Krivitchi, at the advice of the elder Gostomysl, sent ambassadors in 862 to the Russo-Varagians across the Baltic with this message: 'Our country is great and blessed; but order is wanted in it; come then and be our rulers and reign over us.' The three brothers, Rurik, Sineus, and Truvor accepted this invitation; they came over and settled at Novgorod, Bielosero, and Isborsk, and thus laid the foundations of the Russian Empire, which Rurik united under his own sceptre after the death of his brothers.

life has been so passionately aroused by the events of the last twenty years, that some scope must be allowed for its exercise. One of the symptoms of the dangers that arise from a violent suppression of this desire, is the growth of that excrescence of the Revolutionary spirit which passes by the name of Nihilism, and about which recent events have brought to light the most surprising revelations. If the morbid restlessness which has seized the popular mind of Eastern Slavdom is to be prevented from preying upon the nobler parts of the social body, some outlet must be found for it, such as was found, fifteen years ago, in the Russification of Polish Lithuania, and since 1875 in what is called at Moscow and St. Petersburg the 'solution of the Slav question.' That the instinct which points to national expansion and the development of national power is stronger than any other instinct in the Slavonic race, and more imperious than even the law of self-interest, is a fact which Tcherkasski's public life brings out with a distinctness not to be disputed. Twice has he been called on to act as champion of the National cause; and twice has he succeeded in diverting the passionate excitement of his party. Although unable to effect more during his Polish administration than the destruction of the Latin forms of life which he found on the Vistula, this failure did not prevent his fellow-countrymen and partisans from entrusting him with another and far more extensive mission in a field quite as important as the first. The ill success that attended this last enterprise has been as quickly forgotten as the failure of Miliutin's policy in Poland—a failure which, in spite of all proof, the National party even now will not confess. M. Ivan Aksakoff, in a speech made in memory of Tcherkasski on the anniversary of the Slavonic Benevolent Society, still declared that the reproaches heaped upon his Bulgarian administration were all calumnies; and accounted for the extraordinary measures that 'National statesman' devised, by the incapacity for 'administrative work' peculiar to the Bulgarians. The Russian National party cannot renounce the means to which it owes its rise, and the part it played between 1860 and 1870. They must put these means in motion, unless they wish to be condemned to absolute inaction. That party which has inscribed on its flag 'Organic development,' 'Maintenance of true Nationality,' 'Liberation of society from the yoke of State doctrines,' and which in the name of these principles calls in question the Russian history of the last century and a half—that party has now advanced so far as to regard the compulsory absorption of kindred races as their nearest practical task; and, in the name of the Russian State-principle, to arrest the free development of those whom they think it is their duty to emancipate. That party found its incarnation in the man who, as the champion of national independence and the freedom of the peasants, had gained his way to power; who thereupon made use of this power as a despot, recognising no higher law than his own will; and who finally arrived at preaching his ideas of liberty and equality, first in Poland and then in Bulgaria, with the *Nagaika* in his hand.

CHAPTER VIII.

THE RUSSIAN UNIVERSITIES.

I.

Imperial Ukase of 1849—Universities of Dorpat and Helsingfors—of Moscow—of St. Petersburg—The Medico-Chirurgical Academy—Universities of Charkoff, Kasan, and Kieff—Statute of 1835—Government restrictions—Tyranny of provincial curators and inspectors—Unenviable position of professors—Paucity of competent teachers explained—Invidious treatment of students.

II.

Personal reminiscences of the author at St. Petersburg University—Fellow-candidates for matriculation—The 'Marchirovka'—Political apathy of the students—Social characteristics of student life—The Curator—Academical restrictions—Legal studies.

III.

Reforms under Kowalevski's ministry—Liberal movement at the Universities—Reactionary policy of Count Putiätin—His successor Golownin—The Statute of 1863—Instability of academical rights—Vacillating policy of the government—Consequent distrust of the students—Their fondness for conspiracies explained.

I.

It is just thirty years ago that the Emperor Nicholas, frightened by the events of 1848, and under the influence of his intimate adviser, General Buturlin, conceived the plan of abolishing all the Russian Universities, long suspected as the homes of liberal ideas, and of replacing them with special schools for the various branches of learning, to be formed on a military model and removed to different provincial cities. This plan was never fully realised; but the Czar was bent on giving it partial effect. Uvaroff, the Minister of Instruction, gave place to Prince Schirinski-Schichmatoff, and the restriction of academical freedom began. A Ukase was issued, which deprived the universities of the right of electing their rector, abolished the professorships of European international law, placed the teaching of philosophy in the hands of Greek-Orthodox priests, made the supervision both of teachers and students considerably more stringent, limited the number of students to 300 for each university, and virtually excluded the lower classes from academical study. The number of medical students alone remained undiminished, on account of the deficiency of army surgeons; and the Universities of Dorpat and Helsingfors were allowed to retain the chair of Philosophy, which was necessary for the study of Protestant theology, and to educate as many Lutheran ministers as they pleased.

This Ukase, notwithstanding the short period of its operation (from 1849 to 1856), produced very lasting results. It has largely determined the development of the entire system of higher education in Russia, and has been the source of all the difficulties and complications now existing at St. Petersburg, Moscow, Kieff, and Charkoff.

The Russian Empire, including Poland, Finland, and the Baltic provinces, possessed at that time seven universities and several departmental schools, on a like footing, amongst which the Medico-Chirurgical Academy, the School of Law, and the Lyceum at St. Petersburg, the Richelieu at Odessa, and the Besborodko Lyceum at Nekin, were the most important. Two of the universities, Dorpat and Helsingfors, were not taken into account, when the means of educating sixty millions of people came to be considered. Dorpat was purely German in character, Helsingfors was exclusively Swedish. Both of them were outside of Old Russia; both were subject to special regulations, and prided themselves on representing the culture of Protestantism and Western Europe. Dorpat, after its restoration in 1802,[1] became the distinctive University of Livonia; but the few Russians, belonging mostly to the higher ranks of society, who studied there, looked upon it as a foreign university, and adopted the usages of German student-life so completely, that for several years they formed a body of their own, the 'Ruthenia.' Polish students went to Dorpat for two reasons; first, because it was not a Russian university, and secondly, because they found here the spirit of *Burschenschaft* which in Russian universities was then unknown. At Helsingfors the only students were Swedish Finns, since the study of Protestant theology formed the introduction to all other departments of learning. The only Russian professor at Dorpat or Helsingfors was a lecturer on Russian language and literature, whose ample fees consoled him for the paucity of employment.

Among the Russian universities proper, that of Moscow undoubtedly occupied the first place, not only from its age (it had been founded in 1755), but from its superior number of students, and the greater liberty they enjoyed. Even in the days when university study was looked upon in court and military circles as *mesquin* and dangerous,[2] there were always among the students at Moscow a large number of the sons of good families, who went thither for real study, ' living in

---

[1] A Swedish university had existed at Dorpat from 1632 to 1709, but it never exactly prospered.

[2] Prince Obolenski, the last Liberal Curator of Moscow University, was dismissed about 1830, and his place supplied by Prince S. M. Galytzin.

lodgings in the town, but being regularly matriculated, not mere pupils of the university 'boarding-houses for young nobles,' or attending only such lectures as they chose. Among the professors there were always some men of independent thought and genuine culture, and impressed with the dignity of their calling—men who treated the students as comrades, not as mere subordinates; who recognised as their duty the nurture of knowledge, not the mere preparation of the students for their examination as servants of the State; and who sought to promote with all their power the freedom of academical life. All those who, between 1830 and 1850, desired a higher and more liberal cultivation than they could find elsewhere, went to Moscow University,[1] where the chairs of Philosophy and Natural Science in particular were filled by really able men. Well-nigh all the most conspicuous representatives of modern Liberal and National Russia, such as Herzen, Belinski, Granovski, Ivan Turgenieff, the two Aksakoffs, Prince Tcherkasski, M. N. Katkoff, and others, have belonged to this university, which was broad enough to embrace parties as widely different as the Nationalists, the European-Liberals, and the Socialists, while maintaining its position as the centre of national and intellectual life at Moscow.

The University of St. Petersburg, founded in 1819, ranks second in importance; it has not yet succeeded in becoming a real *Universitas litterarum*. It has never possessed a medical faculty (theological faculties do not exist in Russia proper). Students of philology were 'interned' in the pedagogic Institute, affiliated to the university, and a place of strict discipline. The juris-

---

[1] In 1847 the number of students at Moscow had increased to nearly 1,200; but in consequence of the Ukase of 1849 it fell to 821 in the next year. At present there are between 1,500 and 2,000.

tic faculty was of minor esteem, the sons of grandees being usually put into the Law School, which was endowed with exceptional privileges, or else into the Lyceum—to each of which establishments separate gymnasia were attached. The university students consisted of men who could find no other place to go to; or whose parents, at the risk of incurring the displeasure of society, gave them the advantage of greater liberty and a wider intellectual culture than could be met with in the other 'institutions of the Crown.' At St. Petersburg, as at Moscow, the majority of the students were the sons of nobles, officials, or learned men—all of independent mind, who thought of something beyond securing a 'grand career;' who possessed a genuine desire for culture, and regarded an academical degree as an honourable distinction. Most of the students belonged to the Faculty of Law and Politics, in which the German element at times was pretty strongly represented. To study at the German University at Dorpat was for many years considered too dangerous for a young man to risk who aimed at high office.

The Medico-Chirurgical Academy was an institution of a peculiar kind. It was separated from the university, being subject to the Minister of War, and was relegated to a distant suburb of the capital. Three-fourths of the students, who numbered altogether from 1,200 to 1,500, were 'Crown students.' They lived in a large barrack; they were not allowed to appear abroad, except in the regular uniform with red facings, and with helmet and sword; and they were under strict military discipline. They were supposed to have a certain *penchant* for Radical ideas, even in the days of merciless severity towards everything that had a tinge of Liberalism; nor was it strange that young medical students of the nineteenth century, and living in the metropolis, should parade their materialism with a certain air of cynical affectation. They were recruited exclusively from the poorer families of the middle classes and the Jews; the few men of higher rank who wished to study medicine went regularly to Moscow.

The three provincial universities of Charkoff, Kasan, and Kieff resembled that of Moscow in respect of their organisation. They possessed medical faculties, it is true; but, as regards both professors and students, they were decidedly inferior to the universities at Moscow and St. Petersburg, where the surroundings of higher civilisation and the presence of a larger foreign element produced a superior degree of culture and more intellectual activity. At Kasan the neighbourhood of Asia made its effect felt in a considerable influx of students of Siberian and Tartar descent. Kieff, which had taken the place of Vilna, when that university was closed in 1832, was largely frequented by Polish and Polonised students, and for this reason was watched over with extraordinary severity. Even after the limitation Ukase of 1849, the number of students at this university amounted on an average to 600, whilst that at Kasan and Charkoff rarely exceeded from 300 to 400. The constitution of all these universities was the same. It was based on the Statute of 1835, which Nicholas had had drawn up by Uvaroff, the Minister of Instruction, to counteract the mischief which Alexander I. was supposed to have brought about by having founded too many universities and by the liberal decree of 1804. Externally, the German model was adhered to. There was an Academical Senate and a Rector whom the Senate elected. There were faculties which elected their own deans. The university in each case enjoyed a separate jurisdiction; and the faculties had the right of nominating to the vacant chairs. There were professors, ordinary and extraordinary, and private tutors and lecturers. The students were matriculated; they resided, at least in part, in houses of their own choice; they enjoyed a certain amount of liberty with regard to attendance at lectures; they were not flogged; and they possessed the rights of nobles. But all these high-sounding privileges meant in reality very little. The actual ruler of the university was the Curator, appointed by the emperor, usually an ex-officer, whose word in all matters was final. His right of confirmation virtually dictated the elections; he annulled or altered at pleasure the sentences of the university Courts; he controlled the political conduct and the teaching of the professors, who regulated their lectures and the use of lesson-books at his nod; and he regarded it as his chief duty to exercise the strictest discipline over the students, who were looked after by special inspectors. Professors, as well as students, enjoyed the 'right of wearing the Imperial uniform'—in other words, they were forbidden under heavy penalties to appear in public without the regulation coat, hat, and sword. All social, literary, or scientific meetings were interdicted; a friendly intercourse between professors and students was considered improper and inconsistent with the difference of their rank. Especial zeal was shown in maintaining a 'decent decorum,' which meant a regular attendance at church, the loyal celebration of the State festivals, reading limited to Russian works, and as tidy an appearance as possible of the various collections of which the students were allowed a 'moderate use.' Above all, the greatest possible care was taken to accustom the young men early to strict subordination.

At St. Petersburg the emperor himself undertook the inoculation of this cardinal virtue. Woe to the student who ventured to pass a general without saluting him, or who was seen in a cap instead of a hat (the former being allowed only outside the city), or who neglected to wear a sword, or who went to the theatre otherwise than in his costly and gold-embroidered gala uniform! About the year 1840 the emperor personally ordered three youths to be put under arrest, who, with the thermometer at 30° of freezing, had attempted to steal quietly to the university buildings across the Neva, not being dressed in the prescribed uniform, and had omitted to salute the Imperial sledge. The emperor being also a general, the required salute was as follows. The cloak was to be removed off the left shoulder as far as the hilt of the sword ; the left hand placed upon the seam of the trousers (*ruki po schwam*), and the hat touched with two fingers of the right hand. 'You must accustom yourselves from earliest youth to obey your superiors and do them honour,' was the admonition the emperor gave to the young deliquents, whom he had summoned before him, and dismissed with a generous pardon.

To conform to the standard of discipline, thus prescribed by the highest personage in the empire, was an understood duty of honour with the Curators of the provincial universities. It was certainly a duty which they performed with incomparable zeal, and often with far greater severity than their brethren in the capital, where some external homage at least was claimed by literature and science. Magnitzki, the Curator at Kasan, ordered the bodies prepared for dissection to be solemnly interred, deeming it highly irregular that the mortal remains of orthodox Christians, destined for the Resurrection, should remain unburied! Prince Sergei Galytzin, the Curator of Moscow, was so consummate a genius of order, that to prevent the possibility of any lectures being omitted from the programme, he gave instructions that in the event of any professor being hindered by illness or any other cause from attending, one of his colleagues from another faculty—no matter which—should step in and take his turn. Alexander Herzen tells us that he proposed in all seriousness that M. Ternovski, a priest and professor of logic, should give the lectures on clinical science and midwifery, as occasion might require, and that Richter, the accoucheur, should lecture on the doctrine of the Conception.

At Kieff the scholars and teachers were in the worst plight of all. Owing to the large intermixture of Polish elements at this university, General Bibikoff, the Curator, thought fit to establish, so to speak, a permanent state of siege, and to suppress by means of barbarous punishments the least tendency to freedom of thought or action. In spite of the general submissiveness and pliancy of behaviour which he succeeded in enforcing, scarcely a year passed by without some flagrant instance of tyranny. 'Suspected' students were suddenly arrested on the absurdest pretexts, and either sent to the barracks or banished into distant provinces. Professors, who had chanced to incur his displeasure, were 'removed to other branches of the service,' or forbidden to lecture on 'doubtful subjects,' such as political economy. It is true that instances of this sort have not happened at Kieff alone. In 1833 three students of the Moscow University, who were supposed to have had dealings with a 'suspected' Pole,[1] were degraded

---

[1] Antonovitch, one of these students, became afterwards a Lieutenant-General in the army, and has been Curator of the University of Kieff since 1876.

to the rank of common soldiers by a court-martial, specially summoned, and banished to the Caucasus. In 1835 Herzen, then a student of philosophy, was sentenced to be a clerk in the Government of Perm for having been present at a banquet where revolutionary songs were sung. About the same time Belinski, famous afterwards as a liberal writer and critic, received the *consilium abeundi* on the ground of 'incapacity.' Professor Granovski, the most eminent Russian historian of that time, owed it entirely to the protection of his distinguished patron, the kind-hearted Curator, Count S. G. Strogonoff, who was deposed in 1847, that he was suffered to retain his chair, and to escape any serious consequences from the repeated 'warnings' he received. Katkoff, the celebrated National journalist of to-day, and the editor of the 'Moscow Gazette,' voluntarily resigned his professorship, being unable to endure any longer the constant interference of Strogonoff's successor. Pirogoff, the famous surgeon and anatomist, who had removed from Dorpat to St. Petersburg shortly after 1840, repeatedly threatened to quit his chair and go abroad, and was only enabled by these threats to avoid the meddlesomeness of Curators with their mania for regulations. Even at Dorpat, which was treated exceptionally and envied for its liberty, things happened which would have been impossible under the administration of Klinger and Liven. Ulmann,[1] the professor of theology, was cashiered in 1842, at the instance of the Curator, General Craffström,

---

[1] The present government has worthily rehabilitated this honourable but ill-used man by appointing him Vice-President of the Lutheran General Consistory. During his rectorship he made earnest efforts to check duelling, and took the first step in that direction by instituting courts of honour for the students, by whom he was loved and revered.

simply because, at a torch-light serenade, given him by the students' corporation, on his vacating the office of Rector, he had uttered such treason as 'Health and happiness to the students!' and had accepted a goblet presented to him. Ulmann's colleagues, Von Bunge, the celebrated legal historian, and the professors Volkmann and von Madai shared the same fate for venturing to defend his conduct. In 1850 Professor Osenbrüggen, the jurist, who died a short time ago, and the tutor Hehn were dragged off to St. Petersburg for having corresponded with a female friend of Kinkel.

And yet, in spite of such instances of high-handedness, which might be multiplied further, the condition of the Dorpat University at that time was superior, beyond all comparison, to that of the universities in the interior of Russia. Here, at any rate, there existed liberty of teaching, and a collegiate and compact fraternity of professors. Here the folly of examinations was confined to the acquirement of certain learned degrees; and the students retained sufficient liberty, notwithstanding all the senseless regulations, to be able to associate in corporations of a semi-public character.

At St. Petersburg, Moscow, Kieff, and other universities, every kind of learned or social gathering was interdicted. The students there were told precisely what lectures they were to attend. The notes of the professors and the text-books in use were subject to strict control, and if not approved of, cashiered. Every year the student had to attend a prescribed 'course' of lectures, any deviation from which was an act of high treason. At the end of the first course he had to pass an examination before he was qualified to commence the next, and so on until the entire course of studies was completed.[1] If the professor ever noticed any irregularity of attendance at his lectures and reported it to the Inspector, the delinquents were punished in disciplinary fashion. Professors who clung to the old traditions of student liberty, both personally and in respect of their choice of studies, had to expect to be excluded from all promotion or reward, and, if re-elected when their term of office expired, to have their re-election annulled.[2] No wonder, that from year to year these academical professorships, with their moderate salaries in the bargain, became less attractive; that learned men of any independent spirit declined to accept them, and preferred a more modest but less irksome position in life; and that, notwithstanding the offers of new stipends and special courses of lectures, numbers of chairs either remained empty, or were filled provisionally by ungraduated *dilettanti*. In the faculties of Medicine and Natural Science a remedy, if needed, was at hand, by calling in Germans from Dorpat or foreign countries, who in course of time learned to express themselves, however imperfectly, in Russian, and supplied by their knowledge of the subject their defective power of communication. Half the professorships of Russian law, Russian history, philology and archæology, were either not filled up at all, or filled by lecturers and *adjoints*, appointed as stop-gaps, and only waiting for the first opportunity to accept other employment.

---

[1] This system, which dates from the time of Uvaroff, has since been abolished. [Tr.]

[2] A rule prevails in Russia, that professors and teachers after twenty-five years of service are pensioned off on full salary. The colleagues of these *Emeriti* may be elected twice for a period of five years each time, in which case the person so re-elected is entitled to salary and pension. After thirty-five years' service, the pension becomes irrevocable. This arrangement no doubt is open to abuse, but on the whole it has worked successfully.

This paucity of competent professors was due to a certain extent to the difficulty in Russia of obtaining the degree of Doctor, indispensable for the higher educational posts. No one, except a medical man, can be made a doctor, unless he has first been a 'candidate,' and then a 'magister.' To be a candidate he must have completed his courses at a university, passed a somewhat difficult State examination with a certificate of 'very good,' and composed a learned essay to the approval of the faculty. To be a magister, he must have been a candidate for a whole year, have passed an examination in all the chief subjects embraced by the particular faculty, have written another dissertation, and defended it in public. These proceedings, as expensive as they are tedious, are repeated a third time before the degree of doctor is conferred. Naturally, the number of those who possess both the inclination and the talent for fulfilling these complicated conditions is extremely small. Among the Slav race, whose tendencies are decidedly realistic, idealism and devotion to the cause of learning are far more rare than in other races; and even now, when the requirements for a university appointment are reduced to a reasonable standard, and the salaries considerably improved, the number of Russians who embrace an academical career is still extremely small.

In the days of the Emperor Nicholas, indeed, nothing but an actual fanaticism for the cause of learning would have induced any man to spend either time or money on preparing for a career which stamped the candidate as a suspicious character, which he could only pursue at the price of a life-long subjection to the whims of uneducated officials and the mistrust of a suspicious government; and, which, moreover, brought a very moderate pecuniary gain. Those who filled the chairs of Natural Science had at least the opportunity of doing service to their branch of learning, and of acquiring reputation and honour. But for the historian, the jurist, or the political economist such a prospect was hopeless. If he stooped to conform to the ruling system, he rendered himself useless for scientific knowledge; if he attempted to follow his own bent, he was sure to fall into the snares of the secret police. Hence, as a matter of course, professors of eminence, especially those who had risen under the *régime* of the old liberal statute of 1804, learned to regard the later system with aversion, and in this sense became 'political malcontents;' while their younger successors fell off every year both in numbers and ability. It gradually became more common for professors, out of sheer disgust at their position, to accept inferior posts in the administration, while young men, educated at the expense of the government, were forcibly made to accept professorships assigned to them.[1] Thus the real power fell into the hands of inferior men of routine, who owed their promotion to the favour of Curators and Inspectors. Accordingly, patronage and corruption began to regulate the matriculation and graduation of students; and the more independent among the teachers were daily made to feel the suspicious surveillance not only of the Inspectors, but of servile colleagues who hungered for promotion. The case of the smaller universities was the worst in this respect. Here the influence of the Curator was all-powerful, and academical life dege-

[1] The Excise Administration, instituted of late years, has had a fatal effect upon the universities and other learned establishments. Numbers of young men of education and talent have quitted the academical career to seek employment in this department, so much sought after for its high salaries.

nerated into a system of the most miserable adulation and petty intrigue. Added to these evils, came the constant jealousy and national hatred shown by the Russian professors towards their foreign colleagues, who were treated as interlopers and heretics, though, from the dearth of native learning, their services could not be dispensed with.

Great, however, as was the discontent among the professors and tutors with the system prevailing from 1840 to 1860, and with those who supported it, this discontent was still more deeply implanted in the students. Everything seemed to have been purposely designed to make these young men, the future mainstays of intellectual culture, feel that they were the mere stepchildren of the government and the ruling caste. It was understood that a university student ranked socially beneath an officer, in many cases even beneath the pupils in the Page corps and the schools for young nobles, and he was treated no better than a mere schoolboy. With regard to future service in the State, the pupils of the Lyceum and the Law School enjoyed a double advantage over them. Not only were their examinations notoriously far easier than those at the universities, but they had also the privilege of receiving the titular rank of councillor after the termination of their course of study, and were qualified at once to enter any of the ministries. The student, on the contrary, even after he had gained the degree of 'candidate,' became merely a 'college secretary.' Only after serving for three years in the province could he obtain any ministerial employment; and even then he knew well that any former pupil of the Law School would be preferred before him. The special favour shown to the latter was a publicly accepted fact, the reason being that they were looked upon in high quarters as particularly pliable and, moreover, not open to 'corruption.'

To this neglect of university students as a class were added the most humiliating distinctions made among the students themselves. Those who were poor and educated at the expense of the Crown, either at the universities or the Medico-Chirurgical Academy, were subject to restraints of liberty and measures of control unknown to their more favoured comrades. If they failed to pass the examinations, they ran the risk of being made mere barber-surgeons in the army, or even common soldiers. Rank and property were rewarded in all respects with an indulgence as invidious as unjust. Nothing was more provoking and vexatious than the constant interference of the Inspectors with the social conduct of the students. Bitter experience had amply taught these victims of official tyranny that any derelictions of duty on their part were more severely punished and more harshly judged, in consequence of the emperor's distrust of the universities, than the excesses of young men in other classes.

So intolerable was the rigour of discipline at some of the universities that numbers of young men, fully qualified in other respects to take their place as students, preferred to enter as 'voluntary scholars,' and though exposed to the satire of their comrades, imitated the example of the officials and persons advanced in life, who attended the lectures without being matriculated. These restraints grew doubly unbearable, when compared with other countries. Little as anyone cared in general to know about Western Europe or the difference between Russian and foreign institutions, still at times even the students at Kasan or Charkoff got to hear of the greater freedom and higher social position enjoyed by their brethren at Dorpat and Helsingfors, of the more favourable treatment accorded to French and German students by their governments, and of the advantages of the old Liberal Statute of 1804, compared with the hateful regulations of 1835. The more enlightened and humane of the professors did not conceal their own and the students' opinion that such treatment was unworthy. The government, on the other hand, took good care to let the universities know the reason for these oppressive restrictions, and it was no secret to anyone after 1848 that the emperor had been most reluctant to abandon his intention of closing every university in the empire. All the world knew, moreover, that the limitation of the number of students to 300 at each university had originated with Nicholas, and that Uvaroff, his Minister of Instruction, notoriously a pliant statesman, had resigned because he considered it inconsistent with his honour to agree either to this measure or to the abolition (decreed at the same time) of instruction in the Greek language at most of the gymnasia. It appeared, indeed, as if everyone connected with the universities was intended to be brought up in systematic hatred towards the government, which treated the highest institutions of science and culture as so many necessary evils, and more than once seemed ready to turn into bitter earnest the words put by Griboyedoff into the mouth of the military blusterer Skalosub :—

> Had I my way, I'd shut up all the schools,
> Turn out professors and such learned fools.
> Plague on their teaching ! for their A B C
> I'd have drill-sergeants with their ' One, two, three.'
> Books should be kept to please an idle crew
> On feast-days, when there's nothing else to do !

II.

The state of things above described can hardly be illustrated better by the writer of these pages than by a short account of his own personal impressions, as a student in the University of St. Petersburg in the year when Sebastopol was taken (1855).

The circumstances which induced him to enter the university serve to exemplify the relations then existing, but fortunately now hastening to an end. The University of Dorpat, where lectures were given only in German, was bound to require from candidates for admission an amount of acquaintance with the Russian language, which the writer was not able to muster. At St. Petersburg, on the contrary, where all examinations and lectures were conducted in Russian, the knowledge of that language was a matter of minor importance, and there was no difficulty, with the help of a moderate power of speaking French, in getting through the entrance examination. Philologically, this examination was on a par with that of a third class at an average grammar-school in Germany. As for Greek, the would-be young jurist found it was not wanted; and when the writer insisted on being examined in that language, so impressed was the examiner with his knowledge of the first ten verses of the Odyssey, that he immediately gave him full marks. In Latin it was enough to be able to translate a few sentences from Cæsar or Livy; the candidate could choose which of these writers he pleased. The only things that seemed to be required in real earnest were mathematics and an examination in Russian history. The latter was conducted by M. Usträloff, the State historiographer and panegyrist of the Emperor Nicholas—an old man universally hated for his arrogancy and servility, whose main employment was to see that the candidates showed due respect to him as a Privy-Councillor—the other professors being simply Councillors of State—by standing when they gave their answers. The rector Pletneff, who only showed himself for a moment during the examination, was not honoured with any particular notice either by the teachers or the pupils. All the world knew that this amiable, mild-mannered friend and executor of Pushkin was there simply for decorum's sake, and that all the real power and authority was centred in 'Alexander Ivanovitch,' the State-Councillor von Eckstädt, the all-powerful Inspector of the students, and the declared favourite of the Curator Mussin-Pushkin. This man was a curious character in his way. Totally uneducated, of course, but, despite the roughness that occasionally came to the surface, on the whole good-natured, he owed his influence and the consideration paid to him to the energy with which he had taken discipline in hand, and had inculcated in teachers and students the punctilious observance of form—in other words, the due wearing of the cocked hat and sword, the shaving of beards, and the avoidance of the treasonable 'stand-up' collars with sharp corners, which are said to have been formerly the terror of all loyal subjects. So well recognised was this punctilio, as essential to the prosperity of the 'Alma Mater,' that the worthy 'Alexander Ivanovitch' knew of no better or more suitable expression for announcing to us the happy result of the three days' entrance examination than the classical formula, 'You may order your uniforms' (*Prikashite sebjä formu shitj*).

The company, in which I received this joyful intelligence, was of so motley a composition, that it deserves especial mention. We had repaired, four of us, to the room where 'Alexander Ivanovitch' and his assistants reckoned up the results of the examination. So mechanical was this process, that each examiner simply marked a cipher against the name of each candidate, and the total was then divided, three being the minimum necessary to qualify for admission. My companions were a Georgian prince, tall as a tree, with a high Circassian cap, edged with lamb's wool, a red Armenian coat and a dagger as an ornament, who spoke Russian even worse than his neighbour, a Jew of the Karaim sect, who 'paced with melancholy mien,' in a splendid robe of violet coloured silk, but who had the advantage of being able to speak French with some fluency. Both of these intended to devote themselves to the study of Oriental languages, as did also, according to his own statement, the third of my fellow-candidates, a young man with a German name, who was anxious, as he said, to study Protestant theology in earnest, but had never been able to carry out this intention. He was the son of an Imperial official of the kitchen, and, as such, belonged to a class who had been expressly excluded, by an order of the Emperor Nicholas, from academical studies.[1] At the Protestant Universities of Dorpat and Helsingfors the authorities had been sufficiently pedantic and conscientious to regard this Imperial edict as binding, and accordingly had declined to admit my companion. But on the Neva Tartuffe's maxim, 'Il y a des

---

[1] This prohibition—now, of course, long rescinded—was by no means an isolated one at its time. Attendance at any higher institutions of learning than the so-called district or burgher schools had been forbidden, for example, to the children of serfs by the Ukases of 1827 and 1837 (May 9).

accommodements avec le ciel,' had been practised too long and too effectually to allow this young man to be excluded on account of his father's relations with the emperor. Considering that his two elder brothers were already students, and that ' there was no reason for treating brothers unequally,' my friend found no difficulty in matriculating.

The matriculation this time was surrounded with special solemnities, being combined with the ceremony of inaugurating the newly established faculty for the study of Oriental languages. The new professors were, of course, the chief attraction of the day. Half of them at least were Mohammedans, and had come from the Asiatic frontier—the leading *savants*, however, were the actual State-Councillor Kasem-Bek, a Persian by birth, and Dr. Chwolsohn, a German Jew. The proceedings were opened with the Kyrie-Eleison (*Gospodi pomilui*), chanted by a number of plump ' popes ' and choristers. Next came an oration, beginning and ending with an eulogy of the Czar, and other exalted patrons of the university, and then a prayer for the Imperial family. To complete the ceremony, all persons present, including my three companions and myself, were sprinkled with holy water.

The next day the lectures began. The Inspector had taken care that even we novices should appear in the prescribed uniform, which was to symbolise academical freedom and to efface all distinctions between the subjects of his Imperial Majesty, whether Georgian, Crimean, Russian, or German.

On entering for the first time the long, dark corridor, which served as a waiting-room for the students, I was surprised by seeing two pieces of artillery in position, with some persons, busily occupied around them, who looked like non-commissioned officers. I was asked by one of my comrades, whether I thought of taking part in the 'Marchirovka,' as none but the older students were obliged to do so. On my inquiry what it meant, I was told that the late Emperor Nicholas, of blessed memory, on his last visit to the university shortly after the outbreak of the Crimean War, had shown his satisfaction at the proper conduct of the students by presenting them with two cannons, and had expressed his desire that they should prepare themselves for the possibility of having to defend their native country, by exercises in drill and marching. At first, the popularity of these exercises, conducted by two veterans of the Guards, had been extraordinary; but since the death of Nicholas (March 2, 1855) they had lost much of their interest, and took place only occasionally.

This information, given casually in answer to my query, was the only reference to the Crimean War that I heard at the university during the eight months of my residence at St. Petersburg. It is impossible to conceive a more absolute indifference than that with which the students received the bad news that arrived almost daily from the Crimea. We learned, as if nothing had happened, of our defeat at the Tchernaya on August 16, of the storming of the Malakoff on September 8, and two days later of the occupation of the south side of Sebastopol by the French. Just as if we were living in a time of profound peace, conversation turned solely on the petty gossip of the town, the daily doings of the students, small squabbles with professors or inspectors, the difficulties of examinations, tavern incidents, and such like trivialities. On the very day when the news of the capture of Sebastopol arrived, there were the usual billiard matches going on at Dominique's, with the usual betting on the result; there was the breakfast at Wolf's, and the talk about the public balls—or 'dancing classes,' as they were called—which formed a clandestine resort of the students. If any of them cared to touch on public topics, he would first look round him to see if any listener were near, and then exchange the usual sarcasms and expressions of profound contempt for all the higher powers. Nowhere was the slightest trace to be found of any patriotic sympathy for the disasters of the Russian arms, still less of any indignation against the enemies of their country. A few words would pass perhaps about the incapacity (which seemed to be taken for granted) of 'our' generals and the superiority of the French army organisation over that of Russia; and then the conversation fell back into its wonted groove. So completely had this system of stifling all interest in public affairs succeeded, that even during the most critical days of the empire, Mademoiselle Mila's latest admirer, or Fanny Cerito's best part, or some piquant anecdote of the ignorance of the chief Inspector, or of the brutality of the Curator Mussin-Pushkin towards all *péquins* or civilians, interested these young men far more than the fortunes of their country, for whose service they were supposed to be preparing themselves. Science and learning were topics of conversation as unheard-of as politics; the only sources of knowledge were the prescribed manuals and class-books bequeathed from one generation to another, unless perhaps some forbidden book aroused a passing curiosity or stimulated the ever lively pleasure in tales of scandal about the Court and the higher circles of society. The poorer and more industrious students attended the lectures pretty regularly; the rest were quite content to put in an occasional appearance in the corridor, just to remind the officials that they were members of the university.

Roughly speaking, the students, of whom there were then 399, might be divided into three classes. First, there were the young men of rank, who mostly lived with their parents or relations, and who in the morning were seen at elegant *cafés*, in the evening in the drawing-rooms or the theatre, and frequently would drive up to the university gates in their well-appointed sledges. Next, there were the young men from the provinces and the sons of small officials or tradesmen at St. Petersburg, who never visited any decent society, but passed their days in smoking and drinking at obscure taverns or dancing at low music-halls, and never looked at books or papers till a few weeks before the examinations. Lastly, there were the poor wretches who lived by giving private tuition, and sought by a blameless demeanour and submission to their superiors, to gain the privilege of attending the lectures gratis, or to obtain, if possible, a 'Crown stipend.' There was also a small *coterie* of Germans, who, together with about a dozen pupils of the Medico-Chirurgical Academy, residing outside the barrack for medical students, lived in the obscurity of the Viborg quarter, leading a regular wild student's life. In other words, they would sit on free evenings with closely fastened shutters, drinking and singing German songs; they delighted in parti-coloured caps; they were not above sharing the dissipations of Russo-French students, and were equally well acquainted with the music-halls.

As regards the relations between the professors and the students, anything like social intercourse was rare and exceptional. Relations of a friendly kind were discountenanced by the authorities, and required to be handled with great caution. Among the older teachers there were many men of superior culture and refinement, who had studied at Dorpat or abroad, but being considered liberal, had to be careful in their conduct. The younger tutors, who had been brought up under the ruling system, were for the most part the types of dullness, timidity, and awkwardness.

Whoever wished to find favour with the Curator and establish a reputation did well to parade his severity to the pupils placed under him. The then Curator, one Alexander Ivanovitch, was a man with a wooden leg, and decorated with the Kulm Cross, who in his old age had exchanged a general's uniform for the title of privy-councillor and the blue frock-coat of the Ministry of Instruction. I learned to know him under the following circumstances. One day we happened to be kept longer than usual in the lecture-room, when a terrible noise was heard in the adjoining corridor. Opening the door, we stepped out and saw standing before us an old man, glittering with stars, who was raising his crutch with threatening gestures and thundering out unmeasured abuse upon the students, who were escaping on all sides from his fury. His Excellency had entered unperceived and unannounced, while the young fellows were enjoying the interval between the lectures, in running about, laughing and shouting; and so terribly shocked was he with such levity of conduct, so wholly against the rules, though innocent in itself, that he thought fit to fulminate his displeasure in this manner. Full of fright, the Rector, the chief Inspector with his four assistants, and even the old porter, hastened to the spot, and by dint of their joint efforts succeeded at length in quieting this wrathful Boanerges, promising that a strict investigation should be made. Alexander Ivanovitch made a speech the next day, and, after threatening the culprits for the hundredth time with 'serious measures,' the occurrence, like others before it, was consigned to oblivion; and the usual short imprisonment for the ringleaders was omitted.

My life here as a student was altogether very quiet and retired. I had enough indeed of one *soirée* to which a brother pupil of mine—a good-natured fellow with a French name—had invited me. Of this *soirée* I may mention, that the guests appeared in gala uniform and polished boots, sipped tea and lemonade, exchanged a few sentences in French with the Count, who was master of the house, and returned home, about eleven o'clock, after a pleasant conversation flavoured with cigarettes. Once only did I have a brush with the authorities. This was in the middle of one November, when Lablache appeared for the first time at the opera, and I was anxious to go and hear him. My gala uniform not being ready, and the ordinary dark coat with blue collar and brass buttons being forbidden under pain of punishment, I determined to run the risk of going in civilian costume. No sooner had I taken my seat, when to my surprise I saw one of the inspectors sitting just in front of me. My companion told me that these gentlemen were obliged by the duties of their office to spend every evening of their lives at one or other of the theatres, and to look out for students who were dressed against the rules. His watchful eye at once detected the irregularity of my dress. At the next pause in the acting he ordered me to leave the house immediately, and on the morrow I was sent for by the Curator. It was no use my attempting to explain. 'Next time this happens,' was his reply, 'I will have you arrested.'

So much for what was called academical liberty at St. Petersburg in 1855. And what were the advantages held out to students by the Faculty of Jurisprudence in the first metropolis of the empire? The first course of lectures was confined to a general survey of jurisprudence, to logic, and the history of Russian law, public and private, on which subjects notes were dictated to the students. The professor of logic was a fat Russian ecclesiastic, with a face as red as fire, who read off his notes, as approved by the Holy Directing Synod, who looked upon old Wolf as the central luminary of all philosophy, and who was laughed at, but feared by all his pupils. My neighbour, the Mohammedan Georgian, informed me that '*ce grédin*' used to keep his classes filled by 'plucking' students who failed to attend his lectures. Russian public law was represented by a thin and fair-haired young tutor, M. Andrejevski, who had only just entered upon his office. He showed the correctness of his disposition by wearing the blue regulation waistcoat with metal buttons, besides the blue trousers and frock-coat of the proper cut. He became known afterwards by some excellent treatises on the history of Russian law, and his general good qualities I have no wish to impeach. His inaugural address, however, was comical in the extreme, and I have not forgotten the impressions it left upon me. In a high tenor voice, swelling with pathos, he conjured his hearers to follow him, with unselfish devotion to the cause of knowledge, into the sanctuary of learning, and to tread indefatigably and fearlessly its thorny paths till the wished-for goal, the knowledge of truth, was reached. This exhortation formed the preamble to an analysis of the constitution of the Russian Estates and the relation of Imperial decrees to existing law. By

Part I. of 'Russian Public Law' was understood a compilation of essays on the defects of bureaucratic organisation throughout the world; by Part II. a dissertation on the political 'rights' of the different Estates; and so all-important was this knowledge, that none could hope to gain the maximum of marks unless familiar with the details of business belonging to each particular Ministry of State. As the first course of lectures did not extend to the study of Roman law and its history, the theoretical exposition of law in general was confined to the so-called Encyclopædia of Jurisprudence and the history of Russian Law in particular. This last branch of study, under the able conduct of M. Kalmykoff, inspired a certain amount of interest, especially in those parts which treated of more ancient times. It was a pity only that no attempt was made to connect the ancient law of Russia with the contents of the Ukases embodied in the Code of Nicholas, and that a knowledge of the old 'Pravda Russkaya,' and of the theory of its origin, passed for nothing by the side of the measureless mass of dead lumber which in examinations determined the issue, and engrossed the attention of both teachers and pupils. Several circumstances, independent of the quality of the teachers, contributed to render the Encyclopædia of Jurisprudence useless for the purposes of real knowledge. To touch on the public law of Europe was forbidden, and any explanation of the influence of Roman law was rendered impossible, since its history and very existence were unknown to the students of the first course. These branches of study altogether played a very inferior part. Was it not the boast of the Nationalists, no less than twenty-five years ago, that the soil of Holy Russia had remained free from the contamination of the Corpus Juris and the

Canon Law of all ages, and that for this reason, if for no other, the study of legal antiquity was altogether useless for Russians? Add to this, that three-fourths of all the leading works on history, politics, and law were prohibited, and that the only foreign newspapers and journals admitted by the censorship were the 'Nord,' the 'Kreuzzeitung,' and half-a-dozen other papers of like colour and tendency; that the Russian press, besides the official papers, issued only two so-called 'independent' organs, the 'Northern Bee,' and the proverbially absurd 'Son of the Fatherland'; and an approximate idea will be arrived at of what constituted the learned and intellectual life at the University of St. Petersburg. And yet it was generally acknowledged that the 399 students at that university in 1855 [1] were far better off, and enjoyed a far higher degree of intellectual development, than the 483 at Charkoff, the 340 at Kasan, or the 616 at Kieff, who from their geographical position (there were no railways then to those towns), were not even indirectly influenced by the world of culture, and among whom the number of poor and dependent students was much larger than among their more favoured brethren at the 'aristocratic' (as it was called) *Alma Mater Petropolitana*.

III.

A few years later, and comparatively nothing was left of the state of things we have been describing, or of those who had been its chief promoters. At the first puff of the fresh breeze which, after the first prelimi-

---

[1] In 1848, shortly before the publication of the limitation Ukase already mentioned, the total of students at St. Petersburg had amounted to 731, and that of Kieff to 603.

naries for serf emancipation and the other measures of reform, was wafted over the Sarmatian plains, the old system of education and of university life tumbled down like a house of cards. In the spring of 1858, Kowalevski from Kasan, the most liberal of all Curators, succeeded Noroff as Minister of Instruction. The mere tidings of this change sufficed to sound the knell for Mussin-Pushkin and his friends, to paralyse the dreaded activity of the Curator, to show the door to the popes who had been made professors of philosophy, to restore the suppressed faculties of Civil Law and other forbidden sciences, and to alter all at once and altogether the position of teachers and pupils. Even before the new statute, which Kowalevski had ordered to be elaborated, was prepared or promulgated, the restriction imposed in 1849 on the number of students was cancelled, the academical senates received back the former right of electing their own rector, the regulations as to appearing in uniform were repealed, and limits were put to the Chinese method of examinations. These reforms had now become possible, from the altered policy of the government. The old restrictions on foreign travel were removed. The *Index prohibitorum*, which had swoln under the censorship to a portly folio, was laid aside. The press suddenly showed an exuberant growth, and advocated doctrines of advanced radicalism; and finally Herzen's 'Kolokol' had now become a power in the State, more dreaded than even the political police. All at once the old maxims of authority were reversed; the slighted and neglected student became the 'herald of a better future,' and thus the pet of popular opinion. Young men, whose liberal views were well known, crowded to fill the posts of professors and tutors. The leaders of the academical senate were no longer the veterans of the old *régime*, but those youthful and energetic enthusiasts who openly proclaimed war against all traditional ideas of authority, without anyone venturing a protest. Within a few years the number of students at St. Petersburg, Moscow, and Kieff was nearly doubled,[1] multitudes from the middle and lower classes of society, especially pupils of the ecclesiastical schools, having flocked to these universities.

No doubt these young students were frequently as poor as they were illiterate; but they brought with them very decided opinions upon politics. Hitherto, the display of any active interest in public affairs had been forbidden under penalties at the universities; henceforward no student was considered a 'man' unless he was familiar with all the political problems of the day, and regarded their solution as the chief duty of his position. The formation of student clubs, after the manner of the Germans, was a great point gained by these youths, so suddenly promoted to the full enjoyment of 'freedom of learning.' Political reading societies and newspaper clubs were established; funds were raised for the support of poorer students; and unions for learned and philanthropic purposes were multiplied apace. The 'dancing classes' were deserted for the chess club, the head-quarters of the Radical party; newspaper reading and the discussion of politics were regarded as the most important occupations for the citizens of the future; and inasmuch as all respectable persons vied with each other in the display of liberalism, it was natural enough that these praiseworthy efforts should not only meet with the greatest sympathy

---

[1] In the year 1860 the number of students amounted to 1,278 at St. Petersburg, 1,653 at Moscow, and 1,062 at Kieff.

from the younger professors, but enjoy the support of the public at large. And fiercely did this newly kindled flame burn in the Medico-Chirurgical Academy. This place, so lately despised as a mere veterinary establishment, was now looked up to as the advance guard of the 'new generation,' and became in fact the centre of the Nihilist movement throughout the empire, so well described by Turgenieff. The example set here was imitated with ardour, not only by the higher institutions of learning in the capital, but even by the universities in the provinces, the principal of this Academy, General Miliutin, the Minister of War, being looked upon as the most liberal and popular of the new advisers of the emperor. On all sides, with the sole exception of the two Universities of Dorpat and Helsingfors, formerly so much decried, the self-emancipation of the students from all authority and discipline attracted the notice and admiration of the unreasoning masses, who were incapable of estimating its proper value. Students' *émeutes* became everywhere the fashion; and cadets and pupils at the gymnasia and commercial schools sought to imitate the example set them by their brethren at the universities.

Unfortunately, this liberal excitement reached its climax at the very time when the new University Statute was ready for operation. At Court the party of reaction was still powerful, and they easily succeeded in fixing the whole blame of this confusion and these disturbances upon Kowalevski, the Minister of Instruction. His project, which recommended an imitation of the German University system and the promulgation of a moderately liberal statute, conceived in that spirit, was rejected by the emperor, after being reported against by a special committee. Kowalevski was dismissed from office, and his place supplied by the Admiral Count Putiätin.

The new minister had recently returned from Japan, and was a total stranger to the circumstances and the spirit of the time. As short-sighted as conceited, he attempted to undo by one stroke of the pen all the so-called 'liberal achievements' of the last few years, and to force the students back into their former state of subjection. His mode of proceeding was so brutal and clumsy that in the autumn of 1861 the students of St. Petersburg and Moscow broke out into open revolt. The lecture rooms had to be closed for several months; several of the most popular professors resigned in disgust, and in public lectures to large audiences gave utterance to the doctrines interdicted at the universities. Putiätin had heard from his high Tory friends the praises sung of the English universities and of their connection with the State Church, and he fixed his eyes upon them as a model. With this fancied object, he proposed to deprive the students of their former rights of association, and to withdraw the assistance fund, lately established by the emperor himself. This foolish prohibition in particular excited the utmost indignation. The numerous poor students, deprived of all support but what the bounty of their comrades bestowed, were driven to despair, and the whole of the educated public of St. Petersburg became the allies of the university. Now only could the enormous changes of the last few years be seen to their full extent. Public opinion at the capital declared for the ill-used students in so energetic and enthusiastic a manner, that Count Putiätin and his associates, the odious curator Philippson and the rector Sresnevski, were obliged to yield. A new statute was prepared, in conformity with all the requirements of the time; and the Ministry of Instruction was entrusted to Golownin, the Secretary of State and a well-known Liberal. All doubts as to who had been the victor in this unequal contest were removed when the Governor-General of St. Petersburg, General Ignatieff (the father of the well-known diplomatist), was compelled, through his former compliance with the schemes of Putiätin, to resign his post and give place to Prince Suvaroff, a man generally beloved for his humane disposition, and whose appointment was received with unbounded joy.

The history of this transaction, so fertile in its consequences and so remarkable in its details, has been too often told to be repeated. It is typical of the multitudinous and almost yearly recurring perplexities and confusions, of which the Russian universities, including the newly founded ones at Warsaw and Odessa, have been the theatre down to the present day. An explanation of these is unnecessary; it is simply confirming the old adage about the slave who breaks his chain. The fear that haunted the Russian students of being robbed again of the rights which they had so recently acquired, and of relapsing into the servitude of the old system, coupled with the consciousness of having constantly abused their rights and liberties, has been the source of all the scandalous proceedings of more recent years. Their distrust of the government, though dating back from a former state of things, is fed by the incessant vacillations in the system pursued by the leading statesmen, whose motto is now Liberty and now Strict Subordination—to-day Realism, to-morrow Humanism—who alternately slacken the reins and then suddenly tighten them again. The new statute, ratified by the emperor on the 1st (13th) June, 1863, has made large concessions as regards the self-government of the universities, the freedom of teachers and taught, and the liberty of student life in general. The salaries of the professors are nearly doubled, and the funds for the endowment and support of education are considerably increased. Thirty years ago there would probably have been no end to the pæans on the liberal character of the regulations now in force, and the constant accessions to the ranks of students. As it is, the satisfaction is largely qualified, and for these reasons. The influence of the Curators is still as far-reaching as before, and their practice very unequal and disproportionate. The students' right of forming clubs and meeting together is merely nominal, in so far as they are subject to the university police ; and, lastly, they believe they have no guarantee for the stability of their rights, so laboriously acquired and yet too frequently abused.

The corporate sentiment that exists between professors and students at German universities is entirely unknown by their Russian brethren. The aspirations of the latter go beyond the walls of the *Universitas*, and they demand, in the name of academical freedom, a guarantee for existing privileges, which, in the total absence of State institutions in Russia, guaranteed by a constitution, is simply impossible to concede. The smallest encroachment on what they consider their rights—nay, the merest deviation from usages tacitly permitted, are treated by the Russian students as so many attempts to revive the hateful old system ; and pretensions are advanced in reply, such as in the case of any Russian subject of the present day would be considered illegitimate. At the same time, recent events have clearly shown that the suspicions entertained as to the stability of existing reforms are not unnatural or unfounded. The Medico-Chirurgical Academy at St. Petersburg has been deprived of its liberties by a single stroke of the pen; it has been transformed anew into an 'Internate,' with military discipline, and the number of its members has been reduced to one-third. And why? Just because the students of this institution had ventured to remonstrate against certain new regulations imposed upon the pupils of the Veterinary College at Charkoff. The *esprit de corps* among the thousands of Russian students is strong, and a grievance in one place is sure to elicit a sympathetic response among their colleagues. Between the universities and the other scholastic establishments, some of which lie outside the department of the Ministry of Instruction, there exists a secret bond of union, knit closely together by a common belief among all young Russian students in the solidarity of their interests, which serves as an electric wire to transmit at once to the universities the news of any errors or conflicts either in some other learned institution or some branch of the administration. Some of these institutions are subject to the Ministry of Finance and some to the Ministry of War; but the same Damoclean sword hangs over them all; and hence it is an article of faith with their pupils that they must stand together all for one, and one for all.

The division of the higher scholastic establishments among the different ministries, each conducted on different principles, has been the source of endless mischief and confusion. To repair the consequences of this error, the government seem at present to contemplate subordinating all of them to the Ministry of Instruction, and controlling them all with the same 'energy.' The results anticipated by this measure will not be realised. The movement of the last few years cannot be revoked or ignored, and the former system of tutelage re-established. And yet such is the idea of the latest plans elaborated in the Ministry of Instruction. The evils intended to be checked will only be increased. Of real order and conformity to law the authorities understand as little as the students. The effect of the incessantly recurring disorders on the one hand, and the equally incessant acts of tyranny on the other, has been that hundreds of miserably poor students, who have not completed their studies, are annually thrown upon the world and induced to make a regular trade of displaying their grievances and exciting compassion. These un-classed students, who form a distinct body, the proletariate of intelligence, have for the most part nothing else to do but to urge their former fellow-pupils to commit foolish acts, to hatch petty conspiracies, to keep up a connection with the revolutionary emigrants in Switzerland, and to inoculate the rude proletariate, emancipated women and raw schoolboys, with their own vague and senseless ideas. So classically has Turgenieff depicted this state of things, which a long series of criminal proceedings has recently exposed to public view, that in the trial of the arch-traitor and would-be assassin of the emperor, Solovieff, we recognise at once the truth of his descriptions in the 'Fathers and Sons' and 'New Country.' Three-fourths of the revolutionists with whom this remarkable fanatic was connected were, according to Solovieff's own confession, former students, whom want of means or the pressure of regulations had prevented from finishing their studies. It is, in fact, the poorer classes, such as the clergy and the lower officials, who have furnished for the last twenty years the chief contingent to the total of students. It is vain to attempt to subdue these young men by mere measures of coercion; it has been useless to make the conditions of admission to the universities more severe, or to shut their doors against the pupils of ecclesiastical seminaries. Equally futile has been the endeavour to re-enforce in some educational districts the old rules about the wearing of uniforms, and to reimpose the strict orders about saluting a general, on the pupils of the gymnasia and lycæa and suchlike institutions, which furnish the material for the universities. It is impossible to expect that such puerile and superficial remedies will ever suppress an intellectual movement; nor have the authorities even had the sense to apply their nostrums with consistency or perseverance. As long as the present feeling of insecurity continues, and the students regard themselves as the ill-treated and suspected pariahs of the government, they form a world by themselves, one vast conspiracy against existing order. Solovieff was no isolated specimen of a traitor; his sphere of action extended from St. Petersburg to the provinces south of the Volga; he carried on his intrigues for weeks in the towns and governments of Moscow, Novgorod, Nishni-Novgorod, Vladimir, and Saratoff. Everywhere he met with friends and sympathisers, who not only encouraged but actively assisted him. He had connections at his disposal which secured for him an entrance into the most various circles of society, provided for all his wants, and even procured for him the necessary false passports. He formed and dissolved such connections by the hundred, without ever meeting with a single traitor or ever being troubled by the police. Wherever Solovieff discovered himself as a member of the secret conspiracy, he was at home; for everywhere there are unclassed students who are his born confederates. According to his statement there existed a vast number of 'Radical quarters' at St. Petersburg, where the 'comrades' periodically assembled. At Nishni-Novgorod friends are immediately at hand to nurse their fellow-conspirators who fall ill. On the estate of Voronino the revolutionists go in and out unmolested, and the smithy adjoining this property, which is well known as the trysting-place of revolutionary students, male and female, maintains a regular connection with other workshops of the kind.

It is impossible to see the end of this unsatisfactory state of things, equally dangerous to the Russian State and the universities.. A national proverb, quoted thirty-five years ago by Haxthausen, speaks of having 'left one bank without having landed on the other.' The half-concessions of the government have been as ineffectual as the half measures of repression. The former were regularly abused, the latter were applied only by fits and starts, and then answered by open mutinies which it was impossible to quell. Only in places like the German Dorpat and the Swedish Helsingfors, where a certain degree of liberty and self-government had been preserved without interruption, has the transition from the old to the new period been effected without noise and disturbance. At St. Petersburg, Moscow, Kieff, Charkoff, Kasan, and Odessa matters still look quite as gloomy, if not more so, as they did the day after the collapse of the old system had been announced. No real remedy or redress will be possible until the New Russia has succeeded in establishing such order as will set limits not only to the governed but to the governing, and allay for ever all those apprehensions of the academical *ancien régime* which, coupled with the occasional displays of tyranny by those in power, have been the main causes of all the more recent disturbances at the universities.

Stable arrangements and regulations, guaranteed by law and really respected, are at present wholly wanting, and until these exist, Russia will retain the feeling of not being able to 'endure' academies and academical freedom.

CHAPTER IX.

FEMALE EDUCATION IN RUSSIA.

Private boarding-schools described by Gogol—Superficial requirements at State Institutes—Russian and foreign governesses—Western influences under Catherine II.—Private schools in Wigel's time—Tatjana Passek and her school—Want of religious instruction—Defective education of the middle-classes — Elementary schools — Establishment of female gymnasia—Insufficiency of local efforts—Apathy of the government—Self-emancipating movement—Female medical students—Revolutionary tendencies.

' YOUNG ladies, as is well known, receive a good education in boarding-schools. It is also well known that in Russian boarding-schools for young ladies three things are looked upon as the foundation and pillars of all human virtues: the French language—indispensable to domestic happiness; pianoforte-playing, as an agreeable means of entertainment; and the art of housewifery, by which is meant skill in embroidering purses and other objects wherewith to surprise a fond husband. Our modern period in Russia has been particularly inventive in perfecting this method of education. At one boarding-school the pianoforte studies are first cultivated, then French, and lastly the domestic. At another they begin with the embroidery of purses, then French, and lastly the pianoforte ; and so on, with other variations. There are, in fact, many methods.'

When Gogol made these remarks in his celebrated novel ' Dead Souls,' which was published in 1842, they had still to be taken literally. Up to about twenty years ago the care of the Russian government for female education was confined to a number of institutions intended exclusively for certain members of the higher classes, and accessible only to these on the condition that the parents surrendered to them altogether for several years the education of their daughters. At the seminary of the Smolna convent, as at the Catherine Institute of St. Petersburg, none were received but young girls of noble family, whose fathers had acquired high positions, or distinguished themselves for 'special merit' in either the civil or the military service. The same rule prevailed in the Catherine Institution at Moscow as at its sister establishment for young ladies at Charkoff. The daughters of burghers enjoyed the good fortune of being educated 'at the expense of the Crown,' and under the patronage of Her Majesty the Empress; but only provided they were admitted to the Alexander Institute at Moscow, or the Foundling Hospital (*vospitatelny Dom*) at St. Petersburg. The rest were left practically to themselves, and had either to renounce all higher culture or to take refuge in boarding-schools of the stamp described by Gogol.

The Imperial institutes differed only from these private establishments in their peculiar rules of discipline and the programme of studies. It was a law, laid down by the authorities, that never, not even during the holidays, should the pupils leave the institute which they had entered when little children; that all of them, no matter what their age, should be dressed in an affected childlike costume; and that, on Sundays, they should be paraded two-and-two together past the visitors who assembled to see them. The 'programme' prescribed instruction in every possible and impossible art and science, and took care that the young ladies, on their 'discharge,' being totally estranged from practical life, should be unfit for every useful function within that sphere, and serviceable only as figures in the pretentious *salons*. In this respect, indeed, such a praiseworthy equality was maintained among the pupils, that the young girls marked out for future governesses were scarcely to be distinguished from those whose vocation in life would be that of mere ornaments of society. Both classes developed the same outward *tournure*, imitated from French governesses; both spoke the same French, made the same blunders in spelling, embroidered the same purses, played the same nocturnes of Field and mazurkas of Chopin, and, if they had any voice, sang the same false notes in their performances of Warlanoff's ballads.

The diplomas gained for passing a good examination differed in their degrees of merit, but all of them testified alike that their possessors had obtained a thorough mastery of three languages and as many arts, and were familiar with all the branches of general and natural history. As to the actual amount of knowledge acquired by those young ladies who had gained diploma No. 1, the writer has only conjectures to offer. A lady of his acquaintance, who had been educated at the celebrated Smolna convent, and gained the second degree, repeatedly lamented that she had never had explained to her the difference between a fourth part and a third, and stated that she had taken great pains not to confound Moses with Napoleon. 'Ils ont donc été tous les deux en Egypte,' she added, in all innocence, by way of explanation.

In matters of taste, on the contrary, such as those of the toilet, these *protégées* of Her Majesty displayed the most astonishing talent and knowledge. The ten years spent in a tasteless, grey child's dress, with a high white apron, had been evidently devoted simply to the preparation for this important point. Artificially debarred from real life, and especially from all contact with men, these young girls were no sooner released from the Imperial institute than they flung themselves with all the ardour of novices into the pleasures of society, and made up so quickly and effectively for lost time, that, usually, after a few weeks they could no longer be distinguished from the regular veterans of the *salon*; and those who saw them might well have thought that the intercourse between the institute and the Imperial Court had been of daily occurrence, instead of being limited to two visits in the year from their august patroness.

The large majority of young girls, however, were excluded from these institutions of the State, and, as recently as fifteen years ago, were educated either by governesses at home or at the private boarding-schools already mentioned. The ordinary elementary schools were so inefficiently conducted, and remained so far behind the most modest expectations, that they were quite out of the question for the nobility and middle-class officials, who were left in consequence with nothing but private education to look to. The decrees of January 19, 1812, August 4, 1828, June 12, 1831, and July 1, 1834, had prescribed special examinations and tests as to the conduct and attainments of men and women who wished to devote themselves to private education; but as the demand for teachers was greater than the supply, these regulations were not always adhered to. Of the governesses who had passed these tests, the Russian ones had usually received their education at an institution of the State; the Germans were either from the Baltic provinces or the daughters of German families at St. Petersburg, or else had come from the north of Germany; the Swiss and French were generally in most request, since a correct pronunciation of their native idiom took the place of all other qualities desirable in a governess for young people. Ex-*danseuses* and actresses were also very popular, such persons being generally more useful in regard to *tournure*, conversational qualities, and *esprit de conduite* than the pedantic Germans or the dull Swiss from the Pays-de-Vaud or Neufchâtel. For a time also English governesses became the fashion.[1] In the houses of grandees all three nationalities were frequently represented. A nobleman in the provinces was glad if he only succeeded in obtaining any governess who could speak French; and, beyond this, would not trouble himself as to other acquirements. Pushkin's words—

> We all learned something every day,
> But where or how I cannot say—

were more generally applicable, under the old *régime*, to women than to men. Hence the miseries of governess-hunting play a stereotyped and constantly recurring part in the leading novels and comedies of Russian literature. The insuperable difficulties of intercommunication, and the want of culture in the parents, rendered a choice of able and conscientious governesses next to impossible. The Carolina Ivanovna of Potjechin's play *Otresanni lamot*, and the ex-*danseuse* elevated into a governess in Turgenieff's tale 'Rudin,' who starts

---

[1] During the twenty years that followed the war of 1812 the education of children, both male and female, of the Russian nobility was mostly in the hands of French prisoners of war, whose services were keenly sought for in the various governments of the interior.

up at the mention of the word 'amour,' and pricks her ears 'like a war-horse at the sound of the trumpet,' are types of the class of governesses of former days, which has only given place to a different kind within the last twenty or thirty years.

But before speaking of the Russian governess of to-day, we must once more refer to the private boarding-schools, which played a prominent part in Old Russia, both from their large number and the difficulty of access to foreign institutions of learning. The Old Russian national tradition which, after the Eastern fashion, shut out women from all society, and consequently from all culture, was first broken through by Peter the Great. Now and then a specially enlightened Boyár had his daughters instructed by some pope or other servant of the Church, in the rudiments of knowledge; but, as a rule, girls learned nothing. When the despotism of the Iron Czar broke through this custom, enforced under penalties the attendance of the wives of nobles and officials at Court and State festivals, introduced dancing as a social amusement, and insisted that both sexes should have a share of West-European culture, it was a natural consequence that foreigners should become the medium of imparting European civilisation to Russian ladies. The above-mentioned State institutes were first founded under Catherine II. Until then there were no other educational establishments for the daughters of the nobility except private ones, which, out of regard to the wants of the nobles who lived in the country, were mostly boarding-schools, established first in St. Petersburg and Moscow, and only gradually extended to provincial towns. Those of greatest repute were in the hands of French men and women, who, however, made use of their profession of teaching simply as a preparation for a more enlarged career, or as a means of gaining a livelihood. The best of twenty other boarding-schools of its kind, which existed at Moscow at the end of the last century, was that of Monsieur and Madame Forceville, which Philip Wigel has described in his Memoirs, so invaluable for the history of social life in Russia. This establishment consisted of two parts, one for boys and the other for girls, managed jointly by this married couple. Madame looked after the bodily welfare of her pupils; that is to say, she let cleanliness take care of itself. Monsieur was an itinerant turner, whose study contained neither books, pens, nor ink, who spoke French very incorrectly, and sported Anglomania on the strength of having spent the greater part of his life in England, though he was quite unable to teach English, or, indeed, any other language. 'What was learnt at this establishment, except, perhaps, dancing,' says Wigel, 'I cannot say. The masters came and went, and seemed to think solely of shortening their lesson-hours as much as possible. Our so-called foreign boarding-schools at that time were worse than the elementary schools, and differed from these only in the language used as the medium of instruction.' Twenty years later Tatjana Passek, a cousin of Alexander Herzen, was forced by the embarrassment of her father's circumstances to set up, in concert with her stepmother, an 'institute' for girls in a provincial town. Without any special preparation for the work, this lady—clever, but devoid of any regular education, from having grown up in high circles—gave instruction in history, geography, French, and music. 'I did as my stepmother did,' she herself states in her Memoirs. 'I told the girls stories from ancient history, adding moral applications to practical life. I described the personages, events, and places of Greece and Italy as well as I could, and tried to make up for my defects of knowledge by a warm and lively imagination. I even undertook to explain critically the various philosophical systems of antiquity, though I neither knew nor understood them. As a handbook for the history and geography of ancient Greece I used the "Travels of Young Anacharsis," which I had accidentally come across, an historical novel published in 1788, by J. J. Barthélemy, a French antiquarian. My teaching was wanting, of course, in any sort of order, system, and coherence. All was jumbled together pell-mell; and the vividness of my exposition had to compensate for all deficiencies in other respects. When we came to the history of Sparta our enthusiasm for the young Lacedæmonians grew to such a pitch that we attempted to imitate their hardened mode of life, washed in cold water, walked with bare feet, gave up taking tea, and broke ourselves of the habit of crying. When I look back on those days, I wonder that my pupils kept their health with all these fantastic efforts to educate them. I had also to teach pianoforte-playing, drawing, and dancing; and I invented ballets and comedies, which we performed, to the great amusement of the young girls and myself.' The lady to whom we are indebted for this frank confession tells us further of some friends of her youth, who were also her companions during her time of teaching (1827–1829), that, from sheer weariness of the barren and empty existence of the *salons*, they took refuge in aspirations for emancipation, which they showed by wearing men's clothes, practising horsemanship, going clandestinely to public inns, and drinking champagne.

Ladies, however, who indulged in such eccentricities

were in former days as exceptional as those who, after the manner of Madame Passek, sought to compensate for their want of knowledge and method in teaching by fantastic zeal. As a general rule, the teachers in girls' boarding-schools were as apathetic as they were ignorant, and the education of their pupils was limited to teaching drawing-room gossip in French, and the other liberal arts enumerated by Gogol. These were the articles chiefly in request with a public composed of the provincial nobility and the families of civil and military officers, and the supply was equal to the demand. The utmost ever done by certificated tutors and governesses was to cram their pupils with a certain amount of dead knowledge, and to impart a culture on a par with that given to boys at the ill-reputed cadet schools of Moscow and St. Petersburg. Religious instruction, which in other countries forms the groundwork of all female education, played here a pitiful part. As is well known, the higher, and sometimes really educated, clergy of the Greek Orthodox Church, are all of them monks, and, as such, systematically shut out from all contact with laymen. The cure of souls, and the instruction of the young, are almost exclusively in the hands of the 'white clergy,' as they are called—in other words, of the poor, uneducated, and despised popes. To infuse anything like life into the senseless lumber of set formulas of Greek ecclesiasticism, or to make them at all fertile in moral influence, is in itself a sufficiently arduous task at any time; but it was impossible, and will always remain so, as long as those appointed to the work live and die in ignorance, poverty, and servile obedience to their 'black,' or monastic brethren, and occupy a social position which shuts them out from the ruling and educated class. Moreover, there exists between the Eastern Church and the Western civilisation of the upper classes of Russian society a deep chasm which cannot be bridged over. The language, the science and culture, and the mode of thought of Western Europe are regarded with horror to this day by that very portion of the Russian clergy who are inspired with religious earnestness and zeal. The clergy and the educated laity live in totally different worlds. A pope who attempted to influence the character and disposition of the children of his upper-class parishioner would meet with difficulties impossible to surmount. In the first place, the pupils never see the face of their teacher except in lesson-hours. It is very rarely that a priest even crosses the threshold of an educated family, and, should anything happen to take him there, he has usually to wait in the ante-room. Thus the education of a young girl had no ideal impulse whatever. The sole aim of everything being to train her for the world of hollow appearances and external successes, all serious thought and inward life were scorned as mere pedantry, and her mission was made to consist in the mere ornamentation of existence. 'We educate our daughters,' says Griboyedoff, in his classical comedy 'Sorrow Comes from Sense,' 'as if they were intended to be the wives of the dancing-masters and buffoons to whom we entrust their education.'

The middle-classes were not slow to imitate in this, as they did in other spheres of life, the example of the denationalised higher stratum of society. The private boarding-schools were bad copies of the Imperial institutes at St. Petersburg and Moscow, just as the drawing-rooms of the provincial nobility and bureaucracy were a reflex of the fashionable *salons* on the Neva Avenue at St. Petersburg and the Smiths' Bridge at Moscow. Nowhere has the mania to be fashionable and to ape the outward manners of the higher classes been so morbidly developed as among the middle classes of provincial society in Russia. The same subservience to the forms of fashion which, as Alexander Herzen has remarked, 'gives to the dandies of St. Petersburg, who are dressed in strictly symmetrical equality, the appearance of policemen in disguise,' is found distorted into a caricature in the provinces, and counts as one of the chief sources of the moral and domestic ruin of the bureaucracy.

With the latter ended the middle-class, and that social stratum which could pretend to the appearance of a certain education. The burgher class—that is, the merchants and artisans—had to be satisfied with elementary schools, which only professed to teach reading, writing, and the four rules of arithmetic. Of these schools the larger towns alone furnished an adequate supply. In many places there were none at all, and such as existed were almost entirely ignored by the government. Since a considerable portion of this class were serfs, whose children, therefore, were expressly excluded from the higher institutions of learning by the Ukases of 1827 and May 9, 1837, it was impossible, from the nature of the case, to raise these urban national schools to any higher level.

It was self-evident that such a state of things could not survive the system which had produced it. The miserable condition of female education was so notorious, so indisputable, and had been already, in the days of the Crimean War, a fact so universally lamented, that Noroff, the then Minister of Instruction, was forced to confess it, in his report of 1856, to the emperor, and to ask for an entirely new organisation. The scheme prepared for this purpose was ready in May,

1858, but could not be properly carried into effect, as the Ministry of Finance declared themselves unable to assign the necessary funds. The State therefore turned to the communes, the provincial Estates, and private persons, who, in accordance with a statute ratified by the emperor (it was altered again on May 10, 1860), were authorised to establish higher and lower 'female gymnasia,' after the pattern of similar schools in Germany, each of which, when established, should enjoy the patronage of the Empress. The matter, however, progressed very slowly, the government giving a very lukewarm support, and the communes and provincial diets being already burdened with too many other obligations to be able to raise larger sums. Newspapers and periodicals did all, and more than, they could, by discussing 'the woman's question' and the problem 'How to educate our girls,' and advancing the newest and most daring theories on this subject and its 'connection with our general development.' But, in spite of all this, the number of newly-established schools remained small. At the end of 1872 there were in Russia and Poland 55 female gymnasia and 131 lower gymnasia, with a total of about 25,000 female pupils. Since then no later statistics have been published; but the regulations and directions have become all the more prolix and detailed. They extend to the smallest minutiæ of management; who is to act as curator, and who as honorary curator of each school; who is to nominate and appoint the heads and teachers of the different classes; what functions are to be performed by the conference of curators, composed of representatives of the State Institutes, and what by the 'pædagogic conference,' conducted either by the Director of Schools in the province, or the inspector of the 'circle.' The programme of studies prescribed for the gymnasia includes, besides the usual curriculum, 'arithmetic in relation to book-keeping,' natural science and physics, 'with particular regard to housekeeping and domestic economy.' Instruction in foreign languages (French and German), and in the arts (drawing, dancing, and music), is to be facultative. In short, there is as little lack of directions and regulations as there is of praiseworthy intentions, grand conceptions, and pædagogic theories brought together from all the countries on the earth. Schools alone are wanting, and always will be wanting, as long as Russian society, accustomed as it is to State tutelage, and incapable of any independent initiative, has to depend on its own unassisted efforts, and as long as four-fifths of the income of the State are swallowed up by the army and the interest on the national debt. As regards female teachers, some provision has been made by the establishment of a pædagogic institute at St. Petersburg, where a certain number of young women who have received certificates on leaving the female gymnasia are perfected for the profession of teachers by a two years' course of instruction. But institutions of this kind are still wanting in provincial towns. It is a significant fact that the government has made the greatest sacrifices to establish these female gymnasia exactly where, from the existence of other schools—of course, non-Russian—they are least required, as in Poland and the Baltic provinces, where schools of every kind abound. Whilst in many of the large cities of the empire there are no other but elementary schools for girls, the State expends on the Russian female gymnasia of the Warsaw educational district no less than 14,000 roubles, the largest grant that is given anywhere.

The small interest taken by the State in the higher education of women is one of those things most loudly and most frequently complained of in Russia. It is asserted, and not without reason, that the apathy of the government in this respect arises from other than mere financial motives. The ardour with which young Russian females hastened to the newly-opened sources of education, and the peculiar direction their enthusiasm took, have served rather to deter than to encourage the powers in authority. The heyday of the establishment of female gymnasia was from 1861 to 1866, during the administration of the ultra-liberal Minister of Instruction, Golownin, who, as an enemy of classicism, used his utmost efforts to favour the 'real'[1] schools, and made natural science the chief subject of instruction in the 'real' gymnasia for men. This example was imitated with passionate zeal in the girls' schools at St. Petersburg and Moscow, as well as in the provincial towns. Flattered by an admiring public and by the praises of a press intoxicated with the new ideas of liberalism and emancipation, the young girls of the middle-classes—the daughters, that is to say, of the lesser nobles and officials—flocked in crowds to the newly opened female gymnasia, and, these not sufficing, to the courses for instruction in natural science, which were conducted by learned *dilettanti* of all kinds in the capitals and university towns. With the same one-sided fervour with which they had formerly paid homage to drawing-room display and the vanities of fashion, and had derided any serious occupation as incompatible with pretensions to *bon ton*, they now

---

[1] The *Realschulen* of Germany, the prototypes of these schools in Russia, derive their name from the practical nature of the knowledge there imparted. (TR.)

flung themselves upon the studies and interests of men. Numberless young ladies, who had been accustomed to wile away their days with the busy idleness of society life, and to carry on professionally, as it were, the custom of lounging about in the houses of wealthy relations, and especially childless widows, were suddenly inspired with the idea of becoming 'useful members' of the nation, and of imitating men in work, activity, and education. The very opposite of all that had hitherto been the tradition and the rule now came suddenly into vogue; and as none could deny that idleness, the mania for dress, and intellectual vacuity among the women of the educated classes had been the canker of social life in Russia under the old *régime*, the younger generation deemed themselves released from any consideration for the usages and manners of their mothers, and prided themselves on reversing every precept they had learned. The endeavour, praiseworthy enough in itself, to give a greater purport and dignity to life, became distorted, under the influence of the crassly realistic and democratic tendencies which were dominant in the middle and higher educational institutions for men, into a caricature, at first only ridiculous and out of taste, but subsequently full of danger. A species of radicalism became fashionable among these female enthusiasts for knowledge, which soon outstripped that of the men both in cynicism and determination. The reaction, as usual, proceeded to extremes. Because in the boarding-schools on the old principle the French language, music, dancing, and 'embroidering purses' had excluded all occupation of a more serious kind, it was now to be held a disgrace to have anything whatever to do with art and female work. Because luxury in dress and the worship of fashion had formerly been carried to a mania, the 'young women of the period' ostentatiously exhibited their contempt for ornament or beauty. They took to wearing tight jackets, after men's fashion, cut their hair short, and put on spectacles. Instead of the aristocratically coquettish *tournure*, which the village beauties and the daughters of officials had tortured themselves in former days to imitate, a cynical demeanour was now cultivated, which systematically disregarded the differences of sex, and looked upon a close acquaintance with the mysteries of anatomy and embryology as a matter of course, quite as much as smoking cigars and going to taverns. As was to be expected under the circumstances, it was just the most able, energetic, and mentally gifted young women who embraced this new tendency with the most determination; but this only served to make matters worse and more dangerous. It is no exaggeration to say that the great majority of female students in modern Russia are distinguished by their industry, talent, and willingness to make any sacrifice, and enter upon the pursuit of knowledge with far greater earnestness than the young men. For this very reason the self-emancipated demeanour of female students, which excludes, as it affects to despise, all true feminineness of character, grows more and more fashionable every day. The large mass of the nation, of course, remain true to their better principles, and anxious fathers and mothers regard these extravagances with abhorrence. Those, indeed, who are content to cultivate the cheap arts which constitute the traditional stock-in-trade of the young Russian lady, sink as before into superficiality and a state of semi-culture; but those of stronger minds and more enthusiastic temperaments despise such modest pretensions: their privilege is to disregard the restraints of custom, and to take the more difficult and, since the revolution of 1866, more dangerous road of the emancipated. To imitate these becomes gradually the rule among young women who possess neither fortune nor personal charms, or who welcome any pretext to escape from the irksomeness of parental discipline.

The rapidity with which this movement of emancipation has developed itself is an irrefragable proof of its popularity. Exuberant as is its present growth, its beginning dates only from about 1860. In 1864 the first Russian ladies were inscribed in the medical faculty of the University of Zürich. In 1868, for the first time, a woman, who had completed her studies in midwifery, obtained permission to attend the lectures of the Medico-Chirurgical Faculty at St. Petersburg. The incident created so much sensation, and was received so favourably by the leaders of public opinion, that other ladies soon followed suit, and seven years later the female medical students at Zürich could be counted by dozens, and at St. Petersburg by hundreds. In 1872 special courses for married and unmarried women were opened at the Medico-Chirurgical Academy at St. Petersburg, and more than 500 females attended them. In 1873 there were no less than 77 Russian ladies studying medicine at Zürich. Although the right of practising has not yet been conceded to female physicians, there are now at St. Petersburg several hundreds of female students; and the example thus set by the capital has been copied at the Universities of Moscow, Kieff, Charkoff, and Odessa. A professor or tutor who wishes to become popular has no surer or more comfortable way to gain his object than by instituting a 'course' for females. Special lectures are held and special regulations made for female students. A certificate on their leaving a female gymnasium is the usual condition of their admission. The lectures on anatomy, physiology, and obstetrics are the most numerously frequented, owing to the prospect thus offered of being qualified to act as midwives, and obtaining in this capacity a certain amount of practice among ladies.

That the government will ere long resolve to admit these female medical students to the learned degrees, and allow them the full rights of practitioners, is recognised as inevitable even by the opponents of these emancipatory efforts. The government, in fact, has already gone too far to recede. An inclination to retract is of course not wanting in the circles of authority, the female sex having furnished a frightfully large contingent to the Nihilist and revolutionary societies which so disquiet the government, and the female students having surpassed their male comrades in courage, passionateness, and readiness for making any sacrifice. The mad crowd who made the disturbance before the Kasan Cathedral at St. Petersburg were headed by two Jewess students; General Trephof fell by the hand of a woman; a girl of nineteen shot the 'traitor' Rosenzweig; another girl stood in the front ranks of the rebellious students at Kieff; the female members of secret societies accused of high treason, and arrested and sent to Siberia, within the last few years, amount to many hundreds, and belong to various classes of society. Next to the official noblesse, the female relatives of the Greek clergy have supplied most recruits to the party of discontent, a circumstance which is explained, on the one hand, by the ramification of revolutionary intrigues in the (male) ecclesiastical seminaries and academies,[1] and, on the other, by the old-fashioned idleness, coarseness, and want of education so conspicuously rampant among the lower clergy and servants of the Church.

That it would come to this—that those women who aspired or were compelled to get beyond the deadness and narrowness of the old relations would fall a prey to the dangers of revolutionary demoralisation, unless they were granted some scope and a fitting occupation for their energies—was predicted plainly enough by Schédo-Ferrati ten years ago. In his last work the lamented author of the 'Etudes sur l'avenir de la Russie' proposed to entrust to women the education of the illiterate peasants' children, at least during the period of childhood, and to take the first step towards remedying the want of popular teachers, so much complained of, by establishing large seminaries for that purpose, special reference being had to the daughters of village priests, church singers, and church servants. Had not the originator of this proposal been the author of the pamphlet 'Que fera-t-on de la Pologne?' proscribed by the National party of Moscow, it would perhaps have been considered worthy of attention; as it was, it fell stillborn, and the number of the 'emancipated'—able enough in themselves, but perverted by false doctrines into hostility to the existing order of society—has gone on gradually increasing.

The correctness of the picture we have drawn cannot be verified better than by referring to the verdict passed by the most eminent Russians of our time on the present

---

[1] On account of the prevalence of revolutionary tendencies in ecclesiastical schools, their pupils have recently (April 1879) been deprived of their right to enter a university.

education of the daughters of their country. The truth and subtlety of the pictures drawn by Ivan Turgenieff of the social condition of his native land have become proverbial both in and out of Russia. His 'New Country,' 'Fathers and Sons,' and 'Smoke'—the three foremost creations of this incomparably refined and profound delineator of social life—testify on every page that, in point of education, the mass of Russian girls and women of the present day are still on the level of former times, and that it is mainly their disgust at the low condition they have inherited that drives the more able and energetic natures among them to espouse the criminal follies of the revolutionary sects. Turgenieff has been for years systematically persecuted and slandered by the Russian Radicals as the 'calumniator of the young generation,' whilst the champions of existing order have reproached him with representing, in his 'New Country,' the energetic and devoted Maschurina, the serious and active Marianne, and the other female types of the young emancipated generation, as more dignified and attractive characters than the elegant Irina, the beautiful wife of the privy councillor Sipjägin, and the average Russian ladies who had remained 'feminine.'

That these two types of women, however, are essentially those which the present Russian system of education has produced has not been disputed on any side, and has been confirmed of late by a remarkable testimony, classical in its way. Fresh from the impressions created by the late attempt on the emperor, a patriotic Old Russian writes to the ultra-national and conservative 'Moscow Gazette' (Turgenieff, as is well known, is considered 'Western,' and infected with Liberal opinions) in the following terms:—

What are we to say, moreover, of the education of our children? The intelligent Russian educates his sons and daughters in the spirit of the West. The child babbles from its earliest youth French, German, and English verses; but it does not know the Lord's Prayer. The lowest classes of the people have no notion how their children are guided, and in the village schools the teaching is left to Materialists. Our family life threatens to disappear altogether. The children need only pass into a higher class at their school to look down upon and laugh at their fathers as antiquated. Young maidens of sixteen and seventeen seek for independent work, and become absorbed in the mysteries of natural science. Subjects which in former times could not be demonstrated in the presence of a young girl, the modern maiden analyses in detail, and with a skill such as a man of science does not always possess. But to the work her Creator has assigned her she is a stranger. What she wants is to enjoy equal rights with men, without being able to explain to herself what those rights in reality consist of.

CHAPTER X.

JURI SAMARIN AND THE BALTIC PROVINCES.

The Moscow Slavophils under Nicholas—Samarin appointed to Chanykoff's Commission in Livonia—Suppression of municipal rights—Russification of the Baltic provinces under Golowin—Conciliation policy of his successor Suworoff—Samarin's anti-German tendencies—His interview with Nicholas—Refuses service in the State—His literary labours—His pamphlet on the 'Russian Frontiers'—His advocacy of national democracy—His influence with the government—Causes of his success—Vices of bureaucratic legislation in Russia—Death and character of Samarin.

WHEN the Moscow Slavophils, now forty years ago, first entered the public arena, they figured as a party of opposition. In the system of the Emperor Nicholas there seemed to be no place left for politicians who rejected the bureaucracy of that time, organised after the German pattern, and served in great part by officials and generals of German origin, and who, in their disgust with the nobility and the higher classes in general for their alleged desertion of national traditions, fixed their hopes on the 'pure and uncontaminated peasantry,' and demanded the abolition of serfdom. Men like Aksakoff, Kirejewski, Chomjäkoff, and others, of independent mind, and imbued with a genuine love of liberty, were not to be deceived by the *quasi*-National professors of the old *régime*. They declared, indeed, their assent, when the emperor designated the supremacy of the Greek Orthodox Church and the Russian language, and the expulsion of the Turks from the ancient Byzantium, as the respective objects of his home and foreign policy. But the means employed for the attainment of these ends were as distasteful to them, as to their rivals the 'European Liberals,' with whom at first they were on so friendly a footing, that Alexander Herzen used to call the Slavophils '*nos amis les ennemis.*' The government allowed these young enthusiasts to go on within certain limits, but regarded them in general with suspicion.

The first Slavophil leader who attempted to profit by this partial concurrence of the government with the principles of his party, and to prove that on certain questions it was possible, even under existing circumstances, to bring about a union of all national-minded Russians, was Juri Samarin. He was a wealthy landed proprietor, and of noble parentage. During his years of study at Moscow he had distinguished himself by his zeal for the Greek Orthodox Church, and had published a number of treatises on ecclesiastical history and theology *in majorem gloriam* of Eastern orthodoxy (*Prawoslawije*). After that he entered the civil service, and about the year 1840 went as an official of the Ministry of the Interior to Livonia, to assist the extraordinary Commission, conducted by the Councillor of State, Chanykoff. The duties of this Commission were to study the system of municipal government in the Livonian towns, to remove certain abuses of administration, and to elaborate proposals of reform with a view to stricter centralisation and the more immediate dependence of the corporations of estates on the bureaucracy. And in executing this task Chanykoff and his companions were not idle. When in 1844 they 'advanced before Riga' (this expression of the Minister of Domains, Count Kisseleff, aptly designates the aggressive character of Chanykoff's reforms), the town and the surrounding country offered such numerous points of attack, that the possibility seemed to present itself of overthrowing the entire system of German polity and replacing it by one of Russian bureaucratic ordinances. Under the domination of a patriciate grown lazy, and hindered by government tutelage from gradually readapting their condition to the progress of events, abuses had arisen in municipal administration, and obsolete institutions of the middle ages had taken root, which long since, indeed, required some remedial treatment, but which, in spite of all their defects, represented an incomparably higher state of civilisation, when contrasted with the inveterate misgovernment and lifelessness of Russian towns. Unhappily the duty of remedying these defects had been entrusted to men altogether unfitted for the task. Incapable of understanding even dimly the value and meaning of civic self-government and of a compact municipal organisation; unable also to distinguish between the essence of corporate institutions and their clumsy and partly rotten exterior, these officials of Chanykoff's Commission conceived an aversion against the solemn and self-conscious burgherdom of the Livonian towns, which years of constant friction converted into fierce hatred. Accustomed to concede the ordinary rights of mankind to none but persons of noble origin, and to treat all common citizens as serfs, the imperious satellites of the Ministry at St. Petersburg interpreted the resoluteness and independent spirit of the patrician town councillors and aldermen of the former Hanseatic town as symptoms of a disposition hostile, nay revolutionary, to the State. When at length they learned that there were Russians living at Riga, albeit mostly of the lowest grade of civilisation, and located in a distant suburb, who were excluded from any share in municipal government, and that a local legislature—comparatively well organised, by the way—placed insurmountable legal difficulties in the way of applying Russian principles of administration, the indignation of Chanykoff and his companions knew no bounds, and they revenged themselves by resorting to a system of spies and informers, as unworthy as it was tyrannous. One of the Commissioners, Count Stackelberg, fancying he could magnify some financial errors into a charge of fraud, placed himself in the hands of a set of ill-conditioned rogues, who were supposed to assist him to discover the offence, but who ended by fleecing and betraying him. An open ally of these Commissioners was the Greek Archbishop of Riga and Mitau, who had long been waiting for an opportunity of venting his hatred against the National Lutheran Church, whose ascendency was acknowledged in the Baltic provinces, and which was richly endowed on the basis of Old Swedish regulations. His object was to substitute for this the supremacy of the State Church of Russia. The wished-for opportunity, it seemed, had come, when shortly after 1840 disturbances broke out among the Livonian peasantry, the suppression of which entailed a remodelling of agrarian legislation; and again a little later, in the spring of 1845, when General Golowin, a declared enemy of all that was German, was appointed Governor-General of Livonia, Esthonia, and Courland. Under the sheltering ægis of this dignitary, the Greek clergy sought, by the promise of worldly advantages, to incite the peasants against their landlords, and to induce them to go over to the Russian State Church; while at the same time a fierce attack was made against the continuance of the municipal constitution of Riga and the University of Dorpat. It was hoped, by gratifying the avarice of the lower classes, and vexing with official interference the corporations of the Estates, to annihilate the entire social and political fabric in Livonia, and to establish a Russian administrative bureaucracy upon its ruins. Every germ of provincial independence was to be crushed in honour of Nicholas' system of uniformity.

Favoured, at first, by successes of every kind, the half-democratic, half-absolutist Russianizers, whom Golowin, Chanykoff, and von Stackelberg had assembled around them, met with difficulties, as they proceeded, which they were unable to surmount. Discontent and confusion reached such a pitch that the complaints of the German element in Livonia, whose very existence was imperilled, made their way to St. Petersburg; and Nicholas himself, who had hitherto favoured the policy of Golowin, regarded at the beginning of 1848 a change of system as unavoidable. The further extension of the Church propaganda was prohibited; General Golowin was somewhat unceremoniously recalled after more than two years of service; and Prince Alexander Suworoff, an officer of distinction, who had risen under the humane and enlightened traditions of Alexander I., was appointed Governor-General in his stead, and charged to carry out a policy of 'conciliation.' One of Suworoff's first measures was to release Chanykoff's Commission from their labours, and to 'pigeon-hole' their scheme of municipal reconstitution at Riga with the endorsement that 'it had been elaborated by officials who were totally ignorant of the circumstances of the case, and was therefore altogether unsuitable.'

Whilst the superior members of this Commission submitted, like genuine bureaucrats, in silence, M. Juri Samarin, as a courageous democrat and Slavophil, endeavoured to enforce, in its entirety, the system already partially carried out by his colleagues, and to appeal to Russian public opinion over the head of the 'misguided' government. On his departure from Riga, he wrote and secretly circulated a number of polemical letters, denouncing the institutions of the Baltic provinces as a mass of feudal rubbish, and systematically hostile to the Russian State, Church, and people; reproaching the government for tolerating this German *status in statu*; and demanding a total change in the sense of universal submission to the one national law, the one national Church and language. These letters soon circulated throughout Russia in hundreds of copies, and even penetrated to Court circles. But Nicholas, notwithstanding his love for equality without distinction among all his subjects, was not the man to allow young 'titular Councillors' (Samarin was then vested with this title) to make intellectual politics for themselves. The self-constituted letter-writer—who had, moreover, behaved in a somewhat improper manner towards his chief, Prince Suworoff—was arrested and imprisoned for some days in the fortress. The Czar then summoned him to his presence, and restored him to liberty after a personal interview. Samarin's 'National' fervour seems to have been not altogether unpalatable to the monarch, who never understood a joke; for Nicholas showed himself so peculiarly gracious to him, that, twenty-five years afterwards, Samarin declared his life-long gratitude for this opportunity of a personal acquaintance with the dreaded ruler. 'I enjoyed the privilege,' he writes, 'of seeing the late emperor face to face, of hearing his true-hearted conversation, and of engraving on my memory the image of his historical features, which unexpectedly and only for a short space revealed themselves to my gaze in the stern and noble simplicity of his fascinating grandeur.'

After this edifying interview with the Imperial representative of the old system, Samarin retired for some time to his estates in the province of Moscow. In spite of the painful experiences he had had with the government, and in spite of the predilection of his party for the peasantry, who had ' remained pure,' he seems not to have been able to bear the quiet of a country life for long. At the time of the Crimean War we find him in the Chancellery of the Governor-General of Kieff, the dreaded General Bibikoff, zealously busied again with his ' National mission-work.' This time it was a work not of conquering Germans and Protestants, but of achieving a ' moral ' victory over Little-Russians, Poles, and Catholics, and making them fit into the framework of the ' National State.' But the days of the Crimean War were so little favourable to enterprises of this kind, that Samarin soon turned to another and more fruitful vocation. Rightly anticipating that the government could not avoid, after the restoration of peace, taking in hand a total reform of the condition of the peasants, he began to turn his attention to the agrarian relations of Little Russia, and to publish some highly useful works on the best method of remodelling them. So effective were his labours, that he was summoned about 1859 to assist the preliminary committee of the Grand Commission entrusted with the reorganisation of the agrarian system in Russia, and thereby had an opportunity of giving practical expression to his views in favour of the peasantry. Direct service in the State, however, he could not be induced to accept, perhaps because the general current of the times appeared to be far more favourable to the exercise of literary activity, than to adapting himself to the requirements of a bureaucratic system, the principles of which he only acquiesced in with reservations.

The establishment in 1861 of a special organ of his party, the weekly paper 'Dyen' ('The Day'), under the editorship of Ivan Aksakoff, afforded Samarin so wide a field for his literary ambition, that he resolved to adhere to private life. To this resolution he remained true when, in 1864, a considerable number of his old friends accepted the invitation of Miliutin, the reorganiser of the Polish peasantry, and took part with him in his campaign of Polish and Catholic annihilation. ' Je me réserve pour les provinces Baltiques,' was the answer made by Samarin to a lady of rank who expressed her astonishment that he had not accepted a post in the Government Commission at Warsaw. Samarin had grown wise by experience, and so awaited his hour; and at length his hour arrived. After Poland and Lithuania had been successfully Russianised, the 'Moscow Gazette' gave the long-expected signal for an attack on Finland and the 'separatist' provinces of the Baltic. Samarin now took up again the thread which five-and-twenty years before had been severed by the hand of the Emperor Nicholas. In the autumn of 1867 appeared the first volume of the 'Russian Frontiers,' a book which has made an epoch in the history of Russian journalism, and which occupied public attention so keenly for years, that Prince Gortchakoff called it an *événement*, which might become an ' accident,' and declared that nothing less than the thunders of Wörth and Sedan could divert the public of St. Petersburg and Moscow from the subjects which Samarin had put down on the National orders of the day.

An examination of this remarkable pamphlet, and of the numerous controversial works it gave rise to, is beyond the scope and purport of these pages. It treated in detail of the systematic degradation of the complex relations of law, constitutional polity, and political economy, in a country which, in spite of countless errors committed by the ruling class, had attained to a degree of administrative independence, moral culture, and material prosperity, which might and did indeed attract the envy of the rest of Russia. But this position of advantage, which was in fact only the product of a higher and more ancient civilisation, was now to be destroyed. Under the pretext of revealing to the government and people of Russia a web of intrigues, intended on the one hand to enslave and Germanise the Letts and Esths, and on the other hand to effect a separation of the Baltic provinces from Russian legislation, and, if possible, from the Russian State itself, the author took great pains to denounce all the high officials in Livonia appointed since the downfall of Golowin and his system, as mere blockheads of the selfish Baltic aristocracy, and to stigmatise all the legislative reforms introduced since then by the provincial Estates and confirmed by the government, as reactionary and anti-Russian shams. The method of this indictment was substantially as follows: According as it suited the author's design, the rights conceded to the gentry and the municipalities were either exaggerated beyond all proportion into monstrosities of the middle ages, incompatible with the modern ideas of a State, or else designated as the arrogant pretensions of a stupid aristocracy, fundamentally opposed to law and justice, and tolerated in an incomprehensible manner by a feeble government. To the government itself Samarin spoke in two voices—at one time, as the loyalest of all loyal subjects, who was grieved beyond consolation that the enlightened will of his adored monarch should not be carried out, but frustrated by the machinations of a handful of impudent rebels—at another time in the tone of a haughty demagogue, who, in the name of the 'National Idea' and the will of the people, protests against an absolute monarch not being guided by the will of the majority and of the dominant race, in his relations with a minority of his subjects. On one page he reproaches the Letts, Esths, and Courlanders with having ventured to talk of separate constitutional rights as against the sovereign power of the State; on another, he inveighs against the inconsistency, the want of method, and the recklessness of the absolutist system, which, with all the instruments of power at its disposal, does not even know how to manage a couple of little provinces. Of course his treatment of facts is equally clever and unprincipled. Spontaneous acts of the government are ascribed by Samarin, if they happen to displease him, to the intrigues of the Estates; and, conversely, reforms caused by the Estates, of the value of which no doubt could be entertained, were changed under his hands at once into government measures. Other matters were distorted and falsified with similar unscrupulousness. For instance, the whole of the resolutions of the provincial diet respecting the regulation of peasant farming were passed over in silence; and not a word was said about the great progress made in agriculture and rural education. Samarin wrote and acted as if the Baltic provinces of 1867 had remained just the same as those of 1847, and as if the twenty years' interval, so rich in reforms of every kind, had not changed the condition of that country in the least.

Apart, however, from its influence, hereafter to be explained, this work of Samarin's has been important and symptomatic, so to speak, for reasons which only indirectly relate to the condition of the Baltic provinces. In spite of the unrivalled dexterity with which it calculates on the disposition of the government, and the cautiousness with which it was adapted to the absolutist inclinations of the Czar, it betrayed in more than one place the plans and thoughts for the future which the Russian National party had in mind. Hatred and ill-feeling towards the local German aristocracy are by no means the only motives from which this party and its cleverest spokesmen launch their absurd calumnies and accusations against the Baltic provinces. They are afraid that the continuance of independent and peculiar institutions, developed on an historical basis in one part of the monarchy, might interfere with the realisation of the democratic ideal of the future, at which this party aspires. Samarin and his High-Church and ultra-National friends start, like Alexander Herzen, with the notion that the practical mission of the absolutism of the Czar is to render impossible the establishment of firm, conservative institutions of State, to hinder a development of Russia analogous to that of Western Europe, and thereby to bring about a revolution in a National sense. The 'Petersburg period' of Russian development is shortly to be followed by a National period, during which the orthodox Czar himself is to remain of course untouched, but his sovereign power is to be curtailed by the institution of a system of popular representation (*Semskaya duma*) on democratic principles, and on the broadest basis, starting with the *Mir*, or peasant community, as the collective possessor of the undivided landed property of the commune. For the ultimate realisation of this scheme, all historical institutions existing within the limits of the empire must be swept away, and the danger obviated, of the government hereafter at the critical moment gaining support against the popular will of Russia from the Europeanised and non-Russian portions of the population. To prevent this danger, it is necessary that everything which contains within itself the guarantee of stability, and is independent of the shifting views and currents of opinion in court and government circles, should be ruthlessly destroyed and melted down, so to speak, in the huge but half-broken caldron of the State. Absolutism, incapable of any continuous and lasting action, dwells, as Herzen puts it, behind ' wooden walls;' its acts are mere makeshifts and provisory arrangements. 'Our government,' he says, in his 'History of the Revolutionary Movement in Russia,' ' is infatuated with innovations; nothing is allowed to remain as it is; everything is incessantly being changed. Every new ministry begins by upsetting the doings of its predecessor; the decrees of yesterday are repealed to-day.'[1] Essentially the same story, only in rather different words, is told by Samarin, when he demands ' that the conduct and policy of the government should no longer be determined by the chance medley of events or by the views of this or that individual, be he even the autocrat himself, but should correspond with the requirements of the whole empire.' ' This can only be done,' he goes on to say, ' by the government admitting the people themselves to council, and giving them, in one form or another, a voice in

---

[1] 'In Russian life all is smoke and vapour. Everywhere new forms are being fashioned, one new face succeeds another, but practically all remains as before. There is a general rush and scramble after some visionary aim, but nothing is ever attained to. The wind changes, and the multitude scamper off in the opposite direction, and the same restless, aimless pursuit is recommenced. . . . Smoke and vapour, nothing else.'—Turgenieff's *Smoke*.

the affairs of State.' Till this comes to pass, and 'the solemn moment' arrives when 'a genuine National Assembly of the Russian Empire hails the new era,' the matter must rest with the 'wooden walls.' Let no one attempt to strengthen or perpetuate the present state of things, for they are a denial of the sovereignty of the people, the sole legitimate depositories of power. The Baltic provinces have been guilty of a crime against this people, by anticipating, through the independent exercise of their energies, and the achievement of purely local reforms, the task which properly belonged to the collective representatives of the empire at large. He points out the danger, moreover, of the Baltic separatists making common cause with the Russian Conservatives, and combining, by an understanding with certain politicians devoted to their cause, to effect the overthrow of the Democratic-National party. Language like this, interspersed of course with veiled allusions and covert turns of speech, shows plainly enough what are the real objects pursued by Samarin and his friends, and what is the ultimate aim of that party whose watchword is the Russification of the Baltic provinces.

Wherever Samarin's book penetrated—and it was circulated, as we have said, throughout the Russian empire—this 'deeper meaning' was rightly estimated. There was but one exception, and that was in high places. An attempt was made at first to silence the book which so disconcerted the government and compromised its representatives, and to sweep it off the face of the earth by foolish prohibitions of the censorship. When this attempt failed; when the whole Russian press teemed with quotations, critiques, and panegyrics of the *événement*, and the journalists of the Baltic provinces brought the book, by their replies, before the forum of the public of Europe, the government at length thought fit to profit by Samarin's instruction, and by a right use of the hints he had thrown out, to quiet down public opinion. Instead of keeping in view the real designs of the champion of national democracy, they singled out the very victims he had chosen for the cause of 'National Russia.' Just as a few years before against the rebellious Poles, so now a movement set in against the hostile and Conservative German element in the Baltic provinces, and the bureaucracy and Liberal public outvied each other in resolute devotion to the new crusade. Even those 'Liberal' officials who had not yet confessed the theories of the 'Universal Russian' National Assembly'—their younger brethren would have been only too glad to go to all lengths with Samarin—evinced their readiness to take in hand the work of destruction, which the bold tribune had demanded in the name and on behalf of the 'National idea.' So deeply rooted in the traditions of the higher and middle bureaucracy of St. Petersburg was the aversion against the conservative and historical institutions of the Baltic provinces, which were abhorred, moreover, as creations of the German popular spirit, that no one thought of asking whether these institutions might not in the end be of service to the government and to the dynasty so menaced by subversive designs. In blind obedience to the popular current of the day, and exulting in the prospect of being able to subjugate at least one outpost of Western European civilisation to the Slavonic system of the future, the government began to carry out the programme expounded by the prophet of democratic nationality.

The leading statesmen, without distinction of party, sought to outdo each other in patriotic zeal. One by one all the higher officials were suspended whom Samarin had designated as confederates or dupes of the Livonian intriguers. Waluieff, the distinguished Minister of the Interior, who for years had been persecuted with particular animosity by the Nationalists, was now dismissed. The legislative work, which had been directed to the reconstitution of the Baltic municipalities in conformity with the requirements of the time, to a representation of the Estates, and to the reform of the judicial system, was virtually annulled. Renewed efforts were made to enforce the use of the Russian language in the transactions of the Government authorities of the three provinces.[1] It was attempted even to win over the rural proletariate to the Greek Church by the offer of a distribution of State property. The German press of Livonia, Esthonia, and Courland was gagged by redoubling the severity of the censorship, whilst the anti-German diatribes of the Russian journals were sedulously encouraged. A number of Russian churches and schools were founded; the administration of Livonia (Esthonia and Courland came off much better in this respect) was placed in the hands of governors and high officials who were as incompetent as they were anti-German in sentiment; and all endeavours to maintain constitutional privileges were trampled down with unmerciful severity.

Samarin could now boast of having accomplished, in the name of the 'National idea,' what neither his former chief, the Governor-General Golowin, nor all the other high functionaries whose passion for destruction had been inspired by the absolutism of the Czar, had succeeded in achieving; and this at a time when all 'think-

[1] A similar, and the first edict of this kind, had been issued by Nicholas in 1850, but remained a dead letter, owing to the small number of civil functionaries who understood Russian. (TR.)

ing' statesmen in Russia were striving to get rid of the everlasting policy of makeshifts, and to build firm bulwarks instead of 'wooden walls' to protect themselves against the Russian revolution which was knocking loudly at the doors of the old system of State government.

The secret of Samarin's success as the author of the pamphlet we have described is the secret also of the failure which has attended almost all the organising efforts of the present government. Permanent reforms of any kind have been impossible, just because the government has been incapable of appreciating the meaning and importance of conditions which have become organic, of building on existing foundations, and of setting to work with other than purely bureaucratic tools. Where, indeed, it was simply a question of demolition, and of 'breaking with the past,' they have displayed as much energy as zeal. The smallest push against the social fabric sufficed to kindle quite a flame of enthusiasm for the *tabula rasa*, which was regarded as the preliminary of all genuine reform. The whole of young Russia took up arms when it was a question of abolishing serfdom, of destroying the obsolete machinery of justice, of sweeping away the abominable practice of 'brandy farming,' or of rooting out the old military system. Only a hint was needed to make whole hosts of youths, inspired with the 'National idea,' pour into Lithuania and Poland, in 1863 and 1864, in order to free those territories from 'the bondage of Occidentalism'—in other words, to crush to pieces their ancient organisation. Never has a bureaucracy undertaken with more boldness, intrepidity, and recklessness the task of 'clearing out and extirpating the abuses of feudalism and priestcraft,' than did the officials of Young Russia between 1850 and 1870. Measures, which German or English statesmen and officials would have required whole decades to prepare for, were only mentioned to be at once dispatched. Accustomed to regard existing arrangements as products of mere ephemeral caprice, or the chance ideas of the government; surrounded from their birth by institutions the antiquity of which dated, at the most, by years, and often by months; brought up under the dominion of laws which were frequently issued only by way of experiment (*na opüt*, as the technical expression goes), and about the execution of which people troubled themselves as little as about their amendment or repeal—these Russian government officials of the new school have displayed an amount of light-heartedness and freedom from prejudice which is only surpassed by their overweening self-confidence. Whilst Europe, like the rich man in the Gospel, is 'too wealthy to sacrifice her property for a mere aspiration or idea, Russia resembles the poor fisherman, whom it costs nothing to exchange his poor nets for the beggar's garb of an apostle of the future.'

So it has been under the rule of the Emperor Nicholas, when the millstones of the bureaucratic system ground everything to pieces that came within their reach to secure the 'uniformity' of absolutism. So also it is at present, when the same process is continued for the ostensible advancement of National and Liberal ideas. The moment a word is breathed of creating, instead of destroying—of a positive, instead of a negative line of policy—the machinery, so untiring in the work of demolition, stands still and refuses to act. It is thought to be as easy to build up and organise, without any previous preparation, as it was to pull down and disorganise; and so they never get beyond constructing houses of sand, destitute of any solid foundation. Such, for example, is the hastily extemporised legislation for reorganising the system of education, for establishing local self-government in the provinces, and for creating a new judicial procedure, all of which laws belong to 1863, but not one of which, after sixteen years of operation, has yet assimilated itself with the conditions of national life. So incessantly have they gone on patching these 'fundamental' statutes that not a year passes without the question being mooted of their repeal. It is because Samarin has been intimately acquainted with, and therefore known how to profit by this temper of Russian bureaucracy, that he has succeeded in inducing the government to carry out a work which is as contrary to their own interests as it is favourable to those of the party he represents.

Another circumstance has contributed to his success. Samarin's agitation for effecting a *tabula rasa* in the Baltic provinces was in one sense purely unselfish; it arose simply from his devotion to the cause he served. As for his own personal interests, he desired nothing. Whilst the highest functionaries vied with each other in their exertions to carry out the programme he had sketched, and three-fourths of all the Russian newspapers swore by the name of Samarin, the illustrious journalist remained a simple private individual, and was quite content to be treated by the Court aristocrats and their dependents with coldness and ill-concealed disfavour, on account of the boldness and recklessness of his language. That, at least, is more than the enormous majority of Russian patriots and politicians, 'with tendencies,' can boast of. The virtue of unselfishness is nowhere more rarely met with, and therefore nowhere more prized, than in the country of whose subjects it is said that they are mainly preserved from discontent by the *facilité de faire une carrière*.

Living by turns at Moscow, on his estates, and abroad, Samarin was content with the position of a private literary man. He never sought for title, rank, or order; he never suffered friend or foe to interrupt his labours as a journalist. Incredible to relate, the most influential Russian of his time has died a plain titular councillor without office, and has died on foreign soil. At the prime of life—he had reached the age of fifty-five—Samarin, in the spring of 1875, visited a *maison de santé* near Berlin, in order to restore his failing health. Here death overtook him, while busy with his favourite work, the study of ancient Russian theology.

'Il ira loin; il croit ce qu'il dit,' Mirabeau is reported to have said of Robespierre. The same might be said by his contemporaries and friends of Juri Samarin—the first Slavophil who understood how to put in motion the machinery of bureaucracy and absolutism for preparing new ground for the 'Universal National Assembly' of the Russia of the future, and to deprive the dynasty of the mainstay of support which it possessed in the only firm and historical organism within the limits of the Russian Empire.

CHAPTER XI.

THE RUSSIAN POPULAR VIEW OF THE EASTERN QUESTION.

Antiquity of Russia's connection with Constantinople—Early Slavonic invasions of Byzantium—Influences of Græco-Byzantine Christianity—, Mongol invasions of Russia—Establishment of Turkish supremacy in the East—Marriage of Ivan III. with Sophia—Turkish fears of Russia in the sixteenth century—Growing hostility of the Czars—The Will of Peter the Great—His far-sighted policy of aggrandisement—Treaty of Kutchuk-Kainardji—Premature ambition of Potemkin—Catherine II.'s scheme of a Græco-Slavonic empire—Failure of her designs against Constantinople—Her project thwarted by Austria—Incorporation of Crim-Tartary into Russia—Peace of Jassy—Removal of barriers between Turkey and Russia—Progress of anti-Turkish popular sentiment in Russia.

THE origin of the mutual relations between Russia and Byzantium dates back at least a thousand years. Just as the Germans, before the introduction of Christianity, knew of no more brilliant object for their love of adventure than an invasion of the sunny gardens of the Hesperides, south of the Alps, so piratical incursions against the city of the Byzantine emperor formed the favourite occupation of the heathen Slavonic races who dwelt to the North of the Black Sea. As early as the year 866 after Christ the name of the warlike 'Rūs' ('Ρως), who, under the leadership of Askold and Dir, the comrades in arms of Rurik the Varagian, the founder of the State, had appeared in light boats on the Thracian Bosphorus, filled the inhabitants of Constantinople with terror and dismay, and nothing short of a miracle, according to popular tradition, preserved the golden-domed city from the domination of the Slavs. Fifty years later, Oleg, the successor of Rurik and the murderer of Askold and Dir, led a mighty army along the same route which was taken nine hundred years afterwards by Count Diebitch-Sabalkansky, to the gates of the capital of Leo III.; whilst two thousand rowing vessels, brought down the Dnieper into the Euxine, made their appearance in the Dardanelles; and it was only at the price of a humiliating treaty that Constantinople was saved for a second time from the danger threatened her from the North. In like manner Igor, the successor of Oleg, had to be bought off, when he advanced southward in 944 on his second campaign, to take revenge upon the Emperor Romanus I. for the partial destruction of his fleet three years before by means of Greek fire. It was only after another forty years, when Vladimir the Pious, the grandson of Igor, had embraced the Christianity of the Greek confession, and had received, as a reward for his conversion, the hand of the Greek Princess Anna, a sister of the Emperors Basilius and Constantine, and sister-in-law of the German Emperor Otto II., that the danger of Northern invasion was averted from Byzantium.

So close, however, was the connection now established between the rising Empire of Russia and the Byzantine Empire already verging to decay, that even four centuries ago, the former regarded herself as the providentially-ordained successor of the latter. Whatever moral influences found their way to Russia, and helped to promote the Christianising work begun by Vladimir, were of Græco-Byzantine origin. That the higher ecclesiastical offices, including the superiors of convents and the court confessors, should for centuries be chiefly filled by Greeks, was natural enough, since the Œcumenical Patriarch was regarded as the supreme head of the newly-founded Russian Church, and its government was virtually centred in his hands. Greek was the language in which young ecclesiastical noviciates were instructed; Greek manners prevailed at the Court at Kieff; Greek costumes were the fashion among the higher classes; Greek taste dictated the style of church architecture; Greek architects, machinists, armourers, and teachers directed every undertaking carried on by Vladimir's successors. Byzantium was the model striven after in every department of life. This was the holy city from which everything of value in this or the next world was supposed to emanate. She was the porch of Heaven and the paradise of earth; next to Jerusalem, the place in the universe most pleasing in the sight of God. Such was the consideration which the Greek monk, in particular, enjoyed, that even teachers of false doctrines, notorious scoundrels and fanatics, who had been driven from their southern homes by the indignation of the Œcumenical Patriarch, were able in Russia to play the part of favoured teachers and lights of the Church; nay, so lasting has been his prestige, especially if he hails from Mount Athos, that this sole remaining relic of an age otherwise completely passed away, is looked upon by the Russian peasantry at this day as infinitely more holy and venerable than the native monk.

This connection, though not broken, was considerably loosened in the thirteenth century, at a time when it had already received the double consecration of a politico-historical and an ecclesiastical tradition. The terrible Mongol invasion, which burst over Russia under Juri (George) III. and Swätoslav II., causing her ruin and subjecting for centuries the young and scarcely-founded State to a condition of servile dependence on a rude nomadic people, suppressed so completely all intellectual and political life, that there could be no question during all that period of any relations between Russian princes and other countries, and that the paramount care of the former was to preserve their own existence. It seems well nigh a miracle that Christianity survived this period. The young plants of Christian culture, which Byzantine hands had planted, and which had just begun to blossom, were for the most part uprooted; and for many generations there were no hands left to tend them on the devastated soil of unhappy Russia.

Then followed troubles in the Byzantine Empire itself, still more severe than any which Russia had had to suffer. In the days of Ivan Vasilievitch, who brought about the unity of the Russian State, and freed his country from the yoke of the Mongols, occur the capture of Constantinople by the Turks (1453) and the total annihilation of the Eastern-Roman Empire. Russia, engrossed at that time in the struggle for her own existence, was powerless indeed to save this empire from its fate; but the first Czar of all the Russias, immediately his hands were free, declared himself its heir.. With the expressed intention of acquiring by that means a right to the Byzantine imperial throne, the Grand-duke Ivan III., as the first Czar of this name, accepted the proposal made to him by Pope Pius II., through Ivan Früsin, his Master of the Mint, to sue for the hand of the beautiful Sophia, the niece of the last Greek emperor, who fell in the defence of Constantinople. This marriage was concluded in 1475, and to symbolise the event, the double-headed Greek imperial eagle was added to the arms of the Russian Empire.

Centuries elapsed, it is true, before Russia could think of establishing the title she had tacitly acquired by this alliance. The wars of Ivan the Terrible with Poland, Sweden, and the German and Lithuanian knightly orders; and the confusion brought about by the usurpation of Godunow, the Minister of his son Fedor (1584-91), and subsequently by the appearance of the false Demetrius, seemed to forbid the bare thought of extending the frontiers of the empire in the south, where powerful Tartar races, moreover, barred the way. What intercourse the Czar of Muscovy had with the Sultan was usually of a friendly character; for both rulers had a most uncomfortable neighbour in the Tartar Khan of the Crimea. An alliance was even made in 1570 between Ivan the Terrible and Selim II., whereby both parties made a vow of mutual peace and friendship and the Sultan promised freedom of trade to Russians living on Turkish territory. None the less the Turkish statesmen of the fifteenth and sixteenth centuries were already well aware that Russia in time might become the most dangerous enemy of the Osmanli rule, and that the historical relations of the Northern Empire with Byzantinism and the Greek Church constituted a far more serious menace to the Porte than the 150,000 cavalry and 60,000 infantry whom the Muscovite Grand-duke had at his command. No less than three centuries ago, a competent judge of Oriental men and things, Giacomo Soranzo, the Venetian Ambassador at the Court of Suleiman I., made the following observations on this subject. 'The Grand-duke of the Muscovites,' he wrote, 'is chiefly feared by the Sultan because he belongs to the same Greek Church as do the inhabitants of Bulgaria, Bosnia, Servia, the Morea and Greece, who on that account are thoroughly devoted to him (*divotissimi per ciò al nome*). These populations will always be ready to take up arms to liberate themselves from the Turkish yoke, and to submit themselves to the rule of the Grand-duke.'

This fear of Russia was principally the cause why Suleiman I. and Selim II., after the extinction of the Jagellon dynasty, took such an active part in the resettlement of the succession to the Polish throne. These Sultans, with a true instinct, had foreseen that the frontiers of the Turkish Empire would cease to be secure if a Muscovite were to rule in Poland, and they were wise enough to take their measures and instruct their diplomatic agents accordingly. On the other hand, the Czars of that epoch were generally well aware that, of all the populations which surrounded Russia, the Turks were the only ones whom, under all the circumstances, they had to regard as their enemies, and with whom it was impossible to conclude a sincere and lasting peace. Even in the seventeenth century it was no longer a secret to acute-sighted politicians, that the irreconcilability of this antagonism was in no way confined to the differences between orthodox Christianity and Islamism. ' Le Grand Duc de Moscovie a toujours mieux aimé de demeurer en bonne intelligence avec le roi de Perse, que de donner moyen aux Ottomans de s'aggrandir, ce que luy serait à la fin fort préjudiciable.' Such was the language used by the Frenchman des Hayes in his ' Voyage du Levant,' published in 1622, when referring to the constant refusals of Russia to accept the proffered Turkish alliance against Persia. Equally significant was the firmness with which the Muscovite Grand-dukes declined to concede the same external honours to the Padishah which the States of Western Europe had long ago observed in their diplomatic intercourse with the

Porte. The very first Russian ambassadors at Constantinople—Michael Plesstcheyeff in 1495 and Alexei Golochwastoff in 1499—had refused the customary genuflexion to the Sultan, and had declined to receive any presents as inconsistent with the dignity of orthodox Boyárs. The same haughty demeanour, contrasting so conspicuously with the behaviour of the diplomatists of Western Europe, was observed by all the Muscovite ambassadors who were sent from time to time, during the following centuries, to Constantinople.

About the latter part of the seventeenth century, Russia had finally recovered from the crisis brought about by the extinction of the male line of the dynasty of Rurik; an end had been put for ever to the territorial pretensions of Poland; and an attempt could now be made to carry the Muscovite banner to the Euxine, where the Ukraine Cossacks and the Tartars of the Crimea barred the way. This enterprise was first undertaken in earnest by Peter the Great. His Romanoff predecessors, it is true, had anticipated to some extent his hostility to the Turks; but they had been forced to content themselves with occasional attacks against the mighty empire of the Sultans, who notwithstanding their endless feuds with the Cossacks and the Tartars, regarded these tribes as a convenient barrier against the Northern heiress of Byzantine Imperialism, and treated them accordingly. The struggle, however, was long and arduous. It was not until after a succession of wars, conducted with various alternations of fortune (1677-81, 1686-1702), that the great regenerator of Russia succeeded in obtaining, by the capture of Azof and Taganrog, a temporary footing on the Euxine and a basis of operations for the fleet which Venetian shipwrights had constructed. Even these acquisitions, intended to secure

T

to the Czar the key not only 'to his own house,' but to the inheritance of the last of the Palæologi, had to be surrendered in 1711 by the peace of Falczy, when the Russians were surrounded on the Pruth. But the Turco-Tartar dominion on the northern shores of the Black Sea did not last long. It ceased when Russian influence was firmly established on the Baltic. The heirs of Peter the Great were also the executors of his will.

That this much talked of 'Will' was an invention devised by the official press of Paris in 1811, by order of Napoleon I., is a fact too indisputable to need further comment in these pages.[1] It is equally indisputable, however, that Peter had designated the reconquest of Azof to his confidential advisers as the next task to be achieved, and that his comprehensive intellect had already had visions of the establishment of Russian supremacy on the Euxine, and the consequent possession of Constantinople as the ultimate object of Russian policy. The 'ultimate object,' we say, for a statesman of his astuteness must have known that a prize so high as this was not to be gained at one throw; and that the subjection of Polish Lithuania, and the subjugation of the Cossacks and the Crim Tartars, were previous stages necessary to the Eastern policy of Russia. Article X. of the treaty of peace concluded in 1720 between Russia and the Porte abolished the presents which the Czar had been obliged from time immemorial to pay to the Khan of the Crimea; but Article XII. placed the 'rights and constitution of the royal republic'—the perpetuation, in other words, of Polish anarchy—under the joint guarantee of the two contracting powers.

[1] See *Le testament de Pierre le Grand*, by G. Berkholz. [The reader will find this question treated as an 'historic doubt' by Mr. Thoms in the *Nineteenth Century*, July, 1878.—TR.]

So obvious, indeed, was the close connection between the great Eastern problem and the aims which Russia had before her on the Vistula and the shores of the Crimea, that clear-sighted Russian statesmen in the eighteenth century pursued without exception the line of policy prescribed by Peter. Field-Marshal Münnich, the most active and talented of all the foreigners attracted to Russia by the 'great Czar,' took the first opportunity that offered of continuing his system exactly as it stood. Whilst pointing out Constantinople to the Empress Anna as the ultimate goal of Russian statesmanship, the nearer objects of his ambition coincided with those of Peter the Great. By the occupation of the neighbouring Polish territories, and the capture of Dantzig, he restored the former influence of Russia over the internal affairs of the republic; while the taking of Azof and Otschakof reopened to her the long-coveted road to the Black Sea. The latter town, it is true, was restored to the Turkish possession by the peace of Belgrade (1739), and the Empress Anna renounced for the time the right of fortifying Azof and unfolding the Russian flag on the shores of the Euxine. But forty years later the victorious armies of Catherine II., led by Roumanzow, succeeded in removing these obnoxious restrictions, and by the treaty of Kutchuk-Kainardji (July 16, 1774), a new phase was opened in the Eastern policy of Russia.

By this famous compact the Tartar peoples of the Kuban, the Budjak, and the Crimea, till then dependencies of Turkey, were declared completely free nations. Kertch, Yenikalé, the Great and the Little Kabarda, were transferred to Russia. The princes of Moldavia and Wallachia were placed, at least indirectly, under Russian protection, the Russian ambassador obtaining the right of remonstrating with the Porte on their behalf; and the customary supply of troops from Georgia and Mingrelia was abolished for ever. Lastly, Article VII. contained a stipulation, the full significance of which was never understood at the time, but which has proved far more important than most of the conquests bargained for in the preceding paragraphs. The Article in question ran as follows:—

> The Sublime Porte promises to protect constantly the Christian religion and its churches. It also allows the Ministers of the Imperial Court of Russia to make, on all occasions, representations to the Porte as well in favour of the new church at Constantinople, mentioned below in Article XIV., as on behalf of its officiating ministers; and promises to take such representations into due consideration, as being made by a confidential functionary of a neighbouring and sincerely friendly power.[1]

That this stipulation (which only eighty years later was interpreted in the sense of a Russian protectorate over the Greek Church, as such) should have appeared to the Empress herself as only a very moderate concession, was to be accounted for mainly by the high-soaring designs with which she had entered into the war with Turkey. Potemkin, the most intimate of Catherine's advisers at that time, whom the national imagination of Russia had magnified without any reason into a 'giant' and a type of national strength, had endeavoured for years to persuade the Empress that she was called upon to achieve the highest object of the popular desire, and to bring the task of Russia in the East to a final and victorious issue. The first step towards the achieve-

[1] Article XIV. stipulated that Russia should be allowed to erect, in addition to the private chapel of the Russian Embassy, a public church of the Greek ritual at Galata in the street called Ben Oglu, which should always be under the protection of the Russian Minister and secure from all molestation and injury.'

ment of this purpose was one which Peter the Great and Münnich had regarded as the ultimate result of a long process of development, counting by tens, if not hundreds of years. Catherine's was to be the mission and the power of planting the Greek Cross upon the Bosphorus, of driving the Turks out of Constantinople and Europe, and of founding a Greek Empire ruled over by a Russian Grand-duke. Regardless of the astonishment with which all prudent statesmen around her listened to this anticipation, too early by a century, the ambitious Semiramis of the North had embraced with ardour this chimerical project of her favourite. Her flatterers, in the true spirit of their scheme, adopted a court dress in imitation of the Greek national costume, the so-called *Gretschanka*. Over the eastern gate of the town of Cherson were inscribed the words : 'This road leads to Constantinople.' The second grandson of the Empress was named Constantine, baptized according to the Greek and not the Russian rite, and surrounded with playmates of Greek origin. With truly feminine instinct, this princess of the house of Anhalt-Zerbst recognised that there was no surer way to win the hearts of her people, and to efface the memory of her German extraction, than to identify herself with the fulfilment of an idea which had slumbered for centuries in the popular mind, and was interwoven with the most chimerical fancies just because it had never reached a perfect and public recognition. It was quite immaterial whether Potemkin's extravagant project could be realised or not; the mere fact of its avowal promised to ensure her the popularity she coveted so much at home, and glory and honour abroad. The notion of being able to liberate the Greeks from Turkish thraldom was welcomed by none so enthusiastically as by Voltaire, then the most

influential writer of the civilised world. 'J'aimerais
mieux,' wrote the philosopher of Ferney in 1772 to his
friend the crowned philosopher of Sans Souci, 'que
vous aidassiez l'impératrice à chasser du Bosphore ces
vilains Turcs, ces ennemis des beaux-arts, ces éteignoirs
de la belle Grèce. . . . . C'est parceque les Turcs ont
de très-bons blés et point de beaux-arts, que je voulais
vous voir partager la Turquie avec vos deux associés.'[1]
In exactly the same spirit Voltaire and his friends wrote
to St. Petersburg; and these opinions, together with the
advice given by a Venetian nobleman to Count Alexis
Orloff as to the chances of a rising among the Greeks,
weighed far more with the Empress than the doubts of
her most experienced statesmen and generals. Since
1765 Greece, Roumelia, Thessaly, Macedonia, Monte-
negro, and the islands of the Archipelago swarmed with
emissaries, who preached rebellion against the hateful
Crescent, and promised Russian support, Russian money,
and Russian arms. In 1769 a formal treaty was concluded at Pisa between Orloff and the chiefs of the
warlike Mainotes. In February, 1770, Vice-Admiral
Spiridow appeared at Cape Mazatlan with a fleet of
nearly thirty sail. A few weeks later the Russians and
Greeks were masters of Patras and Navarino; and on
May 2, at a high mass celebrated before the altar of
the mosque at Kolon, which had been hastily transformed into a Greek church, that famous manifesto was
read which declared that 'the orthodox and Holy
Czarina and Empress, Catherine II., will complete what
her great predecessor, the Emperor Peter, of glorious
memory, and the Empress Anna, now resting with God,

[1] The answer given by Frederick the Great to this proposal is not
without its interest. 'Les Grecs,' he wrote, 'pour lesquels vous vous inté-
ressez si vivement, sont—dit on—si avilis, qu'ils ne méritent pas d'être
libres.'—*Œuvres de Frédéric le Gr.* xxiii. p. 265.

have already attempted to perform.' In a pompous proclamation, skilfully calculated to excite the Greek imagination, it was announced that the Empress had declared war against the Sultan, with the intention of conquering Constantinople and liberating the Greeks. Already her victorious armies had defeated 600,000 Turks. The Greek nation should take up their weapons and trust to God and the Empress; for this sacrifice there would be no lack of reward, either now or hereafter, since the Empress was resolved richly to recompense those who 'gave tokens of their obedience and showed themselves worthy of her protection.'

Brilliantly as this programme was ushered in by the naval victory won by Alexis Orloff in June, 1770, in the bay of Chesme, its termination was of doubtful value for the reputation of the Russian name. Russia was forced to abandon her Greek and Slavonic allies, in particular the brave Montenegrins, and to renounce her high-flown promises of Greek ascendency, as well as the coveted acquisition of Moldavia and Wallachia, which she had already treated as conquered provinces, added to the empire. For these losses the peace of Kutchuk-Kainardji offered no adequate compensation; nor could it countervail the painful impressions made throughout the civilised world by the news of the punishment inflicted by Turkey upon the Greek allies of Russia. The Empress had good reason for thinking that the results of her ambitious policy were paid for dearly at the price.

The reasons, indeed, which had led to the conclusion of this treaty, and induced the Empress, at an earlier stage, to renounce the vast scheme she had started with, were of the very highest importance. In the face of an Austrian alliance with Turkey, Catherine had been forced in 1772 to abandon her scheme of Greek sovereignty, and to pledge herself to maintain the independence of Moldavia and Wallachia. It was only on these conditions that Prince Kaunitz had consented to the first partition of Poland, which was of incomparably greater value, in regard even to the great Eastern project of Russia, than all that could be gained in the Bosphorus or the Ægean.

Eight years later, by means of the friendly relations contracted by Catherine with Joseph II., the second of those conditions was fulfilled which we have designated above as 'stages' towards the solution of the Eastern question. On April 4 (15), 1783, the Crimean Tartars were deprived of the remnant of their independence, and the Tauric peninsula was incorporated with the Russian Empire. The immediate effect of this was to make the Russians the potential masters of the Black Sea. To rest content, for the present, with this important result, and to abstain from further interference in Eastern affairs, was so simple and obvious a precept of political wisdom, that all the responsible advisers of Catherine were unanimous on that point; and her refusal to accept their counsel was the greatest error she committed in her reign. None but a political blunderer like the 'giant' Potemkin, as reckless as he was void of conscience, could have advised the Empress, even before her work in Poland was completed, and in the midst of the exertions rendered necessary by the second and third partitions of that country, to compromise the more extensive interests of Russia in the East, by preparations for another war with Turkey, and to force the Porte to declare hostilities in August 1787. It is true that Suworoff's bravery and superior generalship remedied the mischief which Potemkin's cowardice and incapacity had caused. It is true that Russia, by the treaty of

Jassy, in the autumn of 1792, extended once more her south-eastern frontier. But these results were more than counterbalanced by the financial embarrassments into which Catherine had plunged the empire, and which she bequeathed as a *damnosa hæreditas* to her successors; they paved the way to difficulties which have lasted to our days and are not yet entirely overcome.

As our object is not to give a history of the Eastern policy of Russia, we may stop, so far as wars and treaties are concerned, at the peace of Jassy. By the annihilation of the Tartar rule in the Crimea, and the destruction of the Polish-Lithuanian State, the barriers between Russia and Turkey were removed, and the politicians of St. Petersburg conducted to the threshold of an enterprise which the Muscovite Grand-dukes had looked upon as the final goal of national policy. Catherine had not merely put aside the obstacles to the development of Russian power towards the south and south-west, but had attracted once more the national attention to those aims which, in the miseries of Tartar domination and the agonies of civil war, had been wellnigh forgotten. The Græco-Slavonic alliance against Turkey, which began in 1770, was an event which made an epoch in the history of the world, and prepared the way for the great revolutions of the eighteenth century. Russia herself was stirred to her innermost depths by the news of the heroic exploits of Roumanzow and Suworoff. The stories of the lofty schemes of the Taurian (Potemkin), of the proud inscription over the gate of the newly-conquered Cherson, and of the noble intention of the Mother-Czarina to purge those 'holy places' to which Russia owed the blessings of Christianity and of civilisation, from the abominations of the infidels, and to free their brethren in the faith who dwelt on the Bosphorus and the

Danube, from the yoke of those 'Bussurmanny,' whom tradition had taught them to regard as the worst enemies and oppressors of Holy Russia—all these stories had penetrated to the huts of the Russian peasants, and had quickened their feelings of patriotism to the core. Ancient popular traditions, surrounded by the halo of sanctity, were conjured up afresh by the proclamation to the Greeks and by the tidings of the victories of Suworoff and Weissmann. Hopes and desires were kindled, the very vagueness and indistinctness of which served to implant them more permanently in the popular mind, and which promised, even if slowly and at a late season, to bear some fruit. These moral effects were chiefly in the mind of Admiral Tchitchagoff, when, after the conclusion of the peace of Bucharest in July, 1812, he wrote these memorable words to M. von Stourdza, the first Russian governor of the newly-annexed Bessarabia :—' I recommend you, as the administrator of Bessarabia, to attract the attention of the neighbouring peoples to that province, by making its inhabitants happy. The late war had raised great hopes among these populations. . . . The Bulgarians, the Moldavians, the Wallachians, the Servians—all seek a fatherland. You can help them to find one.'

CHAPTER XII.

THE RUSSIAN POPULAR VIEW OF THE EASTERN QUESTION
(*continued*).

Greek influence on the early Russian Church—Hostility between the White and Black clergy—Eastern orthodoxy and the Russian National Church—Byzantine tendencies of the higher clergy—Spiritual affinity with the East—Idea of ethnological unity—Greek jealousy of Slav predominance—The Greek-Bulgarian Church conflict—Decision of the Russian Synod—Recent Origin of Slavo-nationality—The movement of 1876.

DURING the first half-century of the Christian era in Russia, the Œcumenical patriarch was the recognised head of the Russian Church, and most of the higher ecclesiastical offices in that country were filled by Greeks. With only two exceptions, all the 'Metropolitans of Kieff and Russia,' up to the time of the establishment of the Tartar dominion in the thirteenth century, had been Greeks, nominated by the Patriarch on an understanding with the Grand-duke that, in case they should not answer the latter's expectations, they should be again deposed. The bishops, holding office under this Metropolitan, and appointed on his recommendation by the Grand-duke, were as a rule Russians, but it can easily be understood that they adopted the views and habits of life of their Greek primate, and gravitated like him towards Constantinople. Nor was this a matter of surprise, when Greek origin determined all pretensions to higher civilisation and general respect; when the influence of the Œcumenical Patriarch formed the only counterpoise to the absolute power of the Russian rulers; and when the Greek Nomocanon was the basis of Russian ecclesiastical law, the standard that governed the episcopal administration of justice, and the fountain of the privileged jurisdiction of the clergy—the most important privilege they enjoyed. The secular clergy alone—the inferior or 'White' clergy as they were called — possessed a strictly national Russian character. They had a right to marry; but in return were excluded from all the higher dignities, and ranked but low in popular esteem, besides being the absolute dependents of their monastic superiors—the 'Black' or regular clergy.

The antagonistic relations existing for ages between these two classes of ecclesiastics brought about the natural result that the monastic clergy attached the utmost importance to their connection with the Greek mother-Church and its head, the Œcumenical Patriarch, and systematically strove to invest the Byzantine hierarchical system, concealed as it was from the popular eye, with a mysterious halo of sanctity and awe. On their connection with this Church, to which such attributes of superior authority were ascribed, they founded their claims to their own exceptional position. Whoever wished to attain a higher position in the hierarchy at home, must have paid at least one visit to Constantinople and the monastery of Mount Athos, have received the blessing of the 'Patriarch of the World,' and have brought away with him a Byzantine relic. So potent was the attraction of 'New Rome,' that Metropolitans, who had waited for years to become chief pastor of their Church, laid down that dignity in the evening of their life, and returned to the seat of their mother-Church, to acquire a higher degree of holiness.

The immediate connection with Constantinople and the subjection of the Russian Church to the Œcumenical Patriarchate, ceased with the year 1446. Already some years before the annihilation of the Greek Empire and the submission of the Patriarch to the Turkish yoke, Grand-duke Vassily, the Blind, ordered the Bishop of Rjäsan, a Russian by birth, to be elected Metropolitan by the Russian episcopal assembly, and this proceeding became the rule after the fall of Constantinople. Boris Godunow (1598-1605) went a step farther: he made use of the embarrassments of the Eastern Church to obtain, through the mediation of the Patriarch of Antioch, the assent of the Council of the Eastern Church to the establishment of a Russian patriarchate, the right of appointment to which was vested in the Czar. But it was exactly the loosening of the formal connection between the Russian Church and the Œcumenical see which tightened the moral bond of union between Russian monasticism and Byzantium. The farther the absolute sway of the Czar extended, and the more directly his influence was exerted upon the Church and the clergy, the more longingly did the clergy look back upon the days when they were independent of the temporal power and, as subordinates of a hierarchy outside the limits of the empire, were free from the arbitrary dominion of the Czar.

Hand-in-hand with these hierarchical—or, as the modern phrase has it, ultramontane—tendencies of the higher clergy, went a passionate hatred of everything that came from the West and was connected with Western European civilisation. Had not the more enlightened Czars turned their attention chiefly towards this 'West,' and by the help of immigrants from that quarter endeavoured to disturb the sacred and time-honoured customs of their fathers? The Russians, like the Greeks, persecuted the Papacy with redoubled hatred for having taken advantage of the troubles at Byzantium, to urge the union of the Eastern and the Romish Churches. On the Moskwa and on the Bosphorus it was told with horror how the Romish heretics had assisted the truculent Sultan, the hereditary enemy of the only one true faith, at the capture of the Holy City, and how the 'prince of lies of the Western Church,' since the downfall of the 'New Rome' (Constantinople), was about to stretch out his heretical hands towards the 'third Rome' (Moscow).[1]

The events of the sixteenth and seventeenth centuries contributed materially to strengthen this conviction that 'light could only come from the East.' The union of the Greek and Romish Churches, completed in White and Red Russia, but rejected throughout the empire at large; the ascendency of the Czar, which had been steadily increasing since the schism of the Old Believers; and, lastly, the abolition of the Russian patriarchate by Peter the Great, and this sovereign's evident partiality to Western influences, necessarily excited the longing for the good old times, and stimulated the Byzantine tendencies of the clergy all the more because the Greek Church retained a position of far greater independence than the Russian. The Turkish conquest and the decline of the old Roman Empire of the East in no way lessened the authority of the patriarchate of Constantinople; on the contrary, they rather increased it. Had not the Divan systematically aimed at making this prince of

---

[1] The Patriarch of Moscow, in the sixteenth and seventeenth centuries, occupied the third rank of dignity in the Greek Church. The Patriarchs of Constantinople and Alexandria alone took precedence of him. Antioch took the fourth place and Jerusalem the fifth.

the Church the head over all Eastern Christians, and thereby making him responsible for their obedience? No wonder that the higher clergy in Russia clung with zeal to the old connection with 'New Rome,' and continually reminded their faithful people that the deliverance of the centre of the true ancient and apostolic Church was the most sacred of all the duties of the orthodox. In proportion as the State busied itself with the task of Europeanising Russia and of introducing the political system of the West, the more zealously did the clergy endeavour to maintain their old connection with the Christian East.

Thus the idea of the unity of the Eastern Church and faith appears as the most mighty of all those agencies which in former centuries impelled Russia's 'progress to the East.' 'Moscow, the third Rome'—in this phrase, first used by Boris Godunow, is contained the quintessence of all which, according to ecclesiastico-national views, was to constitute the task of Russia in the East. A union of race with the Slav inhabitants of the Balkans, the Western and Southern Slavs, was hardly mooted until far into the present century. These tribes came into account, in the Russia of Alexander I. and during the early days of Nicholas, solely as brethren of the faith, not as brethren of the same race. The interest taken by the Russian Church and nation in the Greek war of independence (1821-29) differed in no respect from that which they had manifested some years earlier in the revolt of the Servians, their kinsmen in race, under Kara George and Milosch. In both cases alike, the objects of their sympathy were the orthodox sons of the Holy Eastern Church; the question was scarcely an ethnological one at all. No doubt the establishment of an independent kingdom of Greece marked an entirely new phase in the policy of the government at St. Petersburg, but of this change the Russian public remained completely ignorant. It was only quite recently that even the most highly-cultivated portion of Russian society learned the possibility of a conflict between Russian and Greek interests on the Bosphorus, and of Greek aspirations for the reconquest of Constantinople being guided by the thought of ultimate emancipation from Russian tutelage.

The origin of the National party of modern Russia— the Slavophils, as they are called—dates, as is well known, from between 1835 and 1840. About the same time the first Panslavist ideas and aspirations began to stir in the bosom of Slavism in Austria. Before then, religious sympathies had formed the only bond of union between that country and Russia. It was not until between 1840 and 1860, and then only within a limited circle, that the belief in the existence of common Slav interests gained ground in Russia, and the traditional sympathy of the nation for their 'brethren in the faith, who were languishing under the yoke of the unbelievers,' became intermixed with views of national Slavism, and gradually extended from the Turkish to the Austrian Slavs. The Hungarian campaign of the summer of 1849 added something to this result, by bringing the Russian soldiers for the first time in contact with people who made the sign of the Greek cross, spoke an idiom kindred to the Russian, and nevertheless were neither Russian nor Turkish subjects. More than this, however, it was impossible to expect, so long as Panslavism, from its revolutionary origin, was outlawed by official Russia; Bakunin, its most ardent champion, stigmatised as a 'traitor to the State;' and the Slav Congress at Prague disliked and ignored in high quarters. It is only since the close of the Crimean War, and the commencement of the new era ushered in by the accession of Alexander II., that Panslavist ideas have acquired a larger field for their display, and begun to play a part in politics. A real significance has been given to them only within the last few years. Even at this day the enthusiasm of Russians for their brethren *of race* beyond the frontiers of the empire is only a kind of pastime or plaything— a modern liberal garb for the ancient and deep-rooted interest which the Orthodox nation really took in her orthodox brethren *in the faith,* and which the clergy— especially the monastic portion, who are still imbued at the present day with this Byzantine ' Ultramontanism '— have consciously and intentionally nurtured. The first Slavophils themselves were ecclesiastical zealots, devotees of Byzantine patristicism, and enthusiasts for that form of ultra-orientalism which they called Russian civilisation. For these reasons they were little inclined to discriminate between the politico-national and the ecclesiastical conceptions of the Eastern question, or to recognise a contradiction of interests between the two.

As regards, however, the policy of the Russian cabinet, this contradiction has been acknowledged for more than half a century. The days, when all the inhabitants of the Balkan peninsula, belonging to the Greek Orthodox Church, felt themselves to be members of an undivided community, have long gone by. Ever since the kingdom of Greece was established, the Greeks—Hellenic as well as those living in Turkey—have distinguished their own from Russian interests as clearly as Russian diplomatists have distinguished between the Slavonic and non-Slavonic members of the ' Orthodox nation.' According to the views of the Hellenic Greeks, it is not Russia, nor yet Slavism, but the kingdom of Greece, which is the predestined heir to the 'sick man.' They are naturally pleased to accept Russia's help in the struggle for freedom against the common enemy; but the fruits of this campaign they mean to keep for themselves. Russia, on her part, makes the most of the fact that the enormous majority of 'Orthodox' Christians, south of the Danube, are of Slav descent, and that the Greeks form an aristocratic minority. Hence, she argues, no reason whatever would exist, when the Slavs in those regions are once freed from their Turkish oppressors, to subject them to Greek dominion and expose them to the danger of being gradually Hellenicised.

This long existing conflict of interests first occupied public attention only nine years ago, when the Œcumenical Patriarch called upon the authorities of the Russian Church to arbitrate in the ecclesiastical dispute in Bulgaria. For a long while the Bulgarians, weary of the dominion of the Greek priesthood and of services conducted in the Greek tongue, had demanded to have bishops, priests, and forms of ritual belonging to their own language and their own nationality; and when the patriarchate refused them this, they had obtained leave from the Porte to constitute a Bulgarian exarchate, nominally subject to the Patriarch, but tolerably independent as regards its own internal affairs. In this dispute, conducted with extreme acrimony by the partisans of Slavo-National principles, Russia sided with the Bulgarians, and adhered firmly to their cause, although, by so doing, she lost all the sympathy of the intelligent Greek party and their ambitious princes of the Church. The decision of the ecclesiastical synod at St. Petersburg was governed by the advice of the ambassador Ignatieff and the wishes of the government, who attached far greater importance to an alliance with Slavism in Turkey than to the favourable opinion of the Greek element, which had long been looked upon at St. Petersburg as a pretentious and intriguing rival. Guided by the influence of the press and of the Slavo-National party, which had gradually attained some importance, that part of the Russian nation who took any interest at all in public affairs expressed their concurrence with the decision of the government. Among the high Russian clergy, on the contrary, opinions were divided, and voices were not wanting which openly proclaimed approval of the position taken by the Greek hierarchy, and condemned the vote of the synod in favour of the Bulgarians.

The sum total of the above considerations points to the conclusion that the idea of freeing the 'holy city,' from which Russia received Christianity, and the belief in the right of inheritance, supposed to have been transferred from the second to the 'third Rome,' were popular among the Russian nation long before anything precise was known about the Slav nationality of their persecuted Orthodox brethren. The Slavo-National idea, viewed as an independent factor in the Eastern policy of Russia, dates, as we have said, from very recent days. It is an additional impulse, but by no means the only one, to be taken into account when estimating the force of the movement which has agitated the Russian people since the summer of 1876. As regards the educated classes of society and the zeal with which they have taken this agitation in hand, the solidarity of Slav interests is a matter, no doubt, of some importance. But the real strength of the popular movement is to be sought elsewhere; it lies in the ecclesiastical past of Russia.

At the same time we must carefully consider the fact, that a movement, like that of 1876, initiated as it was essentially by the nation itself, must have possessed for Russians all the charms of novelty. In a country where for centuries the government had been everything, and society nothing, the effect produced was that of magic, when the nation first felt itself to be the standard-bearer of the policy pursued by the government, and social forces, which had formerly played only a subordinate part, appeared at the head of a great popular movement. All the countless malcontents and Liberals who came to the fore after 1860, and seemed for a while to be masters of the situation, but who were dismissed again from notice after the suppression of the Polish insurrection, now gained fresh scope and an unexpected opportunity for displaying their influence and activity, by this agitation for a direct interference of Russia on behalf of the Servians and the Western Slavs. National and liberal tendencies, moreover, so long intimately connected in Russia, now made common cause, and combined to recover lost ground and to play into each other's hands. For the press of St. Petersburg and Moscow, in particular, disregarded for years, and well-nigh discredited, the opportunity for self-assertion and declamation which was offered by the Servian war was of incalculable value. At last a subject had been found which could command universal interest and sympathy; which had power to charm even the lowest classes of the people; which was sure to enlist the approbation of the clergy; and which could serve as an agreeable and not too perilous means for criticising the action of the government.

CHAPTER XIII.

THE WAR AND THE DYNASTY.

Influence of foreign wars on domestic policy—Absolutist system of Nicholas —The Crimean War and its lessons—National humiliation and popular discontent—Reaction after the Polish revolt of 1863—Centralisation and 'National Development'—Russian parties and the Turkish War— Authors and origin of the war—The Moscow Nationalists and the Servian insurrection—Triumph of Panslavistic doctrines—The so-called Russian popular movement—Ivan Aksakoff and the Czar's speech at the Kremlin—Aspirations of the Moscow National party—Expectations founded on the war—Constitutionalism and revolution.

SINCE the great Napoleonic invasion of 1812, the foreign wars carried on by Russian monarchs have never failed to exercise a permanent and penetrating influence upon the internal policy of the State and the development of national life. Until then, and in fact ever since the days of Peter the Great, the external affairs of the empire had passed by without leaving any trace among the mass of the nation. But in 1812, what Alexander Herzen aptly calls the 'St. Petersburg period' of Russian history came at length to an end; and Moscow, the 'first city of Holy Russia,' became for a short but eventful epoch the centre of the national life, awakened from its long sleep. The firebrands of Rostoptchin kindled for a while the slumbering sparks of Russian patriotism, and made Russians feel proud of their country. This sentiment, however, was short-lived, and changed into a cosmopolitan enthusiasm for freedom and the welfare of peoples, when the officers of 1814 and 1815 returned from Germany and France. 'It was impossible, after the excitement of the national war and the glorious march through a liberated Europe, to go back at once to the dull monotony of despotism at St. Petersburg.' Rash attempts to import institutions of Western Europe into Russia, such as those of the military conspirators of the 'North' and 'South' under Pestel and Rylejeff, and the foolish insurrectionists of December 1825, had to pay, it is true, the full penalties of defeat. But the seeds of change, then scattered, were not lost; the soil they fell on was unbroken, but was all the more fertile for that reason. Whilst outwardly, for full thirty years, there reigned the perfect stillness of the tomb, and the government, discarding altogether the civilising traditions of Peter the Great, ruled more absolutely than ever, a revolution was preparing in the heart of Russian society,—a revolution which was silently maturing and developing the impressions received between 1812 and 1815, and aspiring in every sphere of life to reverse the objects of the Emperor Nicholas.

Towards the end of this period it seemed, indeed, as if the government would hold their own against the Liberals at home as they had done with Europe abroad. The absolutism of the Czar reached its climax with the Hungarian campaign of 1849. Henceforth, those in the Imperial camp looked upon it as a settled thing, that Russia had only to continue in the path she had taken to become the mistress of the world, and to lay Europe prostrate 'at the feet of His Majesty,' just as, in the language of Prince Paskevitch, she had done with conquered Hungary. The emperor's hatred of everything savouring of reform or freedom of initiative rendered him incapable at length of discerning his own responsibilities. The three several projects for relieving the oppressed condition of the peasantry were 'shelved' among the public archives. The most absurd abuses of military and civil administration were pronounced sacred, and declared to be integral parts of the conservative system which was supposed to have accomplished such 'grand results.'

The days of these 'results' were numbered, however, even before the Eastern complications after 1850 culminated in the Crimean War. Was not the gigantic collapse of Russia in this contest mainly due to the fatal influence which the apparent triumph of the Hungarian campaign had exercised upon the mind of the autocrat and the views of his myrmidons? They had talked themselves into a state of self-complacency and an arrogance of infallibility which excluded any serious preparation for the war. If only the Czar remained firm, they said, Europe would once more have to submit to the will of Russia. On the other hand, the small but influential number of cultivated Russians, who clung firmly to the traditions of 1812 and 1825, entertained very different thoughts at the prospect of the coming struggle. At the very outset of the war, they maintained that the real salvation of Russia depended on the failure of an enterprise undertaken in such immeasurable ignorance of their own and foreign resources. In spite of their genuine patriotic grief at the fall of Sebastopol and the misfortunes of its heroic garrison, they held quietly but unyieldingly to their conviction, that the true welfare of the Russian nation had nothing to fear from the victories of the allies at Inkermann and the Tchernaya, and that the capture of the Russian Saragossa would prove of greater service to Russia herself than to those who had stormed the Malakoff.

The succeeding twenty years of Russian history have been so indissolubly connected with the experiences of the Crimean War, that it is unnecessary to enlarge further on this point. With the humiliation of national defeat came an awakening from the dreams of optimism, and a sense of dissatisfaction with the past. Up to the Polish insurrection of 1863 nothing passed for any value in official as well as non-official circles but what was opposed to the old system, and recommended itself, or appeared to recommend itself, as a protest against its errors and vices. But after 1863 the fashion of reform began to pall, and a certain reaction again set in. The system of centralisation, pursued by the government of Nicholas, was condoned, and even patronised to some extent, by the prominent leaders of public opinion as the means best fitted for the establishment and furtherance of 'true national development.' With a view to eliminate as speedily as possible the Polish, German, Swedo-Finnish and other foreign elements of the western half of the empire, the Government, which from 1858 to 1863 had been watched with constant suspicion and thwarted at every step, was once more entrusted for a time with absolute power, and allowed to exercise it without limit in the department of foreign policy. Not, indeed, that this absolute power was granted irrevocably, or intended as unconditional. Young Russia, standing, as it were, upon the ruins of Nicholas's system and the disastrous experiences of 1854–55, still claimed the right of determining her own destinies, and of having a voice in the foreign policy of the government, so far, at least, as seemed necessary in the interests of her internal development. This claim had been dormant for a time and for a definite purpose, but it had not been finally renounced; and the strongest proof of its vitality was afforded by the events which accompanied the recent reopening of difficulties in the East. The declaration of war against Turkey, on April 24, 1877, was the act not of the government of St. Petersburg, but of the Russian nation. It was essentially the product of the internal policy pursued by Alexander II. since 1863 and 1864. Domestic considerations had at least quite as large a share in unchaining the anti-Turkish passions of the Russian people as the ancient ambition to raise the Greek cross upon the Mosque of St. Sophia, or the modern Panslavistic theories of concentrating all Slavonic power in the hands of Russia.

At the outbreak of this war with Turkey, Russian society was divided into four entirely distinct and strongly delineated groups. The *first* was the government and its immediate adherents, who recognised the emperor's will as the supreme law, and the preservation of traditional forms of state and society as the sum and substance of all political wisdom. To this group the independent statesmen of St. Petersburg, who inclined to European views, attached themselves rather from necessity than from preference. The *second* was the great National party, enlarged far beyond its original dimensions. At its head were Prince Tcherkasski, the Civil Commissioner of the Grand-duke Nicholas; Ivan Aksakoff, the President of the Moscow Society of Benevolence (formerly the Slav Committee); Katkoff, the editor of the 'Moscow Gazette;' Prince Meschtcherski, the contributor to the 'Graschdanin;' the journalists Illowaiski and Orest Müller, and others of lesser note. So numerous were the adherents of this party in the army, and among the younger civil officials and the clergy, that it was easy to carry along with it the great mass of the mercantile class, who were more or less uneducated, and to inspire the rural population with a sincere and unselfish enthusiasm for the Slavo-Christian cause. The *third* group was the Socialistic-Revolutionary party, whose principles were directly opposed to those of the Nationalists, though their 'circles' came in contact with those of their opponents. Just as there are Panslavists and National enthusiasts whose views of the National State organisation of the future are decidedly tinctured with Socialism, or at any rate start with the presumption of a pure democracy; so also not a few are to be found among the Socialists and Nihilists, who, like Bakunin, rave for the holy alliance of all emancipated peoples, and for the establishment of a Slavonic State, reaching from the Volga to the western frontier of Bohemia. With these Socialists the more advanced Nationalists (for there are also Nationalists, of course, of an essentially Conservative mould) were and still are allied—much more closely than their leaders had either imagined or desired—by a common hatred of the existing State system and its representatives, and by the common hope of a revolution in favour of government by the masses. *Fourthly*, and far removed from the arena where the government party, the Nationalists, and the Radicals fought out their rivalries, came the Finns, the Germans of the Baltic provinces, and the Poles. These, as separatists and people of foreign race (*Inorodzi*), were hated by the ruling parties, and unceasingly calumniated and attacked; but in spite of the aggression of the Greek Church and the increasing stringency of Russian administration, they preserved that social superiority which made them the really ruling element of the population in the western half of the empire. Separated from each other, though they were, by differences of religion and nationality; agitated in Poland and Lithuania by carefully-nursed ideas of revolution; trained by habit on the Baltic to tire out and finally to checkmate their opponents by a persistent attitude of passive resistance, and tolerably well protected in Finland by an excellent constitution—these 'Inorodzi,' with all their mutual isolation and hostility, were unanimous on one point. They all agreed in the conviction that the triumph of the Russian National party would mean their own ruin, and that the further extension of its influence and power must be combated at any price and with all the means at their disposal.

The war itself was the work of the second and third of the groups above described; it was delayed for nearly a year by the first. The fourth group, consisting, as we have seen, of foreign elements, has either had no voice in it at all, or—as has happened here and there in Poland—has secretly added fuel to the flame, with a view to gaining some advantage from the subsequent confusion. The Court and higher bureaucracy were against the war from the beginning, for they dreaded the newly-created institutions of the State being put to their proof, and saw clearly enough that victory no less than defeat might endanger the ruling system they represented. With the exception of some ladies of the upper classes, who were the creatures of priestly influence, and a few military men, anxious for war as a means of promotion, people of rank and station set their faces against the movement kindled by the Servian war and the bands of Russian volunteers in that campaign. In these circles the names of Tchernayeff and Komaroff were mentioned only with indignation and contempt; and the rhapsodies of the press about the Slavonic mission of Russia were quoted as a proof that the so-called National cause was simply a screen for the mischief-making of the old demagogues. The absolute necessity of peace, on political, financial, and military grounds, and the certainty that the outcry for war would cease the moment the mouths of its most blatant advocates were stopped, were facts as thoroughly understood in these quarters as on the Exchange at St. Petersburg, or even by those foreign journalists and correspondents who clung to the old fiction that in Russia the State and the Government were synonymous. So emphatic was the disapproval of the Servian revolt, expressed by the ruling circles at the capital during the winter of 1876-77, that the Moscow Nationalists formally renounced their hope of an understanding with Prince Gortchakoff, and joined with the volunteers who, on their return from the Timok, were treated with marked disfavour and forbidden to wear their Servian uniforms, in protesting against the government for deserting the sacred traditions of Russia.

Notwithstanding all this, the annihilation of the Servian army gave the signal for the issue of that ultimatum by which Prince Gortchakoff for the first time quitted the European concert. While the Emperor Alexander was inveighing most harshly against Servia, he was forced to mobilise half of his army to continue the very work which Servia had begun. Ostensibly, indeed, the subsequent action of Russia had no connection whatever with the Servian insurrection. But in reality, and as everyone at Moscow and St. Petersburg knew, it was just those battles fought between the Danube and the Timok which had roused the warlike temper of the Russians, and compelled the Czar to the most painful and difficult resolution of his life.

As regards the objects of the National party, in promoting this clamour for public intervention on behalf of the conquered Servians, no doubts whatever could exist. With all their vehement protestations of unlimited devotion to the Emperor and his 'sacred' will, they were forced at times and in the heat of discussion to confess that the war they wished for was simply the logical result of the principle they had proclaimed during the Polish insurrection, and that victory meant to them the crowning of the National edifice begun by Alexander II. The Poles and Germans had been suppressed, and the newborn energies of Russian nationality had been aroused by the abolition of serfdom. Necessity, therefore, demanded that the old system, founded on foreign influence, should be swept away, and the requisite scope afforded for the awakened vigour of the nation. The fortunes of Italy and Germany had taught their Russian countrymen that freedom and national unity were only different names for the same thing. For Russia to be truly free and to direct her own destinies, she must follow the example set before her, and solve the Slav question as her peculiar interests dictated. 'Russian life,' they said, 'has acquired a new meaning and purport. It can only acquire new forms by expanding itself to embrace the collective vitality of Slavdom. Thus only will Russia gain the power of stifling the elements of Romanism and Germanism, which have invaded her frontiers, and of erecting on those frontiers a firm bulwark against the "eastern advance" of Germany, doubly dangerous since the victories of 1866 and 1870.' If the government, they went on to argue, has really used aright the absolute power entrusted to them by the emancipated Russian people, and conscientiously fulfilled their duties of reform, no doubt can be entertained as to the victory of the Russian arms, and even the danger of a European alliance in favour of the Porte need not be feared. But if, on the other hand, the present machinery of government should prove inefficient for this task; if, even after twenty years of peace, it should be unable to stand the test of a larger war, then it would be high time to reorganise the State from top to bottom, and entrust its administration to new and more capable hands. 'Russia must know her own condition; she must learn whether she can count on those promises being fulfilled which were made to her during the critical days of 1861 and 1863-64. The time for waiting and fair promises is past. Our Slav brethren beyond Russia have invoked us to fulfil our historic mission. We must show that we have known how to make good use of the years of respite since the Crimean War; and that, after overcoming our enemies at home, we have learned how to conquer our enemies abroad. The abolition of serfdom, the annihilation of Polish nationality, and the removal of German influence have been useful and important, but only as preliminary measures, as means to an end. The moment has come to gather in the harvest, and to store it in the garner.'

Such were the views and language of the Nationalists on the war they had so strenuously urged. And they shaped their conduct accordingly. It was in vain that the official press continued to point to the danger of a south Slavonic movement of Servian volunteers independent of Russia, and insisted on the necessity of giving to the Austrian cabinet a pledge of the moderation and unselfishness of the Imperial Government, by suppressing the aspirations of Bulgaria. At all such representations the Nationalists merely shrugged their shoulders. 'What our native Pitts and Rouhers prate about our considerations for Austria and Europe,' wrote

Prince Meschtcherski early in 1877 to the 'Graschdanin,' 'may be left to foreign newspaper writers to consider. We knew long ago what to think of such talk. The triumph of the present union of the Czar and his people has taught us some plain truths with regard to the Petersburg camarilla. We have learned, in the first place, that it is useless for the conduct of our State affairs; secondly, that it is absolutely powerless; thirdly, that its chief weapons have been lies and calumnies against the Russian people; and, fourthly, that the policy of these men consisted in offending both the Czar and the people, and representing the national discontent at the humiliation of the emperor as a symptom of a revolutionary temper. This party, which has invented the phrase " ultra-Russian," which cringes to Europe, and cares neither for the Russian Church nor for Russian honour, is capable, in short, of anything—of designs as base as they are seemingly unintelligible.'

Still more plainly spoke Ivan Aksakoff, at a meeting of the Moscow Slavonic Benevolent Committee, on March 18, 1877, while endeavouring to interpret in a Slavo-national sense the emperor's famous speech in the hall of the Kremlin in the previous November. 'The historical conscience of Russia,' he said, 'spoke from the lips of the Czar, and his word thundered forth as " one having authority." . . . On that memorable day he spoke as the successor of the orthodox Grand-dukes, as the descendant of Ivan III., who received from the Palæologi the Byzantine arms, and combined them with the arms of Moscow; as the descendant of Peter and Catherine, and the crowned protector of ancient traditions. From these words there can be no drawing back, unless, indeed, the Russian nation should belie itself and its mission, and sign its own death-warrant.' Passing on to the diplomatic negotiations which had followed the Conference of Constantinople—the 'dark grey clouds,' as he called them, which threatened to 'eclipse the light of historical revelation,' the President of the Committee proceeded as follows: 'Our great and powerful Russia, leaving the straight path of truth, is wandering in the forests and mazes of diplomacy, to the astonishment and satisfaction of all Europe. She has never ceased to labour for the arrangement of a benevolent European concert in favour of the Slavs, and each time, when at her instigation the concert has been arranged, the proceeds of the performance go somehow into the pockets of the Turks. We have witnessed a whole series of consultations, conferences, and diplomatic tours, in which all who took part, without deceiving each other, deceived Russia grossly and openly, without even having recourse to ruse. But no amount of deceit, no injuries or insults, could shake the stubborn meekness and importunately pacific spirit of Russian diplomacy, though the insults made the cheeks of Russia blush for shame. . . . Meanwhile the Turks kill, impale, and violate Bulgarians, Bosnians, and Servians, and hundreds of thousands of Slav families have been starving as fugitives in a foreign land. . . . If the martyred people of Bulgaria, after the promises held forth to them by the popular movement in Russia of 1876, lose their faith in Russia, they will sink to such an abyss of despair that they will be morally ruined, and give themselves up to the power of the foreigner. . . . That precious Russian blood, poured out in torrents on the Servian battle-fields for the Slavonic cause, has not only remained unavenged, but has been as little thought of as if it had been the blood of Hottentots. To crown all, that heroic national exploit has become a subject for ridicule, jokes, and calumnies, and this not only in distinguished circles, where such things would naturally be expected, but even in those social strata which we imagine to be more educated and thoughtful. It has become a strange habit among certain people to ridicule and calumniate the gigantic national exploit of last year. The common people have remained true to the spirit which animated that movement, but the upper classes hasten to get rid of the impressions and enthusiasm to which twelve months ago they involuntarily succumbed. . . . It has come to this, that our volunteers, to whom the emperor himself was pleased to refer in his speech, were, on their return, regarded by many people, especially in the higher classes of St. Petersburg, almost as pariahs. The police, adapting themselves to the influence from above, eagerly stripped them of their Servian uniforms and Montenegrin costumes, so that nothing should recall the "shameful enthusiasm" of last year. Some people even ventured to deny the fact of the spontaneous national movement, and asserted—chiefly in St. Petersburg—that the so-called popular sympathy for our orthodox Slav brethren was simply a myth and an invention; that the whole movement was nothing but a practical joke got up by the Slav Committee, which ought, by the way, to be suppressed. . . . To vilify that outburst of popular feeling, by which Russia enlightened and refreshed herself, is to calumniate Russia, the Committee, and the Slavs. Stupidity and ignorance alone will not explain such calumnies; they denote moral weakness and corruption. Granted that the popular intervention on behalf of Servia produced some disorders; granted that among the Russian volunteers there were some drunkards and worthless fellows. Perhaps there were five per cent. of such men, or a little more; but such disorders could not be avoided, and there were no cowards among our fellow-countrymen.' Then, after insisting at some length that, if the *ultimatum* had appeared one or two months earlier, as the Servian Government had requested, not only would precious blood have been spared, but the confusion caused among the Servians by the non-appearance of the hoped-for Russian assistance would have been avoided, M. Aksakoff concluded as follows: 'Perhaps I have alluded too frequently to the emperor's words; but I do not hesitate to say that they are a great event in the history of the present time. In the grey, joyless twilight which surrounds us—in that chaos of contradictory aspirations and activity, in that lassitude of expectation from which all Russia is suffering—these words alone shine through the darkness as a star to encourage and to guide us. They contain a whole programme of action. These words, and the unanimous, spontaneous popular expression of fraternal love for the oppressed Slavs, form such historical landmarks that, if we only let ourselves be guided by them, we cannot lose our way and cannot fail to fulfil our mission, whatever obstacles we may have to encounter. In the spirit of these indications the Slav Committee has always acted. Though we have found little to console us in the last four months of our activity—having had chiefly to distribute what was previously collected with such labour and effort—still we believe that the seed sown has not fallen in vain on the Russian and Slavonian soil, and that one day it will bear fruit. Let us not lose courage or grow lax in our exertion. Let us rather redouble our efforts to alleviate the bodily and spiritual sufferings of the orthodox Slavs, to strengthen our mutual religious and moral solidarity, to confirm their faith in Russia, to uphold the dignity and honour of the Russian name in the unequal struggle with enemies abroad and at home—a struggle with ignorance and prejudice, and with voluntary and involuntary treason to Russian nationality among Russians themselves. May the historic mission of Russia be fulfilled! Behind us is the people, before us the Czar's words spoken at the Kremlin!'

The effect of this speech, widely circulated by the 'Moscow Gazette,' in spite of an express prohibition by the administration of the press, was immense, because it harmonised with the ruling temper of the public. No one could blame M. Aksakoff for boasting, when war was at last declared, that he alone had correctly interpreted the intentions of the Czar, so carefully concealed as they had been by diplomacy. No one could wonder when, in a speech delivered three weeks after the famous April 24, he concluded with this peroration: 'Already beyond the Russian frontier is unfurled the national standard, raised to give back freedom and the rights of man to the orthodox peoples of the Balkan peninsula, whom Europe, so proud of her enlightenment, has enslaved, humbled, and despised. The slumbering East is now awakened; and not only the Slavs of the Balkans, but the whole Slavonic world, awaits its regeneration. A new epoch is approaching; the dawn of the great Slavonic day has at length begun to break.'

Thus the Russo-Turkish war was regarded by those who were its authors as the key-stone of the national period of reform, represented by Alexander II., and at the same time as the frontispiece and title of a new and more momentous chapter of Russo-Slavonic history.

The war was equally desired by the Radical pupils of Herzen and Bakunin, who had recalled themselves to public remembrance by the prosecution of Netchayeff, the Kasan riot at St. Petersburg (Dec. 10, 1876), and the periodically recurring trials of the Nihilists. This party also hoped that now, as three-and-twenty years before, the foreign war would lead to a change of system at home, and a stripping off of the effete and antiquated forms of life. Some reckoned simply upon a total defeat of the Russian arms, and the consequent prospect of a revolution. Others thought that, if an absolutism of reform proved as incapable as the previous absolutism of despotic power, nothing would remain but to try the experiment of a constitutional system, such as a large portion of the Nationalists and even of the moderate Liberals had long desired and expected. In the event of such a change, the most advanced parties had the most to look for, owing to the fickleness of Russian nature and the want of education among the masses, and on this ground alone had the greatest reason to hope for the defeat of the Russian army and for a revolution at home. Lastly, there were many Radicals who made up their minds that the emperor would remain victor, and would really liberate Byzantium from the centuries of Turkish thraldom. But these Hotspurs believed, like the Nationalists, that nothing short of such a consummation would make their cause secure. 'When the Imperial eagle of Byzantium returns to its fatherland'—so Herzen had said, and so said his pupils—'it will disappear from Russia. When Constantinople is won, then the iron sceptre of Peter I. must break, for it cannot be lengthened to reach to the Dardanelles. . . . St. Petersburg is colder, but also safer than Constantinople; and the

Emperor Nicholas did well in 1829 not to go to Constantinople.' This was substantially the view of the Nationalists as well; its colouring only was darker, and it was rather differently expressed. What Aksakoff and his friends called the broadening of Russian into Slavonic nationality, and the acquisition of new forms of life, meant in the eyes of the Nihilists merely the collapse of all existing systems, the beginning of the 'end,' so long striven for by the revolutionary parties in Russia and Europe.

CHAPTER XIV.

THE WAR AND THE DYNASTY (*continued*).

The war not desired by the Government—The Manifestos of 1854 and 1877 compared—Imitation of Prussian military precedents—Want of competent Russian Generals—Bombastic utterances of Panslavism—Commencement of hostilities—Bad news from Armenia—First repulse at Plevna—Popular discontent and despondency in the army—Pessimist spirit at St. Petersburg—Aksakoff's memorial to the Czarevitch—Blunders of military administration—Increase of paper currency—Second repulse at Plevna—Demoralisation of the public mind—The Grand-duke Michael—Trial of the 183 Nihilists—Revolutionary spirit at Odessa—Poland and Lithuania remain tranquil—The Moscow National party and the war.

ALTHOUGH the declaration of war was hailed with enthusiasm and loyal addresses to the emperor, and even in Finland, Poland, and the Baltic provinces, people thought it necessary to come forward with manifestations of that kind, still the temper of the Court and the influential circles of government was subdued, not to say depressed. Those who were behind the scenes knew well enough that the emperor himself had not wished for war. They knew that his most experienced advisers, such as Count Schouvaloff, the ambassador at London, Von Reutern, the Minister of Finance, Miliutin, the Minister of War, and a large number of the older members of the Council of State, had shared the Czar's disinclination to embark on this adventure. They felt instinctively, like almost all other sober observers of the events of 1876, that the war now declared against Turkey must lead either to a general outbreak of hostilities in Europe, the extent of which no man could foresee, or to a revival of the revolutionary spirit in Russia. It was true that only at the eleventh hour had the Chancellor of the Empire consented to take the side of the Nationalists. But what of that? All the world was aware that the aged statesman, since his successes in 1863 and 1870, could no longer dispense with the applause of the Moscow leaders of opinion, and that he felt the need of being popular at any price.

The temper of the Court and its immediate adherents was plainly reflected in the manifesto of war (April 24, 1877,) and in the circular of the same date, addressed by Prince Gortchakoff to the Russian ambassadors at the Foreign Courts. No sooner had these documents been published, than the Moscow patriots drew attention to the vast difference between this manifesto and the one issued in 1854 by the Emperor Nicholas. Not a syllable was said this time about the 'welfare and safety of the Orthodox Church, of which the Russian nation also is a member, or of the sacred and injured rights of the Church.' The Emperor Alexander recapitulated the course of events as if he had to reckon simply with European diplomacy, and not primarily with the Russian people. He formally announced that Russia, in interfering on behalf of the Christians of the Balkans, had acted in concert with the other Powers; that she had demanded nothing but what had met with the agreement of the other Powers, her friends and allies; and that the rejection of those demands by the Porte was a rejection of the 'unanimous will of Christian Europe.' It is true that towards the close of this manifesto such expressions appeared as 'the justice of *our* cause,' the 'unanimity of *our* people.' But not a word was said about the Servian war; and everything was carefully avoided that might look in the least like an effect of national and religious passions, or like a recognition of the popular will, as expressed by the events of the last few months. Special, as well as general reasons, accounted no doubt for the reticence of the government on this last point. On the day of the declaration of war an article in the 'Golos' had distinctly alluded to the necessity of 'society taking a direct share' in the preparations for the struggle—of playing a part, in other words, in the constitution. So keenly were the suspicions of the government excited by this remark, that the paper in question, which circulated widely and was tolerably popular, was at once suspended; and it was only the painful effect produced by this act of severity, which subsequently caused the prohibition to be modified.

At Moscow, where such high-flown hopes had awaited the publication of this Imperial manifesto, as much notice was taken of its meagre language as of the manner in which the monarch and the members of his family prepared themselves for the coming war. The amateur politicians, both National and Liberal, exhausted their sarcasm in observing that all St. Petersburg could do was to copy, down to its smallest details, the precedent furnished by the Prussian royal family in 1870. Just like his royal uncle, so the Czar, after having issued his manifesto and sent the army before him, departed in person with his Chancellor for the seat of war. Just as in Prussia, so the command of the separate divisions of the army had been given to princes of the reigning family, and the heir to the throne had been sent into the field. Exactly after the Prusso-German pattern, a civil administration had been organised, for the purpose of conducting the government of the provinces intended to be occupied. At St. Petersburg, as before at Berlin, a 'silent automaton' had been discovered to direct the movements of the general staff. Wits prophesied that some of the Russian royal family too might find themselves field-marshals when the war was over.

As for generals of public reputation, men whom the popular voice could have designated for the chief command, there were none. That General Tchernayeff and his brother-officers, who had distinguished themselves in the Servian war, had been sent to the Caucasus and given subordinate positions, people learned with regret, but with no surprise. Outwardly indeed all was loyalty and the bliss of confidence; but within the narrower circles at St. Petersburg and Moscow there prevailed a coldly critical spirit of pessimism, such as would have been impossible twenty years ago. Not one of the men appointed to responsible positions in the army enjoyed the particular confidence of the public. Even the most prominent among them had remained such strangers to the mass of the nation, that it is still a matter of discussion whether General Gourko comes from Little Russia, or, as others assert, from Livonia, and whether General Radetzki, the gallant defender of the Shipka Pass, is of German or Russian origin. To eulogise the Grandduke Nicholas, the generalissimo of the army of the Danube, as a 'born soldier,' and a 'Russian Prince Frederick Charles,' remained the privilege of German, and especially Berlin newspaper writers. At St. Petersburg he was known only for his flirtations and his debts, and years ago it was notorious that his affectation of barrack-manners and *brusquerie*, in which occasionally he indulged, had nothing whatever to do with military education or military talent. His appointment to the chief command, and the active share in the campaign assigned to all the grown-up male members of the Imperial family, with the exception of the Grand-duke Constantine and his unfortunate son, were regarded, even outside Liberal circles, as an unsuccessful attempt to imitate Prussia. There was General Todleben, the heroic defender of Sebastopol, and a most popular man, in spite of his Livonian descent; and great was the disgust when the Grand-duke not only refused to attach him as Adlatus to his engineering staff, but was heard to say openly that he wanted no German military tutor (*Djädka*) about his person in the field. There was also another German, Count Kotzebue, the Governor-General of Poland, who was left behind, because he had been bold enough to doubt the sufficiency of the numerical strength of the army of the Danube.

The generals actually in command of this army had gone through their schooling partly in the Caucasus, partly in the Crimea, and during the Polish insurrection, but none of them had ever distinguished themselves. Others had acquired a somewhat adverse reputation. Levitzki, for instance, a former officer of the Guard, now promoted to the General Staff, was looked upon as a mere theoretician and prosy phrase-maker. General Skobeleff, afterwards lauded to the skies as a Divisional commander, was notorious as a *roué* and incorrigible spendthrift. The only men of decent military repute were Zimmermann, who led the first army corps across the Danube, and gained an honourable name by the conquest of Chokand; and Dragomiroff, who was favourably known by his reports on the German campaign of 1866 in Bohemia. On the other hand, the commanders of the army of the Caucasus, with the single exception of Heimann, were all of them men who had acquired their military experience in subordinate positions. That the Grand-duke Michael should be entrusted with the command of a whole *corps d'armée* nobody had ever dreamed to be possible, and the whole of Russia received the news with amazement.

Amidst the general excitement that prevailed, no one even thought of inquiring whether the appointed leaders in the coming conflict were equal to their task. Unwarned by the experiences of the French, only seven years before, our thoroughgoing patriots were full of the customary phrases of a 'Promenade to Constantinople' and of 'covering Europe with Cossack caps.'. What need was there for a general, when the sacred spirit of the nation seemed to have taken the command; when the war was one which had been preceded by twenty years of preparation, and for which everything 'down to the last button' was in readiness? The Czar himself, obedient to the voice of his orthodox people, had unfurled the banner. At length the summons had gone forth for a 'regeneration of all Slavonic races'— a summons so impatiently awaited by all true patriots already when serfdom was abolished. What mattered technical details and mere personalities, when a new chapter had commenced in the history of mankind; when the Russian people, like the giant in their fable, had awakened in their strength, to make the world tremble with the terror of their exploits, and to solve the problem for which they had reserved their energies since the days of the orthodox Grand-dukes of Muscovy?

Many weeks passed by, however, and still these fine prophecies were unfulfilled, and the heathen West remained unterrified by the footsteps of the awakened giant. It was not until two months after the invasion had actually begun (June 22, 1877) that the telegraph announced that the army had commenced to cross the Danube, that the heights of Budjak were occupied, and that Rustchuk was being bombarded. The bridge of Sistova was not ready till the beginning of July. Though the work had advanced more rapidly in Asia, people at Moscow and St. Petersburg learned the calamitous tidings of defeat at Zewin, Zicharisi and Karaklissa, and the compulsory abandonment of the intended investment of Kars, at the very moment when they were rejoicing over the capture of Tirnova and the internment of the garrison of Nicopolis.

This unwelcome news from a country, which at other times had been the scene of innumerable Russian victories, failed at first, it is true, to create any profound impression. Public attention from the outset of the war had been directed far more to Bulgaria than the highlands of Armenia, and in Bulgaria everything appeared to prosper. The victories of Hankioi and Eski-Sagra, the military achievements of Deroschinski and Prince Swätopolk-Mirski, the taking of Kasanlik, and the occupation of the Shipka Pass, followed each other in rapid succession. Up to the end of July, uninterrupted success had attended the Russian arms; and the result seemed to justify General Gourko's daring project of advancing with his cavalry on Adrianople, and seizing Roumelia before the occupation of Bulgaria had been completed, and a safe basis secured for further operations.

Then came, quite as unexpectedly for Russia as for the rest of Europe, the catastrophe of Plevna, and with it a revulsion in the public mind, more sudden and more powerful than had ever been experienced in Russia. A few days after the first storming of the Shipka Pass, the activity of the telegraph, hitherto indefatigable, suddenly came to a dead stop. The public of St. Petersburg, after revelling in anticipations of the capture of Adrianople, were left for three long days without any news whatever from the seat of war. Then a short official bulletin announced that, in an engagement near Plevna, the Russians had 'not been victorious.' Early in August, the passionately excited capital learned at last, that on the fatal days of July 26 and 31, not only had all the advantages obtained during the previous weeks been lost, but that the prospects of a successful termination of the Bulgarian campaign were as small, if not smaller, than the hopes of success in Upper Armenia. Before even the first impressions created by these terrible tidings had had time to abate, news still worse arrived, which, in spite of all the efforts of the press bureau to prevent it, had found its way from English, French, German, and Austrian newspapers into the journals of St. Petersburg and Moscow. Not only had the Russians been beaten in two great battles, and forced to remove their head-quarters from Tirnova to Biela, but the Commander-in-Chief had lost so completely all composure and self-confidence, that the assistance of the hated and despised Roumanians and the ill-treated Servians was invoked at his request. The Guards were ordered to the Danube, and regardless of the urgency of harvest labour, the government decreed an immediate calling out of the militia (*Opoltschénie*). The private letters from the seat of war contained still worse tidings than the newspapers. The cause of all these terrible reverses, they said, was neither a sinister combination of circumstances nor the superiority of the enemy. They were due solely to the incapacity and recklessness of the Commander-in-Chief. The 'insane attempt against Plevna' had been arranged by the Grand-duke personally, against the advice of his most experienced officers, and although old General Krüdener had been down on his knees before him to dissuade him from the venture. Even then it was continued with criminal obstinacy for two whole days, notwithstanding the palpable impossibility of success. Blinded with immeasurable self-assurance before the repulse, and inaccessible to every objection raised against the premature assaults upon the stronghold, the Grand-duke after the catastrophe is said to have been the most disheartened of them all, and one of the accessories of the panic which revealed to the gaze of Europe the full extent of the disasters. The utter helplessness, confusion, mistrust and mutual recriminations which prevailed throughout the army were openly ascribed to head-quarters. Those who had been as haughty and arrogant in the day of success as they were despondent in the day of adversity had infected all the ranks with their vicious example. No one knew what quarter to look to for an extrication from this labyrinth of apparently hopeless failure. There was not a single ray of light amid the universal gloom and dejection. There was not a single man who inspired confidence or trust; all alike seemed helpless and despondent. Gorny Studen, the head-quarters of the emperor himself, was scarcely mentioned for weeks. The figure of the Czar, who had been the sun of his people, seemed to have vanished in the general confusion. Those who saw him in these days have described him as a man looking ill and aged, and stirred to the very depths of his soul by the misery he saw around him. Even his most devoted servants were forced to confess that for a Russian emperor who is with his army, there is only one position to occupy, that of commander-in-chief, and that it was a mistake for his Majesty to have followed as a simple spectator. Such a step would not only provoke painful comparisons between the Russians and the combatants of 1870, both French and Prussians, but would suggest false ideas to the common people about the position of the Autocrat. It was bad enough already that members of the Imperial family had been placed in positions which exposed them to public criticism and reduced them to the level of common mortals. The person of the Czar at least ought to occupy a pedestal removed from the vicissitudes of war, unless the foundations of all public order were to be endangered.

That these foundations have suffered from a disturbance, unparalleled in Russia within the memory of man, is not indeed to be denied. During those memorable weeks of the departure of the Guard and the calling out of the militia, a spirit of pessimism and bitter disappointment prevailed in Russia, beyond anything which either the two capitals or the provinces had ever witnessed in former days. Newspapers and private persons exhausted the language of reproach in inveighing against the blunders of the government. The commissariat and the recruiting system were defective and badly organised. The course of events had plainly shown how imperfect were the preparations for the war. The calling out of the militia, fixed without any necessity for the season of harvest, gave rise in particular to bad feeling. In an article which was much discussed, the 'Golos' pointed out that a delay of three or four weeks would have sufficed to store the crops and save the rural population from enormous losses. 'But alas! we understand as little how to practise economy as we do how to husband our strength.' And indeed for several weeks the scarcity of labour, caused by this sudden drain on its resources, was felt so severely, that even the shops at St. Petersburg fell short of their necessary servants, and the official press thought it necessary to point out that the militia were not intended to supply the vacancies in the active army, but merely for preliminary service at the depôts of the reserve.

At Moscow and in some of the provincial towns matters looked even worse than at censorious and pessimistic St. Petersburg. Already at the first news of the reverses of the Asiatic army, which were generally ascribed to the interference of the Grand-duke Michael in the plan of the campaign, and to the squabbles between Heimann and Loris-Melikoff, Ivan Aksakoff had spoken publicly of the necessity of a 'change of system,' and had suggested the establishment of a central committee, consisting of provincial representatives, to supervise the proceedings of the government. After the fatal days of Plevna the recognised leader of the National party, and now the President of the Slavonic Benevolent Committee, took a further step in this direction. He drew up a memorial to the Czarevitch, supported by the signatures of numerous friends and sympathisers, demanding the immediate calling together of a central assembly of provincial delegates—in other words, a constituent assembly of the empire. He stated his motive for this proposal: the necessity of placing at the head of affairs 'more capable military commanders' and 'more trustworthy diplomatists' than the present advisers of his Majesty, in order to avert the impending national collapse. This memorial was given to Prince Woronzoff to be forwarded to the Czarevitch, who was known to be not averse to constitutional schemes, and thoroughly disapproved of the chief command having been given to his uncle the Grand-duke Nicholas. Although the desired official use was not made of this memorial, it excited a tremendous sensation at head-quarters and in various parts of the empire. To its influence it was chiefly due that, about the middle of October, another scheme, analogous to that of Aksakoff, was brought forward by the press and in various provincial assemblies in Southern Russia. This scheme proposed that, with a view to reorganise and reform the whole departments of commissariat and victualling, which in the hands of the Greger-Horwitz-Kohan Company had completely broken down, their management should be transferred to a Committee of South Russian provincial associations, charged with final control over the provisioning of the army.

That the government should turn a deaf ear to such proposals was only natural. It was just as natural, however, that public opinion should eagerly catch them up and support them by declaring that 'things could not be allowed to go on as they had gone hitherto.' The 'Vêstnik Evrópy,' one of the leading and most influential organs of the press, took up the same theme with variations, with regard to another department of the administration. In an article confined strictly to statements of fact, but for that reason most effective, this paper pointed out that, in the event of a long continuance of the war, the daily cost of which was 700,000 roubles, the administration of finance, as at present conducted, must inevitably lead to bankruptcy. Within six months alone, besides the regular expenses of the military budget, 280 million roubles had been spent for purposes of the war; 240 millions of this total being derived from loans, and 40 millions from the surplus moneys of the State. 'Had we only been moderately prepared for the war,' it was said, 'it would not have been necessary again to increase, during the first five months of hostilities, the mass of paper money already in circulation, and thus to lower so forcibly the rate of exchange.' Quoting then from the official returns of the Bank, the writer calculated that the total of these new paper issues amounted already to 140 million roubles, in addition to the 779 millions circulating before the war began.

Notice was taken of this article even in circles which usually and on principle regarded the utterances of the Russian press with unconcern. The dislike of a further increase of paper money was quite as strong among the German and English bankers on the St. Petersburg Exchange, and the Jewish sub-contractors, traders, and sutlers of the army, as among the 'genuine National' traders of St. Petersburg and the Moscow bazaar, the superior and inferior officials in the Ministries and the provincial administrations, and the democratic writers of newspapers. All and everyone alike suffered from the depreciation of the paper rouble and the consequent rise in prices. The only gainers, with the exception of certain speculators on the Exchange in the confidence of the government, had been those landed proprietors and traders who were able to export corn abroad and sell at a high premium the German money they received in exchange. But this fortunate class was very limited in number, for all traffic on the Southern railways was suspended for many months, in consequence of the transport of troops.

With the advance of autumn, the general gloom and embitterment of the Russian people increased. About the middle of September, together with the news of the arrival of the Guard in Roumania, came the news of a second unsuccessful assault on Plevna. This fresh disaster aroused universal indignation; and fiercely was the wrath expressed against the Grand-ducal Commander-in-Chief, who was designated as the author of this repeated failure. It was a matter of general and painful regret that the emperor should have let himself be persuaded to give a certain sanction by his presence to this senseless act of rashness, and to look on like a modern Xerxes from his imperial pavilion. Public confidence had sunk so low that the wildest rumours and fables were promulgated and believed. One day it was said that the government, with a view to employ in the field the troops garrisoned in Poland, had requested Prussia—'that Prussia,' said the 'St. Petersburg Journal,' 'whose sympathy for our calamities begins to savour of offensive compassion'—to undertake the provisional occupation of the Russian province. Another day it was reported to have been discovered that the two Poles at headquarters, Nepokoischizki, the chief of the general staff, and General Levitzki, with the connivance of several Russian traitors, of Polish sympathies, were hatching a plot for the total annihilation of the army. Then again it was said that Prince Gortchakoff, who was then at Bucharest, and Baron Jomini, were fully convinced of the impossibility of continuing the present 'system,' and were busy, at the instance of the Czarevitch, in elaborating the scheme of a constitution. Ivan Aksakoff was to have been carried off by gendarmes in the middle of the night for having said 'the dynasty began the war, but the nation alone can and will terminate it.' All these reports, no matter how absurd and self-contradictory, were greedily swallowed and industriously propagated. It was enough that they fed the pessimism, in which the nation absolutely revelled, which was regarded as a token of patriotic independence, and which was most adroitly connected with the general desire for a change of system, for the convocation, in short, of a Constituent Assembly. Even when the situation at the scene of war began to improve, and the first news of Russian success arrived from the Asiatic frontier, these tidings would not relieve the 'dull melancholy' of despair, whose leaden weight oppressed even the naturally sanguine and imperialist correspondent of the 'Journal des Débats.' Even the announcement of the reinvestment of Kars, commenced this time under the most hopeful auspices, failed to counteract the impression on the public mind created by the ridicule heaped in some quarters on the 'chicken campaign' carried on by the otherwise popular Czarevitch in the Dobrudscha; by the opening of the great trial of the 183 Nihilists at St. Petersburg on October 30; by Aksakoff's speech to the Slav Committee, and by the news of a change in the temper of the Poles. It was a significant symptom of the mistrust, the demoralisation, and the mania for popularity, then prevailing in higher circles, that the immediate friends of the Grand-duke Michael found it necessary to repel the notion that the improvement of affairs in Armenia had been brought about suddenly, or by a change of persons. They derided the idea that the Commander-in-Chief of the Asiatic army should have needed in any way the advice of strangers; and that General Obrutscheff, who had been suddenly sent from St. Petersburg to the scene of war, should have turned the scale of fortune. Obrutscheff's mission was nothing else, they said, but an intrigue in high places at St. Petersburg against the Grand-duke and his generals.

The most remarkable event, however, and the one most significant of the state of Russian society, was unquestionably the public prosecution of the 183 Nihilist conspirators. Four years had passed since the trial at Moscow of Netchayeff, the murderer of Ivanoff, first unveiled to the eyes of the nation at large the intrigues of the Socialists and revolutionary Radicals; and this period the party of destruction had made use of with decided success. Over no less than thirty-seven provinces of the empire had the net been spread from St. Petersburg, by means of which the 'people'—in other words, the proletariate in the towns and the peasants in the poorer districts—were to be drawn into the interest of the young enthusiasts, both male and female, who espoused the doctrines of Bakunin and Tschernitchevski. But the Government meanwhile had laid their plans, and at length the swoop was made. On one and the same day, in May 1875, these revolutionary fanatics were seized, according to a prearranged scheme of the Third Section, throughout the limits and corners of the empire. Every class of society, and all the governments of Russia, with the exception of the Baltic provinces and Finland, had furnished its contingent. The main body of the accused, excepting those at St. Petersburg itself, came from certain provinces of the Volga, from Lithuania, and the South of New Russia. Most of them were the sons and daughters of small officials and village priests, and had been at the higher institutes of education. There were not wanting a few, however, who belonged to the high nobility, as well as some of the labouring classes. It was remarked, in particular, that numerous young Jews from Lithuania had taken part in the conspiracy.

The preliminary proceedings, conducted in secret, had lasted for a whole year and a half, owing to the vast mass of materials collected, and the obstinacy with which those chiefly accused refused to give any sort of information. The public trial, however, could now no longer be delayed ; and it came off just at a moment most opportune for these young revolutionists, who wished to create as much noise and display as the occasion permitted. Notwithstanding the strict supervision of the reports in the newspapers, the limited dimensions of the court itself, and the similarity of the various indictments, the interest of the public in this trial was as passionate as the wishes of many people were transparent, to give the most interesting—that is to say, the most palliative— aspect to the offence. Not indeed that this sympathy was of a very practical kind. To interfere directly on behalf of these enthusiasts, who, disguised as workingmen, had 'gone about among the people,' distributing revolutionary tracts, imported from Geneva, to the peasants and artisans in the manufactories and others of the lowest grade of civilisation—such a notion occurred to very few, if any of their admirers. The enterprise in question had too little prospect of success, and had been too childish and too badly prepared, to be of any real service to the cause of 'progress.' On the other hand, the number of those was extraordinary who sympathised with the position, and in part acquiesced in the objects of the accused. They declared the charges made by the Nihilist fanatics against the ruling system to be 'not without cause or justification.' They noted the wide extension of Socialist ideas with a certain pleasure, as a remarkable symptom of the 'increase of the social movement.' They were as much edified by the energy and resolution of the accused as by the embarrassment the whole affair caused to the government. And this embarrassment was not a small one. It was bad enough that some of the most guilty of the prisoners, such as Myshkin from Siberia and Rabinovitch, wrought upon the breathless audience by the passionateness of their demeanour and their wild, declamatory eloquence, and aroused ideas and aspirations which, from the very charm of novelty, produced their effect upon the listeners. It was worse that even the counsel for the defence did all they possibly could to give importance to the cause, to awaken the sympathies of the numerous young women and girls who were among the audience, and to perplex the judges, unaccustomed to scenes of that kind, out of countenance. The demeanour of French advocates under similar circumstances was imitated down to the minutest details. The gestures, the very tricks of that forensic oratory were copied, which had been the fashion in France some thirty or forty years before, whenever a political issue was involved in the trial. The accused were surrounded with a halo of martyrdom, on account of their independent views, erroneous perhaps, but from their consistency very remarkable. When Myshkin claimed the right of expatiating on topics wholly unconnected with the cause, and of unfolding the ' programme of the Social revolutionary party' in detail, his claim was treated as a sacred right of man, and its rejection as a menace of despotism. It was attempted to intimidate the witnesses, and to excite the public against the officials of police and gendarmerie, whose duties bound them to report what they had discovered or observed. And in many cases these disgraceful attempts succeeded beyond the expectations of their authors. Myshkin's counsel was able to remove from the court an officer of gendarmes by the impudent remark, loudly made, that ' the sight of his uniform might excite the public.' He attacked the judges with such warmth and vigour, that they were forced to allow his client to hold forth in a long speech, bristling with the most insane invectives against the government. The noise of the audience—men and women here shrieking and screaming, there convulsed with hysterics—became so tumultuous and intolerable, that the proceedings had virtually been long suspended, when at length the president mustered up sufficient energy (Nov. 27, 1877) to order the Court to be cleared and the prisoners to be removed. But, just as if it had been intended by the government to diffuse as widely as possible the excitement caused by these scandalous scenes, and to give the public the most imposing ideas of the extent and danger of the conspiracy, the utmost importance was attached to the treatment of each particular circle, such as the 'Artillerists,' the 'Orenburgers,' and others, grouped around one mysterious centre, and the proceedings were spun out over weeks. The brevity and meagreness of the reports issued to the public served to stimulate the greed of 'interesting news,' and to awaken curiosity about these strange phenomena of national life. When at last the verdict was given, by which ninety-nine of the accused were condemned, there was scarcely any doubt that the injury caused by the trial had far outweighed all the mischief which was alleged to have caused it. Enough food had been given for scandal and evil-talking, and for the greed of political excitement, to glut the public appetite for months. Authority and order had received a heavy blow by the public manner in which the 'system' had been attacked, and the equally public manner in which it had been defended. Nor was the mischief over with this prosecution. It was known quite well that another must shortly follow, bringing fresh excitement and fresh scandal. The trial of the December rioters in the previous year was near at hand; and news was daily arriving of new revolutionary demonstrations and new imprisonments in consequence. These tidings came from the most distant and different parts of the empire; they came in particular from the South, corrupted to the core as the rendezvous and hotbed of all the riff-raff and idlers of Eastern Europe.

Odessa, founded in 1794 by Catherine II., had, under the wise administration of the Duke of Richelieu, afterwards minister of Louis XVIII., risen rapidly to be the capital of 'New Russia.' For a long time past, however, it has been looked upon as one of the most corrupt points in the Russian Empire. Italians had been the parent stock of the population; the streets only thirty years ago had Italian names. The original inhabitants were soon joined by Russians, Greeks, Jews, Armenians, German colonists, Moldavo-Wallachians, and others; for the most part adventurers and swindlers of the most reckless kind, people who had learned their lessons in scoundrelism at Constantinople, Roumania, and the Levant, and had grown grey in vices and crimes of every description. Since the opening of the South Russian Railway Odessa had become the centre of an extensive trade in wheat, and the most considerable town on the shores of the Euxine. But it was still a place of constant disorder and habitual lawlessness. Hopelessly involved in debt through the recklessness of its municipal administration; prevented from effecting any sort of consolidation by a constantly shifting population; held together by no ties of nationality or religion, and visited, moreover, by periodical commercial crises, easily explained by the precarious nature of the wheat trade, this town had degenerated into a focus of crime and dissolute excess, such as none of the governors-general, town prefects, or heads of police sent from St. Petersburg had ever been able to master. Frauds and thefts of unprecedented extent, and murders and acts of violence committed in broad daylight, were daily occurrences. The attempts to curb the prevailing disorder remained nearly always abortive, the sea and the Roumanian frontier being near, and the number of professional thieves and receivers of stolen goods enormous. Neither the watchfulness and severity of Von Kotzebue, the former Governor-General, nor of Count Steenbock, the Chief of Police, had been able to check the evil; but after their departure it was worse than ever.

No wonder, therefore, that the revolutionary propaganda of the Nihilists found a more congenial soil on the coast of the Black Sea than at the neighbouring Kieff, and that the dominant bad spirit infected the students when a university was founded at Odessa in 1865. Of their revolutionary sentiments the Odessa students had given evidence before the recent war; but after the outbreak of hostilities, which all but destroyed the commercial industry of the seaport, it seemed as if town and university alike were possessed by an evil demon. A portion of the army being provisioned from Odessa, Jewish, Greek, and Roumanian contractors and traders of the most suspicious kind thronged thither, and made the town a scene of orgies, frauds, and crimes, such as surpassed the utmost measure of former iniquities. The emissaries of Nihilism understood quite as well as the professional scoundrels of the place how to profit by this state of insecurity. Some of the police were bribed; the rest were intimidated and prevented from acting with energy. Placards appeared on the walls in public places openly inciting the populace to deeds of violence and disobedience against the government; clandestine printing presses prepared and circulated Socialistic pamphlets; small conspiracies were hatched in secret, whose members attacked with daggers and pistols the police who were sent after them. All this was done during the summer and autumn of 1877, and done with an insolence such as people were only accustomed to meet with among the infamous bands of robbers and thieves who infested subterranean Odessa, who prowled among the numerous caverns and passages beneath the plateau on which the city stands. So deeply had the spirit of insubordination corroded the population, that the Communal Council was impudent enough to take no official notice of the passage of the Guards through the town on their way to the seat of war, and to treat the household regiments of the Czar, accustomed to be welcomed everywhere with patriotic ovations, with a coldness scarcely to be distinguished from hostility.

Meanwhile, in Poland and Lithuania, the most suspected portions of the whole empire, there reigned tranquillity and silence. The leaders of the 'emigration,' aristocratic and democratic, had given the word that all disturbance of public peace and order was to be avoided: any occurrence to the contrary would be regarded by them as treason to the National cause. Strict obedience was paid to this injunction, and not a syllable betrayed that the Russian reverses at Plevna made thousands of Polish hearts beat quicker. These tactics could be explained by various reasons. In the first place, there was the fear lest a premature rejoicing at defeat might afford the government a pretext for redoubled severity; in the second place, there were differences of opinion, deeply entertained, and as yet untested by results, whether this time the Polish cause had not more to gain from Russia than from Turkey. Hatred against Russia had ceased since 1871 to be the motive that determined the conduct of Polish patriots. To them, the increase of German influence in Europe appeared far more dangerous than the brutality of Russian violence—a view which was purposely encouraged at Rome and Paris, and which counted a considerable number of adherents, especially among the Ultramontanes of Cracow. There was a Polish party who actually advocated reconciliation with Russia: the fact was well known since 1870, though considered impossible even a few years before. A part also of the Liberal press in Russia had attempted to make the hostility between Slav and German interests a bridge for effecting a better understanding with the Poles, and had repeatedly discussed the possibility of a compromise to be arranged at the expense of Germany. With a like object, Field Marshal Prince Barjätinski had endeavoured to bring his influence to bear on certain circles of magnates at Warsaw, and to establish friendly relations with the remnants of Wielopolski's party. Wielopolski himself, the former Civil Commissioner of the Grand-duke Constantine, was known to have entertained similar thoughts; and his experiences of 1831 and 1846 [1] had convinced him that the hopes of Polish nationality rested not on Austria, or the Western Powers, but on Russia. His son also, Count Siegesmund, was supposed to share this view. The majority

[1] The Marquis had been sent to London in 1831 as the plenipotentiary of the National Government at Warsaw, and had satisfied himself there that the mass of the English people were indifferent to the Polish cause. The butcheries at Tarnow in 1846 had imbued him with a profound hatred of Austria, which he passionately expressed in a public letter addressed to Prince Metternich (*Lettre d'un gentilhomme Polonais au Prince Metternich*). He fell ill at the time of the Turkish war, and died at Dresden on December 30, 1877, in the seventy-fourth year of his age.

of the 'emigration' party, of course, were of a contrary opinion, and would have liked nothing better than to come to blows at once. Even these enthusiasts, however, could not conceal from themselves that, with a Russo-German alliance, such an enterprise would be hopeless; and that the aristocratic leaders were not altogether wrong in taking into account the possibility of a Russian change of system, which might separate Russia from Germany, and oblige the Liberal elements to make concessions to Polish nationality.

Thus, then, the Poles resolved to wait, and in so doing to preserve their liberty of action intact. If Russia proved victorious in the East, Poland had not compromised herself; if she were defeated, a revolution seemed imminent, and with it, the best opportunity for actively advancing the Polish claims. To act prematurely, and with precipitation, would infallibly result in strengthening the already close relations between St. Petersburg and Berlin. All parties agreed that this eventuality would be the worst imaginable; for all knew that Prince Bismark was their most dangerous enemy, and that the continuance of Berlin influence at the Court of St. Petersburg would offer an insurmountable barrier to Russo-Polish conciliation, the fundamental postulate of a Panslavonic policy of the future.

The leaders of the Moscow National party would listen neither to any concessions to Polish nationality and Catholicism, nor to any other measures of conciliation. Whilst in Western Europe people were naïve and short-sighted enough to speculate on a patched-up peace, in consequence of the difficult position of the Russian Empire and the wide-spread discontent with the government; the spokesmen of Liberal opinion, on the contrary, clamoured for war to the knife. 'Before Plevna it might have been possible to conclude peace on the terms of being satisfied with the liberation of Bosnia and Bulgaria; now we must not halt till we reach Constantinople.' This was the verdict of Moscow, and it was echoed by everyone who laid claim to liberal and patriotic sentiments. The struggle for the possession of Plevna was still going on when Prince Vassiltchikoff, in an article much discussed, laid down as the minimum of conditions to be required the cession of all the territory then occupied in Asia Minor, the recognition by Turkey of an independent Bulgaria, and the opening of the Dardanelles. If Aksakoff, Illovaiski, Dostojevski, and his friends, could have had their way, war would have been declared at once against the Austro-Hungarian government, when, early in November, the first news was learned of the formation of an Austrian party in Bosnia, and of a Magyar-Polish conspiracy discovered in Eastern Transylvania; and a Slav crusade would have been preached against the 'hateful Vienna and Pesth, the allies of the Crescent.' The pessimist views of the situation of the Russian army of the Danube served to strengthen the opinion that it only required a concentration of the national energies, and an appeal to 'Russian society,' to surmount impossibilities, and, by the help of a Slav *levée en masse*, to gain for Russia the entire dominion of the East.

Those who spoke thus seemed purposely to increase the dangers surrounding the empire, and to be bent on creating a position of such urgent necessity as should force the government to extremes. The speech of Ivan Aksakoff to the Moscow Slavonic Benevolent Committee, on October 8, was a laboured indictment against the ruling classes—the 'elder brethren,' as he called them—as the responsible authors of the national disgrace, the punishment for the sins of an anti-National policy and its embodiment diplomacy. The war, which the events of 1876 had made an affair of honour, had been declared against the will of these 'elder brethren' by the Czar, and the 'younger brethren,' his people. These must draw closely together to carry on to the end the great and sacred work they had begun. 'Any receding, or standing still half-way, would mean treason to the sacred legacy bequeathed by our martyred brethren who had fallen in the struggle.'

On the ruling point at issue this opinion of Aksakoff was shared by people who had otherwise nothing in common with his doctrines. The pessimists, and those who inveighed most bitterly against the misconduct of the war, were the fiercest in demanding its prosecution. The worst Chauvinists were those who speculated on fresh defeats and embarrassments of the government, and accordingly called everyone a traitor who ventured to whisper of peace and moderation. For this reason alone, nothing else was left to the Conservatives [1] but to join in the general cry. Even those who after the second repulse at Plevna had urgently demanded the return to St. Petersburg of the emperor, already almost lost to sight amid the tumult of the conflict, were forced to confess that now it was too late. 'If the Czar is not to find his authority repudiated altogether, he must not return to his capital except as a conqueror.'

---

[1] It is extraordinary that the *Moscow Gazette*, notorious for its strict monarchical sentiments no less than for its zeal for the war, should have roundly made the *Golos* and the *Exchange Gazette of St. Petersburg* responsible for the failure of the November loan. The first was supposed to have sinned through pessimism, the second through an unpatriotic desire for peace.

It had come to pass exactly as old M. Thiers had predicted. 'Les Russes vaincus seront plus exigeants que les Russes vainqueurs.' Only these 'exigences' were just as applicable to the internal as to the foreign policy of Russia.

CHAPTER XV.

THE WAR AND THE DYNASTY (*continued*).

Fall of Plevna—The Czar's return to St. Petersburg—His despondency amidst the general joy—Differences of opinion in high quarters—Passage of the Balkans—General desire to continue the war—Treaty of San Stefano—Its effects on Russian society—Russian disappointments—The British Fleet in the Bosphorus—European demand for the revision of the treaty—Schouvaloff alone insists on peace—Attempts to coerce the government—Menacing language of the National party—The Treaty of Berlin—Popular indignation—Damage done to the government and dynasty by the war.

MATTERS meanwhile had been gradually improving for some time past at the seat of war in Europe, and in Asia Minor the capture of Kars had made amends for the reverses in the early spring. But at St. Petersburg there was as yet no trace of any change in the sinister temper engendered by the disastrous occurrences of the summer. So deeply did the indignation at the blunders of the government still rankle in the public mind, so confidently had men counted on a change of domestic policy, that the news of the imminent surrender of Plevna was received with the utmost incredulity and suspicion. It was not until towards the end of November, when the investment was finally complete, and Mehemet Ali's attempt to relieve his brother general had proved too late, that a different aspect was observable at home, and the public learned to do justice once more to the maligned and defeated soldiers of July and September. When at length the news of the fall of

Plevna arrived (December 10), a reaction of popular feeling ensued, which in suddenness and excess surpassed even that of the previous summer. Those who had railed most loudly against the existing system, and predicted its immediate downfall, were now silent for the moment. The spell of disaster which had weighed upon the nation seemed suddenly to be broken. The leaders in the desperate struggle had regained their lost laurels. Servia could again take her place by the side of her ally; and a solemn promise of the Czar guaranteed that Russia would not halt half way, but continue her course of victory to the gates of Constantinople. For the moment the government was once more the leader of public opinion, and seemed to be equally bent on the vigorous prosecution of the war. The loudest demonstrations of joy welcomed the emperor and his sons, when he finally returned to his capital, and received the congratulations of the Court, the municipal authorities, and the Marshals of Noblesse, who had flocked together from all quarters of the empire.

But there was one cloud amidst this general joy. The changed appearance of His Majesty attracted universal notice and regret. His pale and mournful face, his hair now turned completely grey, and the painful efforts he betrayed to maintain his wonted soldierly bearing and upright carriage, troubled as he was with asthma—all this showed only too plainly that the anxious months of the summer and autumn, spent in the peasant's cottage at Gorny Studen, had seriously shaken his health. His asthmatic attacks, not dangerous, indeed, but still extremely troublesome, often came upon him so suddenly as to unfit him for all activity, or even movement; and he was compelled, much against his former wont, to sit down in an armchair on festive occasions, and when giving audience. His state of mind was described as one of settled melancholy and gloom; he seemed only momentarily touched by the joyous excitement of the Court and capital at the tidings of victory from the seat of war. No one knew better than himself, who was burdened with the fate of the Russian Empire, that the terrible time of trial he had just passed through had been something more than a mere bad dream, and that now no bridge of retreat was left for reverting to the state of things abandoned by the declaration of war. The very compassion of the public for the anxieties he had suffered since the fatal days of July wounded him at his most sensitive point. It was no secret that the heir to the throne differed totally from his father on questions of momentous importance, and that he made no attempt to conceal this difference of opinion. The emperor desired a speedy termination of the war, and the conclusion of a peace compatible not only with the maintenance of friendly relations with the Courts of Berlin and Vienna, but with the re-establishment of the former system of government. The Czarevitch, on the contrary, would not listen to any consideration being paid to Germany, nor to any limitation of the object of the war. In his opinion the internal administration of Russia required a searching reform, supported by the co-operation of Russian society, and her foreign policy needed bold and resolute action, bold enough to satisfy the wishes of the National party and disarm all possible elements of opposition.

On this last point, however, the opinions of high Russian dignitaries differed quite as much as those of the Czar and his son. Prince Gortchakoff seemed to incline to the party of reckless advance, represented by

Count Ignatieff and a number of Russian generals. The Minister of Finance counselled prudence and moderation. Count Schouvaloff, who had little sympathy with the Czarevitch and the Nationalists, and who was feared, moreover, for his energy and mental superiority, reported again and again from London that a direct endangering of Constantinople would unquestionably be answered by a declaration of war from England. There were other differences, also, of a more delicate nature. The Czarevitch, whose private and domestic life was exemplary, had never disguised his unfavourable opinion of the character and military qualifications of his uncle, the Grand-duke Nicholas, and since the first disaster at Plevna had become his open and determined enemy. The Czar, on the other hand, who had grown up in the views and habits of a different period, judged his brother more leniently, and was unwilling, for mere reasons of decorum, to deprive him of his chief command. For the present, however, matters continued as they were. The opposition of the 'young Court' remained a well-known fact, and the source of perpetual irritation, causing the sensitive-minded emperor, oppressed with a multiplicity of troubles, many an anxious hour, and preventing either him or his adherents from deriving any peace or satisfaction from the successes lately gained.

These successes, meanwhile, had accumulated so rapidly, that they were near becoming a source of embarrassment. However numerous were the complaints made about the barbarous manner of conducting the passage of the Balkans, showing as it did the utter want of proper preparation—nay, the Grand-duke himself was said to have threatened to shoot anyone who brought him evil news—still, the Balkans were crossed, and the Russian army pushed forward to the holy city on the Bosphorus. Had the personal inclinations and wishes of the emperor been able to prevail, a halt would then have been made at Adrianople, and negotiations would have quietly been opened with the envoys sent for that purpose from Stamboul. But the time for entertaining such counsels was past. The sudden change in the situation had thrown the nation from one paroxysm into another. All classes of society, all parties, were filled with the passionate desire of making the most of the favours of fortune, no matter what the consequences might be. In the wish to continue the war, and reject the Turkish overtures for peace, most of the high dignitaries were thoroughly agreed with the generals, the press, and the Nationalist leaders. The Czarevitch and the Grand-duke Nicholas spoke and acted also in this sense, and conjured the monarch to obey the popular voice, supported as it was by the traditions of a thousand years, and to vindicate by bold and vigorous action the authority of the government, so sadly shaken by the events of the previous summer. No patriotic Russian monarch ought to reject an opportunity, such as was now offered, of satisfying the inmost aspirations of the Slavonic people. To none of the heirs of Rurik the Varagian had fortune ever vouchsafed such favours as the present. Let Russia confront for a moment the feeble menaces of the Western Powers, and she would solve at once the problem of her holiest and most important destiny. A calm consideration of all the bearings of the situation, such as would have corresponded with the habits and inclinations of the emperor, seemed to be rendered impossible by the impetuous progress of events. The few voices which ventured to whisper a *respice finem* were drowned in the general clamour. The war cry of the impassioned multitude served to strengthen the influence of those time-serving politicians whose counsels were all for precipitate resolve. The very temper of the army made it appear hazardous to check their victorious march to Constantinople. The emperor was forced to yield, and the consequences are well known. Ignatieff and M. Nelidoff were entrusted with the conduct of the peace negotiations, which were enveloped in a foolish mystery downright offensive to the friendly Powers; and the Russian nation was left under the delusion that the last word had already been spoken about the future of Constantinople and the East.

This short-sighted policy, involving the empire in the utmost danger both at home and abroad, and far from satisfying the popular wishes, which nothing short of the occupation of Constantinople would have now contented, found its ultimate expression in the Peace of San Stefano. It was concluded the day after the twenty-third anniversary of the emperor's accession. The history of this feeble and abortive attempt to surprise Europe with a *fait accompli*, and to mask the military and financial straits of Russia behind a threatening mien put on for the occasion, lies beyond our present province to discuss. We are only concerned with its effects on Russian society. The first and foremost effect was that this society was confirmed in its unreasoning and overweening self-estimate of its powers and capabilities; the second was that the government had to choose between war to the death or the possible jeopardising of their authority; the third was that the actual results of the campaigns of 1877 and 1878 were diminished and lost their value in the eyes of the nation. When the actual terms of the Treaty of San Stefano were made known, three-fourths of the press and of the public protested that they would have thought such a measure of modesty and unselfishness impossible, that the government had shown a moderation and coyness unknown in the history of the world. The idea of these conditions being revised or reduced never crossed the mind of anyone; all parties considered them final. The only question was whether Russia ought to rest content with them, and not demand, at least, a temporary occupation of Constantinople. In anticipation of this criticism the treaty was represented as a mere instalment; and while the whole of Europe was plunged in excitement by this diplomatic surprise, the attention of the Russian people was diverted from the contemplation of their supposed gains to the spectacle of the Turkish capital surrounded on all sides by the Russian troops.

The first bitter disappointment was prepared for Russia, now intoxicated with the prospect of certain triumph, by the appearance of the British fleet in the Bosphorus, and by the impression produced by this event at the head-quarters of the Grand-duke Nicholas. The 'impossible' had come to pass. The army remained, as if rooted to the spot, outside the gates of that city which since the days of Igor and Oleg had never seen the face of a Muscovite invader. For months the Russian soldiers looked wistfully at the Mosque of St. Sophia, and dared not stretch out their hands to reach the Jerusalem of Slav orthodoxy and take possession of the inheritance of the Comneni. In the eyes of the government the fear of intervention from the 'despised West' outweighed the apprehension of wounding the popular spirit and neglecting the sacred traditions of the past. Aksakoff and his friends raged furiously, but in vain. They were forced to confess that the cause of Western civilisation was not yet defunct, and that the name of England had still some meaning in the world.

The second and more bitter disappointment to Russia was the unanimity with which the other Great Powers of Europe insisted on the demand that the Treaty of San Stefano should be submitted to a Congress for revision, and the Eastern Question treated as a European affair. Even Germany joined in this demand, and thereby refuted the foolish rodomontade about Bismark's 'swimming in the wake of Russian policy.' But, it was said, the Czar will not yield; the Czar cannot yield. He is the embodiment of the popular will of Russia, and the people have spoken their final word. What did the Moscow fanatics and the phrase-mongers of St. Petersburg care that the credit of the State was strained to its uttermost, and the paper currency was becoming more and more hopelessly depreciated? What did they care that M. von Reutern declared it financially impossible to conduct a second great war, and that M. Miliutin, the arch-National Minister of War, the man after Katkoff's and Aksakoff's own heart, declined to be answerable for its military success? What was it to them that there was a suspicious groaning and creaking in all the corners and joints of the State organism, and that the result of Sassulitch's trial, and the disturbances among the Moscow students, showed plainly that even the recent news of victory had not removed the danger of revolution? Was not the honour of the Russian name pledged at San Stefano by the Czarevitch's own words? Had not the government by this treaty burned their bridges and their boats, and barred the way against a European compact? Who would be rash enough to commence a shameful retreat against the unanimous will of the nation in the midst of their fever of excitement? Who would speak the language of calm and sober reflection, after the sacred spirit of the people had given utterance? Even the hoary Nestor of Russian diplomacy—the man who could hear the very grass grow, and was versed in all the secrets of his time—even Prince Gortchakoff had shaken his head and confessed himself unequal to such a venture.

One man there was, indeed, who had never cared for the opinions of the day or its spokesmen, who had never made the *vox populi* a *vox Dei*. This was the former chief of the secret police, the third section of His Majesty's own Imperial Chancellery, Count Peter Andrejevitch Schouvaloff. It was known that he considered a continuation of the war quite as unadvisable as any further concessions to the 'liberal spirit of the times.' It was known that he had warned the emperor that the worst results of the war would be those affecting the situation at home, and that the alternative must be faced, either of arresting the movement already set on foot by a speedy conclusion of peace, or of abandoning the ship of State to the waves of popular excitement. But this dangerous man was in London. He had not been able to prevent the dispatch of the British fleet, which had now taken anchorage off Prince's Island. His presence had for some years been inconvenient to His Majesty; he had never been liked by the brothers and sons of the emperor. Among the ruling classes his enemies were as numerous as in the Liberal and National circles. He had long been regarded with distrust by his own chief, the still powerful and influential Chancellor of the empire. He had become 'impossible' as well by his antecedents as by his uncompromising love of peace.

And yet this was the man whom the emperor now sent for to St. Petersburg, when every expedient had failed for securing a peaceful termination of the struggle! To the terror of his numerous enemies, Count Schouvaloff set out at once for the capital, taking Friedrichsruhe *en route*. Thus, then, the proposals he brought with him had gained the sanction, as his few friends observed, of the first diplomatic authority in the world, and in the opinion of his enemies, of the sworn enemy of Slavdom.

The apprehensions raised at St. Petersburg and Moscow by the news of Schouvaloff's impending appearance on the political stage were only too well founded. Notwithstanding all the difficulties prepared for him by the clique of Ignatieff, the young Court party, and certain high personages, male and female, who patronised the Nationalists, the Count gained his point. In a few days the emperor consented to send him to the Congress. The public learned at the same time that Prince Gortchakoff of course would go to Berlin, but accompanied by his dreaded rival. The sensation caused by this announcement was immense; but it would have been tenfold greater and more passionate if the masses had comprehended what as yet only a small number of clear-sighted persons understood—namely, that a substantial, not a mere formal concession to the will of the rest of Europe, the abandonment, in a word, of the Bulgarian frontiers as agreed on at San Stefano, had been recognised as unavoidable by the Czar. Bitter words, as it was, were spoken in private about the irresolution of the sovereign, who neither in war nor in the Cabinet understood how to play the proper part of a leader. Most people, however, seemed to take comfort in the thought that a congress did not mean the submission of Russia to a congress. There was no occasion, they argued, to fear any further concessions to Europe. The wisdom of the great statesman of the old school, who once before, in 1875, had brought the Berlin 'disturber' to his senses, would this time also hold its own. It must be confessed, indeed, that those who sought by such flattering phrases to inspire themselves and others with courage were not of a very sanguine heart themselves. They had ceased to reckon on the emperor's power of resistance; although they still trusted that, by means of a vigorous agitation and an incessantly repeated appeal to the moral impossibility of any detriment to 'Russian honour,' they would succeed in frightening the government out of submission to the will of Europe.

These hopes and this intention formed the staple of all that was spoken and written during June, 1878,[1] in the political circles of St. Petersburg, Moscow, and the larger provincial towns of Russia. Respect to the sacred person of His Majesty forbade the possibility of Russia ever consenting to the demands put forward—forbade it so absolutely that no one could be wounded by being reminded of the disgrace which the contrary would involve. Under the cover of such tricks of language, care was taken to coerce the government by threats as passionate as they were extravagant, and to dictate in imperious fashion the proper conduct to be pursued. The further the negotiations at the Congress advanced, and the more distinctly it was seen that Russia would yield in the matter of dividing Bulgaria into two parts, as well as on the other points at issue, the more menacing grew the language of the National party and its followers, composed of liberals, malcontents, and *frondeurs* of the most various types and species. Aksakoff, as before,

[1] The Congress began on June 1 (O.S.) and ended on July 1 (O.S.)

was the fugleman of these disappointed patriots. When the news arrived that negotiations were going on with regard to the surrender of Southern Bulgaria, he made a speech on June 22 (July 3), St. Basil's day, to the Slavonic Benevolent Committee at Moscow, some passages of which deserve quotation.[1] 'There are no words,' he said, ' by which to characterise as it deserves this shameful treachery to the duty and historical mission of Russia. Consenting to this condition (the division of Bulgaria into two parts and giving up Bosnia to Austria), is equivalent to renouncing the part of Russia as the great protecting power of Slavism and Eastern Christianity. It is equivalent to depriving us not only of the sympathies, but of the respect of the Slavonic races, who are our nearest, nay, our only allies in Europe. Liberty, and a development peculiar to Slavism is possible only on the assumption of a loving union with the Russian people. But Russian diplomacy has decided otherwise.' Then, addressing in grandiloquent terms the ' orthodox Russian nation ' as the only ' independent and powerful branch of the Slavonic race,' he complains of the blood of so many thousands of her sons being sacrificed to increase the power of her enemies, and to submit orthodoxy to the dominion of Germans and Catholics. 'Thou victorious Power, and yet so befooled ! In the face of such folly in the diplomatic heads of Russia, in the face of such grandiose attempts to temporise, the power of language ceases, and thoughts can find no utterance. Even the most malevolent enemy of Russia and her dynasty could not have in-

---

[1] This speech, delivered on $\frac{\text{June 22}}{\text{July 3}}$, was circulated throughout Russia in a manuscript form, the favourite and indeed the only possible device to elude the watchfulness of the press censure.

vented anything more destructive to her internal peace and tranquillity. There you see the true Nihilists—the men for whom there exists neither a Russia nor Russian tradition, no Russian nationality, no Orthodox Church. Those are the men who, like the Nihilists of the stamp of Bogoljuboff and Sassulitch, are destitute of all historical consciousness, of every spark of living national feeling. . . . Both belong to the same species, the same generation. Decide for yourselves who is the more dangerous for Russia, for her national and moral prosperity, and her dignity as a State. Which of two kinds of Nihilists is the worse—the open or the disguised, the coarse anarchists or the refined statesmen? No—whatever may take place at the Congress, however much the honour of Russia may be degraded, there yet lives our crowned protector, and he will be our avenger. If our own blood chills and curdles at merely reading in the newspapers what is done; what must the Russian Czar endure, who bears before history the responsibility for Russia? Has he not called our war a holy cause? Has he not, since his return from the Danube, solemnly declared to the assembled deputies at Moscow and elsewhere in his empire, that this "holy work would be carried to the end"? Terrible, indeed, are the sufferings of the war, and it cannot be with a light heart that the Czar should see the bloodshed renewed. But, great as these horrors are, they cannot be averted by concessions, or at the cost of honour and conscience. . . . Let us therefore hope and trust! Our hopes in our Czar cannot be shipwrecked. His word has gone forth that the holy work shall be carried to the end, and his word cannot be broken.'

And yet this hope was shipwrecked; it had perished already when the bold orator declared its inviolability.

But it was not the fault of the Czar, it was the fault of the short-sighted authors of the Treaty of San Stefano, that there could be any question raised at all as to a breach of promise. They, not he, were to blame, that the treaty guaranteeing the independence of Servia and the autonomy of Bulgaria, appeared to the majority of Russians a cowardly withdrawal, an act of treason to the cause of Russia and Slavism. The grand beginnings of Ignatieff and Nelidoff, and the noisy war trumpets of the press had so completely confused the public mind, and prevented any correct estimate of the true position of affairs, that the publication of the treaty, signed July 1 (13), raised a storm of moral indignation throughout Russia, and was received like a heavy and altogether unexpected disappointment. The masses woke up from their dreams of cloudland. Their leaders spoke and acted as if the whole thing were simply a retreat without a cause; as if there had never existed any incongruity between the Treaty of San Stefano and the means provided for its execution; as if there was one explanation, and one only, for all that had occurred—namely, a malevolent distrust of his people by the Czar. And this notion was indirectly confirmed by the first adviser of the emperor himself! The fact that Prince Gortchakoff had absented himself from the final negotiations, and in a memorandum, much talked of, to the Congress had thrown upon his colleagues (meaning Count Schouvaloff, of course,), the responsibility for what had taken place, was peculiarly calculated to strengthen the cry about an intrigue against the nation, and a dark attempt to undermine the national power.

It seemed, indeed, as if Aksakoff's prediction would be realised. It seemed likely, as he had said, that the results of the Congress, as brought about by diplomacy, would strike a heavier blow to the peace of Russia and the authority of her government, than could ever have been dealt by the Nihilists. Only the guilty parties were not the diplomatists of June, but those of February, 1878. To Schouvaloff alone belonged the honour of having rescued Russia from the danger of a conflict with the rest of Europe. And yet, so general and so passionate was the popular indignation at the disappointment of their cherished hopes; so openly was this indignation expressed, in spite of all the rigours of the censorship, that the question of summoning him to the helm of State could not be entertained for a moment. The official press attempted to calm down the popular excitement, by putting forward the most daring and most fanciful conjectures. It was not, indeed, a difficult matter to throw the greater share of this odium on the German Chancellor, and to declaim with such violence against German 'intrigues,' that even the most devoted friends of the Berlin alliance began to speak of the necessity of drawing nearer to France. But it was difficult, nay, almost impossible, to disarm the reproaches hurled against the Prussomania of the Court, and in consequence against everything connected with the conduct of the war and the government of the State during the last eventful year. All the old accusations, all the grievances and suspicions which six months ago had made their voice first heard, and were raised on all sides against the 'system' of absolute executive power, were now repeated with redoubled acrimony. 'Matters could not have been worse,' it was said, 'if we had made peace immediately after our first defeat at Plevna.' Now for the first time was seen the full extent of the damage which the authority of the government had suffered the year before. Now for the first time it was seen how deeply discontent and mistrust had eaten into the people, who still hugged themselves with the delusion that they needed only to muster their common strength in order to conquer the world. This delusion could only be maintained by heaping the fault of everything upon the government, by misinterpreting and putting a sinister construction on all its actions. The recall of the Grand-duke Nicholas from his chief command; the studied hostility with which the Czarevitch refused to take part in the festivities given in honour of his uncle; the painful sensation caused by the abandonment of the prosecution against the company of Greger, Horwitz, and Kohan; the malicious reports as to the sources from which it was said his Imperial Highness had drawn the means for paying his debts; the embarrassment evinced by those responsible for Russian diplomacy when asked to account for their confidence at San Stefano, all combined to shake the 'respect and the reserve' due otherwise to the government, and to strengthen the general conviction that it would 'not do any longer to let matters continue as they were.' The moment chosen for the declaration of war, the manner in which it was declared, the mode of preparation for the war, and the way in which it was conducted; the system of alliances relied on; the proceedings of diplomacy, beginning with its mouth full of big phrases, and ending by humbling itself in the dust—everything, in short, was said to have deceived the confidence and the trusting devotion of the nation. Everything had gone differently to what had been expected. No one seemed to have been left who was able to maintain authority. The foundations on which the *régime* of 1863-77 had rested were undermined as completely as the *régime* of Old Russia by the Crimean war. Close upon the conclusion of peace began the era of political assassinations and revolutionary plots. What had previously been whispered only in the circles of the *enragés*, was now publicly proclaimed by the 'Moscow Gazette.' No attempt was made any longer to conceal the fact that the Treaty of Berlin had shaken the existing system of government to its very foundations.

The consequences of the war recoiled upon the dynasty, of whom it was said that it neither wished for nor prevented the war; that it had neither the courage nor the capacity to begin it at the right time, to conduct it properly, or to break it off when the proper moment arrived.

CHAPTER XVI.

INCIDENTS AND LESSONS OF THE WAR.

Popular appetite for news of the war—Complaints of mismanagement—Inferiority of Russian weapons and equipment—Want of trenching tools at Plevna—General absence of maps—Defects of the Field-post and of telegraphic arrangements—Want of telescopes—Breakdown of the Intendance and Commissariat—Jobbery of army contractors—Military peculation—Scandalous condition of the hospitals—Incapacity of the Army Medical Department—Want of transport for the wounded—Admirable arrangements of the Red Cross Society—Excellent behaviour of Russian officers and troops—Absence of military offences early in the war—The nation and the government—Popular estimate of Russian strength.

FOR months before the conclusion of peace, and after the return of the troops from the seat of war, the incidents and stories of the recent campaign formed the staple of conversation and literature in Russian society. Newspapers, periodicals, and private pamphlets outbid one another in communicating what had taken place during the fifteen months between April 24, 1877, and July 13, 1878. The number of people who were anxious and able to contribute to the history of the war was greater this time than ever. The general call to arms had brought thousands of educated and half-educated persons into contact with the common people. To write for the periodical press was a privilege of only recent acquisition, and a thing unknown at the time of the Crimean War. A host of professional and occasional correspondents had followed the different divisions of the army, and the transport and ambulance waggons sent to Bulgaria; and each of these was naturally anxious to describe what he had seen and heard. As the number of journals and printing-presses had increased twenty-fold between 1850 and 1860, and that of the reading public had doubled, there was no end to the demand for this class of literature. Even the uneducated wished to know how it was that things had happened as they did at the theatre of war, and why the high hopes placed on the success of this 'holy crusade' had not been realised to the full. People who formerly had looked on reading and writing as a necessary luxury for the higher classes, seized upon the newspapers whenever they contained the gossip of the camp or chronicles of the war. While the war was actually proceeding, the news, so eagerly demanded by the whole of Russia, came in but scantily and in driblets. But when the war was over, no such restrictions could prevent the public appetite from being fed. A new branch of literature arose, more prolific from its past neglect, which engrossed almost exclusively the attention of the public.

The character of this literature, which came into vogue during the autumn of 1878 and the early months of 1879, can be guessed from the observations already made in the previous chapter on the ruling temper of the public mind. The precedent of 1854 was repeated. It was the 'system' responsible for the conduct of the war and the provisioning of the troops which formed the central object of criticism and the theme of discussion in the newspapers. Granted that men of the stamp of Moltke and Roon are not to be had at a moment's notice. Granted that when the question is one of testing a totally new organisation, mistakes in high places are unavoidable. When the blunders committed at Plevna, and the want of a settled plan for the first advance across the Balkans, were discussed, people were disgusted, but they only shrugged their shoulders when the names of those responsible for these strange errors were mentioned; now and then a remark unfit for publication would be made, or it was hinted that the composition of the general staff had been somewhat unfortunate. But that was really all. Genuine complaints and bitter remarks or remonstrances were only heard when the conversation touched on evils which could have been avoided by some care or conscientiousness on the part of ordinary or even less than ordinary men, and which could only be explained by supposing that each and every 'system' had failed, and that the disorder had been even worse than during the much-abused Crimean War. Our object in this chapter is to represent to our readers what these complaints really were, as made known through the literature of the war.

We Russians are so accustomed, by this time, to the fact that the French, Austrians, and Germans are better prepared for war, better armed, better provided for, and better officered than ourselves, that we look upon it as a matter of course and intended so by Providence. Nevertheless, we feel it to be a grief and a disgrace that the arrangements made by the rude, barbaric Turks on behalf of their army were a thousand times better than our own. Our finances before the war began were in a tolerably good condition—according to official accounts in an excellent condition—whilst the insolvency of the Porte was proverbial. We were told again and again that the Turkish officers were more ignorant and useless than ever, whereas on our part everything worth knowing in military matters had been learned from Germany and France, and everything needful had been provided. How was it possible, under such circumstances, that corrupt and bankrupt Turkey put better weapons into the hands of her soldiers than wealthy and aspiring Russia, with her military representatives at all the great Courts, could furnish to those who fought on her behalf? But so it actually was. The Turkish rifles carried to a distance of 3,000 paces, and could be loaded sixteen times in a minute, whilst six or eight hundred paces only was the range of ours. It was fortunate, however, that we were not able to load as quickly as our enemies, for we were usually provided with such a small supply of cartridges. Every child knows that nowadays the quality of the weapons decides the issue. How came it that our general staff did not know this, and that the Guards alone were armed with Berjanki rifles, which in fact contributed more to victory than all the old-fashioned muskets used by the Line from June to September?

No one can give satisfactory answers to these questions. Excuses might possibly be invented for other shortcomings. But the want of cartridges and ammunition, of which soldiers and officers without exception complained, remains quite inexplicable—the more so, inasmuch as it continued throughout the whole campaign. The Turkish troops, as their own officers confessed, were reckless in wasting their cartridges. Our soldiers, let them husband their ammunition as they would, could never make the supply suffice. Behind the Turkish army marched whole trains of horses, asses, and mules, laden with cartridge-chests. We, on the contrary, had to carry our reserves of ammunition ourselves, and we knew very well that when the store was exhausted, days would pass before it was replenished. In addition to this, our accoutrement was intolerably heavy—heavier far than necessity required. All who have witnessed the war and associated with the common soldiers have dwelt particularly on this last point, and have told us how the most patient and phlegmatic among them would become enraged, when speaking of the burdens packed so senselessly upon them. After the days of Plevna, whole regiments threw away this useless lumber, the loss of which they never afterwards missed, and which never burdened Turkish backs. And yet it was only a few years before, on the occasion of the Franco-German war, that this very point of equipment had been discussed in all the newspapers. The comfortable, but also solid clothing, the light but strong shoes, and, above all, the splendid indestructible tents of the ' unbelieving Bussurmanni,' were the objects of constant envy to their ' orthodox opponents.' The wretched quality of the stuffs of which the coats and shirts provided for the Russian troops were made was only surpassed by the miserable quality of their boots. It can readily be understood that those whose shoes were worn out did not easily find new ones to replace them. At the beginning of the winter of 1877-78, just when the toilsome march over the snow-covered Balkans was about to be commenced, most of the boots were worn to pieces, and the soldiers had to tramp along barefooted or with rags over their bleeding feet. New boots were either wanting altogether, or of such a quality that to put them on appeared ridiculous. Old soldiers, who happened to see samples of these goods on their way through Moscow, knew well enough why these boots nearly proved the death of those who wore them : the soles were made of pasteboard ! So utterly destitute of warm clothing were the troops during their march across the Balkans, that thousands of them, solely for this reason, were frozen to death or perished from exhaustion. Whether it was thought at head-quarters that a winter campaign could be conducted in summer clothing, or whether they had reckoned on settling with the Turks before winter set in, has never been determined. In either case, however, they were guilty of a degree of recklessness bordering on crime, and they have sown the seeds of bitterness and contempt towards the government which will assuredly some day bear fruit.

But we will first allude to those materials of war which the Turks also had in abundance, and the want of which among our troops could not be ascribed by head-quarters to the imperfections of the Intendance or the negligence of contractors. At the time of the blockade of Plevna, the world was suddenly astonished by the announcement that the siege operations must come to a standstill on account of an absolute lack of spades and shovels, and that these tools must be procured from Bucharest. This absence of materials for throwing up earthworks and entrenchments was neither an exceptional case, nor one peculiar to the division of the army before Plevna; it was the general rule. Again and again our men were astonished at the rapidity with which the Turks, as soon as they had taken up their position, had their spades in their hands and were busy at fortifying themselves behind their rampart and trench. All we could do was to look on; for it was always the same story—there were no spades, and so there could be no earthworks made on our part. Of course no one in particular was to blame; for all had been guilty of the same forgetfulness.

And as with spades, so with other things. People even who could not read, had occasionally heard how excellently the Germans during the last war had been provided with maps, and what good use the sub-officers had made of this advantage. Even the 'Syn Otetchesstwa' ('Son of the Country')—a small and insignificant, but yet widely-circulated paper for the people—had discussed the question of these maps at length. To our general staff alone it seems to have remained a secret. The most done was that six maps were distributed among one regiment; and if officers wished to buy any for themselves, they could not get them. The Abramoff map and that of the Austrian general staff, copies of which had been multiplied, were not issued till May— that is to say, when the army had actually taken its departure. Whilst every newspaper reader at home could follow the road taken by the troops, the possession of a pocket-map of the intended scene of war was the privilege of only a small number of those chiefly concerned in the campaign. 'In other matters,' it was said, 'we blindly ape the Germans; why have we not done so in this case?' For ten or twenty thousand roubles the whole army could have been inundated with maps; was it possible that this insignificant sum was not forthcoming?

Among the most remarkable things that happened during this remarkable war were the experiences of the soldiers with regard to the Field-post. Of the hundred thousands of letters sent through this post to and from the army, the greater part never reached their destination. Just as in the days before there was any post at all, it was a rare exception if ever an officer or private in the field received any news of their belongings, or a sign of life sent from the banks of the Danube or the slopes of the Balkans was transmitted to their homes at the proper time. Dozens of enormous sacks lay about on the platforms of the railway stations in Roumania; but it never occurred to anyone to look after them, and to see that those to whom the letters were addressed should receive news from their relatives and friends. There was only one praiseworthy feature in the affair—the bungling had the merit of impartiality, for it was the same to all alike. Just as little care was taken of the letters addressed to generals and other officers as of those for subalterns and common privates. Packets and things of value shared, with few exceptions, the fate of ordinary letters. If they arrived at all, they arrived at least several months too late. No astonishment was excited if the objects of value contained in these packets had been abstracted. Officers who had thousands at their bankers at home, and had counted with certainty on the receipt of remittances from their agents, were often painfully embarrassed by their non-arrival, and glad if they could borrow a few roubles. Still more serious, however, was the anxiety that weighed on those married officers and soldiers who were left for weeks and months without news of wife or child. At times the matter bore a tragical character. At Kazanlik, for instance, an officer had succeeded in getting hold of an old letter-bag intended for his regiment, but which had wandered about aimlessly for weeks. The fortunate finder called his comrades around him, in order to distribute the precious booty. When the names were called out, it was found that nearly all those to whom the letters were addressed had died in battle, without receiving the comfort of news from their homes. So intolerable at length became the evil, that officers and men refused any longer to make use of the postal service in the field; and the letters intended for Russia were addressed in German or French, but on no account in Russian, and if an opportunity offered, were sent to the nearest Austrian post-office. In this way they usually reached their destination in safety; the only pity was that letters directed to the army could not be sent in the same manner.

The telegraph arrangements were as bad as those of the field-post. The mutual isolation of the various divisions of the army, and the absence of any telegraphic communication between them, were matters so well established that individual commanders—as, for example, Colonel Kossitch, the chief staff officer of the Twelfth Corps stationed at Rustchuk—were forced to get information of what had happened in other places from newspapers two or three weeks old. And yet Rustchuk was not seventy miles from head-quarters. Instances of this kind might pass perhaps, and find a sort of excuse in the 'peculiar conditions of the country' which were always brought forward as a plea. But what is to be said of the fact that commanders whose instructions demanded constant co-operation, and who were only separated from each other by a few miles, were entirely without telegraphic communication, even when, as before Plevna for example, they remained for weeks stationary in the same quarters? The natural result of all this was that neglect prevailed on every side, and the mistrust of the generals in command surpassed all bounds. To-day it was said that the fault lay with Gourko; yesterday, the honest old Krüdener had been the scapegoat. At another time the general staff was said to have failed in its duty. In the end, all parties concerned, the innocent as well as the guilty, were included in the common sentence of condemnation. Who was cook and who was butler, as the phrase goes, no one had ever properly known, since the commanders of the different corps and the composition of the corps themselves were perpetually being changed. 'Our corps,' wrote one, 'were treated like dough which required incessant kneading. This man was in command one day and that the next. What chance was there of any steadiness among the men, or how could the commanders become acquainted with their officers and troops?' Not only were brethren-in-arms frequently strangers to each other—as much so, in fact, as if they belonged to different armies—but it often happened, through this constant change of persons, that there were staff-officers without a staff, and staffs without officers, and that whole corps either dispensed with their Intendant altogether, or were ignorant of his name and where he was.

But even this was not all. Together with the spades, trenching-tools, maps, and telegraphic apparatus, the telescopes also had been forgotten. The consequence was this—that officers of all grades and branches of the service were forced to advance blindfold and at haphazard into a country which they did not, and from the want of maps they could not know, and to deliver up literally their soldiers to the slaughter. More than once it happened that divisions, marching from different points to the same goal, failed to recognise each other, and, thinking to have the enemy before them, fired a murderous volley at their brother soldiers! And not a word of reproach could have been said to the officers.

The necessity of having an exact knowledge of the ground on which anything is to be done in war has been amply taught us by the Germans; from the French we have learned what it is to be 'ready' only in imagination. We knew already, six months before war was declared, that we should have to cross the Danube; and yet the country which we were to conquer remained to us altogether a *terra incognita*. From time immemorial the solution of the Eastern Question had been said to be our mission; the liberation of the South Slavonic races our nearest and most natural task. And yet the Commander-in-Chief and the general staff allowed us to take this task in hand before there were any books to instruct us about the country and the people on the other side of the Danube, or any maps to guide us on our way. None of these things had been thought of, just because no one had yet acquired the habit of earnestly and thoroughly considering a question, and because people had surrendered themselves to the illusion that a Russian conquest of the East was the simplest matter in the world. Had the question been simply one of mistakes and inadequate preparation in individual departments of military administration, no reasonable man would deny that this administration was sharing the lot of all human institutions, and that, so far from despairing of the future, the prospect of improvement must be kept steadily in view. But the same inconceivable blunders have recurred again and again in all departments alike. It is idle, therefore, to waste complaints on a single department only, and to confine one's censure to individuals. The whole system has so completely broken down, so entirely failed in its object, that it must be extirpated root and branch. It must be owned, and owned frankly, that there has been no real improvement since 1855, save in one respect, and that an immensely important one. The moral condition of the army has perceptibly improved, and so have the relations between the officers and the men. Everything else has grown during the last twenty years not only not better, but steadily worse.

Up to the present time it has been held, both in and out of Russia, as an undisputed fact that the system of Intendance and Commissariat followed during the Crimean War was the worst and most corrupt system that could possibly have been devised. This judgment now, in certain circles, is considerably modified. Those who have been in both wars are now heard to speak as follows, when a comparison is instituted between the two. 'The officials and contractors,' they say, 'who were entrusted in 1854-5 with the general provisioning of the army, stole like jackdaws; but they were also clever fellows, who knew how to make a fit and practical use of what they did not steal. But this time we have been cheated by blockheads, robbed by people whose incapacity was even greater than their villainy.'

The testimony of our soldiers is naturally not of such a kind as to give a demonstrable confirmation of this assertion. They simply say that the food and fodder during the Crimean War had been eatable, but that this time mouldy meal, putrid bread, and uneatable fodder for the horses had been in very many instances the rule. That exorbitant prices were paid, and millions of roubles fraudulently taken from the Crown, is confirmed, however, on all sides, and is looked upon, strange to say, as quite natural. Our officers, when these matters are talked of, quote the testimony of General Bogdanovitch, the historian of the Crimean War, whose impartiality is acknowledged, to show that Generals Annenkoff and Satler did, in fact, manage, by means of inexorable severity, that the army was on the whole well provided for. The complaints against the commissariat system, which were heard then on every side and recognised even by the government, referred chiefly to the disproportion between the value of the articles provided and the enormous prices paid for them. But even for this some excuses could have been alleged which it is impossible to allege this time. The chief difficulty during the former war, namely, the want of railways and practicable roads, does not now exist. In the autumn of 1854, a waggon-train conveying stores from Perikop to Simferopol, took thirty-four days to accomplish 134 versts (about 90 English miles); and Piragoff, the famous surgeon, spent a day and a-half in travelling with post-horses from Simferopol to Sebastopol, a distance of only 74 versts. With such imperfect means of transport and communication it was perfectly conceivable that the provisions should spoil, and the animals intended for slaughter should die on the road.

But this time the situation of affairs was wholly different. The army waggons could drive close to the banks of the Danube, and only a very moderate amount of common sense and care would have been required to protect the stores and provisions—if good for anything at all—from the effects of weather or decay. Unhappily, the case was this, that the very persons whose duty it was to supply these provisions were but little interested in their condition. The Intendance had, as is well known, made a contract with the firm of Greger, Horwitz, and Kohan; but this contract was so clumsily worded that the quality of the goods supplied was left entirely to the will and pleasure of these persons, whose moral character had better perhaps not be discussed. It is true it had been stipulated that all the articles in question should be of the best quality; but a proviso stated that outside the limits of the empire there must be exceptions, and regard must be had to the quality and kind of local products. Now, as the whole war was carried on 'outside the limits of the empire,' it can easily be understood that the 'exceptions' formed the rule, and that in its main stipulations the contract remained a mere paper-covenant. As regards the prices, it was arranged that the Company should receive payment for their cost of purchase, as proved, together with a commission of ten per cent. for their trouble. The Intendance, consequently, remained just as much at the mercy of Messrs. Greger and Co. with respect to the sums to be paid as they were with respect to the quality of the goods supplied. But the worst thing was that the department in question, even after they had had the opportunity of ascertaining how matters stood, never attempted to get rid of these contractors, who had victimised them so grossly, but rather identified their own interests with those of the Company, and treated every charge made against them as an attack on their own dignity. Inasmuch as the Company, by the terms of their contract, were enabled to exclude all competition and to compel the acceptance of their goods, there was no guarantee at all that provisions would be found when or where they were required.

Neither during the first nor second advance of Gourko across the Balkans was any agent of the Company to be seen near the districts where the operations of the war were going on, and the army in consequence had to provide for itself. Still more extraordinary was the experience of General Sotoff, the Commander of the Fourth Army Corps, at Sistova. His intended arrival there with his division had been announced beforehand to the very day and hour. When he reached the place there were no provisions whatever, and the telegrams sent to the Intendance and the agents of the Company had been so utterly without effect that nothing was left to the General but to apply to the Civil Governor, Prince Tcherkasski, who partially relieved the distressed army by placing at their disposal the crops and provisions belonging to the Turkish inhabitants. In July, 1877, two corps stationed in the neighbourhood of Tirnova shared the same fate, and their commander sent the following telegram to headquarters : 'I am entirely without provisions, or a single bit of bread. Pray send me assistance of some kind.' The Intendance threw all the blame upon the Company, who, again, laid it all upon the Intendance. 'It is stipulated in the contract,' so said the Company, ' that requisitions for fresh supplies must be sent to us at least three days before they are wanted. For this we are prepared ; but not for cases where to-night is ordered what is wanted to-morrow— to say nothing of the fact that in the places appointed for the delivery of supplies, which we have only been able to reach with the utmost labour and difficulty, there is frequently no one to receive them.'

The inevitable consequence of all this has been that the Intendance has been much more harshly judged, and much more suspected, than the Company, whose want of principle was regarded as a matter of course. It has been asserted by word and in writing, in newspapers and journals, by combatants and non-combatants, that certain people of high position had conspired together with ' the Jews,' and that it had been for their advantage that ' the worst possible goods should be supplied at the highest possible price.' If anyone asks for proofs of this assertion, people simply refer him to the contract, and to the fact, vouched for readily by hundreds of witnesses, that the Intendance and the Company were constantly to be found where, in consequence of other expedients being at hand, their expensive services were not required, but that they were invariably absent wherever it was difficult or disadvantageous to procure food. 'Had the Intendance,' they say, ' been earnest in exercising their right of supervision, at least such shameless and unheard-of frauds would not have been possible as were practised against the unfortunate persons who provided carriage transport. The poor Russian peasants who had allowed themselves to be tempted into undertaking to cart the stores to Roumania and Bulgaria, not only received no pay, but were so terribly ill-treated and plundered that they returned half starved or as beggars to their homes.'

One example will suffice to show the measure of the peculation and fraud. In July, 1877, a certain M. Warshawski made a contract for supplying transport waggons, the terms being that he should receive twenty francs in gold, daily, for the cartage. Two months later a similar contract was concluded with Messrs. Kaufmann and Baranoff, at sixteen francs per diem. Nevertheless, M. Warshawski, in April, 1878, succeeded in renewing for some months his first contract on the old terms; and in July of the same year he still received nineteen francs. The lower tender of Messrs. Kaufmann and Baranoff was disregarded by the department, simply because they saw it was for their own interest to contract with M. Warshawski, and to give him a present amounting to something like five million and three-quarters of francs.

Among the few official thieves of the Intendance who were subsequently called to account, was a sub-official named Chwoschtschinski, about whom the 'Molva' newspaper tells as follows. In those happy days—now, alas! no more—when everything was paid for in ready money and in gold, and brilliant strokes of business could be done in the name of patriotism, M. Chwoschtschinski was superintendent of a depôt of forage at Kotroscheni, in Roumania. Notwithstanding his humble position, he was able to embezzle money to the extent of 340,000 roubles, and to allow provisions worth 2,000,000 roubles to go bad. During the usual 'general confusion' attending a war the authorities, under ordinary circumstances, would scarcely have noticed the doings of this functionary. He might quietly and industriously have gathered honey from the stores, in order, like a prudent man, to 'place his family in a secure position.' But the superintendent, unhappily for himself, lavished money without a 'benevolent object.' Instead of sending home his bags of gold to be converted into paper of value, he changed his stores into choice food, and by his luxurious way of living attracted the notice of the authorities. He had the taste of a Lucullus, which was not suitable to the office of a simple superintendent. He once gave a breakfast which cost him 45,000 roubles in coin—it cost him a good deal more in reality, for his breakfast was commented on in a Roumanian newspaper, and thereby caused the inquiry which brought this prodigality to light.[1] A colleague of this man, who was entrusted

---

[1] Official terminology in Russia distinguishes between two sorts of civil functionaries: the 'ordinary man' (*porädotschni tschelowek*), who steals from the Crown and capitalises what he has stolen; and the 'splendid man' (*prekrassni tschelowek*), who steals and allows what he has stolen to profit others—that is, he spends it. M. Chwoschtschinski belonged evidently

with the provisions stored in Rasdelnaja, was convicted of having stolen 180,000 'pud' of hay (1 pud = 36 pounds), and of having allowed 11,000 'chetvert' of oats (1 chetvert = $5\frac{3}{4}$ bushels) to rot. Is it to be wondered at that the worst frauds practised by these rascals on the unlucky peasant carters remained unpunished?[1]

That charges such as these can be alleged at all against the agents of the government is assuredly an evil sign. It is still worse that they are universally believed, and that the government has given, at least indirectly, a support and sanction to this belief. The prosecution of Messrs. Greger, Horwitz, and Kohan before the military tribunal at Odessa is known to have been quashed by 'supreme command,' and the order was given that all accounts should be paid. This crime is unquestionably the worst committed by the government for many a day. Not only has the sense of right and justice among thousands of brave officers and soldiers been grievously outraged, and confidence in the Government once more deeply shaken, but a door has been opened to suspicions of the worst and most damaging kind.

The same want of foresight and order, so conspicuous in most of the administrative departments of the State, was felt in the management of the hospitals and all

---

to the second category, which is usually far more strongly represented than the first. Both classes are simply called 'unlucky persons' if ever they are brought to trial and punished.

[1] Some of these victims of roguery were German colonists from Bessarabia. Great excitement was caused by their pastor, the Protestant minister Lemm, sounding an alarm about the affair in the press, and exerting himself to institute a prosecution at his own cost against those who had fleeced his parishioners. The Russian press were forced to admit with shame that the Russians who had been similarly cheated had no pastors who were willing to step in to their assistance.

the medical arrangements for the war. At first—that is, before there were any wounded—everything appeared to go excellently well. The rooms destined for the reception of the patients made a favourable impression; they were so airy, so clean, so attractively arranged, that people who saw them only at that time are still loud in their praise. Even after bloodshed had begun, and the hospitals were filled with sufferers of every kind, there were some hospitals which left scarcely anything to be desired, and might have served as a pattern for all. Such, in particular, were those at Tirnova and at Gorny-Studen, the headquarters of the emperor. But if the spectator looked behind the scenes, if he went to Sistova or Simnitza for example, a very different picture met the eye; and he involuntarily began to suspect that the hospitals at Tirnova and Gorny-Studen were there for show and for the sake of appearance. We say nothing of the impressions made on lay observers, and their opinion as to the horrible condition of the ordinary field-hospitals. Doctors only can be the proper judges of what, during a bloody war, is possible and attainable in the way of arrangements for mitigating the miseries of its victims. But it is just the doctors who are most severe in their strictures on the Medical Department for the degree of disorder and want of organisation, which surpassed belief. From a mass of other testimony of this kind, we quote the following words of a doctor who had worked at Sistova: 'The hospitals at Sistova consisted of what could hardly be called houses; they were rather holes or dens, bearing every mark of destruction, in which the Turks, their former inhabitants, had left behind them the traces of their intolerable filth. The interiors were still more loathsome, and bore no appearance of ever having been intended for the reception of sick and wounded, to say nothing of hospital arrangements. The food was carried about in pails, which were taken straight, when emptied, to the wells, to receive the water used for preparing more victuals. It was distributed by dirty attendants, whose hands had not been washed for weeks, and whose appearance was enough to fill the most hardened with horror and disgust. The utensils for the food were smeared with fat, dirt, and all manner of unsavoury garbage. " Why am I here at all?" remarked one of the doctors at Sistova; " there is not a single thing to be had—no servants, no medicines, no provisions." More than a score of wounded wretches were lying in hospital No. 50 at the beginning of August, who, after having been jolted about for three hours in springless carts, remained for forty hours without food and without a doctor; and this happened, not in suddenly improvised hospitals near the scene of action, but at regular hospitals in a large town, where arrangements had previously been made, or were supposed to have been made, for the reception of wounded men brought thither from a distance! The Medical Department had simply been incapable of calculating beforehand the requirements of a field-hospital, and even of providing the bare necessaries of the case. Arrangements had been made at Sistova (we say nothing of their miserable character) for from four to six hundred wounded, and yet from 1,000 to 1,500 men were allowed to be penned together there with only about ten doctors, badly provided with assistants, to look after this mass of unfortunate creatures.'

At Simnitza things were even worse than at Sistova. Here there was a hospital (No. 57) with 'arrangements' for 630 sick and wounded, which on September 5, 1877, contained no less than 2,886 inmates, and was accordingly in a state of dirt, stench, and disorder that baffles all description. The doctors, attendants, and sisters of mercy, from their incessant overwork and exertions, found themselves in the same terrible condition as the wounded, who were so closely herded together that they literally pushed against and trod upon each other. Happy indeed was the man who possessed a bed, however filthy and uncomfortable. Many of the wounded lay uncovered, in their dirty and blood-stained clothes, upon the floor, and often lay there for twelve or fifteen hours together without the taste of food or water. At Frajeschty, early in September, a hospital intended for 630 men was packed with 3,000 sick and wounded. Dr. Iljinski, who was employed here, reports that around the barracks about 300 wounded lay along the railway on straw caked and stiff with mud, and exposed to the open air. These poor creatures remained for four-and-twenty hours without seeing a doctor or receiving a morsel of bread. And all this occurred at one of the central places, which were said to have been arranged for the reception of the wounded. No wonder that the complaints heaped upon the Medical Department by the doctors, the voluntary nurses, and the soldiers and officers who were wounded were loud, severe, and bitter; and that the report just alluded to declares the whole organisation of this department to be 'beneath all criticism.' No wonder that a report of Professor Sklifassowski in the 'Medizinski Vêstnik' concludes as follows: 'The selection of the places and buildings intended for hospitals, the composition of the staff, the arrangements of the hospitals and the organisation of the service—all and everything was in incapable hands.'

The means of transport for the wounded was in

keeping with the condition of the hospitals. The unfortunate victims to their bravery lay heaped on one another by dozens in miserable small carts without springs. The mere sight of these crazy vehicles betrayed that they had been hastily scraped together, without the least regard to their fitness or convenience. The Medical Department had evidently not given a thought to providing for the conveyance of the wounded, and had left them entirely to chance. Cases could be given of 300 or 400 wounded being dragged for days along the road under the escort of a single physician and a couple of army-surgeons, to find, when they reached at length their destination, that no preparation whatever had been made for their reception, and that nothing was left to the leaders of this miserable caravan but to continue their journey. Sometimes no conveyance at all was to be had. After the third assault on Plevna 574 wounded men had to march on foot for five days to Simnitza, without receiving on their way any regular food. And among these 'lightly wounded,' as they were called, there were men with broken bones. 'One would have supposed,' says an eye-witness, 'that this war, expected for so many years, had been a surprise, which had rendered preparations impossible.'

That preparations would certainly have been possible — that with some intelligence and care they might have been made with satisfactory results, is shown by the enormous difference that existed between the official medical organisation and that of the 'Red Cross Society.' The hospital arrangements, which were under the control of this society, are a theme of grateful admiration to this day among all who were fortunate enough to come under their nursing. Officers and soldiers, who were removed from the other hospitals to those of the Red Cross, describe the change as one from hell to heaven. Wherever this sign appeared, there reigned, in spite of the same difficulties, order, cleanliness, and a system of treatment as humane as it was methodical. The pity was that the hospitals of the Red Cross, like the above-mentioned 'model-hospitals' at Tirnova and Gorny-Studen, were the exception; and that most of the sick and wounded in 1877 were crowded into places differing but little from those at Simnitza and Sistova.

If the press and the public were unanimous, as we have seen they were, in condemning everything connected with the administration, the organisation, and the Intendance arrangements of the war, they were equally unanimous in their praises of both officers and men. Whether discipline was always as rigorously maintained as during the time of the old *régime*, may be left an open question. That the relations between officers and men have changed for the better since the introduction of universal compulsory service in the army, and the abolition of the severe and degrading corporal punishment of the old system, is a fact beyond dispute. It is equally undeniable that the admixture of numerous elements of culture and education in the army has immensely raised its moral standard. The mere fact that a common soldier could speak of young men of culture and good social position as his comrades; that the ideas of soldier and 'muzhik' are no longer interchangeable; and that the ranks no longer contained vagabonds and criminals, placed there for punishment; showed an enormous progress as compared with the past. Brave, patient, obedient, and unassuming—this the Russian soldier has always been; but the full development of these qualities is due to the influence of that humane treatment, on which the younger officers in particular have prided themselves. Every kind word from their lips, every expression of human sympathy fell on hearts, whose gratefulness can only be appreciated by those who know both the amiability and gentleness of the Slavonic nature, and the enormous gulf which has hitherto separated the educated from the uneducated, the master from his servant. The civilians who accompanied the army are unanimous in their opinion that the altered relations between officers and men have made the exercise of discipline not more difficult but easier. Because rational obedience and personal attachment took the place of fear of punishment, the soldiers many a time fulfilled their duty even where they knew themselves to be unobserved and uncontrolled. Once thoroughly convinced that more was to be gained by personal example and by stimulating a feeling of honour than by mere bullying and commanding, the officers on their part strove to outvie each other in contempt of death and in placing themselves always in the front. The consequence of this was that in numerous cases, where all the officers to a man were killed or wounded, the men marched on of their own accord and plunged into the hottest of the fire, though there was on longer any commander left to lead them.[1] Equally touching as well as numerous traits are told of the gratitude and devotion of the soldiers towards the humanely disposed of their

[1] That the percentage of officers killed in the last war was unusually large, and larger than in former wars, as, for instance, the Crimean, has been officially confirmed. We abstain from entering into the question whether the number of rewards bestowed on officers was proportionately too small, or whether those rewards were, as alleged, frequently bestowed by favour and according to a vicious system. Complaints of this kind are always made, and very probably are unavoidable.

superiors. A correspondent of the 'Vêstnik Evrópy' speaks of officers, who, when visiting the wounded of their division, could scarcely restrain themselves from shedding tears and embracing their men, and who could boast without exaggeration that their troops were devoted to them in life and death, even though they had led them but a short time and under the most difficult and unfavourable circumstances. Hunger, thirst, cold, and privations of every sort—so says all the most veracious testimony in the Russian press—have never been more heroically and patiently endured than by the Russian soldiers on their second march across the Balkans. Every terror was surmounted, because the officers of these troops were foremost in displaying the most unselfish devotion to the interests of their men.

The worship of 'the people' and of the 'common man,' as a being undefiled by the 'corrupt' civilisation of the West, is well known to be one of the weaknesses of our advanced Nationalists, who in this respect go very much further than the professional enthusiasts for 'the people' and 'nationality' in other countries. The accounts, therefore, given by journalists and retailers of camp stories, about the incomparable performances of the 'genuine Russian' private, must be received with a certain amount of caution. Still, it is true beyond cavil or question that the recent war has been rich in episodes illustrative of Russian life and morals. For example, the total number of crimes committed by soldiers and brought for trial before military tribunals, from January 1 to August 1, 1877, was estimated at about three hundred. Taking into consideration the enormous strength of the active forces, the host of irregulars attached to it, and the circumstance that the army had remained four months inactive at Kischeneff, and then had stopped four months on Roumanian and

Turkish territory, this total seems unusually small. It is particularly noticeable that cases of insults offered to women, in the above total of offences, have been extremely few and far between. Matters of course grew worse in this respect as the campaign went on. When the troops advanced farther south and entered purely Turkish territory, they became more or less brutalised by the fatigues of the campaign and the incessant scenes of bloodshed, and so many cases of brutal treatment of women occurred, that it became impossible to punish such offences as they deserved. The excellent conduct of the common soldiers, at least at the beginning of the war, is a gratifying testimony to the growth of national morality and the influence of the educated over the uneducated combatants. It is not yet necessary, therefore, to confine the progress made in the Russian army to the fact that the number of common soldiers who can read and write has increased, and that reading and writing have been encouraged by the Minister of War. The percentage of privates who can write is still extremely small—much smaller, at any rate, than in other armies. But the belief in the moral effects of such acquirements, whatever value may be attached to them, in a military sense, by the rest of Europe, is still adhered to and encouraged in Russia.

A consideration of the incidents of the recent war, as narrated by those who took part in it, and a comparison of this with previous Russian campaigns, leads to the following conclusions. Together with an unsparing criticism and condemnation of all military arrangements, extending from the Commanders-in-Chief to the Intendance, we find an enthusiastic and often exaggerated recognition of all that has been done by officers and soldiers, and of the moral progress achieved by the aid of a humane system of discipline. That this

Russian estimate of the war and its lessons is tinctured with certain prejudices, and betrays the influence of particular 'tendencies,' is evident at first sight. It must be admitted at the same time, when one knows exactly about the matter, that the complaints of unreadiness for the war, of the incapacity of the Intendance administration, and of the want of definite purpose shown by the Commander-in-Chief, are not exaggerated, but justifiable. Politically, however, the circumstance of most importance is this, that the popular verdict on the recent war amounts to a glorification of the warlike resources of the nation, and a condemnation of the way in which they were abused. This verdict coincides with the general direction which our political development has taken for several years, and which daily becomes more threatening. Instead of placing at least some portion of responsibility for the blunders committed to the national account, the sole endeavour is to represent the matter so that everything good is on one side and everything bad on the other—that is, on the side of the government. Existing authority, and the respect for that authority, must be undermined at any cost. These tactics have been successful, and might well have been successful, because an enormous mass of corruption and incapacity have indeed been brought to light, and because the chasm of difference between the terms of San Stefano and those of Berlin is sufficiently broad and deep for even the masses to measure it. That a large share of the guilt proved must be ascribed to an overestimate of Russian strength by the Russians themselves, and that on this point the government and the nation are almost equally to blame, is a truth which the ruling opinion of the day will not acknowledge. And yet it is the key-stone of the whole question.

CHAPTER XVII.

THE NEW SITUATION AND THE NEW MINISTERS.

Acquittal of Vera Sassulitch—Recent frequency of political murders.
—Cases of incendiarism—Ministerial changes—The new Minister of
Finance—Fallacious estimates of the Budget—Urgent need of retrench-
ment—The Eastern Loan of 1877—The Ministry of the Interior—Arbi-
trary restrictions on the Press.—The Plague in Astrachan.—Alleged
cases at St. Petersburg—M. Botkin and the German doctors—The
Minister M. Makoff—Solovieff's attempted assassination of the Czar—
Martial law in Russia—Solovieff's trial—Wide extent of Nihilist con-
spiracies—Apathy of the public—M. Nabokoff, the new Minister of
Justice—Count Tolstoy, the new Minister of Public Instruction—
Tyrannical treatment of the Universities—Turgenieff and Young Russia—
Count Schouvaloff and Constitutionalism—Makeshift policy of the
government—Foreign relations—Russia demands a constitution—Dan-
gers of revolution in case it is refused.

'TOUT m'annonce aujourd'hui la chute de Carthage.' With this line, quoted, I think, from Arnault's 'Regulus,' I heard a young officer conclude his narrative of the trial which ended in the acquittal of Vera Sassulitch amidst the jubilant acclamations of the public. The line might as well form the text of the whole history of recent Russian development as that of the introductory chapter on this *cause célèbre*.

'Monstrous' acquittals on the part of juries have occurred too frequently in modern Russia for the 'Not guilty' of the murderess of General Trephoff to create any peculiar sensation. Considered from a legal point of view, the verdicts of acquittal, given about the same time in the cases of a young person from Saratoff, who had forged her own marriage certificate (March 7,

1878); of Madame Wenezka, who attempted to shoot her faithless lover; or of the Odessa student, who thought proper to box the ears of a professor, are perhaps still more remarkable. The verdict on Vera Sassulitch derived its significance from the time when and the circumstances under which it was pronounced; but above all from the approval it met with throughout the greater part of Russia, and the effects it has since produced.

Vera Sassulitch is a young lady who has been banished from her home by arbitrary acts of the police, and driven to despair by incessantly being expelled and put in prison, although the extent of her crime was reduced to a superficial acquaintance with Netchayeff. She had attempted to assassinate Trephoff, the Chief of the Police, to whom she was personally a total stranger, because he had ordered the political offender Bogoljuboff to be flogged in prison for refusing to submit to discipline. She was put on her trial before a jury, because her crime was not considered a political one, with which a Russian jury has nothing to do. Impressed, no doubt, by the general feeling of indignation aroused by her account of the tyrannical dealings of the police, a special jury, consisting of nobles and high officials, acquitted her, after stormy proceedings and a short deliberation. The public, as we have said, approved the verdict. So also did the young Radicals of St. Petersburg. So also did a portion of the Russian press, such as the 'Severni Vêstnik,' the 'Russki Mir,' the 'Golos,' and the 'Novoé Vremya.' Another portion, including the very moderate and intelligent 'Vêstnik Evrópy,' excused it under existing circumstances. The whole affair took place at a time of feverish excitement in Russian society. It threw such a

new and striking light upon the practice of the police
of imprisoning people 'administratively' who could not
be touched by the law, and of interning and banishing
them extra-judicially to 'eastern provinces,' that even
persons of a conservative turn of mind were constrained
to admit that perhaps it was useful that society for once
should 'make an example.' The further effect was that a
murderess, and the murderess of a man who had been
very popular at St. Petersburg, was celebrated in certain circles as a heroine and a Russian Charlotte Corday
—nay, a Moscow lady of high rank spoke of her at a
large party as a 'grande citoyenne'—and that, thanks
to the sensation produced by her crime, political murders have come into fashion in Russia, and seem likely
to continue so for a long time to come.

Exact statistics of political murders and attempts to
murder in Russia are as yet wanting. But we can
supply some precedents of eminent persons assassinated
during the last fifteen months. There are those of
General Mesenzeff, the Chief of the Gendarmerie, Prince
Krapotkin, the Governor of Charkoff, and Baron
Heyking at Kieff. There are likewise those of a
number of pretended traitors to their revolutionary
confederates, such as Gorinovitch and Tawlejeff at
Odessa, Nikonoff at Rostoff on the Don, Fisogenoff at
St. Petersburg, and Rothenstein (others call him Rosenzweig) at Moscow. There are also the attempts at
assassination made on Kotlerevski, the provincial Pro-
curator at Kieff, on Tchertkoff and Hübbinett, the two
Chiefs of the Kieff administration of Police, on General
von Drenteln, the successor of Mesenzeff, and finally on
the emperor himself. The number of criminal prose-
cutions instituted during this period against political
offenders is countless. The trials of December 1876, of

the first batch of 138 Kieff Nihilists, of Brandt and his confederates, and of the rioters at Poltawa, Charkoff, and Odessa, and so on, have followed each other in unbroken succession. The police are still hunting for those who are concerned with the large sums of money seized in Bessarabia, and collected 'on behalf of exiled political criminals,' and for those who invented and spread the report of an approaching redistribution of land among the peasants by the Czar. This report gave occasion to the decree of June 28, issued by the Minister of the Interior, which produced the utmost excitement, and plainly revealed the fears of the government. It remains to be seen whether the police will have better success this time than in their search for the murderers of Mesenzeff and Krapotkin. Latterly Nihilist bands have made repeated and successful attempts to extort money from wealthy merchants, such as Kokoreff and Elisséieff at St. Petersburg, and a merchant at Moscow not named,[1] in order to procure the funds necessary for their designs. Finally they have tried a third political remedy, an application of

[1] These persons had anonymous letters sent them by 'the Committee' asking them for considerable sums, from twenty to thirty thousand roubles, and threatening them with death in case of refusal. Elisséieff and the anonymous Moscow merchant complied with the demand, and by so doing have drawn upon themselves many reproaches and accusations. The *St. Petersburg Journal*, in particular, tried to make these gentlemen understand that they had acted in an unpatriotic manner, had made themselves guilty of a heavy offence by 'filling revolutionary coffers,' and had shown an unnecessary fear for their lives. M. Elisséieff is said to have replied to such remonstrances and to the remark that the government would know how to protect him, in these simple words: 'If the chief of the gendarmerie has been unable to protect himself against murderers, how will they protect me?' Here is a distinct proof that the public do not consider the danger yet overcome, and that even persons of education and position fear the secret propaganda even more than the police. That M. Elisséieff and his companions will not remain unpunished is regarded by the Russian press as a matter of course.

which has long ago been mentioned by Hippocrates.
Quod medicamina et ferrum non sanant, ignis sanat.
The towns of Irkutsk, Irbit, Orenburg, Kosloff, and
Uralsk have experienced that the Russian revolutionary
party manages the handling of a blazing torch as
skilfully as that of the dagger and the pistol.[1] The
pauses between these outbreaks of revolutionary and
Nihilist violence have been filled up by scandalous
trials, illustrating the moral degradation of all classes of
the population in the towns; by attempts to revive
the waning confidence and loyalty of the nation by
some new move in Eastern politics, which always failed
at the critical moment; by experiments in taxation
and finance which have proved abortive; and finally
by arbitrary measures, the reactionary shortsightedness
of which was only exceeded by the fitful and lukewarm
manner of their execution.

During this eventful period, which must be numbered among the most difficult epochs of modern Russian history, and which is marked by a general disturbance of authority, four of the most important branches of the administration have been placed in the hands of new ministers. Moreover, by the appointment of a Governor-General of Bulgaria and Eastern Roumelia, furnished with extensive powers, an office has been created which in importance is not inferior to that of a Minister of State. Nothing is so significant of the present situation as the choice of the persons

---

[1] Respecting the fires which have occurred during June alone of this year, the *Official Messenger* has the following:—' Altogether there have been 3,501 fires, of which 930 arose from carelessness, 310 were caused by lightning, 508 by incendiarism, either proved or suspected, and 1,753 were due to causes unknown. The total damage amounts to over twelve millions of roubles; viz., more than two millions at St. Petersburg, one and a half millions at Uralsk, &c.'

entrusted with these appointments. No sooner had peace been declared than M. von Reutern resigned the Ministry of Finance, which he had held for sixteen years. He had been anxious to resign at the beginning of the war, and it was only in deference to the personal wish of the emperor that he consented to continue in office provisionally. The last ten years of his administration, which at first had been anything but successful, were followed by results so marked and solid that intelligent persons of all parties viewed his retirement with regret. But von Reutern had resolved voluntarily to resign his portfolio, an act scarcely ever known in Russia, for he found his occupation gone. He saw the labour of his life, which had been spent in the endeavour to equalise the budget, hopelessly destroyed by the war. He was succeeded by his former assistant, General Greig, who had been appointed Controller of the Empire in 1878, in the place of Tatarinoff. Formerly a Chevalier of the Guard, he had served for a time in the Ministry of Marine, a department considered as singularly enlightened and progressive between 1858 and 1862, from its having been the first to abolish corporal punishment, and having adopted a liberal tone in its official organ the 'Mosskoi Sbornik.' He afterwards removed to the Administration of Finance, where he was a candidate for the post of minister, as early as 1863. He was considered personally a highly honourable man, and was a general favourite in society, from his elegant and amiable manners.[1] In ordinary times

---

[1] The famous naval battle in the Bay of Chesme (July 7, 1770), which ended in the annihilation of the Turkish fleet, and for which Count Alexis Orloff was rewarded with the first class of the Order of St. George, a grant of 100,000 roubles, and the title of 'Chesmenski,' was in reality won by the English captain Greig, who had recently entered the Russian service, and his two countrymen, Elphinstone and Dugdale. Orloff, who bore the

the capacity of this well-meaning official might perhaps have sufficed for the management of Russian finances; but that he was unequal to the task of administering the difficult inheritance of his predecessor was notorious to everyone when he received his appointment, and was proved by his very first measures. In order to restore the exhausted credit of the State, Greig ordered a preliminary budget estimate to be prepared for the year 1879, which showed an anticipated surplus of one-third of a million of roubles, but failed of course to deceive the public or the Exchange as to the true position of affairs. No sooner had this document been published, than its contents were subjected to scrutiny; and calculations showed that the nominal surplus had only been arrived at by including in the computation of receipts, contrary to all precedent and usage, the proceeds of new taxation and the additions to already existing taxes, and by treating the probable yield from these sources as income actually secured. This increase of problematic receipts is put down at $21\frac{1}{2}$ millions of roubles, of which 18 millions are to be realised in the course of this year. Inasmuch, however, as the total increase of the Imperial revenue, as compared with last year, has been estimated at only 400,000 roubles, it follows that the proceeds of the old taxes have decreased to about $17\frac{3}{4}$ millions, and that the new imposts would only suffice, assuming the most favourable case, to cover

---

title of Admiral-General, and is still treated in Russian history as a great naval hero, was hiding during the engagement in the cabin of a frigate outside the line of battle. Trembling and terrified, he fainted during the cannonade, and prevented full use being made of the victory. Philip Hackert, the friend of Goethe, was commissioned to represent in two pictures the chief moments of the battle. In order to give the artist a correct idea of the blowing up of the Turkish Admiral's vessel, Count Orloff, no less extravagant than vain, ordered a Russian frigate to be blown up, which was lying at anchor before Leghorn.

these losses. It was further pointed out to M. Greig that his estimate of receipts from the new taxes, as well as that of the expenditure to be incurred, was based on erroneous premisses. The minister had assumed that the income derived from stamps would remain the same, in spite of the duty being increased by fully a third; and that the duty to be levied on railway traffic would not affect the traffic in passengers and goods. Still more naïve was the assumption that the tax on the licence to retail spirits, raised as it was to 500 roubles, would not be followed by any decrease in the number of public-houses, or diminution in the consumption of brandy. The excise receipts had increased by 21 millions in 1877, in consequence of the war. M. Greig assumed that, notwithstanding the restoration of peace, and notwithstanding, that is to say, the discharge of a vast number of soldiers, and the diminution of their pay, the consumption of brandy would yield a further addition of 16 millions to the excise, and consequently 37 millions more than in 1876. It was noticed also that the minister had largely underestimated the margin for unexpected and extraordinary expenditure, and that, in spite of the enormous increase of taxation, the means were wanting for covering even these expenses. Had not M. Greig himself published the accounts of the administration of control, which showed that in the year 1877 alone nearly 40 millions had gone to defray unforeseen expenses, entirely apart from the extraordinary expenditure caused by the preparations for the war?

The minister has been equally unfortunate hitherto in his attempts to bolster up Russian finances by introducing a new proportional tax, and by diminishing the amount of 'prospective' expenditure, to do away with the anomaly that three-fifths of the total revenue should be spent on the army and in payment of debts, and only two-fifths should be available for other purposes. Out of 595 millions, 156 go to the account of debt, and 206 into the military and marine budget. The project of a classified income-tax, elaborated by his order, has proved a complete fiasco. No one would listen to a tax which, in the most favourable event, would yield only 15 millions; least of all the party of reform, who feared that so *dilettante* and fantastic an experiment might endanger the prospect of any fiscal reform. As regards the first point, a reduction of expenses, a special Commission has been appointed to revise the whole system of expenditure, consisting of Count Baranoff, Baron Nicolai, hitherto the Civil Commissioner of the Governor of the Caucasus, and the Privy-Councillors MM. Sablotzki, Grot, and Ostrovski, and a Secretary of State. It is a pity, however, that retrenchment and economy, to be of any value, can only be effected at the expense of the ruling classes, and that these are more than ever resolved not to tolerate any interference with the enjoyment of their privileges. It is also a great pity that not a single person trusts the amiable ex-Chevalier of the Guard to have sufficient capacity and independence of spirit to lessen the incomes of those from whose circles he himself has sprung. The subordinates in every department, that of the Excise alone excepted, are so badly paid, that any reduction of their salaries, in the face of a constant increase of prices, would be a downright injustice. Successful retrenchment could only be effected in those quarters where retrenchment will not be made—in the salaries, that is to say, of the innumerable ministerial and Court officials, governors-general, commandants, governors, and generals out of office, who derive all their pensions and emoluments from the favour of the emperor, or receive salaries varying from ten to thirty thousand roubles, under the titles of inspectors-general of infantry, cavalry, artillery, fortresses, &c., without giving any but a purely nominal service. Of what use is it that men like Stassulevitch, with a thorough knowledge of affairs, have pointed out that the military expenditure might be reduced, without prejudice to efficiency, by 30 millions; and that out of the 24 millions put aside for pensions, a large, if not the largest, part is bestowed on persons who either have no legal claim to support by the State, or are only entitled by law to receive small sums, but who nevertheless go on drawing their fathers' pensions by virtue of special favour? The habit of 'open-handedness' in this department is too deeply rooted to be eradicated in a moment. The statement made in the 'Golos,' that the sum total of 'extraordinary pensions and gratifications' amounts annually to 14 millions, is perhaps an exaggeration of the truth. At the same time it is notorious that there are persons who, on account of their fathers' merits, are in receipt of pensions threefold greater than the ordinary pensions of generals; that the majority of officials work scarcely three or four hours a day; and that a reduction in the number of officials in nearly every department might be effected without any trouble, and with profit to the public service. The provincial administration alone, notwithstanding the proverbially low salaries of the second-rate and third-rate officials, swallows up nearly 100 millions of roubles per annum; of which $24\frac{1}{2}$ millions are paid to subordinates of the Ministry of the Interior, 20 millions to those of the Ministry of Finance, 5 millions to those of the Ministry of Domains, and so on.

To judge from experience hitherto, a reduction in the number of officials is the most improbable of any measure of retrenchment or reform. It is an axiom among all of the old, and a large number of those of the new school, that the influence of the government depends directly on the number of its functionaries. It would require the labours of a Hercules to cleanse the Augean stables of abuses and malpractices, which in this province of public life have become inveterate, and date back by decades. For undertaking a task of these proportions our tatesmen and financiers, ex-officers of the white-uniformed Garde de Cheval, are far too dapper and elegant; the work is one for men of sterner mould. M. Greig, when Chief Controller of the Empire, had abundant opportunity for rectifying such abuses, and for continuing the difficult task begun by his predecessor, the late Tatarinoff; but even there he never got beyond beginnings and good intentions. No wonder, then, that as Minister of Finance he knew of nothing better than to go on in the old comfortable groove, and as soon as circumstances would permit, to take refuge in a new 'Eastern loan'—the third one of its kind. As no money could be got this time from foreign countries, an appeal was made to the nation itself, and with more success, indeed, than could have been expected. The loan announced for issue on May 24–26 (O.S.) was subscribed for more than double. Instead of the 300 millions required, 744½ millions were offered. The St. Petersburg Exchange alone had subscribed no less than 577,624,200 roubles of this total.

As to whether the mass of subscriptions to this loan came from Russia herself, or, as the 'Vêstnik Evrópy' asserted it was prepared to prove, from foreign countries glutted with Russian paper money; whether the proceeds were really applied for calling in notes of credit, or merely for paying off war debts still outstanding; and whether the result of the loan, as the 'Moscow Gazette' contends, can really serve as an argument in favour of a paper currency—on these points of controversy we cannot enter. It is enough to remark that this third Eastern loan has for the present strengthened M. Greig's position, and that the government and its friends think they have tided over the next financial troubles. His promise to substitute for the poll-tax other taxes more equitable and convenient has not yet been redeemed; though he has rendered a continuance of this oppressive impost morally next to impossible. His 'grand success' then is limited at present to having happily carried through a third loan, and having thereby effected a momentary improvement in the value of Russian stock. Notwithstanding this success, however, there is no sign or question of any increase or strengthening of confidence. Nor indeed can there or will there be any question of this kind, so long as the management of finances remains a mystery, which is only partially and periodically unveiled—and then merely for fixed purposes, and to a very limited extent—and so long as no trace is to be found of any guarantee against the discontinuance of the preliminary budget estimate. The necessity of such a guarantee is the great theme, although never called by its name, of all that has been written and said in Russia about the state of finance. It is the most telling argument, and one not refuted to this hour, of those who declare that any real improvement in the economic condition transmitted from the past is incompatible with the present system of government.

Even people prepared to give full credit to the praiseworthy intentions of M. Greig are convinced that, after the experience made by contact with M. von Reutern, the continuance of a Department of Finance—uncontrolled in its action, dependent on the influence and dictation of the Court and the high bureaucracy, and slavishly creeping in the ruts of routine—must infallibly result in bankruptcy. 'If not even the necessities of the present situation,' so people argue, 'have led to a resolve to reform the head and members of the State, and to draw together men capable of dealing with the case; if matters have been again allowed to rest with routine and a *routinier*, there is no hope for us whatever of being spared the fate which overtakes the finances of almost all modern great States under absolute rule. We may go on as we are for a while, but we cannot go on for ever. Therefore——' and after this *quos ego* follows a conclusion, which in writing is carefully and discreetly disguised, but in conversation is stated nakedly and intelligibly enough; the form of it may differ, but the substance and meaning are always the same.

Shortly after M. von Reutern had made room for General Greig, it was reported that General Timascheff, the Minister of the Interior, had also grown tired of his labours, and was desirous of transferring to a successor the portfolio he had accepted in February 1868. Several months, however, passed before this step was carried out. The true reason was not any 'fatigue' on the part of this, the gayest and most jovial of all the ministers, but the disordered condition—an unusual circumstance even in Russia—of one of the most difficult and extensive of all the departments of government. General Timascheff was a man of intelligence, a kind of *bel esprit*. He was deservedly popular in society as a retailer of spicy anecdotes, as a talented and agreeable composer of French and Russian verses, and as a clever draughtsman of caricatures. His alleged striking resemblance to the German emperor, and his facetious and spirited official reports, had often served to cheer the Czar. An amiable *garçon*, he was thoroughly at ease with the ladies, and knew how to appreciate their charms. No right-minded man could blame him for not always showing the patience needed for the troublesome and tedious details of administration and official life, enjoyable only to *roturiers*. His career had differed very little from the customary career of Russian statesmen. He had passed his youth in a regiment of the Guard; and after spending some years at Paris, where he was attached to the embassy as a military agent, he quitted diplomacy for the Gendarmerie, and left the latter again to enter the Ministry of the Interior. Finally, before his appointment as minister, he presided over the Post Office after the death of Count Tolstoy, the first and last Minister of that department. His promotion as successor to Waluieff was due to his qualities as a statesman, such as we have just described, and to the favour of the National party. This party looked upon him as one of themselves, and may possibly have expected 'decided views' from him in favour of their scheme for the Baltic provinces. And, indeed, it was due to him that one of the earliest and most beneficial institutions of his department, the Governorship-General of Livonia, Esthonia, and Courland, was abolished in 1876, after an existence of more than half a century; and that Russian municipal institutions were chartered upon the towns of these provinces in May 1878, in the place of the Hanseatic constitution guaranteed to them in former days. In other respects his administration was remarkable only from the fact that it paralysed and discredited the action of the provincial assemblies, by constant attempts at tutelage and interference, and that the press, through incessant persecution, was forced into the Radical camp. In other branches of his department things were even worse. The state of the police and public safety had been far from satisfactory; but under his management it steadily deteriorated, and in the capitals alone a certain semblance of order was maintained. Here, too, matters had taken so unfavourable a turn since the war, that Timascheff's own National friends' could no longer deny the fact of a confusion worse confounded, and an internal dissolution of society. Of course, it was not the fault of the Minister of the Interior alone that none of the Nihilist conspirators could be traced, who carried on their work as assassins, as itinerant preachers of Socialism, or as printers and circulators of revolutionary placards and tracts. Ever since Count Schouvaloff's retirement, the 'third section,' whose particular province was the conduct of the political police, had been less satisfactorily managed from year to year. Twice it had changed its chief—Potapoff, the successor of Schouvaloff, having lost his reason in the summer of 1876, and Mesenzeff having been assassinated in the summer of 1878; and in consequence largely of these changes it had given very small support to the head of the ordinary police. The latter, on the other hand, had been left with all the greater liberty of action, and had had the chance of gaining a monopoly of power. But of this chance no use whatever was made. The number of common crimes which remained undetected increased quite as rapidly as that of political offences; and in both respects the administration of the police betrayed an imbecility and a want of intelligence beyond all precedent. When at length all inquiries failed to discover the murderers of Heyking and Mesenzeff, the public lost all faith and patience. At St. Petersburg the feeling was so strong that people began to doubt the sincerity and earnestness of the department itself, and to propagate reports which were apt to become more dangerous to those in authority than the political crimes which remained unpunished. People would simply no longer believe that not one of those crimes which had terrified Russian society during the summer and autumn of 1878 had been brought to light. The same evil gossip which had fastened on the withdrawal of the prosecution against Messrs. Greger, Horwitz and Co., and accused the government of robbing justice of her victims from fear of publicity, was now again astir, and astir with the same damaging results. The moral credit of the department had sunk so low, that persons readily believed the report that every clue which might have led to the discovery of Mesenzeff's murderers had been dropped intentionally, because these murderers had been hired by a person in high position and compromised by Mesenzeff!

Such a distrust, surpassing all belief, could only be increased by the behaviour of a minister, who, although, as chief of the police, so unfortunate as never to hear until the eleventh hour things which were of public notoriety in town and country, yet in his position as head of the supreme administration of the press ruled with the most foolish and capricious severity, and restricted and abridged, whenever it was possible, the slender modicum of publicity in Russia. Outside the two capitals there existed a preventive censorship, which negatived altogether the free action of journalism, and made the public absolutely dependent on the papers of St. Petersburg and Moscow. Even these papers were regularly interdicted from discussing those subjects which were of most interest to their readers. Besides this, the publication of unpleasant news, inconvenient to the minister and his friends, was surrounded with so many dangers that the press carefully avoided such topics, even when the facts in question had become the theme of daily conversation. It is true the papers could not be permanently prevented from toying with Radical, National, and Socialist theories, nor from making a profit out of the scandal which was daily being amassed in the proceedings of the law courts. A subject might be perfectly innocent in itself, but it was quite enough to ensure its exclusion from their columns if it happened to be unpalatable to this or that person in power. Two instances may be quoted, among numberless others of this kind. A certain M. Korsch, one of the most cultivated and honourable representatives of the Russian press, was a victim of such outrageous ill-treatment and chicanery on the part of the censorship, that he was forced to throw up the editorship of the 'St. Petersburg Gazette,' which he had taken on lease—thus losing a considerable part of his small fortune, earned by hard literary work—and to expatriate himself for several years at Heidelberg, simply because he had criticised the classical gymnasial system pursued by Tolstoy, the Minister of Public Instruction. Again in the spring of 1879 the 'Golos' received a warning for having expressed surprise that a boy of eleven should have been excluded from the gymnasium at Odessa for his 'political opinions.' Similar instances might be quoted, not by dozens, but by hundreds. Scarcely anything has contributed so much to poison public opinion, and inflame the hostility entertained by even moderate Liberals against those in power, as the despotic and yet hypocritical system pursued in the treatment of the press under Timascheff's administration. On paper, so to speak, and so far as theoretical questions are concerned, there is absolute liberty; but in the practice of daily life there are vexations of the pettiest and the most perverse description—vexations which are felt the more deeply as they are practised without method, without any fixed purpose or consistency.

This 'press system' was, and still remains, only a part of a larger system. In the administration of justice, we find, on the one hand, publicity and ample show of discussion during the proceedings and in the jury-box; on the other, a practice which removes inconvenient persons from the cognisance of a tribunal, and sends them 'administratively' to Siberia. In the administration of finance we find, on the one hand, the yearly publication of a preliminary estimate of the budget; on the other, an utter absence of all control over its preparation. On the one side we find the abolition of corporal chastisement as a criminal and disciplinary punishment; on the other, incessant flogging in secret; on the one side, a recognition of the principle of self-government in the provinces, towns, and circles; on the other, the impossibility of turning this self-government to any practical use, through the fear of displeasing the governor, the chief of the provincial gendarmerie, or the minister, or some ministerial councillor. On the one side we find a strict demarcation of power among the various authorities, and a distinct separation of judicial from administrative functions, down to the smallest communal authorities of the peasants; on the other, an unbounded exercise of arbitrary power among the higher officials of the department, who make no difference between the independent tribunals and the police authorities immediately under their control; and who are ruled over in turn by a mysterious supreme direction, the 'third section,' which, like certain heathen deities, is never mentioned by name, and, according to circumstances, acts at one and the same time as administrator and judge—*judex a quo*, and *judex ad quem*. 'When a supreme command is given, everything else of course ceases to exist'—so a well-known professor of Russian public law used to say in the 'good old days' at the conclusion of his lectures; and this classical dictum has been raised to the rank of a leading principle under the administration of Timascheff, only with this difference, that the commands, at which 'everything ceased,' needed not always to emanate from 'supreme' authority, it being enough that they came from 'high' quarters.

Already in the autumn of last year the disorder, confusion, distrust, and uneasiness had reached so painful a climax, that the dismissal of a Minister of the Interior, once so dear to his Majesty, was considered a mere question of time. A new misfortune occurred during the last days of Timascheff's administration. As if the department of this minister were not burdened enough already with its ordinary cares and difficulties, a disease broke out at a Cossack station, situated in the eastern part of the government of Astrakhan, which, after much bandying of discussion among the doctors, turned out to be the Asiatic plague, and produced not only in Russia, but throughout Europe, a state of panic. Europe, whose hostility was the theme of daily complaint, contented herself with sending several physicians to the seat of the disease, and with instituting, when it began to assume a threatening character, certain measures of precaution on the German and Austrian frontiers of the empire. But by far the chief difficulties the Ministry had to encounter in stamping out the epidemic were those caused by the prevailing spirit of distrust and opposition at home. In educated and 'liberal' circles, to ridicule the efforts of the authorities threatened to become *bon ton*. It seemed to be the proper thing to shrug one's shoulders when any favourable news was reported from Wetlianka; to declare the measures of quarantine to be either inadequate or illusory; to sneer at official reports on the progress of the disease as worth nothing more than all other official news; and to remark that it was quite as easy to invent fables about the small number of victims to the plague as about the trifling casualties among the Cossacks in their battles with the Circassians. No sooner was it seen what embarrassments the epidemic was causing to the government than pessimist views about the malady came into fashion, and people tried to make capital even out of this misfortune. This evil temper was illustrated when, early in this year (March 2), an instance of the plague was supposed to have occurred at St. Petersburg, in the case of one Prokoffieff, a porter at the School of Artillery. For weeks the diagnosis of his malady formed the subject of political controversy. The Imperial physician, contrary to the wish of the government and the opinions of the German doctors, had given his opinion that the Asiatic plague had appeared in the capital, and it was a national duty to accept his verdict.

The physician in question, M. Botkin, was in fact a

man of some political importance. His scientific merits were undoubted; and his reputation was enhanced by his resolute advocacy of Russian science, independent of foreign influences, in opposition to his German colleagues. For many years he had been regarded as the representative of a new movement, as a Slav pioneer in the province of medicine, which was also the cause of the people. It is true there had long been at St. Petersburg national Russian physicians; they had frequently been appointed to important posts; they had enjoyed a certain influence at Court; and had gained orders and ribbons. But the heads of the medical profession had been from time immemorial Germans, either from Germany or the Baltic provinces, men who laid stress on their nationality, called themselves 'German' physicians with a certain emphasis, and had almost a monopoly of practice among persons of rank and education. In the old days the relations between these men and their Russian colleagues were undisturbed by national differences. The superiority of the German physicians, including, now and then, a small sprinkling of Poles and Frenchmen, was a recognised fact at St. Petersburg, as throughout the empire, and the Russian physicians readily confessed it. Now it had been M. Botkin's grand merit in the eyes of his admirers to have rebelled against this tradition. He had come forward just about the time when the new-fashioned fanaticism of nationality began to make a noise. Skilfully turning the prevailing sentiment to account, and assisted by his natural talents and energy, he declared himself the 'Russian physician' *par excellence*, and the opponent of the German hegemony, to crush which, as he announced, was the great task of his life. He succeeded in becoming so far the fashionable physician as to compete with the most popular of his German colleagues, and to bring the grandees round to the opinion that his services were indispensable to a man of rank. He founded a medical society of his own; he became Imperial Physician, Professor, Director of Chemical Science at the Medico-Chirurgical Institute, and honorary member of various learned societies in Russia and abroad. In the eyes of a large number of his countrymen he was the type and embodiment of true Russian genius.

To support such a man against a government that shunned the light, and to take his part against the intrigues and servility of the German physicians and their abettors, was regarded as a sacred duty by every patriotic Russian, conscious of his vocation as a Slav. Almost all the chief organs of the 'independent' and national press took the side of M. Botkin. He was lauded in these journals as a man of independent spirit, of undaunted love of truth, and of loyalty to his convictions, who had been the salvation of society. He was encouraged to stand firm to his principles. He was assured that the sympathies of all men of intelligence and right feeling were with him; honorary diplomas were showered upon him; his praises were sung in addresses and at public meetings. Just as a hundred years ago the rival Piccinists and Gluckists at Paris had represented political parties, so it was at St. Petersburg in 1878. The government would not admit that Prokoffieff was sick with the plague; this was quite enough to make their enemies assert the contrary. The 'Golos' and some other papers had been forbidden to be sold in the streets, on the ground that they had exaggerated the danger of the plague on the Lower Volga; this was sufficient reason, for all who had the honour of the press at heart, to copy their example. The Medical Council had entered the lists against M. Botkin; this was enough to arouse the suspicion that the government were seeking to prejudice the freedom of scientific inquiry. The 'Germans' had given the lie to the great national Botkin;—who could doubt that these men were influenced by considerations 'such as none of independent mind should entertain'?

All this, of course, was ridiculous and childish in itself. But as an index to the situation it was highly significant; for it furnished a striking proof of the divided state of society, and the incessant growth of a spirit of popular opposition to the government. That people who for a thousand reasons would be interested in seeing the hypothesis refuted as to the existence of a case of plague in their capital should do their utmost to support this hypothesis, and praise its author as a patriot for having advanced it; that they should do this solely from national zeal, and with the intention of harassing the government—this is a sign of the times which, taken in connection with many others pointing in the same direction, is ominous to the last degree.

When this ugly piece of scandal, particularly painful and compromising to the Ministry of the Interior, was made public, General Timascheff had already for some months resigned his office 'from reasons of health.' Several of his proposals and 'representations' had been left unnoticed by the emperor; and at his departure for the Crimea in the autumn of 1878, his Majesty had said to the general, 'Your health will perhaps not allow you to come to Livadia.' This was quite enough for Timascheff: he quietly slipped off the political stage, after having been numbered among its chief actors for nearly twelve years. It had been expected that M. Waluieff, the Minister of Domains, would be ready to resume the office he administered from 1861 to 1868.

But he declined the proffered post; and as no other suitable successor was at hand, M. Makoff, the second assistant of the late minister, and a Secretary of State and Privy Councillor, undertook for the present to conduct the department so beset with difficulties.

M. Makoff differed so far from his predecessors that he laid no special claims to being 'intellectual.' But he had a reputation for greater industry and zeal, and had the advantage of having served in the light, instead of the heavy, cavalry of the Guard. Both men had gone through the same course of education and the same school. M. Makoff had begun his career in a Uhlan regiment of the Guard. Only a few years ago he had exchanged the saddle for a seat in the Ministry of the Interior; and now, without the slightest knowledge of the duties of his department or the machinery of district and provincial administration, he commenced his business as a ruler.

The attempt upon the Czar's life (April 14, 1879) occurred only a few months after M. Makoff had been in office, and immediately created an exceptional situation, which has deprived the Minister of the Interior of the largest and most important part of his authority, and reduced him to playing for the present the part of a mere spectator. A few days after that attempt, when the emperor returned pale and terrified to the Winter palace from his customary morning walk, a decree was issued, placing the greater part of European Russia under the authority, *ad interim*, of six military governors-general, armed with full powers to suspend the ordinary functions of the police and the courts of law, and to substitute a state of siege in the broadest meaning of the term.

It is needless to dwell on the details of this exceptional edict, which is in the hands of all the world. From the Minister of the Interior it took the management of the police and of the press. From the Minister of Public Instruction it took the administration and control of education. It paralysed, or rather superseded, the action of the courts of law, leaving them only the semblance of jurisdiction. It placed the whole power in the hands of the governors-general and their subordinates, the military and gendarmerie officers. For weeks it constituted the house porters (*dvorniks*) at St. Petersburg the responsible overseers of the conduct of the whole population of the capital. It attempted to regulate the sale of fowling-pieces and pocket-knives in the largest city of Eastern Europe; and threatened the proprietors of printing-offices, who allowed their lead types to be taken from them, with the loss of their licence. Of the state of things which followed upon this miserable *loi d'exception*, too plainly indicative of the helplessness and mortal anxiety of the government, no one but an actual eye-witness can form an idea. The first moment it seemed as if all those in power had lost their wits, and as if their only object was to extend discontent further and further, and to convince more people how hopeless it was to look for a peaceful extrication from the present chaos of disorder, corruption, and arbitrary rule. The public, as in the worst times of the Emperor Nicholas, received their foreign newspapers, however moderate or friendly to Russia might be their tone, half-blackened with the obliterations of the Press-Censure. The articles written in the 'Nord-Deutschen Allgemeinen Zeitung,' the 'National-Zeitung,' and the 'Journal des Débats,' on the subject of the attempted assassination, were immediately suppressed. Directly any topic, no matter what, began to interest the public, its discussion was prohibited by the supreme administration of the press, and every public expression of opinion was stifled in these days of feverish excitement. The universities and other higher institutions of education were watched with a severity and suspicion which robbed both teachers and pupils of every spark of cheerfulness, and made them tremble for the existence of these places of learning. Day after day students or schoolboys were dismissed on the most trifling pretext; professors were cautioned, reprimanded, or dictated to; books and lectures, which had been allowed for years, were interdicted. A whisper or hint against the system of Count Tolstoy, the Minister of Public Instruction, was regarded as high-treason, and treated accordingly.

This subjection of the universities and the press to the provisional Governors-General produced a state of insecurity and confusion which baffles all description. Nor was the evil lessened or concealed by the senseless instructions which were issued to regulate the behaviour of young men in the streets and public places, or when meeting high officials. The request sent in by the professors of the universities at St. Petersburg to be allowed to resign *en masse* was hailed with universal assent, and with the approbation of persons to whom no one had ascribed anarchical or even mere radical tendencies. The state of criminal jurisdiction was still worse. For weeks past it had become the rule—hitherto it had been only the exception—for persons politically suspected not to be taken before a judge, but to be interned 'administratively'—in other words, without any previous examination, and banished either to the eastern provinces or to Siberia. The same government which had been unable to suppress the secret press and to detect a conspiracy to which dozens of higher and lower officials had been sacrificed, now persecuted with relentless passion whatever seemed in the remotest way to be a criticism of existing regulations or measures of administration. The provincial assemblies were virtually silenced; and the functionaries of the government greedily seized the opportunity, under the pretext of its being necessary to repress 'a few misguided men,' of trampling down every barrier of the law. While the official press was continually assuring the public that all that was wanted was to get hold of a small number of hardened miscreants, who had already been tracked, the extent of the measures taken by the government betrayed plainly their belief in a conspiracy embracing half the empire, and their disbelief in the loyalty of anyone. So tormented were the Czar and those about him with the fear of a renewed attempt upon his life, that when he left St. Petersburg it was under the protection of a strong military escort. The railway stations on the route looked like fortified places; and the district in which the Court resided in the Crimea was practically shut off from the whole outer world, much to the amazement of its harmless and loyal inhabitants.

At St. Petersburg and Moscow the aspect of affairs was even worse. General Gourko's only notion of maintaining the fidelity of the garrison stationed in the capital was to tighten the reins of discipline, and to infringe the provisions of the law respecting service in the army, by making the admission to the St. Petersburg division depend on the fulfilment of special conditions, the first of which was the production of testimonials to absolute 'moral trustworthiness'—that is to say, politically orthodox views. Similar fears were testified at

Moscow by an order issued by the Governor-General, issued about the same time, whereby public officers on duty in the streets were enjoined ' to direct their whole attention to the maintenance of order and tranquillity, and not to divert it by paying military honours to the Governor-General when he happened to drive past them.' The government evidently felt the necessity of continued efforts being made by those responsible for public safety, in order to prevent any excesses of the revolutionary party, and to inspire the public, now tormented by the most ridiculous apprehensions, with at least some feeling of security. That such a feeling was equally desirable in the provinces is shown by the panic which seized the town of Kostroma on May 25 (June 6), and the preceding days. A number of anonymous letters, written in the name of the revolutionary party, had threatened the town with a conflagration on that day, and had produced such a state of terror, that the insurance offices were besieged by persons anxious to insure their property. At Kieff and Odessa there seemed to be no lull in the excitement caused by the innumerable political trials before the military tribunals in those cities. In the towns east of the Volga fires began to break out early in May. At St. Petersburg, the fear of the domestic porters, whose insolence had increased with their powers, alternated periodically with the dread of Orsini bombs, until the discoveries and non-discoveries in the affair of the traitor Solovieff put for a moment every other interest aside.

The excitement created by this trial was only too well justified, for it excluded completely any comparison with the deeds of Moncasi, Hödel, Nobiling, as well as any parallel between the conditions of Russia and those of the 'corrupt' West of Europe. This was no case of a good-for-nothing fellow, having sunk through vanity and dissipation, standing singly, so to speak, and obeying solely the dictates of a diseased brain. Here was a cold, resolute fanatic of reflection, supported by a vast confederacy, and acting by deliberate design, who had raised his hand against the Russian State-system and its representative the Czar. This would-be assassin, who, from the hour of his arrest down to his latest breath, had been willing to sacrifice his own life, and whose sole anxiety was to save his party from injury, and to demonstrate the immovable strength of his convictions; this was a criminal who had evidently believed that he was serving a fixed cause—a cause dependent on his life and death—and that, although his attempt had failed in its object, it had been of signal advantage to his party. His dearest wish was to prove himself worthy of the confidence of his confederates. And this confidence he justified to the full. Not only in the preparation and attempted execution of the horrible deed did Solovieff display a presence of mind, an inflexibility and energy of purpose, quite unexampled, but down to his last breath he continued the part of a voluntary instrument of the revolutionary idea, determined thereto solely by enthusiasm for his cause, and untouched by personal considerations or motives of self-interest. He gave a simple, clear, and precise account of the programme of his party, and the motives of his crime. But to give any information about the persons who had known of it, and with whom he had been connected during the last months of his residence at St. Petersburg, he obstinately refused. By a consistent practice of reserve he prevented even his relations from knowing or suspecting anything of this connection. About his antecedents and personal concerns he said nothing beyond what would have been known without his avowal. Those persons only were named, who had already fallen into the hands of the police, or had disappeared without leaving a trace behind them. As to the most interesting part of his knowledge concerning the revolutionary agitation—namely, the organisation, the composition, and the doings of the Committee which was hidden somewhere in St. Petersburg, and had undoubtedly been privy to the plan of assassination— not a word of confession could be extorted from his lips. Who provided him with money; from whose hands he had received the proclamations and copies of the newspaper 'Semlja i Volja;' what was the connection between Dr. Weimar and those from whom the latter was said to have purchased the revolver with which the Czar was shot at—these were questions which he resolutely refused to answer. Whenever any specific point of inquiry was raised, he alluded to the mysterious 'Ivan, surnamed the Wolf,' an expression which, as a French correspondent acutely observed, was probably intended to personify the Committee. What inspired, however, the greatest terror was the fact that Solovieff wielded agencies ramifying over every part of the vast empire, and that for many months he had been carrying on his trade of revolution and conspiracy, without having once come into contact with the officers entrusted with the public safety. Of all the numerous arrests which had been taking place for months, not one had led to a trace of this arch-criminal and his friends.

The existence, indeed, of Nihilist intrigues, to an extent far beyond what even the suspicions of the 'third section' had surmised, was testified not by Solovieff's trial, but by the events which followed it. Some secret printing-presses were discovered one day in the sheds of the Custom-house on the quays. A few days passed and the compositors again were busy. To-day revolutionary placards were torn down by the police, and all suspected persons were supposed to have been arrested. To-morrow the same placards reappeared upon the walls. The greater part of this subterranean machinery, as proved by the reports from the South, had remained as good as untouched by the measures for a state of siege. Nothing, in fact, had been interrupted but the monotonous series of murderous attempts on high officials; and even this interruption was only temporary. Of the persons who had been arrested during the first fever of excitement, and lodged in the Peter and Paul fortress or the Liteinaja, those of higher station and the 'more interesting' were released again after a few days. The mass of the common rabble which filled the prisons, to be sent off in troops to the Eastern provinces, were of little use for the purposes of discovery, since the Nihilists of the lower grades are mostly pickpockets or criminals by profession.[1]

The worst of this affair was, that the fright occasioned by the first edicts issued by Gourko did not last very long; that the instruments of law and order grew tired much sooner than their enemies; and that altogether the bow had been strung too tightly to allow

---

[1] The proceedings at the trial of the 133 conspirators at Kieff furnish some interesting information on this point. Amongst others the following facts were proved. A Socialist young woman, Idalia Pohlheim, was commissioned to ingratiate herself with a rich old country gentleman, with the object of poisoning and then robbing him for the benefit of the secret society to which she belonged. It came out at the trial of Ituschin that the Revolutionists of the Moscow circle had urged a boy to murder and rob his own father, and then to let the spoils go to further the cause of the revolution. The functionary who acted as prosecutor in the Kieff trial declared he had ample evidence to show that Russian Socialists belonged to the class of professional thieves and impostors.

of its being gradually slackened. Scarcely two months after the order of the Governor-General had gone forth, insisting on watch being kept day and night without interruption by the domestic porters at St. Petersburg, the negligent or disobedient could be counted not by dozens but by hundreds, and it was perfectly well known that the threatened penalties could no longer be inflicted to their full extent. Here, where the presumption of a reaction, such as in other countries would have followed on a crime like that of Solovieff, could not be entertained for a moment, it was idle and worse than idle to think of carrying out a system of suppressing by force every movement which might possibly lead to excesses. The public neither seemed desirous of supporting the exceptional measures of the government, nor did they regard the suppression of revolutionary intrigues as the most urgent and all-important task of the moment. Not a finger was stirred to assist the authorities; on the contrary, a universal outcry was raised if they exceeded by an inch the legitimate measure of their power; a general sympathy was aroused for the 'innocent' victims of the new despotic rule. Scarcely was the lawyer M. Stassoff released, than he was elected President of the Chamber of Advocates at St. Petersburg; and just because the demonstrative character of his election was evident to all, it was received by the public with the greatest approbation. In vain did the press exhort the public actively to support the guardians of the public safety. People knew too well that the free action of the press was paralysed, and that any discussion of really burning questions was impossible. They knew that even in the most moderate and respectable of the monthly periodicals, the usual column devoted to 'internal affairs' was left a blank; and that in the daily papers articles on Egypt or the French law of education had to take the place of discussions on the domestic problems of the day. This fact was enough to deprive the few Conservative papers of all their influence. The feebleness of their criticism was pitied as much as the tendency of the young to liberal vagaries and Socialist dreams was deplored. There is no doubt that the attempt on the emperor's life had excited general indignation. But now, when the first impression was over, still greater was the indignation that not the smallest attempt was made to restore the social equilibrium, to strengthen the self-confidence of the nation, to check existing evils, and to furnish society itself with the means of resisting lawlessness, corruption, and arbitrary rule. Whilst everyone was convinced of the impossibility of making any real progress by following the customary path of exceptional measures and mere paper legislation, and by leaving the administration of this vast empire in the hands of half a dozen badly-informed officials, the government declared this exceptional rule *en permanence*, by attempting to keep half the empire in a state of siege, the maintenance of which exhausted all the resources of authority at their command. How could the nation hope for the removal of even the smallest of the evils laid bare by the results of the war, so long as the *ipse dixit* of six Governors-General, each armed with extraordinary powers, formed the supreme law of the land? What prospect was there of improvement or reform, so long as a whisper about financial embarrassments, military disorganisation, the absolute barrenness of the provincial institutions, and the lamentable state of the public establishments for education, was regarded as high treason and punished with all the rigour of despotism? By far the greater portion of educated Russians shared the opinion, which the provincial delegates of Tschernigoff had wished to express in their loyal address to the emperor, but which was expunged at the urgent desire of the Governor, M. Daragan. 'It is an illusion,' so ran the original text, 'to think that anarchical ideas can be destroyed by measures of violence. These ideas live and flourish so long as they find a favourable soil; and the persons whom it is attempted to suppress are replaced by others.' These expressions, of course circuitously divulged, have interested thousands of people far more than the multitude of loyal addresses which for months have filled the columns of the official papers, and whose form and contents betray their manufacture from models of 1866 and 1867, carefully preserved since then as precedents for the constantly recurring cases of that kind.

We need not discuss the part played by the Minister of the Interior, who had been a compulsory witness of these proceedings. Substantially, it was the same as that which fell to the share of the third new minister appointed during 1878, namely, the Minister of Justice, M. Nabokoff. Both had allowed themselves to be so completely pushed into the background and ignored, as if the object were to demonstrate practically to the public, how in the Russia of to-day, things might go on just as well without a Minister of the Interior and of Justice at all, as with the customary class of officials who had previously filled these posts. Nabokoff's predecessor, Count Pahlen, a descendant of the well-known noble Esthonian family, had shipwrecked his reputation over the trial of Vera Sassulitch, after having incurred repeated odium from his over-zealous advocacy for the independence of justice, and his patronage of the young

Liberal school of judges. Afflicted with those leanings to optimism which seem to be a general weakness among 'Liberal' statesmen in Russia, the Count himself had guaranteed to the emperor the issue of the trial of Vera Sassulitch, and was the cause of her not being treated as a political criminal, but arraigned on an ordinary charge of murder before the jury of notables at St. Petersburg. The mischief done to the government by this miscalculation could not be repaired, and Count Pahlen had sufficient tact to request the acceptance of his resignation immediately the unfortunate verdict of acquittal was pronounced. That this request would at once be granted was known to everyone beforehand, and Pahlen himself had expected it. His endeavours to create an honourable, independent, and incorruptible class of judges had been attended with some success. But in his well-intentioned zeal for purging the old administration of justice from its innumerable abuses, he had committed the error of trusting chiefly to the young generation, who for the most part were passionate Oppositionists, and of filling many posts with men who traded, so to speak, on their independence of government influence and freedom from aristocratical bias. These men not unfrequently exposed themselves to the suspicion of favouring, in accordance with their tendencies, the peasant before the nobleman, the poor before the rich, and of allowing their legal abstractions to override the interests of the State and the existing system.[1] Complaints had been heard for some years past that Count Pahlen did not hold the reins over these young men sufficiently tight,

---

[1] An excellent sketch of this school of 'liberalising' Russian judges is given in Mackenzie Wallace's *Russia*, ii. pp. 381, 399. They are especially numerous among the justices of the peace.

and that in his zeal for the utmost independence of justice, he was neglecting to exercise proper discipline over its servants and assistants, the much-blamed advocates. It was above all the numerous senseless acquittals pronounced by juries, and ascribed to the lax conduct of the presiding judge, which had undermined so completely the position of the Minister of Justice, that only a slight push was needed to bring him to the ground.

These facts were too well known to the public at large, not to make the position of Pahlen's successor a difficult one from the very outset. This successor, as we have said, was M. Nabokoff. He had served at Warsaw under the Grand-duke Constantine and the Marquis Wielopolski, and, on Miliutin's illness, had carried on the duties of Secretary of State for Poland. Since then, he had held the rank of a Secretary of State at home and the position of a member of the Committee of Ministers. From him, as an older and more experienced man, was expected that pliability and bureaucratic severity in which Pahlen had been deficient, and the want of which was supposed to have been the cause of the failure of judicial administration in Russia.

What and who he really is, M. Nabokoff has hardly had the opportunity of showing; since that branch of the administration of justice towards which the national attention is principally directed, has not rested with him for some months past, but has been and still remains in the hands of the Governors-General and the military tribunals under their control. Should justice ever reassume her former rights, the minister who consented to their suspension will scarcely ever rise to the position of a man who enjoys the public confidence. In the eyes of those who represent public opinion at present, the doom of all those ministers is already sealed, who acquiesced in the overthrow of established order and legality. M. Nabokoff will have to share the fate of his colleagues in the Ministries of the Interior and of Public Instruction.

Count Tolstoy, the representative of this last-named department, may be pronounced at once the most unpopular of all the present advisers of the emperor. The brutality with which he has attempted to carry out his system, to destroy the independence of the professorial body at the Universities, and to silence every expression of criticism on his actions, is only surpassed by the subservience of his demeanour towards the Governors-General and the Third Section. For a long while those subject to his department — teachers and students alike—have been exposed to ill-treatment and acts of violence of the most disgraceful kind; and have been tyrannised over by governors and police-officers, without the smallest regard being paid to their privileged position. And never did the minister once raise his finger to protect those committed to his care, or even affect a wish to win the confidence of the young by the exercise of a just and equable discipline. No man now in office is so detested as he; no man is more constantly criticised by professors of influence and popularity. When, in December 1878, he demanded a report from the Academical Senate at St. Petersburg on the causes of the bad spirit prevailing among the students, the Senate told him in plain words that it was due simply and solely to the harshness and tyrannical folly of his dealings with them. 'Matters have gone so far,' said the report, ' that the smallest number of students can no longer meet in social intercourse, but immediately a great noise is made about the meeting, and the landlord or his porter is ordered to report it to the police, and describe minutely what the young people are about. .... We are scarcely able any longer to visit any trifling irregularity or excess on the part of the students in the manner prescribed by law, because we have at once to fear the summary interference of the police, who add " administrative " punishments out of all proportion to the petty character of the offence. Thus it happened that the student Organoff was removed in 1876 to a distant town by administrative procedure, without our hearing at all what had become of him. In 1878 he suddenly returned; and this was a young man who had always been remarkable for his good character and industry. Not long ago, three students, after having had to undergo a preliminary imprisonment for several years, were acquitted after trial by a court of law; whereupon General Silverstoff at once ordered them to be administratively exiled. The Council of the University had the greatest trouble in procuring permission for two of these students to continue their studies under the personal guarantee of the Rector. Occurrences of this kind do not tend to increase the respect for the laws among the young.' The justice of these complaints was strikingly confirmed by a communication addressed to Count Tolstoy a few weeks later. ' Your Excellency has nothing to fear from us,' wrote the revolutionary Chief Committee to the Minister of Instruction. 'We know how to appreciate the services you have rendered, and still are rendering, to our cause; and we promise you that your life shall always be dear to us.'

We have already spoken of the regulations introduced by Count Tolstoy during the last few months, with a view of rendering the admission to the Universities more difficult, and of keeping the young spirits under check by strict orders as to uniform and discipline. Short-lived as these and other edicts, such as those relating to the Medico-Chirurgical Academy, will unquestionably be, they have created far too unpleasant a sensation, and been far too widely condemned, to make it likely that the minister appointed in 1866 will be able permanently to preside over this department. Even now Count Tolstoy's resignation is regarded as a mere question of time. Not, indeed, that any great hopes can be built on his retirement; since other experiences have shown that, with circumstances as they are at present, the old method of selecting Ministers and statesmen is the only one possible. Of the candidates most likely to succeed him, Saburoff, the Curator of the Dorpat University, a son-in-law of the poet Count Solohub, has been mentioned *en passant*. Prince Andreas Lieven, the former Civil Governor of Moscow, and a colleague of the Minister of Domains, is said to have the best chance of success. Prince Lieven is scarcely forty years of age; he is a perfect stranger to the department; but he is considered to be a very pliant person from the unexampled quickness of his promotion. The probable results of his appointment may be guessed at once. No branch of the administration so urgently requires a chief who shall be independent of the petty gossip of the day, and shall rule according to fixed principles, as that department which for twenty years has been the field for embryonic statesmen to experimentalise on. The disrespect of our students for authority, which has become a byword, is very easily explained. It is the direct consequence of the fact, that nearly every one of the Ministers of Instruction during the last twenty years has absolutely reversed the policy of his predecessor; and that all these ministers alike—whether Liberals like Golownin, or so-called Conservatives of the stamp of Putiätin and Tolstoy—have never regarded the welfare of the students as their chief task and duty, but have been anxious merely to satisfy the official or popular powers of the day.

Add to this, that the higher institutions of learning are not under one supreme administration, but under half-a-dozen different departments, whose heads have been constantly changing and are scarcely ever of one mind. The students of the Medico-Chirurgical Academy at St. Petersburg are forbidden by the Minister of War what was allowed to their brethren at the Universities of Moscow, Kieff, Charkoff and Kasan, and those subject to the Ministry of Instruction. The agricultural academies placed under the Ministry of Domains are administered on principles as little in harmony with those observed at the Universities as at the Polytechnic Institutes controlled by the Ministry of Finance. The young men, who are transferred from the ecclesiastical seminaries and academies belonging to the department of the Synod, to a lay institution, find themselves transplanted into a new world, where every former precept has to be unlearned. The student youth of all these higher establishments of learning are ruled indeed by the spirit emanating from the Universities; but these Universities have not yet acquired a settled system or repose. According to the quarter the wind was blowing from, there came into fashion either classicism or realism, a repression or a worship of the liberal ideas of the day, a childish mania for tutelage or a passion for unlimited freedom; and the thoughts which stirred the growing generation were stigmatised to-day as the sources of ruin, and hailed to-morrow as so many guarantees for a better future. Under Tolstoy's administration the young students have been dealt with in a manner so unequal and so foolish, that they can scarcely be blamed for complaining that in Russia it has become a crime to be a young man at all, and after the manner of young men to indulge in ideal aspirations. The blind prejudice with which the press and the public espouse in all cases the part of the students, and put a favourable construction on their excesses, even those of the most dangerous kind, forms in fact the only counterpart to the mistrust with which the present government regards every free movement in this portion of Russian society.

An incident which happened not many months ago, illustrates better than any argument the present situation in this respect, and the extent of the changes which have recently taken place. The famous Russian novelist Ivan Turgenieff, whose criticisms on Young Russia have long exposed him to the most acrid attacks of Russian Radicalism, paid a visit in April and May to St. Petersburg and Moscow. In both capitals he has been almost overwhelmed with ovations by the young students and their friends. If anything could compensate him for the indignities he had formerly endured, it was the enthusiastic character, beyond all precedent, of his welcome. Professors and journalists, and students both male and female, have been taught by the oppression under which they groan, that the man who was the first to warn them against a misuse of liberty, and who, in spite of his clear insight into the abysses of Radicalism, never wavered in his belief in a better future—that this man, after all, has been their best friend. Academical honorary diplomas and laurel wreaths have been showered upon the writer who was said to have been the first to raise in his 'Fathers and Sons' an accusation of Nihilism against the Russian students, and who was reproached with having, in his blind idolatry of Western culture, pulled down the national sanctuaries and declared everything Russian to be 'Smoke.' The bitter experiences of the last few years have had a sobering effect; and the interest Turgenieff has taken in the aspirations and errors of his young countrymen, by not condemning them off-hand, but by exhorting the students to serious self-examination, whilst acknowledging the legitimate origin of their aspirations, is already numbered among his cardinal merits. 'You have never calumniated us; you have never given us up,' the young men and women again and again exclaimed to the writer who in his time had told them the bitterest truths, but who, in so doing, had acknowledged that it was the sins of the fathers which were being visited on the sons, and that from the sons alone could salvation be expected. And in him too above all—in him the foremost Russian writer of the day—his countrymen celebrated the loyal man of the Opposition, who in the days of serfdom had confessed the cause of true liberty, of culture, and of the dignity of man as courageously as in the days of ultra-Radical and national eccentricities. It was known what Turgenieff thought of the present situation and of the exceptional measures in which the government in its helplessness had taken refuge. This was quite enough to make people forgive his former attacks upon Radicalism and the narrowness of the Moscow Nationals; it was enough to make a national hero of the man, who only a twelvemonth ago had been thinking of laying aside his pen from sheer despair at the unsympathetic attitude of his fellow-countrymen. The same keynote ran through all the speeches and toasts in honour of the champion of old Liberalism; one sentiment, however disguised or diversely expressed, pervaded all the addresses and marks of honour which were showered upon him. It was impossible, his admirers all agreed, to advance any farther on the path of arbitrary rule, or to plunge deeper into chaos. Only 'one ray of light from above' was needed to scatter all the clouds which darken the future of Russia and of her rising generation.

What is meant by this 'ray of light' will be obvious to those who are familiar with the previous chapters of this book; nor need we remind our readers that the light which is intended to illuminate, runs the danger of being turned into a light that burns. Turgenieff's friends and admirers had at heart the same desire which had inspired, and serves largely to explain, the events of the last three years. This desire is simply that society should have a voice in the destinies of the State, that the nation should control the men who conduct her affairs. The government, therefore, acted with perfect consistency when they expressed to Turgenieff, through the medium of the 'Moscow Gazette,' their disapproval of the movement, the 'dupe' of which, it was said, he had become, and gave him to understand that he would do well to avoid further outbursts of national gratitude for his undoubted services, and to consider that these outbursts might lead to painful consequences, if not to him, yet to those who were their authors. As to the 'decisive' point at issue, there is no difference of opinion between the programme of Turgenieff and his friends and that of the advanced party. But, measured by the standard of absolutism, all are equally dangerous and equally criminal which, in whatever form, speak or even whisper of limiting the omnipotence of the Czar. And yet to this side are pressing the most vital forces, the best intellects of the Empire, whatever is inspired with inward life, whoever has a will independent of the daily whims of the government. Nay, the government itself cannot help testifying by its own example to the fact that the desire of the governed to enjoy a share in the government, is too deeply rooted in the requirements of the time to be left unsatisfied for ever. The very day after the young principality of Bulgaria was established, she received from the hands of Russia a constitution, such as would have gladdened the hearts of innumerable Russians, and perhaps have satisfied most of the educated. That it creates a painful impression to see political institutions made *articles d'exportation*, and yet kept at home under lock and key, as if they were dangerous commodities, is a fact which not even the most ardent supporters of the government can any longer deny.

Meanwhile in ruling circles, the spirit of anxiety and mistrust increases day by day. No more effective argument could have been adduced by the enemies of Count Schouvaloff against his being eventually called to the helm of State—a question repeatedly mooted—than the fear of his insisting, as a necessity, on some unity in the ministry, and the subordination for that purpose of the separate chiefs of departments to a single minister-president. Nothing more was needed but to remind the emperor of the fact that an arrangement of this kind would be inseparable from the idea of a 'responsible' government, and that minister-presidents were only possible in constitutional States, to silence any plans for employing Schouvaloff as his chief adviser.

The aversion to any change which might possibly be interpreted as a concession to modern ideas, weighed heavier in the balance than the pressing want, felt on all sides, of putting an end to the internal chaos produced in the administration by a number of independent and isolated ministers, each working on opposite principles and pursuing contradictory aims.

Nor is the want of a clear and consistent system of foreign policy less powerfully felt. If things go on as they have gone hitherto, we must inevitably fall, so to speak, between two stools and be entangled at the first opportunity that offers, in some endless and aimless adventure. In Western Europe Prince Gortchakoff is chiefly busied with impressing on Prince Bismarck, by means of petty tricks and *méchancetés*, the independent action of Russian diplomacy, with a view to securing the cheap applause of his National friends at Moscow. In the East, for kindred reasons, the absence of a system seems intended to become the one system now in favour. Towards a State like Germany, whose friendship we cannot do without, and whose alliance the present Russian Emperor will never suffer to slip from his hands, so long as he and his uncle, the German Emperor, are alive, our press, otherwise fettered hand and foot, teems with hostile invective and challenges, the meaning of which is apparently ignored on purpose at Berlin, but is perfectly well understood at St. Petersburg. Certain diplomatic *dilettanti* and *dilettanti* diplomatists of our foreign policy, baffled in their hopes of effecting a Franco-Russian alliance, are doing their best, by declaring against Prussian ingratitude in 1878, to destroy all prospects of a German alliance, and morally to pave the way for a new National policy. The East remains, as before, the arena for fantastic adventures. Prince Dondukoff-Korssakoff, known ever since his conduct as Governor-General of Kieff as an able administrator and a liberal aristocrat, thoroughly averse to national vagaries, has had to undertake the office of rocking the Bulgarians of Eastern Roumelia into dreams from which a very 'rude awakening' has ensued, dreams which have prepared extraordinary difficulties for pacifying this country, without profiting in the least the Bulgarian cause. The project of revising the Berlin Treaty having fallen to the ground, as also that of a prolonged occupation of Eastern Roumelia by the Russian troops, a retreat had again to be made, resulting once more in bitter disappointment at St. Petersburg and Moscow, and a material damage to Russia in her relations with the other Great Powers. The Nestor of our diplomacy seems to regard as the perfection of wisdom the same system that controls our internal policy. We live in fact from hand to mouth. One never looks beyond the morrow, but comforts himself with the reflection, to which the late Emperor Francis gave expression when he said, 'It will last my time and Metternich's.'

How long, indeed, this state of things will 'last,' how long, in other words, the convulsion of Russian society produced by the late war can endure, is a question on which it would be idle to speculate. To determine a problem of this kind certain factors are requisite, and these are wholly wanting. The Russia of to-day has no institutions whose existence is a guarantee of their permanent vitality. She has no men who have the stuff for braving the storms which have gathered on the horizon since the recent war. The state of siege, under which the government have sought refuge since the attempted assassination of the

Czar, is a mere temporary shelter, and does not pretend to be anything more. That a 're-establishment of the normal state of things' may be expected from day to day, and that it will be followed by a reorganisation on a much larger scale than hitherto, are assurances repeatedly given by the official press, and given in the most conclusive form. And this for a very good reason. After only four months of active work, the officials burdened with the enforcement of this exceptional *régime* betray a fatigue which clearly indicates their despair of a 'reaction' such as they would desire. Their sole anxiety is to keep going from hour to hour the regular functions of the body, politic and social, thus galvanised into artificial life. We know, and all the world knows, what the thinking part of Russian society aspires to. How the government intend to master these aspirations is a secret of the government alone. Their promises to resume the interrupted labour of readjusting the machinery of State have borne no fruit, and have met with no response. There was a time when most Russians who took an interest in their country's fortunes, believed in the sufficiency of purely administrative reforms. But they cherish this belief no longer; for experience has shown them that the essence and nature of this administration are unchangeable, so long as the conditions of its existence remain the same. The cornucopia of such reforms, held forth by Alexander II. early in his reign, is now exhausted, without these conditions being changed, which form the latest ground for popular discontent. Whatever could be done under the rule of unlimited absolutism, has undoubtedly been done. So much indeed has been done, that only one thing more remains. But this one thing apparently the government of Alexander II. cannot bring themselves to do. One more step lies before them, which they have evidently not the resolution to take. Urgently and universally as it is demanded, the effect of taking it would, indeed, be so tremendous, that it can well be understood that a monarch in his sixty-second year, who for nearly a quarter of a century has guided the destinies of Russia, and who has experienced disappointments beyond number, should shrink from laying a new responsibility upon his shoulders. The mere fact that the most important and exposed portion of the empire is inhabited by people whose nature and institutions are essentially West-European, whose political emancipation might imperil the unity of the State, and whose superior civilisation might again be called in question by the purely Russian population, seems sufficient in itself to make the Autocrat of 'All the Russias' the irreconcileable enemy of those aspirations which are stirring the hearts of his people, and of many who immediately surround him. Apart from all other objections, have not, it is argued, the latest experiences of Austria distinctly shown what efforts it cost to maintain the unity and cohesion of a State, made up of various nationalities, by any form of government other than that of absolutism? And in Austria the population is little more than half that of Russia, while the leading nationality, moreover, is the most cultivated of all. Add also this further consideration. The present ruler of the Russian empire is fairly entitled to assume that he may ultimately succeed in staving off for the remainder of his life the movement now set afloat, and in sparing for a while the empire, with the aid of the authority he has acquired—an experiment which would involve the issue of life or death. On the other hand, it must be considered, that for a ruler who, like the present emperor, can look back upon a long series of external triumphs, and who has been able to abolish serfdom, it would be far easier than for his successor to determine the measure of concessions to the national desire for political emancipation. At any rate, it is not too late to make the attempt. Things are still in this position, that any and every limitation of absolutism would suffice to arrest, at least for several years, the movement now begun. All that is demanded now, is that society in Russia should have a controlling share in the administration; that some apparatus should be devised to check the tendency and habit of the government to indulge in incessantly changing experiments in legislation, and to guarantee in some measure more uniformity, more method, and more legality, in administrative and financial matters. Should the present emperor have the courage to make such a concession; should he have the wisdom to reconcile to his dynasty the Western provinces of his empire, by enlisting in his support their national, ecclesiastical, and historical peculiarities, then there is a hope that this dynasty may keep the power in their hands, and be powerful enough to stem the rising flood of discontent. But if, on the other hand, the internal dissolution of Old Russia continue as at present; if the system of Russian legislation and administration remain subject to mere accident or personal caprice; if the government persist in their endeavour to combine legality with arbitrary rule, European civilisation with old-fashioned doctrines of isolation, and to yoke together maxims which are mutually suicidal; then indeed the end is not far off. 'The old order changeth, giving place to new;' but in this case the change will be vast and violent; and ere long the government will have difficulties and dangers to confront, such as find no parallel even in the present situation. But the masses, it may be said, have remained unstirred by the currents which agitate the educated classes. This reflection may comfort some, but it can only comfort those who are not aware that the fickleness and irresolution of the masses are nearly unlimited, while their material condition is as unsatisfactory as it well can be, and that within the two classes, which act as mediators, so to speak, in the relations between the government and the governed—namely, the bureaucracy and the clergy—the younger elements are far more deeply infected with revolutionary ideas than all the rest. Those who immediately surround the government, and with whom the first reckoning must be made, have for a long while had nothing in common with the traditions of the peasants. In Russia, as in other European countries, the determining influence is centred in the towns and in those of urban sympathies and education. The masses pour into whatever channel is prepared for them. Every hour of delay, every further moment allowed to the internal dissolution and decomposition now apparent, only tends to increase the danger. Should it come to pass that not Alexander II., but the heir to his crown, who is pledged already to fulfil the desires of his future subjects, undertakes the 'great reform,' then the probability is that this reform will open the door to a revolution, the like of which has never yet been witnessed in Russia. The materials for such a revolution have been accumulating in masses; the events of the last few years have enormously increased them ; and, as is well known, in a political inheritance the available assets scarcely ever suffice to meet the most pressing encumbrances.

CONCLUSION.

SINCE the preceding chapters of this book were written, three important events have taken place, each of which has confirmed the anticipations of the author. The experience of last October has proved beyond dispute that the follies of the Russian National party have caused the Russo-German alliance to be dissolved, and have forced Prince Bismarck to turn to Austria, the old and natural ally of every sensible German, and indeed of every reasonable English statesman. Again, the recently attempted murder of the Czar has shown that neither the internal dissolution of the old society in Russia has been arrested, nor the courage of the revolutionary party been broken. And, lastly, the fact that the Emperor Alexander II has retained his hitherto advisers, including Prince Gortchakoff, and has removed only Count Schouvaloff, the most capable among them, from his position, points with tolerable certainty to the conclusion, that the same vicious system, as impotent and untenable at home as it is fraught with dangers to the rest of Europe, will be blindly persevered in for the present.

The fears expressed by the author last July, when foreboding a larger and more menacing extension of the revolutionary movement throughout Russia, have been only too sadly and strikingly confirmed. Nay, it would seem that these fears are destined to be realised to the full. The prospect, indeed, is gloomy, and the situation critical in the extreme. If nothing is done to relieve the intolerable pressure of arbitrary rule, and to respond to the wishes for reform entertained by all Russians of sense and moderation; and if the Government persists in a foreign policy, intended solely and incessantly to distract the attention of the National party towards abroad—then the only question to be decided, and to be decided very shortly, will be this: Whether Europe will live to see, first the collapse of the old system of Absolutism, and then a foreign war for the purpose of diverting the national mind, or whether a war is to come first (begun with the help of France), and the revolution is to follow at the news of the first defeat. Every day serves to illustrate more clearly the enormous ravages of discontent and internal decomposition, and yet nowhere in Russian society are the vestiges or symptoms of a reaction discernible. Even those who speak of a reaction do not believe in its possibility, and manifest by their conduct, that the measure of the evils under which the nation groans is greater than the measure of those difficulties and disturbances which they think are to be feared from a violent overthrow of the present system. This is the real reason why the Courts of Justice, whenever they are placed in a position to act at all, act with leniency towards even the most dangerous of political criminals. This explains the apparent apathy of the party of order, who refuse to rally round a government which they distrust and fear. This is the reason why even the moderate organs of the press criticise the existing state of things in a manner which entails such heavy penalties; and why the Professors at the Universities deplore the uncertain and short-sighted action of the government still more loudly and bitterly than the students, who have been sent back to their uniforms, and subjected again to the old ridiculous dry-nursing and surveillance. That such a disposition of the public mind should be possible at a time when the very foundations of social order and security are imperilled, and the fear of assassination threatens to become permanent, would be incredible and inconceivable in the absence of facts to prove it.

But such facts exist, and are notorious. At St. Petersburg it is no secret that Mirsky, the young man of twenty-three, who shot at General von Drenteln, and who has recently been tried before a military tribunal in the capital, has been able, by the moderate yet determined manner of his defence, as well as by his searching exposure of the defects of the existing government, to produce an alarmingly favourable impression, not only upon a large portion of the impressionable public, but also upon his judges; and that his strictures upon the intolerable tyranny of the police, the venality of officials, and the incongruity between the liberal laws and the arbitrary manner of their execution, have gained far more applause to the accused than the prosecution has brought to the official accuser. Eye-witnesses of the trial speak of the drastic effect produced when Mirsky, upon the President asking him 'Why, after devoting himself to death, as the agent of his party, and undertaking to execute so perilous a deed, he had taken to flight?' replied that the clumsiness and stupidity of the police who pursued him offered a temptation which he was not able to resist. But, as had happened before with Solovieff, not one syllable escaped the lips of this young fanatic, to betray the 'secret government,' by whose orders he confessed he had acted; not a word of repentance has he uttered or even hinted. Notwithstanding this silence and this avowal, General Gourko, the Governor-General of the capital, commuted his sentence of death, and this decision was received with downright jubilation by public opinion, and registered by a portion of the press as a sign of our improved condition, which no longer requires the former rigour and severity of penal discipline. This commutation, announced as it was on the day after the attempt on the Czar's life at Moscow, was only rendered possible by the fact that the news of that attempt had been kept back from St. Petersburg for more than twenty-four hours. So critical was the situation considered, that for some hours at least the government thought of ignoring the outrage altogether, and of passing over in perfect silence the terrible fact of a fourth attempt upon the life of the Sovereign, in order to spare the public this fresh excitement. And yet not only this, but still further excitement was aroused. While the Nihilists, disappointed, but not discouraged, were supposed to be preparing the destruction of the Winter Palace, the Censorship renewed its insane persecution of the press by virtually silencing, on trivial pretexts, the 'Golos' and the moderate and peaceable 'Molva,' two of the chief newspapers of St. Petersburg. Already, as is probably well known, the Provincial Assemblies had been stripped of the remnant of their importance by a law which made the election of their members depend on the confirmation of the governors; the military uniforms of the University students had been reintroduced as a matter of compulsion; and the public libraries had been forbidden to lend any books to the pupils at the various institutions of learning. It is equally well known, at least in Russia, that, of all the projects of fiscal reform which M. Greig, the Minister of Finance, has promised, not one has been carried out, and that this Minister, on his visit to Moscow and Nishni-Novgorod, has been obliged repeatedly to confess that the abolition of the hateful salt-tax could not be thought of for the present.

If, with all these direct and indirect evidences of the seemingly incurable decomposition of the Russian State and society, it were only a question of the greater or less probability of a violent internal cataclysm, then the rest of Europe might afford to contemplate the struggle as spectators who had no interest in its issue. But such is not the case. The very fact that all these domestic events in Russia, which have so immeasurably increased the severity of the present crisis, and threaten to make it fatal, are closely connected with the question of her foreign policy, serves to hasten the probability that, if all other remedies are found of no avail, an attempt will be made, after the well-known French method, to occupy the feverish elements of society by a foreign war. Add to this the fact that such a war is most eagerly desired by the discontented themselves, and that the first use which emancipated Russian society would make of its liberty would consist in taking up again the policy of Eastern conquest, forcibly arrested by the Berlin Congress, and declaring a war of revenge against those who brought that Congress about. Frequent mention of such a war is made even now by the Russian press, and the sentiment which prompts such utterances still remains. Not that the Emperor Alexander II. desires another war; he is sick and weary of the name, and contemplates such an event with anxiety and dread. And indeed, so long as the Austro-German alliance can reckon on seeing its policy of peace, which constitutes its *raison d'être*, supported by an English Government, strong at home and respected abroad, whose influence with France is powerful enough to wean or to deter her from an armed coalition with the Northern Empire, even the most warlike Russians are forced of necessity to keep still. But if, on the other hand, an unhappy fate should will that a revolution in Russia should be accompanied by a relapse of England into indifference to Continental interests, then the first result of this would be that France, deprived of the peaceful counsels of her English neighbour, would reach her hand to Russia for an alliance; and the next result, that the whole of Europe would be taught to know, what only a few know at present, that the revolution now imminent in Russia implies a terrible danger to European peace and civilisation.

39 Paternoster Row, E.C.
LONDON, *July* 1879.

GENERAL LIST OF WORKS

PUBLISHED BY

MESSRS. LONGMANS, GREEN & CO

HISTORY, POLITICS, HISTORICAL MEMOIRS, &c.

A History of England from the Conclusion of the Great War in 1815. By SPENCER WALPOLE, Author of 'Life of the Rt. Hon. Spencer Perceval.' VOLS. I. & II. 8vo. 36*s.*

History of England in the 18th Century. By W. E. H. LECKY, M.A. VOLS. I. & II. 1700–1760. 2 vols. 8vo. 36*s.*

The History of England from the Accession of James II. By the Right Hon. Lord MACAULAY.

STUDENT'S EDITION, 2 vols. cr. 8vo. 12*s.*
PEOPLE'S EDITION, 4 vols. cr. 8vo. 16*s.*
CABINET EDITION, 8 vols. post 8vo. 48*s.*
LIBRARY EDITION, 5 vols. 8vo. £4.

Critical and Historical Essays contributed to the Edinburgh Review. By the Right Hon. Lord MACAULAY.

CHEAP EDITION, crown 8vo. 3*s.* 6*d.*
STUDENT'S EDITION, crown 8vo. 6*s.*
PEOPLE'S EDITION, 2 vols. crown 8vo. 8*s.*
CABINET EDITION, 4 vols. 24*s.*
LIBRARY EDITION, 3 vols. 8vo. 36*s.*

Lord Macaulay's Works. Complete and uniform Library Edition. Edited by his Sister, Lady TREVELYAN. 8 vols. 8vo. with Portrait £5. 5*s.*

The History of England from the Fall of Wolsey to the Defeat of the Spanish Armada. By J. A. FROUDE, M.A.

CABINET EDITION, 12 vols. cr. 8vo. £3. 12*s.*
LIBRARY EDITION, 12 vols. 8vo. £8. 18*s.*

The English in Ireland in the Eighteenth Century. By J. A. FROUDE, M.A. 3 vols. 8vo. £2. 8*s.*

Journal of the Reigns of King George IV. and King William IV. By the late C. C. F. GREVILLE, Esq. Edited by H. REEVE, Esq. Fifth Edition. 3 vols. 8vo. price 36*s.*

The Life of Napoleon III. derived from State Records Unpublished Family Correspondence, and Personal Testimony. By BLANCHARD JERROLD. In Four Volumes, 8vo. with numerous Portraits and Facsimiles. VOLS. I. to III. price 18*s.* each.

The Constitutional History of England since the Accession of George III. 1760–1870. By Sir THOMAS ERSKINE MAY, K.C.B. D.C.L. Fifth Edition. 3 vols. crown 8vo. 18*s.*

Democracy in Europe; a History. By Sir THOMAS ERSKINE MAY, K.C.B. D.C.L. 2 vols. 8vo. 32*s.*

A

Introductory Lectures on Modern History delivered in 1841 and 1842. By the late Rev. T. ARNOLD, D.D. 8vo. price 7s. 6d.

On Parliamentary Government in England; its Origin, Development, and Practical Operation. By ALPHEUS TODD. 2 vols. 8vo. price £1. 17s.

History of Civilisation in England and France, Spain and Scotland. By HENRY THOMAS BUCKLE. 3 vols. crown 8vo. 24s.

Lectures on the History of England from the Earliest Times to the Death of King Edward II. By W. LONGMAN, F.S.A. Maps and Illustrations. 8vo. 15s.

History of the Life & Times of Edward III. By W. LONGMAN, F.S.A. With 9 Maps, 8 Plates, and 16 Woodcuts. 2 vols. 8vo. 28s.

History of the Life and Reign of Richard III. To which is added the Story of PERKIN WARBECK, from Original Documents. By JAMES GAIRDNER. With Portrait and Map. Second Edition. Crown 8vo. 10s. 6d.

Memoirs of the Civil War in Wales and the Marches, 1642-1649. By JOHN ROLAND PHILLIPS, of Lincoln's Inn, Barrister-at-Law. Second Edition, in One Volume. 8vo. 16s.

The Life of Simon de Montfort, Earl of Leicester, with special reference to the Parliamentary History of his time. By G. W. PROTHERO. Crown 8vo. Maps, 9s.

History of England under the Duke of Buckingham and Charles I. 1624-1628. By S. R. GARDINER. 2 vols. 8vo. Maps, 24s.

The Personal Government of Charles I. from the Death of Buckingham to the Declaration in favour of Ship Money, 1628-1637. By S. R. GARDINER. 2 vols. 8vo. 24s.

Popular History of France, from the Earliest Times to the Death of Louis XIV. By ELIZABETH M. SEWELL. With 8 Maps. Crown 8vo. 7s. 6d.

The Famine Campaign in Southern India, (Madras, Bombay, and Mysore,) in 1876-78. By WILLIAM DIGBY, Secretary of the Madras Famine Committee. With Maps and many Illustrations. 2 vols. 8vo. 32s.

A Student's Manual of the History of India from the Earliest Period to the Present. By Col. MEADOWS TAYLOR, M.R.A.S. Third Thousand. Crown 8vo. Maps, 7s. 6d.

Indian Polity; a View of the System of Administration in India. By Lieut.-Col. G. CHESNEY. 8vo. 21s.

Waterloo Lectures; a Study of the Campaign of 1815. By Colonel C. C. CHESNEY, R.E. 8vo. 10s. 6d.

The Oxford Reformers—John Colet, Erasmus, and Thomas More; a History of their Fellow-Work. By F. SEEBOHM. 8vo. 14s.

General History of Rome from B.C. 753 to A.D. 476. By Dean MERIVALE, D.D. Crown 8vo. Maps, price 7s. 6d.

The Fall of the Roman Republic; a Short History of the Last Century of the Commonwealth. By Dean MERIVALE, D.D. 12mo. 7s. 6d.

Carthage and the Carthaginians. By R. BOSWORTH SMITH, M.A. Second Edition. Maps, Plans, &c. Crown 8vo. 10s. 6d.

History of the Romans under the Empire. By Dean MERIVALE, D.D. 8 vols. post 8vo. 48s.

The History of Rome. By WILHELM IHNE. VOLS. I. to III. 8vo. price 45s.

The Sixth Oriental Monarchy; or, the Geography, History, and Antiquities of Parthia. By G. RAWLINSON, M.A. With Maps and Illustrations. 8vo. 16s.

The Seventh Great Oriental Monarchy; or, a History of the Sassanians. By G. RAWLINSON, M.A. With Map and 95 Illustrations. 8vo. 28s.

The History of European Morals from Augustus to Charlemagne. By W. E. H. LECKY, M.A. 2 vols. crown 8vo. 16s.

History of the Rise and Influence of the Spirit of Rationalism in Europe. By W. E. H. LECKY, M.A. 2 vols. crown 8vo. 16s.

The History of Philosophy, from Thales to Comte. By GEORGE HENRY LEWES. Fourth Edition. 2 vols. 8vo. 32s.

Zeller's Stoics, Epicureans, and Sceptics. Translated by the Rev. O. J. REICHEL, M.A. Cr. 8vo. 14s.

Zeller's Socrates & the Socratic Schools. Translated by the Rev. O. J. REICHEL, M.A. Second Edition. Crown 8vo. 10s. 6d.

Zeller's Plato & the Older Academy. Translated by S. FRANCES ALLEYNE and ALFRED GOODWIN, B.A. Crown 8vo. 18s.

Epochs of Modern History. Edited by C. COLBECK, M.A.

Church's Beginning of the Middle Ages, 2s. 6d.
Cox's Crusades, 2s. 6d.
Creighton's Age of Elizabeth, 2s. 6d.
Gairdner's Houses of Lancaster and York, 2s. 6d.
Gardiner's Puritan Revolution, 2s. 6d.
———— Thirty Years' War, 2s. 6d.
Hale's Fall of the Stuarts, 2s. 6d.
Johnson's Normans in Europe, 2s. 6d.
Ludlow's War of American Independence, 2s. 6d.
Morris's Age of Anne, 2s. 6d.
Seebohm's Protestant Revolution, price 2s. 6d.
Stubbs's Early Plantagenets, 2s. 6d.
Warburton's Edward III. 2s. 6d.

Epochs of Ancient History. Edited by the Rev. Sir G. W. COX, Bart. M.A. & C. SANKEY, M.A.

Beesly's Gracchi, Marius & Sulla, 2s. 6d.
Capes's Age of the Antonines, 2s. 6d.
———— Early Roman Empire, 2s. 6d.
Cox's Athenian Empire, 2s. 6d.
———— Greeks & Persians, 2s. 6d.
Curteis's Macedonian Empire, 2s. 6d.
Ihne's Rome to its Capture by the Gauls, 2s. 6d.
Merivale's Roman Triumvirates, 2s. 6d.
Sankey's Spartan & Theban Supremacies, 2s. 6d.

Epochs of English History. Edited by the Rev. MANDELL CREIGHTON, M.A. Fcp. 8vo. 5s.

Browning's Modern England, 1820-1874, 9d.
Cordery's Struggle against Absolute Monarchy, 1603-1688, 9d.
Creighton's (Mrs.) England a Continental Power, 1066-1216, 9d.
Creighton's (Rev. M.) Tudors and the Reformation, 1485-1603, 9d.
Rowley's Rise of the People, 1215-1485, 9d.
Rowley's Settlement of the Constitution, 1688-1778, 9d.
Tancock's England during the American & European Wars, 1778-1820, 9d.
York-Powell's Early England to the Conquest, 1s.

Creighton's Shilling History of England, introductory to the above. Fcp. 8vo. 1s.

The Student's Manual of Modern History; the Rise and Progress of the Principal European Nations. By W. COOKE TAYLOR, LL.D. Crown 8vo. 7s. 6d.

The Student's Manual of Ancient History; the Political History, Geography and Social State of the Principal Nations of Antiquity. By W. COOKE TAYLOR LL.D. Cr. 8vo. 7s. 6d.

BIOGRAPHICAL WORKS.

Memoirs of the Life of Anna Jameson, Author of 'Sacred and Legendary Art' &c. By her Niece, GERARDINE MACPHERSON. 8vo. with Portrait, price 12s. 6d.

Memorials of Charlotte Williams-Wynn. Edited by her Sister. Crown 8vo. with Portrait, price 10s. 6d.

The Life and Letters of Lord Macaulay. By his Nephew, G. OTTO TREVELYAN, M.P.
CABINET EDITION, 2 vols. crown 8vo. 12s.
LIBRARY EDITION, 2 vols. 8vo. 36s.

The Life of Sir Martin Frobisher, Knt. containing a Narrative of the Spanish Armada. By the Rev. FRANK JONES, B.A. Portrait, Maps, and Facsimile. Crown 8vo. 6s.

Gotthold Ephraim Lessing, his Life and Works. By HELEN ZIMMERN. Crown 8vo. 10s. 6d.

The Life, Works, and Opinions of Heinrich Heine. By WILLIAM STIGAND. 2 vols. 8vo. Portrait, 28s.

The Life of Mozart. Translated from the German Work of Dr. LUDWIG NOHL by Lady WALLACE. 2 vols. crown 8vo. Portraits, 21s.

Life of Robert Frampton, D.D. Bishop of Gloucester, deprived as a Non-Juror in 1689. Edited by T. S. EVANS, M.A. Crown 8vo. 10s. 6d.

The Life of Simon de Montfort, Earl of Leicester, with special reference to the Parliamentary History of his time. By G. W. PROTHERO. Crown 8vo. Maps, 9s.

Maunder's Biographical Treasury; a Dictionary of Universal Biography. Latest Edition, thoroughly revised and for the most part re-written, with over Fifteen Hundred additional Memoirs, by WILLIAM L. R. CATES. Fcp. 8vo. 6s.

Felix Mendelssohn's Letters, translated by Lady WALLACE. 2 vols. crown 8vo. 5s. each.

Autobiography. By JOHN STUART MILL. 8vo. 7s. 6d.

Apologia pro Vitâ Suâ; Being a History of his Religious Opinions by JOHN HENRY NEWMAN, D.D. New Edition. Crown 8vo. 6s.

Isaac Casaubon, 1559-1614. By MARK PATTISON, Rector of Lincoln College, Oxford. 8vo. 18s.

Leaders of Public Opinion in Ireland; Swift, Flood, Grattan, O'Connell. By W. E. H. LECKY, M.A. Crown 8vo. 7s. 6d.

Essays in Ecclesiastical Biography. By the Right Hon. Sir J. STEPHEN, LL.D. Crown 8vo. 7s. 6d.

Cæsar; a Sketch. By JAMES ANTHONY FROUDE, M.A. formerly Fellow of Exeter College, Oxford. With Portrait and Map. 8vo. 16s.

Life of the Duke of Wellington. By the Rev. G. R. GLEIG, M.A. Crown 8vo. Portrait, 6s.

Memoirs of Sir Henry Havelock, K.C.B. By JOHN CLARK MARSHMAN. Crown 8vo. 3s. 6d.

Vicissitudes of Families. By Sir BERNARD BURKE, C.B. Two vols. crown 8vo. 21s.

MENTAL and POLITICAL PHILOSOPHY.

Comte's System of Positive Polity, or Treatise upon Sociology:—

Vol. I. General View of Positivism and Introductory Principles. Translated by J. H. Bridges, M.B. 8vo. 21s.

Vol. II. The Social Statics, or the Abstract Laws of Human Order. Translated by F. Harrison, M.A. 8vo. 14s.

Vol. III. The Social Dynamics, or the General Laws of Human Progress (the Philosophy of History). Translated by E. S. Beesly, M.A. 8vo. 21s.

Vol. IV. The Theory of the Future of Man; with Comte's Early Essays on Social Philosophy. Translated by R. Congreve, M.D. and H. D. Hutton, B.A. 8vo. 24s.

De Tocqueville's Democracy in America, translated by H. Reeve. 2 vols. crown 8vo. 16s.

Analysis of the Phenomena of the Human Mind. By James Mill. With Notes, Illustrative and Critical. 2 vols. 8vo. 28s.

On Representative Government. By John Stuart Mill. Crown 8vo. 2s.

On Liberty. By John Stuart Mill. Post 8vo. 7s. 6d. crown 8vo. 1s. 4d.

Principles of Political Economy. By John Stuart Mill. 2 vols. 8vo. 30s. or 1 vol. crown 8vo. 5s.

Essays on some Unsettled Questions of Political Economy. By John Stuart Mill. 8vo. 6s. 6d.

Utilitarianism. By John Stuart Mill. 8vo. 5s.

The Subjection of Women. By John Stuart Mill. Fourth Edition. Crown 8vo. 6s.

Examination of Sir William Hamilton's Philosophy. By John Stuart Mill. 8vo. 16s.

A System of Logic, Ratiocinative and Inductive. By John Stuart Mill. 2 vols. 8vo. 25s.

Dissertations and Discussions. By John Stuart Mill. 4 vols. 8vo. price £2. 6s. 6d.

Philosophical Fragments written during intervals of Business. By J. D. Morell, LL.D. Crown 8vo. 5s.

The Philosophy of Reflection. By S. H. Hodgson, Hon. LL.D. Edin. 2 vols. 8vo. 21s.

The Law of Nations considered as Independent Political Communities. By Sir Travers Twiss, D.C.L. 2 vols. 8vo. £1. 13s.

A Systematic View of the Science of Jurisprudence. By Sheldon Amos, M.A. 8vo. 18s.

A Primer of the English Constitution and Government. By S. Amos, M.A. Crown 8vo. 6s.

A Sketch of the History of Taxes in England from the Earliest Times to the Present Day. By Stephen Dowell. Vol. I. to the Civil War 1642. 8vo. 10s. 6d.

Principles of Economical Philosophy. By H. D. Macleod, M.A. Second Edition in 2 vols. Vol. I. 8vo. 15s. Vol. II. Part I. 12s.

The Institutes of Justinian; with English Introduction, Translation, and Notes. By T. C. Sandars, M.A. 8vo. 18s.

Lord Bacon's Works, collected & edited by R. L. Ellis, M.A. J. Spedding, M.A. and D. D. Heath. 7 vols. 8vo. £3. 13s. 6d.

Letters and Life of Francis Bacon, including all his Occasional Works. Collected and edited, with a Commentary, by J. Spedding. 7 vols. 8vo. £4. 4s.

The Nicomachean Ethics of Aristotle, translated into English by R. WILLIAMS, B.A. Crown 8vo. price 7s. 6d.

Aristotle's Politics, Books I. III. IV. (VII.) Greek Text, with an English Translation by W. E. BOLLAND, M.A. and Short Essays by A. LANG, M.A. Crown 8vo. 7s. 6d.

The Politics of Aristotle; Greek Text, with English Notes. By RICHARD CONGREVE, M.A. 8vo. 18s.

The Ethics of Aristotle; with Essays and Notes. By Sir A. GRANT, Bart. LL.D. 2 vols. 8vo. 32s.

Bacon's Essays, with Annotations. By R. WHATELY, D.D. 8vo. 10s. 6d.

Picture Logic; an Attempt to Popularise the Science of Reasoning. By A. SWINBOURNE, B.A. Post 8vo. 5s.

Elements of Logic. By R. WHATELY, D.D. 8vo. 10s. 6d. Crown 8vo. 4s. 6d.

Elements of Rhetoric. By R. WHATELY, D.D. 8vo. 10s. 6d. Crown 8vo. 4s. 6d.

On the Influence of Authority in Matters of Opinion. By the late Sir. G. C. LEWIS, Bart. 8vo. 14s.

The Senses and the Intellect. By A. BAIN, LL.D. 8vo. 15s.

The Emotions and the Will. By A. BAIN, LL.D. 8vo. 15s.

Mental and Moral Science; a Compendium of Psychology and Ethics. By A. BAIN, LL.D. Crown 8vo. 10s. 6d.

An Outline of the Necessary Laws of Thought; a Treatise on Pure and Applied Logic. By W. THOMSON, D.D. Crown 8vo. 6s.

Essays in Political and Moral Philosophy. By T. E. CLIFFE LESLIE, Hon. LL.D. Dubl. of Lincoln's Inn, Barrister-at-Law; late Examiner in Polit. Econ. in the Univ. of London; Prof. of Jurisp. and Polit. Econ. in the Queen's University. 8vo. price 10s. 6d.

Hume's Philosophical Works. Edited, with Notes, &c. by T. H. GREEN, M.A. and the Rev. T. H. GROSE, M.A. 4 vols. 8vo. 56s. Or separately, Essays, 2 vols. 28s. Treatise on Human Nature, 2 vols. 28s.

The Schools of Charles the Great, and the Restoration of Education in the Ninth Century. By J. BASS MULLINGER, M.A. 8vo. price 7s. 6d.

MISCELLANEOUS & CRITICAL WORKS.

The London Series of English Classics. Edited by JOHN W. HALES, M.A. and by CHARLES S. JERRAM, M.A. Fcp. 8vo.

Bacon's Essays, annotated by E. A. ABBOT, D.D. 2 vols. 6s. or in 1 vol. without Notes, 2s. 6d.

Ben Jonson's Every Man in His Humour, by H. B. WHEATLEY, F.S.A. Price 2s. 6d.

Macaulay's Clive, by H. C. BOWEN, M.A. 2s. 6d.

Marlowe's Doctor Faustus, by W. WAGNER, Ph.D. 2s.

Milton's Paradise Regained, by C. S. JERRAM, M.A. 2s. 6d.

Pope's Select Poems, by T. ARNOLD, M.A. 2s. 6d.

Miscellaneous Writings of J. Conington, M.A. Edited by J. A. SYMONDS, M.A. 2 vols. 8vo. 28s.

Selected Essays, chiefly from Contributions to the Edinburgh and Quarterly Reviews. By A. HAYWARD, Q.C. 2 vols. crown 8vo. 12s.

WORKS *published by* LONGMANS & CO.   7

Literary Studies. By the late WALTER BAGEHOT, M.A. and Fellow of University College, London. With a Prefatory Memoir. Edited by R. H. HUTTON. 2 vols. 8vo. with Portrait, 28s.

Short Studies on Great Subjects. By J. A. FROUDE, M.A. 3 vols. crown 8vo. 18s.

Manual of English Literature, Historical and Critical. By T. ARNOLD, M.A. Crown 8vo. 7s. 6d.

Lord Macaulay's Miscellaneous Writings:—
LIBRARY EDITION, 2 vols. 8vo. 21s.
PEOPLE'S EDITION, 1 vol. cr. 8vo. 4s. 6d.

Lord Macaulay's Miscellaneous Writings and Speeches. Student's Edition. Crown 8vo. 6s.

Speeches of the Right Hon. Lord Macaulay, corrected by Himself. Crown 8vo. 3s. 6d.

Selections from the Writings of Lord Macaulay. Edited, with Notes, by G. O. TREVELYAN, M.P. Crown. 8vo. 6s.

The Wit and Wisdom of the Rev. Sydney Smith. Crown 8vo. 3s. 6d.

Miscellaneous and Posthumous Works of the late Henry Thomas Buckle. Edited by HELEN TAYLOR. 3 vols. 8vo. 52s. 6d.

Miscellaneous Works of Thomas Arnold, D.D. late Head Master of Rugby School. 8vo. 7s. 6d.

German Home Life; a Series of Essays on the Domestic Life of Germany. Crown 8vo. 6s.

Realities of Irish Life. By W. STEUART TRENCH. Crown 8vo. 2s. 6d. boards, or 3s. 6d. cloth.

Max Müller and the Philosophy of Language. By LUDWIG NOIRÉ. 8vo. 6s.

Lectures on the Science of Language. By F. MAX MÜLLER, M.A. 2 vols. crown 8vo. 16s.

Chips from a German Workshop; Essays on the Science of Religion, and on Mythology, Traditions & Customs. By F. MAX MÜLLER, M.A. 4 vols. 8vo. £2. 18s.

Language & Languages. A Revised Edition of Chapters on Language and Families of Speech. By F. W. FARRAR, D.D. F.R.S. Crown 8vo. 6s.

The Essays and Contributions of A. K. H. B. Uniform Cabinet Editions in crown 8vo.

Recreations of a Country Parson, Three Series, 3s. 6d. each.

Landscapes, Churches, and Moralities, price 3s. 6d.

Seaside Musings, 3s. 6d.

Changed Aspects of Unchanged Truths, 3s. 6d.

Counsel and Comfort from a City Pulpit, 3s. 6d.

Lessons of Middle Age, 3s. 6d.

Leisure Hours in Town, 3s. 6d.

Autumn Holidays of a Country Parson, price 3s. 6d.

Sunday Afternoons at the Parish Church of a University City, 3s. 6d.

The Commonplace Philosopher in Town and Country, 3s. 6d.

Present-Day Thoughts, 3s. 6d.

Critical Essays of a Country Parson, price 3s. 6d.

The Graver Thoughts of a Country Parson, Three Series, 3s. 6d. each.

DICTIONARIES and OTHER BOOKS of REFERENCE.

Dictionary of the English Language. By R. G. LATHAM, M.A. M.D. Abridged from Dr. Latham's Edition of Johnson's English Dictionary. Medium 8vo. 24s.

A Dictionary of the English Language. By R. G. LATHAM, .M.A. M.D. Founded on Johnson's English Dictionary as edited by the Rev. H. J. TODD. 4 vols. 4to. £7.

Roget's Thesaurus of English Words and Phrases, classified and arranged so as to facilitate the expression of Ideas, and assist in Literary Composition. Revised and enlarged by the Author's Son, J. L. ROGET. Crown 8vo. 10s. 6d.

English Synonymes. By E. J. WHATELY. Edited by R. WHATELY, D.D. Fcp. 8vo. 3s.

Handbook of the English Language. By R. G. LATHAM, M.A. M.D. Crown 8vo. 6s.

Contanseau's Practical Dictionary of the French and English Languages. Post 8vo. price 7s. 6d.

Contanseau's Pocket Dictionary, French and English, abridged from the Practical Dictionary by the Author. Square 18mo. 3s. 6d.

A New Pocket Dictionary of the German and English Languages. By F. W. LONGMAN, Ball. Coll. Oxford. Square 18mo. 5s.

A Practical Dictionary of the German and English Languages. By Rev. W. L. BLACKLEY, M.A. & Dr. C. M. FRIEDLÄNDER. Post 8vo. 7s. 6d.

A Dictionary of Roman and Greek Antiquities. With 2,000 Woodcuts illustrative of the Arts and Life of the Greeks and Romans. By A. RICH, B.A. Crown 8vo. 7s. 6d.

The Critical Lexicon and Concordance to the English and Greek New Testament. By the Rev. E. W. BULLINGER. Medium 8vo. 30s.

A Greek-English Lexicon. By H. G. LIDDELL., D.D. Dean of Christchurch, and R. SCOTT, D.D. Dean of Rochester. Crown 4to. 36s.

Liddell & Scott's Lexicon, Greek and English, abridged for Schools. Square 12mo. 7s. 6d.

An English-Greek Lexicon, containing all the Greek Words used by Writers of good authority. By C. D. YONGE, M.A. 4to. 21s.

Mr. Yonge's Lexicon, English and Greek, abridged from his larger Lexicon. Square 12mo. 8s. 6d.

A Latin-English Dictionary. By JOHN T. WHITE, D.D. Oxon. and J. E. RIDDLE, M.A. Oxon. Sixth Edition, revised. 1 vol. 4to. 28s.

White's College Latin-English Dictionary, for the use of University Students. Medium 8vo. 15s.

A Latin-English Dictionary for the use of Middle-Class Schools. By JOHN T. WHITE, D.D. Oxon. Square fcp. 8vo. 3s.

White's Junior Student's Latin-English and English-Latin Dictionary. Square 12mo. ENGLISH-LATIN DICTIONARY, 5s.6d. LATIN-ENGLISH DICTIONARY, 7s.6d. COMPLETE, 12s.

M'Culloch's Dictionary of Commerce and Commercial Navigation. Re-edited by HUGH G. REID. With 11 Maps and 30 Charts. 8vo. 63s.

Keith Johnston's General Dictionary of Geography, Descriptive, Physical, Statistical, and Historical; a complete Gazetteer of the World. Medium 8vo. 42s.

The Public Schools Atlas of Ancient Geography, in 28 entirely new Coloured Maps. Edited by the Rev. G. BUTLER, M.A. Imperial 8vo. or imperial 4to. 7s. 6d.

The Public Schools Atlas of Modern Geography, in 31 entirely new Coloured Maps. Edited by the Rev. G. BUTLER, M.A. Uniform, 5s.

ASTRONOMY and METEOROLOGY.

Outlines of Astronomy.
By Sir J. F. W. HERSCHEL, Bart. M.A. Latest Edition, with Plates and Diagrams. Square crown 8vo. 12s.

Essays on Astronomy.
A Series of Papers on Planets and Meteors, the Sun and Sun-surrounding Space, Star and Star Cloudlets. By R. A. PROCTOR, B.A. With 10 Plates and 24 Woodcuts. 8vo. 12s.

The Moon; her Motions, Aspects, Scenery, and Physical Condition. By R. A. PROCTOR, B.A. With Plates, Charts, Woodcuts, and Lunar Photographs. Crown 8vo. 10s. 6d.

The Sun; Ruler, Light, Fire, and Life of the Planetary System. By R. A. PROCTOR, B.A. With Plates & Woodcuts. Crown 8vo. 14s.

The Orbs Around Us;
a Series of Essays on the Moon & Planets, Meteors & Comets, the Sun & Coloured Pairs of Suns. By R. A. PROCTOR, B.A. With Chart and Diagrams. Crown 8vo. 7s. 6d.

Other Worlds than Ours;
The Plurality of Worlds Studied under the Light of Recent Scientific Researches. By R. A. PROCTOR, B.A. With 14 Illustrations. Cr. 8vo. 10s. 6d.

The Universe of Stars;
Presenting Researches into and New Views respecting the Constitution of the Heavens. By R. A. PROCTOR, B.A. Second Edition, with 22 Charts (4 Coloured) and 22 Diagrams. 8vo. price 10s. 6d.

The Transits of Venus;
A Popular Account of Past and Coming Transits. By R. A. PROCTOR, B.A. 20 Plates (12 Coloured) and 27 Woodcuts. Crown 8vo. 8s. 6d.

Saturn and its System.
By R. A. PROCTOR, B.A. 8vo. with 14 Plates, 14s.

The Moon, and the Condition and Configurations of its Surface. By E. NEISON, F.R.A.S. With 26 Maps & 5 Plates. Medium 8vo. 31s. 6d.

A New Star Atlas, for the Library, the School, and the Observatory, in 12 Circular Maps (with 2 Index Plates). By R. A. PROCTOR, B. A. Crown 8vo. 5s.

Larger Star Atlas, for the Library, in Twelve Circular Maps, with Introduction and 2 Index Plates. By R. A. PROCTOR, B.A. Folio, 15s. or Maps only, 12s. 6d.

A Treatise on the Cycloid, and on all forms of Cycloidal Curves, and on the use of Cycloidal Curves in dealing with the Motions of Planets, Comets, &c. and of Matter projected from the Sun. By R. A. PROCTOR, B.A. With 161 Diagrams. Crown 8vo. 10s. 6d.

Dove's Law of Storms,
considered in connexion with the Ordinary Movements of the Atmosphere. Translated by R. H. SCOTT, M.A. 8vo. 10s. 6d.

Air and Rain; the Beginnings of a Chemical Climatology. By R. A. SMITH, F.R.S. 8vo. 24s.

Schellen's Spectrum
Analysis, in its Application to Terrestrial Substances and the Physical Constitution of the Heavenly Bodies. Translated by JANE and C. LASSELL, with Notes by W. HUGGINS, LL.D. F.R.S. 8vo. Plates and Woodcuts, 28s.

NATURAL HISTORY and PHYSICAL SCIENCE.

Professor Helmholtz' Popular Lectures on Scientific Subjects. Translated by E. ATKINSON, F.C.S. With numerous Wood Engravings. 8vo. 12s. 6d.

Professor Helmholtz on the Sensations of Tone, as a Physiological Basis for the Theory of Music. Translated by A. J. ELLIS, F.R.S. 8vo. 36s.

Ganot's Natural Philosophy for General Readers and Young Persons; a Course of Physics divested of Mathematical Formulæ and expressed in the language of daily life. Translated by E. ATKINSON, F.C.S. Third Edition. Plates and Woodcuts. Crown 8vo. 7s. 6d.

Ganot's Elementary Treatise on Physics, Experimental and Applied, for the use of Colleges and Schools. Translated and edited by E. ATKINSON, F.C.S. Eighth Edition. Plates and Woodcuts. Post 8vo. 15s.

Arnott's Elements of Physics or Natural Philosophy. Seventh Edition, edited by A. BAIN, LL.D. and A. S. TAYLOR, M.D. F.R.S. Crown 8vo. Woodcuts, 12s. 6d.

The Correlation of Physical Forces. By the Hon. Sir W. R. GROVE, F.R.S. &c. Sixth Edition, revised and augmented. 8vo. 15s.

Weinhold's Introduction to Experimental Physics; including Directions for Constructing Physical Apparatus and for Making Experiments. Translated by B. LOEWY, F.R.A.S. With a Preface by G. C. FOSTER, F.R.S. 8vo. Plates & Woodcuts 31s. 6d.

A Treatise on Magnetism, General and Terrestrial. By H. LLOYD, D.D. D.C.L. 8vo. 10s. 6d.

Elementary Treatise on the Wave-Theory of Light. By H. LLOYD, D.D. D.C.L. 8vo. 10s. 6d.

Fragments of Science. By JOHN TYNDALL, F.R.S. Sixth Edition, revised and augmented. 2 vols. crown 8vo. 16s.

Heat a Mode of Motion. By JOHN TYNDALL, F.R.S. Fifth Edition in preparation.

Sound. By JOHN TYNDALL, F.R.S. Third Edition, including Recent Researches on Fog-Signalling. Crown 8vo. price 10s. 6d.

Researches on Diamagnetism and Magne-CrystallicAction; including Diamagnetic Polarity. By JOHN TYNDALL, F.R.S. New Edition in preparation.

Contributions to Molecular Physics in the domain of Radiant Heat. By JOHN TYNDALL, F.R.S. Plates and Woodcuts. 8vo. 16s.

Six Lectures on Light, delivered in America in 1872 and 1873. By JOHN TYNDALL, F.R.S. Second Edition. Portrait, Plate, and Diagrams. Crown 8vo. 7s. 6d.

Lessons in Electricity at the Royal Institution, 1875-6. By JOHN TYNDALL, F.R.S. With 58 Woodcuts. Crown 8vo. 2s. 6d.

Notes of a Course of Seven Lectures on Electrical Phenomena and Theories, delivered at the Royal Institution. By JOHN TYNDALL, F.R.S. Crown 8vo. 1s. sewed, or 1s. 6d. cloth.

Notes of a Course of Nine Lectures on Light, delivered at the Royal Institution. By JOHN TYNDALL, F.R.S. Crown 8vo. 1s. sewed, or 1s. 6d. cloth.

Principles of Animal Mechanics. By the Rev. S. HAUGHTON F.R.S. Second Edition. 8vo. 21s.

WORKS *published by* LONGMANS & CO.   11

Text-Books of Science,
Mechanical and Physical, adapted for the use of Artisans and of Students in Public and Science Schools. Small 8vo. with Woodcuts, &c.

Abney's Photography, 3s. 6d.
Anderson's (Sir John) Strength of Materials, 3s. 6d.
Armstrong's Organic Chemistry, 3s. 6d.
Barry's Railway Appliances, 3s. 6d.
Bloxam's Metals, 3s. 6d.
Goodeve's Mechanics, 3s. 6d.
——— Mechanism, 3s. 6d.
Gore's Electro-Metallurgy, 6s.
Griffin's Algebra & Trigonometry, 3/6.
Jenkin's Electricity & Magnetism, 3/6.
Maxwell's Theory of Heat, 3s. 6d.
Merrifield's Technical Arithmetic, 3s. 6d.
Miller's Inorganic Chemistry, 3s. 6d.
Preece & Sivewright's Telegraphy, 3/6.
Rutley's Study of Rocks, 4s. 6d.
Shelley's Workshop Appliances, 3s. 6d.
Thomé's Structural and Physiological Botany, 6s.
Thorpe's Quantitative Analysis, 4s. 6d.
Thorpe & Muir's Qualitative Analysis, price 3s. 6d.
Tilden's Systematic Chemistry, 3s. 6d.
Unwin's Machine Design, 3s. 6d.
Watson's Plane & Solid Geometry, 3/6.

Light Science for Leisure
Hours; Familiar Essays on Scientific Subjects, Natural Phenomena, &c. By R. A. PROCTOR, B.A. 2 vols. crown 8vo. 7s. 6d. each.

An Introduction to the
Systematic Zoology and Morphology of Vertebrate Animals. By A. MACALISTER, M.D. Professor of Comparative Anatomy and Zoology, University of Dublin. With 28 Diagrams. 8vo. 10s. 6d.

The Comparative Ana-
tomy and Physiology of the Vertebrate Animals. By RICHARD OWEN, F.R.S. With 1,472 Woodcuts. 3 vols. 8vo. £3. 13s. 6d.

Homes without Hands;
a Description of the Habitations of Animals, classed according to their Principle of Construction. By the Rev. J. G. WOOD, M.A. With about 140 Vignettes on Wood. 8vo. 14s.

Wood's Strange Dwell-
ings; a Description of the Habitations of Animals, abridged from 'Homes without Hands.' With Frontispiece and 60 Woodcuts. Crown 8vo. 7s. 6d.

Wood's Insects at Home;
a Popular Account of British Insects, their Structure, Habits, and Transformations. With 700 Woodcuts. 8vo. 14s.

Wood's Insects Abroad;
a Popular Account of Foreign Insects, their Structure, Habits, and Transformations. With 700 Woodcuts. 8vo. 14s.

Wood's Out of Doors; a
Selection of Original Articles on Practical Natural History. With 6 Illustrations. Crown 8vo. 7s. 6d.

Wood's Bible Animals; a
description of every Living Creature mentioned in the Scriptures, from the Ape to the Coral. With 112 Vignettes. 8vo. 14s.

The Sea and its Living
Wonders. By Dr. G. HARTWIG. 8vo. with numerous Illustrations, price 10s. 6d.

Hartwig's Tropical
World. With about 200 Illustrations. 8vo. 10s. 6d.

Hartwig's Polar World;
a Description of Man and Nature in the Arctic and Antarctic Regions of the Globe. Chromoxylographs, Maps, and Woodcuts. 8vo. 10s. 6d.

Hartwig's Subterranean
World. With Maps and Woodcuts. 8vo. 10s. 6d.

Hartwig's Aerial World;
a Popular Account of the Phenomena and Life of the Atmosphere. Map, Chromoxylographs, Woodcuts. 8vo. price 10s. 6d.

Kirby and Spence's Introduction to Entomology, or Elements of the Natural History of Insects. Crown 8vo. 5s.

A Familiar History of Birds. By E. STANLEY, D.D. Fcp. 8vo. with Woodcuts, 3s. 6d.

Rocks Classified and Described. By BERNHARD VON COTTA. An English Translation, by P. H. LAWRENCE (with English, German, and French Synonymes), revised by the Author. Post 8vo. 14s.

The Geology of England and Wales; a Concise Account of the Lithological Characters, Leading Fossils, and Economic Products of the Rocks. By H. B. WOODWARD, F.G.S. Crown 8vo. Map & Woodcuts, 14s.

Keller's Lake Dwellings of Switzerland, and other Parts of Europe. Translated by JOHN E. LEE, F.S.A. F.G.S. New Edition, enlarged, with 206 Illustrations. 2 vols. royal 8vo. 42s.

The Primæval World of Switzerland. By Professor OSWAL HEER, of the University of Zurich. Edited by JAMES HEYWOOD, M.A. F.R.S. With Map, 19 Plates, & 372 Woodcuts. 2 vols. 8vo. 16s.

The Puzzle of Life and How it Has Been Put Together; a Short History of Praehistoric Vegetable and Animal Life on the Earth. By A. NICOLS, F.R.G S. With 12 Illustrations. Crown 8vo. 3s. 6d.

The Origin of Civilisation, and the Primitive Condition of Man; Mental and Social Condition of Savages. By Sir J. LUBBOCK, Bart. M.P. F.R.S. 8vo. Woodcuts, 18s.

A Dictionary of Science, Literature, and Art. Re-edited by the late W. T. BRANDE (the Author) and the Rev. Sir G. W. COX, Bart., M.A. 3 vols. medium 8vo. 63s.

The History of Modern Music, a Course of Lectures delivered at the Royal Institution. By JOHN HULLAH, LL.D. 8vo. 8s. 6d.

The Transition Period of Musical History, from the Beginning of the 17th to the Middle of the 18th Century. A Second Series of Lectures. By the same Author. 8vo. 10s. 6d.

Loudon's Encyclopædia of Plants; comprising the Specific Character, Description, Culture, History, &c. of all the Plants found in Great Britain. With upwards of 12,000 Woodcuts. 8vo. 42s.

De Caisne & Le Maout's System of Descriptive and Analytical Botany. Translated by Mrs. HOOKER; edited and arranged according to the English Botanical System, by J. D. HOOKER, M.D. With 5,500 Woodcuts. Imperial 8vo. 31s. 6d.

The Treasury of Botany, or Popular Dictionary of the Vegetable Kingdom; with which is incorporated a Glossary of Botanical Terms. Edited by J. LINDLEY, F.R.S., and T. MOORE, F.L.S. With 274 Woodcuts and 20 Steel Plates. Two Parts, fcp. 8vo. 12s.

Rivers's Orchard-House; or, the Cultivation of Fruit Trees under Glass. Sixteenth Edition, re-edited by T. F. RIVERS. Crown 8vo. with 25 Woodcuts, price 5s.

The Rose Amateur's Guide. By THOMAS RIVERS. Latest Edition. Fcp. 8vo. 4s. 6d.

Town and Window Gardening, including the Structure, Habits and Uses of Plants; a Course of Sixteen Lectures given out of School-Hours to Pupil Teachers and Children attending the Leeds Board Schools. By Mrs. BUCKTON, Member of the Leeds School Board. With 127 Woodcuts. Crown 8vo. 2s.

CHEMISTRY and PHYSIOLOGY.

Miller's Elements of Chemistry, Theoretical and Practical. Re-edited, with Additions, by H. MACLEOD, F.C.S. 3 vols. 8vo.
PART I. CHEMICAL PHYSICS. 16s.
PART II. INORGANIC CHEMISTRY, 24s.
PART III. ORGANIC CHEMISTRY, New Edition in the press.

Animal Chemistry, or the Relations of Chemistry to Physiology and Pathology: a Manual for Medical Men and Scientific Chemists. By CHARLES T. KINGZETT, F.C.S. 8vo. price 18s.

Health in the House: Twenty-five Lectures on Elementary Physiology in its Application to the Daily Wants of Man and Animals. By Mrs. BUCKTON. Crown 8vo. Woodcuts, 2s.

A Dictionary of Chemistry and the Allied Branches of other Sciences. By HENRY WATTS, F.C.S. assisted by eminent Scientific and Practical Chemists. 7 vols. medium 8vo. £10. 16s. 6d.

Third Supplement, completing the Record of Chemical Discovery to the year 1877. PART I. 8vo. 36s. PART II. completion, in the press.

Select Methods in Chemical Analysis, chiefly Inorganic. By WM. CROOKES, F.R.S. With 22 Woodcuts. Crown 8vo. 12s. 6d.

The History, Products, and Processes of the Alkali Trade, including the most recent Improvements. By CHARLES T. KINGZETT, F.C.S. With 32 Woodcuts. 8vo. 12s.

The FINE ARTS and ILLUSTRATED EDITIONS.

In Fairyland; Pictures from the Elf-World. By RICHARD DOYLE. With a Poem by W. ALLINGHAM. With 16 coloured Plates, containing 36 Designs. Folio, 15s.

Lord Macaulay's Lays of Ancient Rome. With Ninety Illustrations on Wood from Drawings by G. SCHARF. Fcp. 4to. 21s.

Miniature Edition of Macaulay's Lays of Ancient Rome, with Scharf's 90 Illustrations reduced in Lithography. Imp. 16mo. 10s. 6d.

Moore's Lalla Rookh. TENNIEL'S Edition, with 68 Woodcut Illustrations. Fcp. 4to. 21s.

Moore's Irish Melodies, MACLISE'S Edition, with 161 Steel Plates. Super-royal 8vo. 21s.

Lectures on Harmony, delivered at the Royal Institution. By G. A. MACFARREN. 8vo. 12s.

Sacred and Legendary Art. By Mrs. JAMESON. 6 vols. square crown 8vo. price £5. 15s. 6d.

Jameson's Legends of the Saints and Martyrs. With 19 Etchings and 187 Woodcuts. 2 vols. 31s. 6d.

Jameson's Legends of the Monastic Orders. With 11 Etchings and 88 Woodcuts. 1 vol. 21s.

Jameson's Legends of the Madonna. With 27 Etchings and 165 Woodcuts. 1 vol. 21s.

Jameson's History of the Saviour, His Types and Precursors. Completed by Lady EASTLAKE. With 13 Etchings and 281 Woodcuts. 2 vols. 42s.

The Three Cathedrals dedicated to St. Paul in London. By W. LONGMAN, F.S.A. With numerous Illustrations. Square crown 8vo. 21s.

The USEFUL ARTS, MANUFACTURES, &c.

The Art of Scientific Discovery. By G. GORE, LL.D. F.R.S. Author of 'The Art of Electro-Metallurgy.' Crown 8vo. 15s.

The Amateur Mechanics' Practical Handbook; describing the different Tools required in the Workshop. By A. H. G. HOBSON. With 33 Woodcuts. Crown 8vo. 2s. 6d.

The Engineer's Valuing Assistant. By H. D. HOSKOLD, Civil and Mining Engineer, 16 years Mining Engineer to the Dean Forest Iron Company. 8vo. 31s. 6d.

Industrial Chemistry; a Manual for Manufacturers and for Colleges or Technical Schools; a Translation (by Dr. T. H. BARRY) of Stohmann and Engler's German Edition of PAYEN's 'Précis de Chimie Industrielle;' with Chapters on the Chemistry of the Metals, &c. by B. H. PAUL, Ph.D. With 698 Woodcuts. Medium 8vo. 42s.

Gwilt's Encyclopædia of Architecture, with above 1,600 Woodcuts. Revised and extended by W. PAPWORTH. 8vo. 52s. 6d.

Lathes and Turning, Simple, Mechanical, and Ornamental. By W. H. NORTHCOTT. Second Edition, with 338 Illustrations. 8vo. 18s.

The Theory of Strains in Girders and similar Structures, with Observations on the application of Theory to Practice, and Tables of the Strength and other Properties of Materials. By B. B. STONEY, M.A. M. Inst. C.E. Royal 8vo. with 5 Plates and 123 Woodcuts, 36s.

A Treatise on Mills and Millwork. By the late Sir W. FAIRBAIRN, Bart. C.E. Fourth Edition, with 18 Plates and 333 Woodcuts. 1 vol. 8vo. 25s.

Useful Information for Engineers. By the late Sir W. FAIRBAIRN, Bart. C.E. With many Plates and Woodcuts. 3 vols. crown 8vo. 31s. 6d.

The Application of Cast and Wrought Iron to Building Purposes. By the late Sir W. FAIRBAIRN, Bart. C.E. With 6 Plates and 118 Woodcuts. 8vo. 16s.

Hints on Household Taste in Furniture, Upholstery, and other Details. By C. L. EASTLAKE. Fourth Edition, with 100 Illustrations. Square crown 8vo. 14s.

Handbook of Practical Telegraphy. By R. S. CULLEY, Memb. Inst. C.E. Seventh Edition. Plates & Woodcuts. 8vo. price 16s.

A Treatise on the Steam Engine, in its various applications to Mines, Mills, Steam Navigation, Railways and Agriculture. By J. BOURNE, C.E. With Portrait, 37 Plates, and 546 Woodcuts. 4to. 42s.

Recent Improvements in the Steam Engine. By J. BOURNE, C.E. Fcp. 8vo. Woodcuts, 6s.

Catechism of the Steam Engine, in its various Applications. By JOHN BOURNE, C.E. Fcp. 8vo. Woodcuts, 6s.

Handbook of the Steam Engine, a Key to the Author's Catechism of the Steam Engine. By J. BOURNE, C.E. Fcp. 8vo. Woodcuts, 9s.

Examples of Steam and Gas Engines of the most recent Approved Types as employed in Mines, Factories, Steam Navigation, Railways and Agriculture, practically described. By JOHN BOURNE, C.E. With 54 Plates and 356 Woodcuts. 4to. 70s.

Encyclopædia of Civil Engineering, Historical, Theoretical, and Practical. By E. CRESY, C.E. With above 3,000 Woodcuts. 8vo. 42s.

Ure's Dictionary of Arts, Manufactures, and Mines. Seventh Edition, re-written and enlarged by R. HUNT, F.R.S. assisted by numerous contributors. With 2,604 Woodcuts. 4 vols. medium 8vo. £7. 7s.

Practical Treatise on Metallurgy. Adapted from the last German Edition of Professor KERL'S Metallurgy by W. CROOKES, F.R.S. &c. and E. RÖHRIG, Ph.D. 3 vols. 8vo. with 625 Woodcuts. £4. 19s.

Anthracen; its Constitution, Properties, Manufacture, and Derivatives, including Artificial Alizarin, Anthrapurpurin, &c. with their Applications in Dyeing and Printing. By G. AUERBACH. Translated by W. CROOKES, F.R.S. 8vo. 12s.

On Artificial Manures, their Chemical Selection and Scientific Application to Agriculture; a Series of Lectures given at the Experimental Farm at Vincennes in 1867 and 1874–75. By M. GEORGES VILLE. Translated and edited by W. CROOKES, F.R.S. With 31 Plates. 8vo. 21s.

Practical Handbook of Dyeing and Calico-Printing. By W. CROOKES, F.R.S. &c. With numerous Illustrations and specimens of Dyed Textile Fabrics. 8vo. 42s.

Mitchell's Manual of Practical Assaying. Fourth Edition, revised, with the Recent Discoveries incorporated, by W. CROOKES, F.R.S. Crown 8vo. Woodcuts, 31s. 6d.

Loudon's Encyclopædia of Gardening; the Theory and Practice of Horticulture, Floriculture, Arboriculture & Landscape Gardening. With 1,000 Woodcuts. 8vo. 21s.

Loudon's Encyclopædia of Agriculture; the Laying-out, Improvement, and Management of Landed Property; the Cultivation and Economy of the Productions of Agriculture. With 1,100 Woodcuts. 8vo. 21s.

RELIGIOUS and MORAL WORKS.

Four Lectures on some Epochs of Early Church History. By the Very Rev. C. MERIVALE, D.D. Dean of Ely. Crown 8vo. 5s.

A History of the Church of England; Pre-Reformation Period. By the Rev. T. P. BOULTBEE, LL.D. late Fellow of St. John's College, Cambridge. 8vo. 15s.

Sketch of the History of the Church of England to the Revolution of 1688. By T. V. SHORT, D.D. Crown 8vo. 7s. 6d.

The English Church in the Eighteenth Century. By CHARLES J. ABBEY, late Fellow of University College, Oxford; and JOHN H. OVERTON, late Scholar of Lincoln College, Oxford. 2 vols. 8vo. 36s.

The Human Life of Christ revealing the Order of the Universe, being the Hulsean Lectures for 1877; with an APPENDIX. By G. S. DREW, M.A. Vicar of Holy Trinity, Lambeth. 8vo. 8s.

An Exposition of the 39 Articles, Historical and Doctrinal. By E. H. BROWNE, D.D. Bishop of Winchester. Eleventh Edition. 8vo. 16s.

A Commentary on the 39 Articles, forming an Introduction to the Theology of the Church of England. By the Rev. T. P. BOULTBEE, LL.D. New Edition. Crown 8vo. 6s.

Historical Lectures on the Life of Our Lord Jesus Christ. By C. J. ELLICOTT, D.D. 8vo. 12s.

Sermons preached mostly in the Chapel of Rugby School by the late T. ARNOLD, D.D. Collective Edition, revised by the Author's Daughter, Mrs. W. E. FORSTER. 6 vols. crown 8vo. 30s. or separately, 5s. each.

The Eclipse of Faith; or a Visit to a Religious Sceptic. By HENRY ROGERS. Fcp. 8vo. 5s.

Defence of the Eclipse of Faith. By H. ROGERS. Fcp. 8vo. 3s. 6d.

Nature, the Utility of Religion and Theism.
Three Essays by JOHN STUART MILL. 8vo. 10s. 6d.

A Critical and Grammatical Commentary on St. Paul's Epistles.
By C. J. ELLICOTT, D.D. 8vo. Galatians, 8s. 6d. Ephesians, 8s. 6d. Pastoral Epistles, 10s. 6d. Philippians, Colossians, & Philemon, 10s. 6d. Thessalonians, 7s. 6d.

Conybeare & Howson's Life and Epistles of St. Paul.
Three Editions, copiously illustrated.

Library Edition, with all the Original Illustrations, Maps, Landscapes on Steel, Woodcuts, &c. 2 vols. 4to. 42s.

Intermediate Edition, with a Selection of Maps, Plates, and Woodcuts. 2 vols. square crown 8vo. 21s.

Student's Edition, revised and condensed, with 46 Illustrations and Maps. 1 vol. crown 8vo. 9s.

The Jewish Messiah;
Critical History of the Messianic Idea among the Jews, from the Rise of the Maccabees to the Closing of the Talmud. By JAMES DRUMMOND, B.A. 8vo. 15s.

The Prophets and Prophecy in Israel;
an Historical and Critical Inquiry. By Prof. A. KUENEN, Translated from the Dutch by the Rev. A. MILROY, M.A. with an Introduction by J. MUIR, D.C.L. 8vo. 21s.

Mythology among the Hebrews
and its Historical Development. By IGNAZ GOLDZIHER, Ph.D. Translated by RUSSELL MARTINEAU, M.A. 8vo. 16s.

Bible Studies. By M. M. KALISCH, Ph.D.
PART I. *The Prophecies of Balaam.* 8vo. 10s. 6d. PART II. *The Book of Jonah.* 8vo. 10s. 6d.

Historical and Critical Commentary on the Old Testament;
with a New Translation. By M. M. KALISCH, Ph.D. Vol. I. Genesis, 8vo. 18s. or adapted for the General Reader, 12s. Vol. II. Exodus, 15s. or adapted for the General Reader, 12s. Vol. III. Leviticus, Part I. 15s. or adapted for the General Reader, 8s. Vol. IV. Leviticus, Part II. 15s. or adapted for the General Reader, 8s.

Ewald's History of Israel.
Translated from the German by J. E. CARPENTER, M.A. with Preface by R. MARTINEAU, M.A. 5 vols. 8vo. 63s.

Ewald's Antiquities of Israel.
Translated from the German by H. S. SOLLY, M.A. 8vo. 12s. 6d.

The Types of Genesis,
briefly considered as revealing the Development of Human Nature. By A. JUKES. Crown 8vo. 7s. 6d.

The Second Death and the Restitution of all Things;
with some Preliminary Remarks on the Nature and Inspiration of Holy Scripture. By A. JUKES. Crown 8vo. 3s. 6d.

Commentaries, by the Rev. W. A. O'CONOR, B.A.
Rector of St. Simon and St. Jude, Manchester.

Epistle to the Romans, crown 8vo. 3s. 6d.
Epistle to the Hebrews, 4s. 6d.
St. John's Gospel, 10s. 6d.

Supernatural Religion;
an Inquiry into the Reality of Divine Revelation. Complete Edition, thoroughly revised, with New Preface and Conclusions. 3 vols. 8vo. 36s.

Lectures on the Origin and Growth of Religion,
as illustrated by the Religions of India; being the Hibbert Lectures for 1878, delivered at the Chapter House, Westminster Abbey, in 1878, by F. MAX MÜLLER, M.A. Second Edition. 8vo. price 10s. 6d.

Introduction to the Science of Religion,
Four Lectures delivered at the Royal Institution; with Two Essays on False Analogies and the Philosophy of Mythology. By MAX MÜLLER, M.A. Crown 8vo. price 10s. 6d.

The Four Gospels in Greek,
with Greek-English Lexicon. By JOHN T. WHITE, D.D. Oxon. Square 32mo. 5s.

Passing Thoughts on Religion.
By ELIZABETH M. SEWELL. Fcp. 8vo. 3s. 6d.

Thoughts for the Age.
by ELIZABETH M. SEWELL. New Edition. Fcp. 8vo. 3s. 6d.

Preparation for the Holy Communion; the Devotions chiefly from the works of Jeremy Taylor. By ELIZABETH M. SEWELL. 32mo. 3s.

Bishop Jeremy Taylor's Entire Works; with Life by Bishop Heber. Revised and corrected by the Rev. C. P. EDEN. 10 vols. £5. 5s.

Hymns of Praise and Prayer. Corrected and edited by Rev. JOHN MARTINEAU, LL.D. Crown 8vo. 4s. 6d. 32mo. 1s. 6d.

Spiritual Songs for the Sundays and Holidays throughout the Year. By J. S. B. MONSELL, LL.D. Fcp. 8vo. 5s. 18mo. 2s.

Christ the Consoler; a Book of Comfort for the Sick. By ELLICE HOPKINS. With a Preface by the Bishop of Carlisle. Second Edition. Fcp. 8vo. 2s. 6d.

Lyra Germanica; Hymns translated from the German by Miss C. WINKWORTH. Fcp. 8vo. 5s.

The Temporal Mission of the Holy Ghost; or, Reason and Revelation. By HENRY EDWARD MANNING, D.D. Crown 8vo. 8s. 6d.

Hours of Thought on Sacred Things; a Volume of Sermons. By JAMES MARTINEAU, D.D. LL.D. Crown 8vo. Price 7s. 6d.

Endeavours after the Christian Life; Discourses. By JAMES MARTINEAU, D.D. LL.D. Fifth Edition. Crown 8vo. 7s. 6d.

The Pentateuch & Book of Joshua Critically Examined. By J. W. COLENSO, D.D. Bishop of Natal. Crown 8vo. 6s.

Lectures on the Pentateuch and the Moabite Stone; with Appendices. By J. W. COLENSO, D.D. Bishop of Natal. 8vo. 12s.

TRAVELS, VOYAGES, &c.

A Voyage in the 'Sunbeam,' our Home on the Ocean for Eleven Months. By Mrs. BRASSEY. Cheaper Edition, with Map and 65 Wood Engravings. Crown 8vo. 7s. 6d.

A Freak of Freedom; or, the Republic of San Marino. By J. THEODORE BENT, Honorary Citizen of the same. With a Map and 15 Woodcuts. Crown 8vo. 7s. 6d.

One Thousand Miles up the Nile; a Journey through Egypt and Nubia to the Second Cataract. By AMELIA B. EDWARDS. With Plans, Maps & Illustrations. Imperial 8vo. 42s.

The Indian Alps, and How we Crossed them; Two Years' Residence in the Eastern Himalayas, and Two Months' Tour into the Interior. By a LADY PIONEER. With Illustrations. Imperial 8vo. 42s.

Discoveries at Ephesus, Including the Site and Remains of the Great Temple of Diana. By J. T. WOOD, F.S.A. With 27 Lithographic Plates and 42 Wood Engravings. Medium 8vo. 63s.

Memorials of the Discovery and Early Settlement of the Bermudas or Somers Islands, from 1615 to 1685. By Major-General Sir J. H. LEFROY, R.A. With Maps, &c. 2 vols. Imp. 8vo. 60s.

Eight Years in Ceylon. By Sir SAMUEL W. BAKER, M.A. Crown 8vo. Woodcuts, 7s. 6d.

The Rifle and the Hound in Ceylon. By Sir SAMUEL W. BAKER, M.A. Crown 8vo. Woodcuts, 7s. 6d.

Guide to the Pyrenees, for the use of Mountaineers. By CHARLES PACKE. Crown 8vo. 7s. 6d.

The Alpine Club Map of Switzerland, with parts of the Neighbouring Countries, on the scale of Four Miles to an Inch. Edited by R. C. NICHOLS, F.R.G.S. 4 Sheets in Portfolio, 42s. coloured, or 34s. uncoloured.

The Alpine Guide. By JOHN BALL, M.R.I.A. Post 8vo. with Maps and other Illustrations.

The Eastern Alps, 10s. 6d.

Central Alps, including all the Oberland District, 7s. 6d.

Western Alps, including Mont Blanc, Monte Rosa, Zermatt, &c. Price 6s. 6d.

On Alpine Travelling and the Geology of the Alps. Price 1s. Either of the 3 Volumes or Parts of the 'Alpine Guide' may be had with this Introduction prefixed, 1s. extra.

The Fenland Past and Present. By S. H. MILLER, F.R.A.S. F.M.S.; and S. B. J. SKERTCHLEY, F.G.S. of H.M. Geological Survey. With numerous Illustrations and Maps. Royal 8vo. 31s. 6d. Large Paper, fcp. folio, 50s. half-morocco.

WORKS of FICTION.

Novels and Tales. By the Right Hon. the EARL of BEACONSFIELD, K.G. Cabinet Editions, complete in Ten Volumes, crown 8vo. 6s. each.

Lothair, 6s.	Venetia, 6s.
Coningsby, 6s.	Alroy, Ixion, &c. 6s.
Sybil, 6s.	Young Duke &c. 6s.
Tancred, 6s.	Vivian Grey, 6s.

Henrietta Temple, 6s.

Contarini Fleming, &c. 6s.

Tales from Euripides; Iphigenia, Alcestis, Hecuba, Helen, Medea. By VINCENT K. COOPER, M.A. late Scholar of Brasenose College, Oxford. Fcp. 8vo. 3s. 6d.

Whispers from Fairyland. By the Right Hon. E. H. KNATCHBULL-HUGESSEN, M.P. With 9 Illustrations. Crown 8vo. 3s. 6d.

Higgledy-Piggledy; or, Stories for Everybody and Everybody's Children. By the Right Hon. E. H. KNATCHBULL-HUGESSEN, M.P. With 9 Illustrations. Cr. 8vo. 3s. 6d.

Stories and Tales. By ELIZABETH M. SEWELL. Cabinet Edition, in Ten Volumes, each containing a complete Tale or Story:—

Amy Herbert, 2s. 6d. Gertrude, 2s. 6d. The Earl's Daughter, 2s. 6d. The Experience of Life, 2s. 6d. Cleve Hall, 2s. 6d. Ivors, 2s. 6d. Katharine Ashton, 2s. 6d. Margaret Percival, 3s. 6d. Laneton Parsonage, 3s. 6d. Ursula, 3s. 6d.

The Modern Novelist's Library. Each work complete in itself, price 2s. boards, or 2s. 6d. cloth.

By Lord BEACONSFIELD.
 Lothair.
 Coningsby.
 Sybil.
 Tancred.
 Venetia.
 Henrietta Temple.
 Contarini Fleming.
 Alroy, Ixion, &c.
 The Young Duke, &c.
 Vivian Grey.

THE MODERN NOVELIST'S LIBRARY—continued.

By ANTHONY TROLLOPE.
Barchester Towers.
The Warden.

By Major WHYTE-MELVILLE.
Digby Grand.
General Bounce.
Kate Coventry.
The Gladiators.
Good for Nothing.
Holmby House.
The Interpreter.
The Queen's Maries.

By the Author of 'The Rose Garden.'
Unawares.

By the Author of 'Mlle. Mori.'
The Atelier du Lys.
Mademoiselle Mori.

By Various Writers.
Atherstone Priory.
The Burgomaster's Family.
Elsa and her Vulture.
The Six Sisters of the Valleys.

The Novels and Tales of the Right Honourable the Earl of Beaconsfield, K.G. Complete in Ten Volumes, crown 8vo. cloth extra, gilt edges, price 30s.

POETRY and THE DRAMA.

Lays of Ancient Rome; with Ivry and the Armada. By LORD MACAULAY. 16mo. 3s. 6d.

Horatii Opera. Library Edition, with English Notes, Marginal References & various Readings. Edited by Rev. J. E. YONGE, M.A. 8vo. 21s.

Poems by Jean Ingelow. 2 vols. fcp. 8vo. 10s.
FIRST SERIES, containing 'Divided,' 'The Star's Monument,' &c. Fcp. 8vo. 5s.
SECOND SERIES, 'A Story of Doom,' 'Gladys and her Island,' &c. 5s.

Poems by Jean Ingelow. First Series, with nearly 100 Woodcut Illustrations. Fcp. 4to. 21s.

Brian Boru, a Tragedy. By J. T. B. Crown 8vo. 6s.

Festus, a Poem. By PHILIP JAMES BAILEY. 10th Edition, enlarged & revised. Crown 8vo. 12s. 6d.

The Iliad of Homer, Homometrically translated by C. B. CAYLEY, Translator of Dante's Comedy, &c. 8vo. 12s. 6d.

The Æneid of Virgil. Translated into English Verse. By J. CONINGTON, M.A. Crown 8vo. 9s.

Bowdler's Family Shakspeare. Genuine Edition, in 1 vol. medium 8vo. large type, with 36 Woodcuts, 14s. or in 6 vols. fcp. 8vo. 21s.

Southey's Poetical Works, with the Author's last Corrections and Additions. Medium 8vo. with Portrait, 14s.

RURAL SPORTS, HORSE and CATTLE MANAGEMENT, &c.

Annals of the Road; or, Notes on Mail and Stage-Coaching in Great Britain. By Captain MALET. With 3 Woodcuts and 10 Coloured Illustrations. Medium 8vo. 21s.

Down the Road; or, Reminiscences of a Gentleman Coachman. By C. T. S. BIRCH REYNARDSON. Second Edition, with 12 Coloured Illustrations. Medium 8vo. 21s.

Blaine's Encyclopædia of Rural Sports; Complete Accounts, Historical, Practical, and Descriptive, of Hunting, Shooting, Fishing, Racing, &c. With 600 Woodcuts. 8vo. 21s.

A Book on Angling; or, Treatise on the Art of Fishing in every branch; including full Illustrated Lists of Salmon Flies. By FRANCIS FRANCIS. Post 8vo. Portrait and Plates, 15s.

Wilcocks's Sea-Fisherman: comprising the Chief Methods of Hook and Line Fishing, a glance at Nets, and remarks on Boats and Boating. Post 8vo. Woodcuts, 12s. 6d.

The Fly-Fisher's Entomology. By ALFRED RONALDS. With 20 Coloured Plates. 8vo. 14s.

Horses and Riding. By GEORGE NEVILE, M.A. With 31 Illustrations. Crown 8vo. 6s.

Horses and Stables. By Colonel F. FITZWYGRAM, XV. the King's Hussars. With 24 Plates of Illustrations. 8vo. 10s. 6d.

Youatt on the Horse. Revised and enlarged by W. WATSON, M.R.C.V.S. 8vo. Woodcuts, 12s. 6d.

Youatt's Work on the Dog. Revised and enlarged. 8vo. Woodcuts, 6s.

The Dog in Health and Disease. By STONEHENGE. With 78 Wood Engravings. Square crown 8vo. 7s. 6d.

The Greyhound. By STONEHENGE. Revised Edition, with 25 Portraits of Greyhounds, &c. Square crown 8vo. 15s.

Stables and Stable Fittings. By W. MILES. Imp. 8vo. with 13 Plates, 15s.

The Horse's Foot, and How to keep it Sound. By W. MILES. Imp. 8vo. Woodcuts, 12s. 6d.

A Plain Treatise on Horse-shoeing. By W. MILES. Post 8vo. Woodcuts, 2s. 6d.

Remarks on Horses' Teeth, addressed to Purchasers. By W. MILES. Post 8vo. 1s. 6d.

The Ox, his Diseases and their Treatment; with an Essay on Parturition in the Cow. By J. R. DOBSON, M.R.C.V.S. Crown 8vo. Illustrations, 7s. 6d.

WORKS of UTILITY and GENERAL INFORMATION.

Maunder's Treasury of Knowledge and Library of Reference; comprising an English Dictionary and Grammar, Universal Gazetteer, Classical Dictionary, Chronology, Law Dictionary, Synopsis of the Peerage, Useful Tables, &c. Fcp. 8vo. 6s.

Maunder's Biographical Treasury. Latest Edition, reconstructed and partly re-written, with above 1,600 additional Memoirs, by W. L. R. CATES. Fcp. 8vo. 6s.

Maunder's Treasury of Natural History; or, Popular Dictionary of Zoology. Revised and corrected Edition. Fcp. 8vo. with 900 Woodcuts, 6s.

Maunder's Scientific and Literary Treasury; a Popular Encyclopædia of Science, Literature, and Art. Latest Edition, partly re-written, with above 1,000 New Articles, by J. Y. JOHNSON. Fcp. 8vo. 6s.

Maunder's Treasury of Geography, Physical, Historical, Descriptive, and Political. Edited by W. HUGHES, F.R.G.S. With 7 Maps and 16 Plates. Fcp. 8vo. 6s.

Maunder's Historical Treasury; Introductory Outlines of Universal History, and Separate Histories of all Nations. Revised by the Rev. Sir G. W. COX, Bart. M.A. Fcp. 8vo. 6s.

The Treasury of Botany, or Popular Dictionary of the Vegetable Kingdom; with which is incorporated a Glossary of Botanical Terms. Edited by J. LINDLEY, F.R.S. and T. MOORE, F.L.S. With 274 Woodcuts and 20 Steel Plates. Two Parts, fcp. 8vo. 12s.

The Treasury of Bible Knowledge; being a Dictionary of the Books, Persons, Places, Events, and other Matters of which mention is made in Holy Scripture. By the Rev. J. AYRE, M.A. Maps, Plates & Woodcuts. Fcp. 8vo. 6s.

A Practical Treatise on Brewing; with Formulæ for Public Brewers & Instructions for Private Families. By W. BLACK. 8vo. 10s. 6d.

The Theory of the Modern Scientific Game of Whist. By W. POLE, F.R.S. Tenth Edition. Fcp. 8vo. 2s. 6d.

The Correct Card; or, How to Play at Whist; a Whist Catechism. By Captain A. CAMPBELL-WALKER, F.R.G.S. New Edition. Fcp. 8vo. 2s. 6d.

The Cabinet Lawyer; a Popular Digest of the Laws of England, Civil, Criminal, and Constitutional. Twenty-Fifth Edition, corrected and extended. Fcp. 8vo. 9s.

Chess Openings. By F.W. LONGMAN, Balliol College, Oxford. Second Edition. Fcp. 8vo. 2s. 6d.

Pewtner's Comprehensive Specifier; a Guide to the Practical Specification of every kind of Building-Artificer's Work. Edited by W. YOUNG. Crown 8vo. 6s.

The English Manual of Banking. By ARTHUR CRUMP. Second Edition, revised and enlarged. 8vo. 15s.

Modern Cookery for Private Families, reduced to a System of Easy Practice in a Series of carefully-tested Receipts. By ELIZA ACTON. With 8 Plates and 150 Woodcuts. Fcp. 8vo. 6s.—

Food and Home Cookery. A Course of Instruction in Practical Cookery and Cleaning, for Children in Elementary Schools, as followed in the Schools of the Leeds School Board. By Mrs. BUCKTON, Member of the Leeds School Board. With 11 Woodcuts. Crown 8vo. 2s.

Hints to Mothers on the Management of their Health during the Period of Pregnancy and in the Lying-in Room. By THOMAS BULL, M.D. Fcp. 8vo. 2s. 6d.

The Maternal Management of Children in Health and Disease. By THOMAS BULL, M.D. Fcp. 8vo. 2s. 6d.

The Farm Valuer. By JOHN SCOTT, Land Valuer. Crown 8vo. price 5s.

Economics for Beginners By H. D. MACLEOD, M.A. Small crown 8vo. 2s. 6d.

The Elements of Banking. By H. D. MACLEOD, M.A. Fourth Edition. Crown 8vo. 5s.

The Theory and Practice of Banking. By H. D. MACLEOD, M.A. 2 vols. 8vo. 26s.

The Resources of Modern Countries; Essays towards an Estimate of the Economic Position of Nations and British Trade Prospects. By ALEX. WILSON. 2 vols. 8vo. 24s.

Willich's Popular Tables for ascertaining, according to the Carlisle Table of Mortality, the value of Lifehold, Leasehold, and Church Property, Renewal Fines, Reversions, &c. Also Interest, Legacy, Succession Duty, and various other useful tables. Eighth Edition. Post 8vo. 10s.

The Patentee's Manual; a Treatise on the Law and Practice of Letters Patent, for the use of Patentees and Inventors. By J. JOHNSON, Barrister-at-Law; and J. H. JOHNSON, Assoc. Inst. C.E. Solicitor and Patent Agent, Lincoln's Inn Fields and Glasgow. Fourth Edition, enlarged. 8vo. 10s. 6d.

INDEX.

Abbey & Overton's English Church History	15
———'s Photography	11
Acton's Modern Cookery	21
Alpine Club Map of Switzerland	18
Alpine Guide (The)	18
Amos's Jurisprudence	5
——— Primer of the Constitution	5
Anderson's Strength of Materials	11
Armstrong's Organic Chemistry	11
Arnold's (Dr.) Lectures on Modern History	2
——— Miscellaneous Works	7
——— Sermons	15
——— (T.) English Literature	7
Arnott's Elements of Physics	10
Atelier (The) du Lys	19
Atherstone Priory	19
Autumn Holidays of a Country Parson	7
Ayre's Treasury of Bible Knowledge	21
Bacon's Essays, by *Abbott*	6
——— by *Whately*	6
——— Life and Letters, by *Spedding*	5
——— Works	5
Bagehot's Literary Studies	7
Bailey's Festus, a Poem	19
Bain's Mental and Moral Science	6
——— on the Senses and Intellect	6
——— Emotions and Will	6
Baker's Two Works on Ceylon	17
Ball's Alpine Guides	18
Barry on Railway Appliances	11
Beaconsfield's (Lord) Novels and Tales	18
Beesly's Gracchi, Marius, and Sulla	3
Bent's Republic of San Marino	17
Black's Treatise on Brewing	21
Blackley's German-English Dictionary	8
Blaine's Rural Sports	20
Bloxam's Metals	11
Bolland and *Lang's* Aristotle's Politics	6
Boultbee on 39 Articles	15
———'s History of the English Church	15
Bourne's Works on the Steam Engine	14
Bowdler's Family *Shakespeare*	19
Bramley-Moore's Six Sisters of the Valleys	19
Brande's Dictionary of Science, Literature, and Art	12
Brassey's Voyage of the Sunbeam	17
Brian Boru, a Tragedy	19
Browne's Exposition of the 39 Articles	15
Browning's Modern England	3
Buckle's History of Civilisation	2
——— Posthumous Remains	7
Buckton's Food and Home Cookery	21
——— Health in the House	13
——— Town and Window Gardening	12
Bull's Hints to Mothers	21
——— Maternal Management of Children	21
Bullinger's Lexicon to the Greek Testament	8
Burgomaster's Family (The)	19
Burke's Vicissitudes of Families	4
Cabinet Lawyer	21
Capes's Age of the Antonines	3
——— Early Roman Empire	3
Cayley's Iliad of Homer	19
Changed Aspects of Unchanged Truths	7
Chesney's Indian Polity	2
——— Waterloo Campaign	2
Church's Beginning of the Middle Ages	3
Colenso on Moabite Stone &c.	17
———'s Pentateuch and Book of Joshua	17
Commonplace Philosopher	7
Comte's Positive Polity	5
Congreve's Politics of Aristotle	6
Conington's Translation of Virgil's Æneid	19
——— Miscellaneous Writings	6
Contanseau's Two French Dictionaries	8
Conybeare and *Howson's* St. Paul	16
Cooper's Tales from Euripides	18
Cordery's Struggle against Absolute Monarchy	3
Cotta on Rocks, by *Lawrence*	12
Counsel and Comfort from a City Pulpit	7
Cox's (G. W.) Athenian Empire	3
——— Crusades	3
——— Greeks and Persians	3
Creighton's Age of Elizabeth	3
——— England a Continental Power	3
——— Shilling History of England	3
——— Tudors and the Reformation	3
Cresy's Encyclopædia of Civil Engineering	14
Critical Essays of a Country Parson	7
Crookes's Anthracen	15
——— Chemical Analyses	13
——— Dyeing and Calico-printing	15
Crump's Manual of Banking	21
Culley's Handbook of Telegraphy	14
Curteis's Macedonian Empire	3
De Caisne and *Le Maout's* Botany	12
De Tocqueville's Democracy in America	5
Digby's Indian Famine Campaign	2
Dobson on the Ox	20
Dove's Law of Storms	9
Dowell's History of Taxes	5
Doyle's (R.) Fairyland	13
Drew's Hulsean Lectures	15
Drummond's Jewish Messiah	16
Eastlake's Hints on Household Taste	14
Edwards's Nile	17
Ellicott's Scripture Commentaries	15
——— Lectures on Life of Christ	15
Elsa and her Vulture	19
Epochs of Ancient History	3
——— English History	3
——— Modern History	3
Ewald's History of Israel	16
——— Antiquities of Israel	16
Fairbairn's Applications of Iron	14
——— Information for Engineers	14
——— Mills and Millwork	14
Farrar's Language and Languages	7
Fitzwygram on Horses and Stables	20
Frampton's (Bishop) Life	4
Francis's Fishing Book	20
Frobisher's Life by *Jones*	4
Froude's Cæsar	4
——— English in Ireland	1
——— History of England	1
——— Short Studies	7
Gairdner's Houses of Lancaster and York	3
——— Richard III. & Perkin Warbeck	2

WORKS published by LONGMANS & CO. 23

Ganot's Elementary Physics	10
——— Natural Philosophy	10
Gardiner's Buckingham and Charles	2
——— Personal Government of Charles I.	2
——— First Two Stuarts	3
——— Thirty Years' War	3
German Home Life	7
Goldziher's Hebrew Mythology	16
Goodeve's Mechanics	11
——— Mechanism	11
Gore's Art of Scientific Discovery	14
——— Electro-Metallurgy	11
Grant's Ethics of Aristotle	6
Graver Thoughts of a Country Parson	7
Greville's Journal	1
Griffin's Algebra and Trigonometry	11
Grove on Correlation of Physical Forces	10
Gwilt's Encyclopædia of Architecture	14
Hale's Fall of the Stuarts	3
Hartwig's Works on Natural History and Popular Science	11
Haughton's Animal Mechanics	10
Hayward's Selected Essays	6
Heer's Primeval World of Switzerland	12
Heine's Life and Works, by Stigand	4
Helmholtz on Tone	10
Helmholtz's Scientific Lectures	10
Herschel's Outlines of Astronomy	9
Hobson's Amateur Mechanic	14
Hodgson's Philosophy of Reflection	5
Hopkins's Christ the Consoler	17
Hoskold's Engineer's Valuing Assistant	14
Hullah's History of Modern Music	12
——— Transition Period	12
Hume's Essays	6
——— Treatise on Human Nature	6
Ihne's Rome to its Capture	3
——— History of Rome	2
Indian Alps	17
Ingelow's Poems	19
Jameson's Sacred and Legendary Art	13
——— Memoirs	4
Jenkin's Electricity and Magnetism	11
Jerrold's Life of Napoleon	1
Johnson's Normans in Europe	3
——— Patentee's Manual	21
Johnston's Geographical Dictionary	8
Jonson's (Ben) Every Man in his Humour	6
Jukes's Types of Genesis	16
Jukes on Second Death	16
Kalisch's Bible Studies	16
——— Commentary on the Bible	16
Keller's Lake Dwellings of Switzerland	12
Kerl's Metallurgy, by *Crookes* and *Röhrig*	15
Kingzett's Alkali Trade	13
——— Animal Chemistry	13
Kirby and *Spence's* Entomology	12
Knatchbull-Hugessen's Fairy-Land	18
——— Higgledy-Piggledy	18
Kuenen's Prophets and Prophecy in Israel	16
Landscapes, Churches, &c.	7
Latham's English Dictionaries	8
——— Handbook of English Language	8
Lecky's History of England	1
——— European Morals	3
——— Rationalism	3
——— Leaders of Public Opinion	4
Lefroy's Bermudas	17
Leisure Hours in Town	7
Leslie's Essays in Political and Moral Philosophy	6
Lessons of Middle Age	7
Lewes's Biographical History of Philosophy	3
Lewis on Authority	6
Liddell and *Scott's* Greek-English Lexicons	8
Lindley and *Moore's* Treasury of Botany	21
Lloyd's Magnetism	10
——— Wave-Theory of Light	10
London Series of English Classics	6
Longman's (F. W.) Chess Openings	21
——— German Dictionary	8
——— (W.) Edward the Third	2
——— Lectures on History of England	2
——— Old and New St. Paul's	13
Loudon's Encyclopædia of Agriculture	15
——— Gardening	15
——— Plants	12
Lubbock's Origin of Civilisation	12
Ludlow's American War	3
Lyra Germanica	17
Macalister's Vertebrate Animals	11
Macaulay's (Lord) Clive, by *Bowen*	6
——— Essays	1
——— History of England	1
——— Lays, Illus. Editions	13
——— Cheap Edition	19
——— Life and Letters	4
——— Miscellaneous Writings	7
——— Speeches	7
——— Works	1
——— Writings, Selections from	7
McCulloch's Dictionary of Commerce	8
Macfarren on Musical Harmony	13
Macleod's Economical Philosophy	5
——— Economics for Beginners	21
——— Theory and Practice of Banking	21
——— Elements of Banking	21
Mademoiselle Mori	19
Malet's Annals of the Road	19
Manning's Mission of the Holy Spirit	17
Marlowe's Doctor Faustus, by *Wagner*	6
Marshman's Life of Havelock	4
Martineau's Christian Life	17
——— Hours of Thought	17
——— Hymns	17
Maunder's Popular Treasuries	20
Maxwell's Theory of Heat	11
May's History of Democracy	1
——— History of England	1
Melville's (Whyte) Novels and Tales	19
Memorials of *Charlotte Williams-Wynn*	4
Mendelssohn's Letters	4
Merivale's Early Church History	15
——— Fall of the Roman Republic	2
——— General History of Rome	2
——— Roman Triumvirates	3
——— Romans under the Empire	2
Merrifield's Arithmetic and Mensuration	11
Miles on Horse's Foot and Horse Shoeing	20
——— on Horse's Teeth and Stables	20
Mill (J.) on the Mind	5
Mill's (J. S.) Autobiography	4
——— Dissertations & Discussions	5
——— Essays on Religion	16
——— Hamilton's Philosophy	5
——— Liberty	5
——— Political Economy	5
——— Representative Government	5

WORKS published by LONGMANS & CO.

Mill's (J. S.) Subjection of Women	5
———— System of Logic	5
———— Unsettled Questions	5
———— Utilitarianism	5
Miller's Elements of Chemistry	13
———— Inorganic Chemistry	11
———— & *Skertchley's* Fenland	18
Mitchell's Manual of Assaying	15
Milton's Paradise Regained, by *Jerram*	6
Modern Novelist's Library	18-19
Monsell's Spiritual Songs	17
Moore's Irish Melodies, Illustrated Edition	13
———— Lalla Rookh, Illustrated Edition	13
Morell's Philosophical Fragments	5
Morris's Age of Anne	3
Mozart's Life, by *Nohl*	4
Müller's Chips from a German Workshop	7
———— Hibbert Lectures on Religion	16
———— Science of Language	7
———— Science of Religion	16
Mullinger's Schools of Charles the Great	6
Neison on the Moon	9
Nevile's Horses and Riding	20
Newman's Apologia pro Vitâ Suâ	4
Nicols's Puzzle of Life	12
Noiré's Müller & Philosophy of Language	7
Northcott's Lathes & Turning	14
O'Conor's Scripture Commentary	16
Owen's Comparative Anatomy and Physiology of Vertebrate Animals	11
Packe's Guide to the Pyrenees	18
Pattison's Casaubon	4
Payen's Industrial Chemistry	14
Pewtner's Comprehensive Specifier	21
Phillips's Civil War in Wales	2
Pole's Game of Whist	21
Pope's Select Poems, by *Arnold*	6
Powell's Early England	3
Preece & *Sivewright's* Telegraphy	11
Present-Day Thoughts	7
Proctor's Astronomical Works	9
———— Scientific Essays (Two Series)	11
Prothero's De Montfort	2
Public Schools Atlas of Ancient Geography	8
———— Atlas of Modern Geography	8
Rawlinson's Parthia	3
———— Sassanians	3
Recreations of a Country Parson	7
Reynardson's Down the Road	19
Rich's Dictionary of Antiquities	8
Rivers's Orchard House	12
———— Rose Amateur's Guide	12
Rogers's Eclipse of Faith	15
———— Defence of Eclipse of Faith	15
Roget's English Thesaurus	8
Ronalds' Fly-Fisher's Entomology	20
Rowley's Rise of the People	3
———— Settlement of the Constitution	3
Rutley's Study of Rocks	11
Sandars's Justinian's Institutes	5
Sankey's Sparta and Thebes	3
Schellen's Spectrum Analysis	9
Seaside Musings	7
Scott's Farm Valuer	21
Seebohm's Oxford Reformers of 1498	2
Seebohm's Protestant Revolution	3
Sewell's History of France	2
———— Passing Thoughts on Religion	16
———— Preparation for Communion	17
———— Stories and Tales	18
———— Thoughts for the Age	17
Shelley's Workshop Appliances	11
Short's Church History	15
Smith's (Sydney) Wit and Wisdom	7
———— (Dr. R. A.) Air and Rain	9
———— (R. B.) Carthage & the Carthaginians	2
Southey's Poetical Works	19
Stanley's History of British Birds	12
Stephen's Ecclesiastical Biography	4
Stonehenge, Dog and Greyhound	20
Stoney on Strains	14
Stubbs's Early Plantagenets	3
Sunday Afternoons, by A. K. H. B.	7
Supernatural Religion	16
Swinbourne's Picture Logic	6
Tancock's England during the Wars, 1778-1820	3
Taylor's History of India	2
———— Ancient and Modern History	3
———— (Jeremy) Works, edited by *Eden*	17
Text-Books of Science	11
Thomé's Botany	11
Thomson's Laws of Thought	6
Thorpe's Quantitative Analysis	11
Thorpe and *Muir's* Qualitative Analysis	11
Tilden's Chemical Philosophy	11
Todd on Parliamentary Government	2
Trench's Realities of Irish Life	7
Trollope's Warden and Barchester Towers	19
Twiss's Law of Nations	5
Tyndall's (Professor) Scientific Works	10
Unawares	19
Unwin's Machine Design	11
Ure's Arts, Manufactures, and Mines	14
Ville on Artificial Manures	15
Walker on Whist	21
Walpole's History of England	1
Warburton's Edward the Third	3
Watson's Geometry	11
Watts's Dictionary of Chemistry	13
Weinhold's Experimental Physics	10
Wellington's Life, by *Gleig*	4
Whately's English Synonymes	8
———— Logic	6
———— Rhetoric	6
White's Four Gospels in Greek	16
———— and *Riddle's* Latin Dictionaries	8
Wilcocks's Sea-Fisherman	20
Williams's Aristotle's Ethics	6
Willich's Popular Tables	21
Wilson's Resources of Modern Countries	21
Wood's (J. G.) Popular Works on Natural History	11
———— (J. T.) Ephesus	17
Woodward's Geology	12
Yonge's English-Greek Lexicons	8
———— Horace	19
Youatt on the Dog	20
———— on the Horse	20
Zeller's Plato, Socrates, &c.	3
Zimmern's Lessing	4

Spottiswoode & Co., Printers, New-street Square, London.

www.ingramcontent.com/pod-product-compliance
Lightning Source LLC
Chambersburg PA
CBHW022100300426
44117CB00007B/534